FOOD, NUTRITION AND CLIMATE

International Symposium organised by The Rank Prize Funds and held at the Dormy Hotel, Ferndown, Dorset, UK, on 5–9 April, 1981

FOOD, NUTRITION AND CLIMATE

Edited by

SIR KENNETH BLAXTER

Director, The Rowett Research Institute,
Bucksburn, Aberdeen, UK

and

LESLIE FOWDEN

Director, Rothamsted Experimental Station,
Harpenden, Herts, UK

APPLIED SCIENCE PUBLISHERS
LONDON and NEW JERSEY

APPLIED SCIENCE PUBLISHERS LTD
RIPPLE ROAD, BARKING, ESSEX, ENGLAND
APPLIED SCIENCE PUBLISHERS, INC.
ENGLEWOOD, NEW JERSEY 07631, USA

British Library Cataloguing in Publication Data

Food, nutrition and climate.
1. Meteorology, Agriculture—Congresses
I. Blaxter, *Sir* Kenneth   II. Fowden, Leslie
630   S600.5

ISBN 0-85334-107-9

WITH 39 TABLES AND 89 ILLUSTRATIONS

Printed in Northern Ireland at The Universities Press (Belfast) Ltd

Foreword

The Rank Prize Funds were constituted by the late Lord Rank shortly before his death in 1972. The Funds were endowed by grants of £2·5 million from the J. Arthur Rank Group Charity (now known as The Rank Foundation) which is a major charity set up by the late Lord and Lady Rank in 1953 as one of many charitable activities with which they were involved during their lifetime. The Funds exist to further Lord Rank's wish to encourage research and provide awards for significant advances in human and animal nutrition and crop husbandry and in opto-electronics. These two fields relate to the flour milling industry and to the film industry with which Lord Rank became so clearly identified. The aims of The Rank Prize Funds are:

To award prizes to persons who have made notable advances in the above mentioned sciences

To grant moneys for the purposes of research in these sciences

To sponsor seminars or conferences for the discussion of any aspects of these sciences

This volume is the publication of the proceedings of the fifth symposium organised by the Advisory Committee on Nutrition and Crop Husbandry of The Rank Prize Funds. In organising these symposia, the Advisory Committee has sought to achieve more than is usually possible in a symposium organised by a scientific society bound by the specialisation of its members. The Committee has deliberately chosen subjects of considerable breadth so as to bring together members of scientific disciplines which do not, customarily, have much opportunity to meet. Thus, this symposium on *Food, Nutrition and Climate* brought together a wide group of human and animal nutritionists, plant breeders, marine biologists, meteorologists, physiologists, biochemists, plant pathologists, soil scientists and agricultural economists from 13 countries.

The success of such a mixture of experts from so many fields was again endorsed by the quality of the papers and by the discussion which they provoked. This volume provides the record of those proceedings.

A matter for further note is that three of the participants, each an eminent plant physiologist, had already been selected for the award of a Rank Prize for their fundamental work in crop bioenergetics. The three recipients of a shared prize of £60 000 were Dr Hugo Peter Kortschak, Dr Marshall Davidson Hatch and Dr Charles Roger Slack. The awards were presented by Sir John Davis, Chairman of the Trustees of The Rank Prize Funds in recognition of the prize winners' contributions towards the discovery of the C_4 mechanism of photosynthesis in plants.

SIR WILLIAM HENDERSON

Chairman, Advisory Committee on Nutrition and Crop Husbandry, Rank Prize Funds, London

Contents

Introduction

Climate and man interact in many ways. Climate obviously affects man's food supply, for in the long term it dictates what species of crop or animal can be used as sources of food. In the short term the variation in the climate from year to year may be sufficient to affect the yields obtained, either through direct effects on the plants and animals or indirectly by encouraging diseases, pests and parasites.

Additionally, man reacts to his physical environment; climate certainly modifies his nutritional needs and it also appears to account for many of the cultural differences between peoples in the methods they adopt to prepare the food they consume. The interaction is a two way process. Man can modify the climate, particularly by the provision of irrigation and protective climates within buildings.

This symposium was designed to explore many of these effects of climate on the nutrition and well-being of man—an immense subject which was, in part, limited by requesting speakers to give greatest emphasis to the northern temperate regions of the world.

A primary requirement in any study of the effects of climate, is the precise measurement of its components. Here the use of standard meteorological measurements, while useful and justifiable in dealing with some aspects of the biological implications of climate, can be of limited value in the precise definition of the microclimates of plants and animals in other contexts. In an introductory lecture L. P. Smith outlined some of the problems involved in the use of meteorological measurements and drew attention to the considerable effects of modifying factors such as topography and elevation on their interpretation, together with attributes of climate which involved the colligative effects of components.

1

Climate and the Soil

L. J. PONS

Department of Soil Science and Geology,
Wageningen Agricultural University, The Netherlands

INTRODUCTION

Soil conditions form only a part of the factors that determine the productivity of a piece of land. Sums of solar energy on days with temperatures high enough to allow plant growth determine potential yields. Soil characteristics, in association with the climate, combine to give land qualities that limit the potential to maximum yields that may be obtained locally. A number of economic, social and political conditions, that direct capital and labour input and knowledge, may further limit the maximum to actual yields. In many cases these limitations are so great that the actual yields are only a small fraction of the maximal yields. Because soil conditions themselves are also closely related to climate, the whole complex of climate, soil and productivity is very complicated.

A number of fundamental requirements that plants, and especially crops, demand from soils, are presented first in order to see which aspects of soils are important. In the second part of the paper, I will discuss the distribution of soils and their characteristics in relation to climate. Finally, I will show why actual yields, maximum land productivity and potential productivity are sometimes similar, but in most cases differ greatly.

THE LAND REQUIREMENTS OF CROPS

Plant growth and productivity are mainly determined by climate, but it is useful to speculate about the role soils play in this context. The whole production of organic matter (OM), which is the primary and

3

secondary source of our food and also provides the soil with organic material, depends upon the assimilation process occurring in the green leaves of plants. A simple equation reads as follows:

$$
\underset{\substack{\text{(From the} \\ \text{air)}}}{CO_2} + \underset{\substack{\text{(From the} \\ \text{soil)}}}{H_2O} + \underset{\substack{\text{Small amounts} \\ \text{of a variety} \\ \text{of major and} \\ \text{minor nutrients} \\ \text{(From the soil)}}}{} + \underset{\substack{\text{Radiation} \\ \text{energy} \\ \text{(Sunlight)}}}{} \rightarrow \underset{\substack{\text{CHO} \\ \text{(OM)} \\ \text{(Plant} \\ \text{material)}}}{} + \underset{\substack{O_2 \\ \text{(To the air)}}}{}
$$

When enough nutrients are supplied, living plants may develop in water as is shown by aquatic plants and hydroponics. Although some products of intensive cultivations such as vegetables and flowers are cultivated in nutrient solutions, soils will always be the most economic growing medium for food production.

The environmental requirements that both wild and cultivated plants demand from the soil, so that they can realise the above assimilation process, may be summarised in the following general points (Schlichting, 1964):

1. Soils have to act as a medium in which seed may germinate and roots may develop. This means that soils must have structure and porosity, protect against drying out, too high temperatures, etc.
2. Soils must provide the growing plant with an anchorage, to allow it to expose its leaves to sunlight in the most economic way.
3. Soils must be well drained to ensure that the pore system stays partly filled with air to sufficient depths. Roots consume oxygen and produce carbon dioxide and there must be a ready diffusion of gases.
4. Soils have to act as emergency water reservoirs in times of drought or between irrigations. The water storage capacity depends on the soil colloids (clay and humus) and the finer soil pores.
5. Soils must be able to provide the plant with sufficient and well balanced amounts of a number of macro- and micro-nutrients required in biosynthetic processes of plant materials. The soil colloids (clay and humus), the organic matter content, and the amount of weatherable minerals are most important in this respect.

To produce food, plants are cultivated under economic management on defined pieces of land with specific soil conditions. Nobody can produce food continuously if the outputs are lower than the inputs. Outputs are measured in kilograms per hectare, so at this point we have to consider the surface of the soil, which we term 'land'; i.e. a certain piece of the earth's surface that includes not only the soils but also other physiographic characteristics such as slope, climate, groundwater, etc. (Brinkman and Smyth, 1973).

Agricultural land use infers that the land is conditioned for optimal productivity. Every crop or group of crops will make specific demands on the management of the land (Beek, 1978) and certain management requirements have to be added to the environmental ones. In this respect, soils or land must allow:

1. A good seedbed to be prepared and the crop to be sown.
2. Management measures required to safeguard the crop from hazards, pests, diseases and weeds.
3. The possibility that the crop may be harvested, transported and processed even under bad weather conditions.

To facilitate these needs, a certain piece of land should be fairly homogeneous with respect to soil conditions (Pons, 1977).

It is not only economically important to the cultivator but also to the country and possibly to the world that the ability of a certain area of land to produce food is not lost by erosion or other soil degradation. For this reason, conservation requirements may be formulated, to ensure that agricultural or other types of land use do not result in degradation of the land (soil) by (a) erosion; (b) silting up; (c) worsening of drainage; (d) increase in salinity; (e) desertification; etc. Where food production is secondary (i.e. via livestock production), additional land requirements should be listed, but I shall not cover this aspect of food production.

SOME DEFINITIONS OF PRODUCTIVITY

As will be understood from the foregoing, the influence of the climate on production via the intermediary of the soil is very complicated. In an attempt to simplify this complicated subject, some basic terms relating to the principles mentioned earlier may be helpful. The potential productivity (PP) of a certain area is determined by radiation and temperature (independent from the soil), the rainfall and the evaporation. However, actual land and weather conditions are seldom

ideal and thus the concept of potential productivity has to be rational-
ised and the maximum land productivity (MP), a more realistic version
of the same concept, is used in practice. In modern land evaluation
(Beek, 1978), it is possible to indicate the extent to which crop and other
land use requirements are met by the land qualities present and to estimate, at least for some types, how much PP will be limited by the land
and weather conditions. Sometimes just one soil quality will depress
yields so much that the land is classified as unsuitable for a specific
type of land use. Some examples might show how local weather conditions may influence land use and yields.

Frequent high rainfall during harvest time will cause serious difficulties especially if occurring more than 3 years out of 10. Land with
heavy textured clay soils will be unsuitable for arable use although all
other land qualities may be favourable. On the other hand, on
shallow soils with limited amounts of available water, even short
periods without rainfall will damage crops, making such land also
unsuitable for arable use.

The reductions in PP caused by inadequate land qualities and
climate characteristics determine MP: this will be emphasised later in
this paper. However, only on relatively small areas will yields actually
obtained closely approach the MP. Nearly everywhere, actual yields
are far below the MP for economic, social and political reasons. The
gravest reason, and direct cause of hunger in developing countries, is
the poverty of the majority of the small farmers and the low prices
paid for agricultural products even in richer countries (Buringh, 1981).

SOILS AND CLIMATE IN THE TEMPERATE ZONE

It was only in the second half of the 19th century that Russian soil
scientists learned that soil formation depends on parent material,
climate, topography, drainage, flora and fauna, and time. Dokuchayev
(1886) and Sibirtsev (1899) distinguished the genetical horizons of the
soil profile: A, B and C. This simple original concept was accepted in
nearly every country and rapidly extended, as shown in Fig. 1 (US
Department of Agriculture, 1938). Unfortunately adaptions to local
conditions are causing more and more deviations from the original
concept. Modern soil science has introduced the concept of the soil
pedon, defined as the smallest soil volume that can be recognised as a
soil individual (Buol et al., 1973). Figure 2 shows how a soil pedon is
related to a soil individual forming part of the landscape.

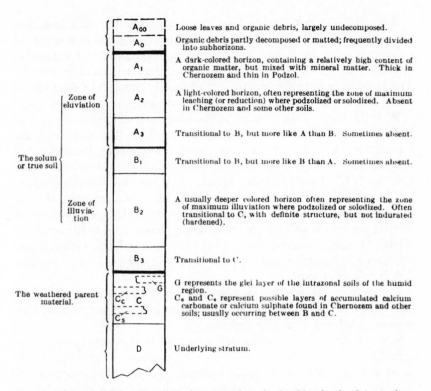

A_{00}		Loose leaves and organic debris, largely undecomposed.
A_0		Organic debris partly decomposed or matted; frequently divided into subhorizons.
A_1		A dark-colored horizon, containing a relatively high content of organic matter, but mixed with mineral matter. Thick in Chernozem and thin in Podzol.
A_2		A light-colored horizon, often representing the zone of maximum leaching (or reduction) where podzolized or solodized. Absent in Chernozem and some other soils.
A_3		Transitional to B, but more like A than B. Sometimes absent.
B_1		Transitional to B, but more like B than A. Sometimes absent.
B_2		A usually deeper colored horizon often representing the zone of maximum illuviation where podzolized or solodized. Often transitional to C, with definite structure, but not indurated (hardened).
B_3		Transitional to C.
C, C_c, C_s, G		G represents the glei layer of the intrazonal soils of the humid region. C_c and C_s represent possible layers of accumulated calcium carbonate or calcium sulphate found in Chernozem and other soils; usually occurring between B and C.
D		Underlying stratum.

Zone of eluviation

Zone of illuviation

The solum or true soil

The weathered parent material.

FIG. 1. The subdivision in soil horizons as given in the *Yearbook of Agriculture* (US Dept. of Agriculture, 1938).

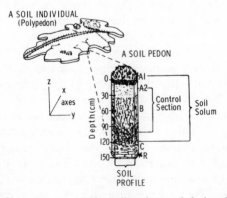

A SOIL INDIVIDUAL (Polypedon)

A SOIL PEDON

z, x, y axes

Depth(cm)

Control Section

Soil Solum

SOIL PROFILE

FIG. 2. A soil profile as an aspect of a soil pedon and their relationships with a soil individual (polypedon), forming a natural unit in the landscape (after Buol *et al.*, 1973).

Both Russian pedologists also formulated for the first time soil zonality in comparable parent materials; under the same topographical conditions (flat land) and under free drainage, the soil formation depends only on the climate and the related vegetation and animal life. The zonal soils form the abiotic part of mainly climatically determined ecosystems, and are arranged in climatic zones.

With the birth of the concept of the zonal soil type, soil science was born as a branch of the natural sciences and, at the same time, the foundation was laid for the genetic classification of soils. Parallel to the development in Russia, zonality principles were also formulated in the USA by Hilgard (1833–1906). Zonality as a base for soil classification was introduced in the USA by Marbut (1928). Apart from the class or order of zonal soils, a second class or order of intrazonal soils was introduced, which reflects the dominating influence of local factors of relief, drainage or parent material over the zonal effects of climate and vegetation. The azonal soils, a third order, includes soils too young to reflect soil formation.

Latitudinal soil zonality is best developed in extended flat areas covered by moraines, loess or other medium textured parent materials, showing gradually changing climates.

Western Russia and eastern and northern North America, where soil formation is only Holocene and young Pleistocene and at most 40 000 years old, provide the classical examples. Knapp (1979) shows the relationship between some major groups and the two major characteristics of the climate, temperature and humidity in a simple theoretical diagram (Fig. 3). Figure 4 presents a comparison of the distribution of very broad climatic zones, the principal vegetative types and the principal zonal soil groups for Europe and North and Central Asia following Strahler (1960). On this very small scale, striking correlations are apparent between climate, vegetation and soils. On a larger scale Fig. 5 compares the Köppen-Geiger climates for North America (Strahler, 1960) with the distribution of the generalised great soil groups in the USA (Knapp, 1979); patterns may also be compared.

The same sequence of zonal soils can occur along mountain slopes, as shown in Fig. 6. This altitude zonality, reported from many mountainous areas, is sometimes of more than local importance.

The process of soil formation involves numerous events, occurring simultaneously or in sequence, which may mutually reinforce or counteract each other. Thus a given process may tend to change the soil or maintain it in its current condition.

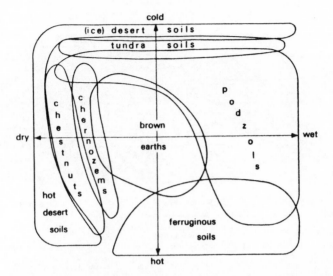

FIG. 3. A simple diagram showing the world distribution of some major soil groups in relation to two aspects of climate: temperature and wetness: humidity (after Knapp, 1979).

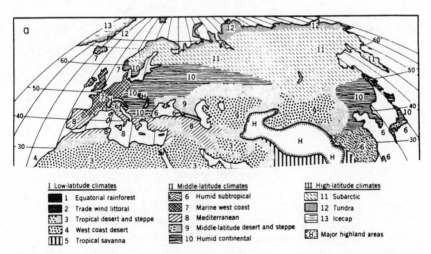

I Low-latitude climates
1 Equatorial rainforest
2 Trade wind littoral
3 Tropical desert and steppe
4 West coast desert
5 Tropical savanna

II Middle-latitude climates
6 Humid subtropical
7 Marine west coast
8 Mediterranean
9 Middle-latitude desert and steppe
10 Humid continental

III High-latitude climates
11 Subarctic
12 Tundra
13 Icecap

Major highland areas

FIG. 4. A comparison of broad climatic zones, the principal vegetative types and the principal zonal soil groups of Europe and northern Asia (after Strahler, 1960).

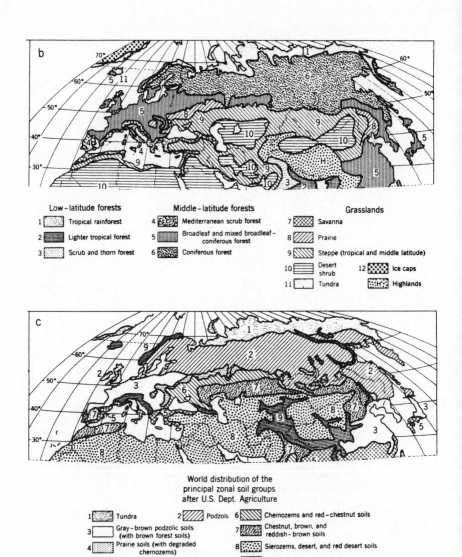

Low - latitude forests

1 Tropical rainforest

2 Lighter tropical forest

3 Scrub and thorn forest

Middle - latitude forests

4 Mediterranean scrub forest

5 Broadleaf and mixed broadleaf - coniferous forest

6 Coniferous forest

Grasslands

7 Savanna

8 Prairie

9 Steppe (tropical and middle latitude)

10 Desert shrub

11 Tundra

12 Ice caps

Highlands

World distribution of the
principal zonal soil groups
after U.S. Dept. Agriculture

1 Tundra

2 Podzols

3 Gray - brown podzolic soils (with brown forest soils)

4 Prairie soils (with degraded chernozems)

5 Latosols and red - yellow soils

6 Chernozems and red - chestnut soils

7 Chestnut, brown, and reddish - brown soils

8 Sierozems, desert, and red desert soils

9 Azonal (mountain) soils

FIG. 4.—*contd.*

In the temperate climatical zone, a number of soil processes are taking place, providing each zonal and intrazonal soil with their typical characteristics. Buol *et al.* (1973) list such pedogenetical processes, and the most important ones acting in temperate climates are given in Table 1. The table also indicates the resulting soil horizons and the soils in which they occur.

In the temperate climates, the soils are relatively young. Figure 7 shows the maximum spread of the ice sheets in Europe and North America during the Pleistocene. In these areas, all poor, older soil covers are eroded. Fresh parent material was laid down as moraine deposits, most of mixed composition. The same change took place south of the ice sheets in the Pleistocene periglacial zone where river terraces, loess and solifluction layers (also mostly of mixed composition) form the parent materials of the greater part of the land surfaces. Weathering has been mainly physical in type. Minerals are only slightly chemically weathered and new formation of clay minerals has been weak. The relatively low temperatures contribute in part to the weak chemical weathering. Decomposition of organic matter also is depressed, so that relatively high amounts of organic matter and humus are present in the top soils and, because of their youth, many soils are relatively rich in plant nutrients. Mountainous areas and the higher parts of the hills with thin covers of parent material show shallow and mostly stony soils.

Table 2 lists the zonal, intrazonal and azonal soils and shows their most important characteristics in relation to the land qualities necessary for crop growth. From this table and the previous figures, the following summary of the soil conditions of the temperate areas may be given:

The humid temperate areas include very important areas of medium to light textured, well-drained, rather deep to medium-deep soils (grey-brown podzolics, brown podzolics and related soils). Their fertility is medium to rather poor but they respond well to fertilisers. Soil working is not very difficult and the topography is nearly flat to undulating. North of this zone extensive areas of podzols are to be found with mostly light textures and medium root depths. They are rather poor in fertility but in being not stony they are easy to manage. Their response to added fertilisers is good but they tend to have water shortages. The northern part is not suited to crop growth because of the low temperatures.

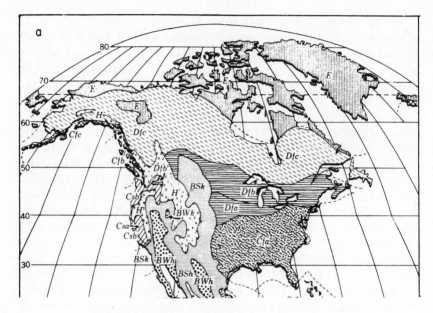

Key to letter code designating climate regions:

FIRST LETTER

A, C, D Sufficient heat and precipitation for growth of high-trunked
            trees.
A Tropical climates. All monthly mean temperatures over 64.4°F
                                                              (18°C).
B Dry climates. Boundaries determined by formula using mean annual
                            temperature and mean annual precipitation
                            (see graphs).
C Warm temperate climates. Mean temperature of coldest month:
                  64.4°F (18°C) down to 26.6°F (−3°C).
D Snow climates. Warmest month mean over 50°F (10°C).
                        Coldest month mean under 26.6°F (−3°C).
E Ice climates. Warmest month mean under 50°F (10°C).

SECOND LETTER

S Steppe climate. } Boundaries determined by formulas (See graphs).
W Desert climate. }
f Sufficient precipitation in all months.
m Rainforest despite a dry season (i.e., monsoon cycle).
s Dry season in summer of the respective hemisphere.
w Dry season in winter of the respective hemisphere.

THIRD LETTER

a Warmest month mean over 71.6°F (22°C).
b Warmest month mean under 71.6°F (22°C). At least 4 months have
                    means over 50°F (10°C.)
c Fewer than 4 months with means over 50°F (10°C).
d Same as *c*, but coldest month mean under −36.4°F (−38°C).
h Dry and hot. Mean annual temperature over 64.4°F (18°C).
k Dry and cold. Mean annual temperature under 64.4°F (18°C).

FIG. 5. Comparison between (a) the Köppen–Geiger climates and (b) the
generalised major soil groups of North America (Knapp, 1979).

b

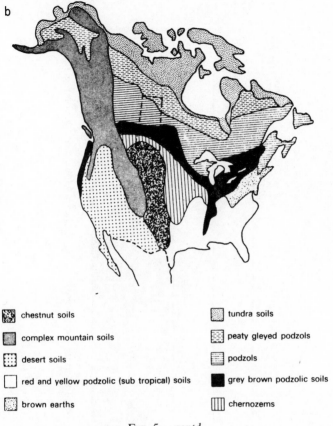

chestnut soils

complex mountain soils

desert soils

red and yellow podzolic (sub tropical) soils

brown earths

tundra soils

peaty gleyed podzols

podzols

grey brown podzolic soils

chernozems

FIG. 5.—*contd.*

In the subhumid to subarid areas of the temperate zone good to excellent quality soils are present. They show well-drained, deep profiles with medium textures, and deep A_1 horizons with very favourable structures. The natural fertility is medium to high and they respond very well to fertilisers. Water shortage is a problem, but the high water storage capacity of the profiles make irrigation economic. Soil labouring and harvesting of root crops do not form limitations.

The lithosols of the mountains and higher hills sometimes occupy important areas as in Europe, middle and eastern Siberia, and western USA and Canada.

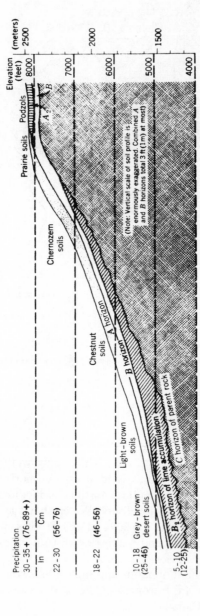

FIG. 6. Diagram showing the altitude zonality along the slopes of the Bighorn Mountains, Wyoming (after Thorpe, 1931).

TABLE 1
THE MOST IMPORTANT PROCESSES OF SOIL FORMATION IN THE TEMPERATE ZONE, THEIR RESULTING HORIZONS AND THE SOILS IN WHICH THEY OCCUR

Process term	Brief description	Horizon	Soils
Littering	The accumulation on the mineral soil surface of organic litter and associated humus to a depth of less than 30 cm	0_l 0_f 0_h	Tundra soils Podzols Forest soils Gley soils
Humification	The transformation of raw organic material into humus and the incorporation with clay	Mollic A_1 Umbric A_1	Chernozem Prairie soil Chestnut soil Rendzina Gley soil
Decalcification	Reactions that remove $CaCO_3$ from one or more soil horizons	Cambic B	Tundra soils Podzols Grey-brown podzolic soils Prairie soils
Braunification	Release of iron from primary minerals, dispersing of iron oxide in increasing amounts and dehydration, giving the soil mass brownish colours	Cambic B Argillic B	Brown forest soils Grey-brown podzolic soils Chestnut soils
Lessivage	The migration of small mineral particles from the A to the B horizon producing in the B horizon relative enrichment of clay	Argillic B	Grey-brown podzols Planosols
Podzolisation	The formation of chelates and the migration of organo-Al and/or Fe oxides, resulting in the concentration of silica in the eluviated layer	Albic A and part of podzol B	Podzols
Pedoturbation	Biological, physical (freeze–thaw and wet–dry cycles) churning and cycling of soil materials	Cambic B Mollic A	Acid brown soils Brown forest soils Chernozems Chestnut soils Some alluvial soils
Gleysation	The reduction of iron under anaerobic soil conditions (bluish-greenish grey colours) with or without brown and other mottles of ferric concretions	Wet Cambic B Wet Argillic B	Gley soils Pseudo gley soils Planosols
Salinisation and alkalinisation	The accumulation of salinity in soils and/or the accumulation of Na ions on the exchange sites in a soil	Natric B	Solonchak Solonetz

TABLE 2

ZONAL, INTRAZONAL AND AZONAL SOILS AND THEIR MOST IMPORTANT SOIL
CHARACTERISTICS IN RELATION TO CROP GROWTH

Zonal and intrazonal great soil group	Native vegetation	Drainage	Natural kind of A_1	Texture	Structure
Tundra soils	Moss, flowering plants	Poor	Peaty	Medium to light	—
Podzols	Coniferous or mixed forests	Good	0 horizon, shallow	Light	Favourable
Brown podzolic soils	Deciduous and mixed forests	Good	0 and A_1 horizons, shallow	Light to medium	Favourable
Grey-brown podzolic soils	Deciduous and mixed forests	Good	A_1 horizon, shallow	Medium to heavy	Favourable
Prairie soils	Tall grass	Good	A_1 thick and well developed	Medium	Very favourable
Chernozems	Tall and mixed grass	Good	A_1 thick and well developed	Medium	Very favourable
Chestnut	Mixed tall and short grass	Good	A_1 thick to medium and well developed	Medium to heavy	Very favourable
Saline and alkaline soils	Halophytic grasses and shrubs, prairie	Poor to imperfect	A_1 very thin	Medium to heavy	Very poor to poor
Rendzinas	Grassland to forest	Good	Well developed, thin	Medium	Very favourable
Lithosols	Grass, shrubs	Good	A_1 thin	Medium to light	Medium
Alluvial soils	Wide range	Poor to good	A_1 thin	Light to heavy	Favourable to medium
Planosols	Grass to forest	Poor to imperfect	A_1 very thin	Light to medium to heavy	Very poor

TABLE 2—*contd.*

Rooting depth	pH	Chemical fertility	Other characteristics	Present land use
Shallow	Medium to low	Medium to low	Sometimes strong	Nature or very extensive pastures
Shallow to medium	Low	Low	Sometimes strong	Cropland, grassland, forests
Medium to deep	Low	Low to medium	—	Cropland, grassland, forests
Deep	Medium to low	Medium	—	Crops on small farms
Deep	Medium	Medium to high	—	Crops on medium farms
Deep	High	High	—	Grain crops on large units
Medium to deep	High	High	—	Grain crops, extensive grassland
Shallow	High	Poor	Saline impermeable	Waste to grazing to poor crop land
Shallow	High	Medium	Sometimes strong	Pastures, regional crops
Shallow	Medium	Medium to low	Very strong	Forests, barren, or grazing (extensive)
Medium to deep	Wide range	Medium to high	—	Wide range of land use
Shallow	Medium to low	Very poor	Impermeable	Pasture, some crops, forests

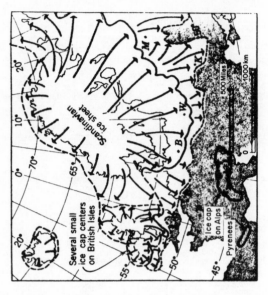
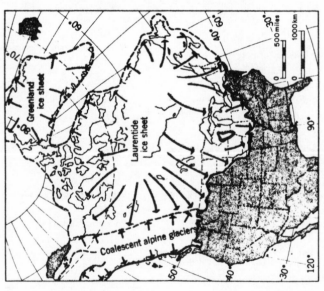

FIG. 7. The Pleistocene ice sheets of North America and Europe at their maximum spread. Solid lines show limits of ice in the last glacial stage; dotted line on land shows maximum extent at any time.

SOILS AND CLIMATES IN THE SUBTROPICAL
AND TROPICAL ZONE

Soil classifications founded on zonal concepts are very attractive to soil surveyors, geographers and ecologists and this possibly accounts for their continued use (Fitzpatrick, 1980). In modern classification systems, however, the infallibility of the zonal system has been challenged, for many reasons. The main practical reason is that the system was based largely on environmental factors rather than on intrinsic properties of soils, and in most cases the tendency was to use virgin soils. Other reasons were the impossibility of distinguishing between some zonal and intrazonal soils, e.g. podzols, the relative abundance of intrazonal and azonal soils in some countries, and the strong emphasis placed on colour. Also, for theoretical reasons, the zonal concept must be abandoned as soon as subtropical and tropical soils are incorporated.

Whereas the temperate land areas on which the zonal system was developed are always of young Pleistocene origin and mostly about 10 000 years (maximum 40 000 years) old, the subtropical and tropical land surfaces are 100 000–1 000 000 years and sometimes even older. In fact, the subtropical and tropical soils form at least two other categories of zonality to be added to the zonal, azonal and intrazonal categories of the old system, as shown in Table 3. The terms juvenile, mature and senile (adapted from Carter and Pendleton, 1956) describe the overall development of soils with age.

Although this and other simplifications have to be used with care and in a limited way, because exceptions are numerous, this adapted zonal system does give a clear explanation of the distribution of soils on earth and their important characteristics. The age-differentiated zonality is one of the cornerstones of the morphometric soil classification system developed in *Soil Taxonomy* (US Dept. of Agriculture, 1975) with its 10 Orders.

Whereas the distribution of zonal soils in the northern hemisphere is related to the present climate, the distribution of the juvenile, mature and senile soils on earth has its origin in long-term climatic changes. As already shown (see Fig. 7) the present temperate zones of the earth roughly coincide with zones that were glacial and periglacial during the Pleistocene glacial periods.

Periodically, the vegetation vanished partly or completely, and tremendous erosion occurred. The old, senile soil cover of Tertiary age was eroded and the parent rocks were denuded.

TABLE 3
ZONAL SOILS AND SOIL ORDERS CLASSIFIED IN AN AGE DIFFERENTIATED ZONAL-
ITY SYSTEM

Soil category	Estimated ages (years)	Zonal, intrazonal and azonal soils	Soil taxonomy, orders and suborders
Zonal soils	0–±5 000	Alluvial soils, lithosols, peat soils	Entisols, inceptisols, histosols, some aridisols
Juvenile zonal soils	±5 000– ±50 000	Tundra podzols, prairie soils, chernozems, G.B. podzolic soils, brown podzolic soils, brown soils, rendzina's, pseudogley, andosols, reddish prairie soil	Inceptisols, spodosols a majority of mollisols, young alfisols, andepts
Mature zonal soils	±50 000– ±500 000	Black cotton soils, feriallitic soils, red and yellow podzolic soils, reddish-brown savanna soils, red and brown Mediterranean soils, planosols	Ultisols, vertisols, palaeo-alfisols
Senile zonal soils	±500 000– ±5 000 000	Reddish-brown lateritic soils, latosols, laterite soils, ferrallitic soils, white sands	Oxisols

Very strong physical weathering processes, together with transportation of this fresh material by water, wind and gravity provided a totally
new and fresh parent material cover over more than 90% of the
surface of the temperate areas.

The soils in the present temperate zone are relatively young, rich in
chemical components and, depending on their parent materials, of
medium texture and physically rather favourable (as shown in Table 2).

South and north of the Sahara in the subtropical and tropical
savanna zones climates fluctuated in response to the glacial and inter-
glacial periods in the northern hemisphere. In these areas, however,
climates with strong dry seasons alternated with wet climates. Periodically the vegetational cover became sparse and erosion took place, but
not on scales comparable with the erosion in the glaciated and peri-
glaciated areas.

The majority of the soils in this area have not been eroded or have only been partly eroded. This means that together with the accelerated soil formation that resulted from the higher temperatures, the soils are much more developed and may be considered as mature soils. The main soil-forming processes are listed and briefly described in Table 4.

TABLE 4

IMPORTANT PROCESSES OF SOIL FORMATION, WORKING OVER LONG PERIODS AND EFFECTIVE IN THE SUBTROPICAL AND TROPICAL ZONES, WITH THEIR RESULTING HORIZONS AND SOME SOILS IN WHICH THEY OCCUR

Process term	Brief description	Horizons	Soils
Chemical weathering	Chemical disintegration and decomposition of rocks and minerals including oxidation, reduction hydration, hydrolysis and solution of the substances formed	Older cambic B, wet cambic B, wet argillic B, red argillic B, oxic B	Planosols, red Mediterranean soils, ultisols, oxisols
Eluviation	Progressive movement of material out of a portion of the soil, or out of the whole soil, causing extreme low plant nutrient contents	Argillic B with low base sat., oxic B	Ultisols, oxisols
Rubification and ferrugination	Continued release of iron from primary minerals, progressive oxidation, dehydration and crystallisation, giving the soil matrix reddish and red colours	Older cambic B, and argillic B, oxic B	Red inceptisols, red alfisols, ultisols oxisols
Laterisation (desilication, ferrallitisation)	Chemical migration of silica out of the soil solum and thus concentration of the sesquioxides in the solum	Oxic B, plinthite	Oxisols, white sands

The table also shows the resulting soil horizons and the soils in which they occur. In Table 5 the most important soil characteristics are listed for some mature soils.

Soil conditions in the subtropical subhumid to arid climate zones may be summarised based on Tables 4 and 5 as follows:

In the arid tropical areas, azonal soils such as lithosols, sands, etc.

TABLE 5

SOME MATURE AND SENILE ZONAL SOILS AND THEIR MOST IMPORTANT CHARACTERISTICS IN RELATION TO CROP GROWTH

Zonal great soil groups	Native vegetation	Drainage	A_1	Texture	Rooting depth	pH	Chemical fertility	Other characteristics	Present land use
Red and yellow podzolic soils	Deciduous and some mixed forms	Good to medium	Weak	Medium	Deep	Low	Low	Responsive to fertilisers	Cropland and forests
Reddish-brown savanna soils	Tall grass and shrubs	Good to medium	Weak	Medium (to heavy)	Moderate to deep	Medium	Low	Responds well to irrigation	Grazing in large units
Red and brown Mediterranean soils	Winter green forests	Good to medium	Weak	Heavy	Deep	Medium to low	Medium	—	Cropland, fruits
Black cotton soils	Grass and some shrubs	Poor	Weak	Very heavy	Poor	High to medium	Medium	Responsive to irrigation	Grazing, irrigated crops
Reddish-brown lateritic soils	Tropical rain forest	Good	Weak	Medium to light	Very deep	Very low	Very low	Response low to fertilisation	Fruit plantations, subsistence crops
White sands	Savanna	Good to poor	Weak	Light	Deep to shallow	Very low	Very low	—	Extensive grazing

are covering the major land surfaces. As a result of the shift of the arid zone, fossil well-developed red soils are occurring.

The semi-arid and semi-humid zones include partly reddish soils of heavy textures, and medium to deep root depths. The drainage is good to medium but the poor permeability together with the extreme climatic conditions give major problems in relation to erosion. Relatively high amounts of fertilisers are needed on the chemically poor soils. Other important parts of this zone are occupied by flat land with very heavy textured black cotton soils, now mostly under extensive grazing. Upon irrigation and application of fertilisers, however, these very difficult soils may give reasonable yields, if properly managed (Blokhuis, 1980). The main difficulties in the semi-arid and semi-humid subtropical and tropical areas are unstable climatic conditions, land labouring, erosion hazards, fertility problems and danger of salinity.

On both sides of the equator, in the areas still covered by humid tropical forests, dense vegetation has covered the soils for a very long period. The land surfaces are stable and only slightly eroded and here senile soils are found. They are completely leached and chemically degraded and their clay colloids are broken down or are inactive. Only aluminium and iron oxides are left giving the soils an excellent stable structure (Tables 4 and 5). In this zone senile zonal soils are occurring, indicated as lateritic or latosols and in the modern classifications as oxisols. All are deeply rootable, beautifully structured soils, physically very favourable, but extremely poor from a chemical point of view. A further difficulty arises from their low absorption capacity that, together with the high rainfall, makes the application of fertiliser very uneconomic.

Large land surfaces are occupied by planosols which are mostly used for irrigated crops such as rice. These are also very poor soils, both from a physical and a chemical point of view (Brinkman, 1980).

The best soils in the tropical zones are the azonal soils derived from volcanic materials and from rich alluvium, on which the majority of the population of the tropics depend.

POTENTIAL PRODUCTIVITY

To obtain a clear idea about the maximum land productivity of a certain soil it is necessary to know the local potential level of production. As mentioned earlier, the basis of all crop production is dependent upon radiation from the sun, which provides the energy for photosynthesis. Moving in a northern direction, temperature will progressively limit the length of the growing season, and the total effective amount of radiant energy will also decrease.

The theoretical potential production for the latitude at Wageningen was determined by de Wit (1965) as being about 200 kg dry organic matter per day per hectare. This represents the production of a standard crop, well supplied with nutrients, oxygen and water in a stable soil, under the weather conditions of a sunny summer's day in England and in Holland. Under these conditions the conversion of CO_2 and H_2O into carbohydrates depends only on the number of days of growth of the plant, the day length and the intensity of the light during each day (clear days or overcast days). With the help of the formulas of de Wit (1965) and relatively simple climatical data, the 'mean monthly gross photosynthesis product', expressed in 'kg carbohydrates per hectare per month' can be computed for every place. To calculate the 'amount of plant dry matter with a standard chemical composition' a reduction factor of 0·65 is applied (Penning de Vries, 1973).

Buringh et al. (1975) determined the potential production of dry matter (PPDM) for their 'broad soil regions' of the world. PPDM is the sum of the average potential production of each month. Only months with a mean temperature of 10°C or higher during at least 3 months are taken into consideration, because a growing season of less than 3 months does not allow arable farming.

The PPDM of a theoretical standard crop includes roots, stems, leaves, flowers and fruits. To convert PPDM into the potential production in grain equivalents (PPGE), e.g. of wheat or rice, Buringh et al. (1975) made assumptions leading to a reduction factor of 0·43. Now, however, this treatment is considered too simple for such a complex situation. In recent literature (Buringh, 1980), this reduction factor is studied in relation to the kind of crop varieties, management practices, finer climatic variations, etc. and is found to vary greatly, but to avoid complications, the factor of 0·43 will be retained.

The value obtained for PPGE is the absolute maximum yield produced by an ideal variety of a theoretical crop, growing during the whole period at temperatures $\geq 10°C$, on an ideal soil, not threatened by adverse weather conditions, diseases or lack of water. In Figs 8, 9, 10 and 11 the PPGE is shown for broad soil regions (see later) in relation to Europe, northern and central America, South America and Asia.

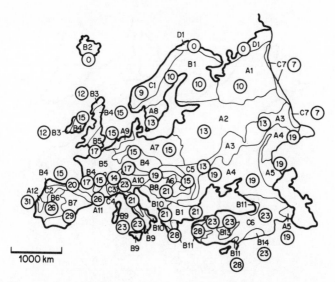

FIG. 8. Europe. Broad soil regions (after Buringh *et al.*, 1975) with potential productivity in grain equivalents per hectare (PPGE).

In Europe (Fig. 8) the PPGE is increasing from 0 in Iceland and the tundras of northern Russia, to 10 t ha^{-1} in Finland and middle Sweden, 12–13 t ha^{-1} in southern Sweden, Scotland, western Ireland and central Russia, 15–17 t ha^{-1} in England, Holland, western and northern France and south-western Germany, 19 t ha^{-1} in southern Russia, and 26–31 t ha^{-1} in the Mediterranean areas of southern Turkey, Greece, Italy, Spain and Portugal.

In North and Central America (Fig. 9) the same tendency is found. The PPGE increases from 9 to 13 t ha^{-1} in Canada, to 19 t ha^{-1} in the northern chernozem area, 23–30 t ha^{-1} in the Gulf Coast States, 26–28 t ha^{-1} in California and 34 t ha^{-1} in central Mexico, the central American countries and the Caribbean Islands. In South America (Fig. 10) the high level of PPGE of 32–34 t ha^{-1} is continued until Uruguay and Argentina, where its value is 24–21 t ha^{-1}. In Africa the PPGE is between 32 and 34 t ha^{-1} over the whole continent.

Asia (Fig. 11) shows wide variations. In this continent the PPGE changes from 0 in northern Siberia and 5–8 t ha^{-1} in western and central Siberia, to 20 and 21–27 t ha^{-1} in Japan and central China respectively, 23 t ha^{-1} in Tibet, and to the same tropical level of

FIG. 9. North and Central America. Broad soil regions (after Buringh *et al.*, 1975) with potential productivity in grain equivalents per hectare (PPGE).

32–34 t ha^{-1} in Saudi Arabia, Iran, India and the whole of South-east Asia.

Australia also shows a high PPGE value of 32–34 t ha^{-1} except in the south where it drops to 26 t ha^{-1} in Victoria. In New Zealand the value falls from 23 in the northern Island to 16 t ha^{-1} in the south.

Areas with high temperatures and clear skies all the year round exhibit maximum PPGE values of 36–38 t ha^{-1} as a result of maximum radiation. Examples are the desert around the Arab Lake, the West Coast of northern South America, in north-eastern Brazil, the eastern Sahal zone, some East African coastal areas, western Madagascar and central Australia. These values have little practical significance, however, because in these areas the lack of water is also maximal.

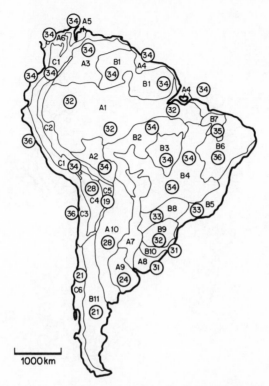

FIG. 10. South America. Broad soil regions (after Buringh *et al.*, 1975) with potential productivity in grain equivalents per hectare (PPGE).

LAND QUALITIES, REQUIREMENTS OF LAND USE TYPES AND BROAD SOIL REGIONS

The potential productivity, both the PPDM as well as the PPGE, although governed by the radiation energy and temperature, is in practice limited by a number of physical factors. These include 'pure' adverse climatical conditions and 'pure' soil conditions, but interacting soil and climatical limitations are more important.

Damage resulting from nightfrost, strong winds, hailstorms, dry winds or heavy rains is due mainly to pure climatical constraints but soils also play some role. On the other hand physical limitations such as poor drainage, impermeable soil layers, stoniness and low chemical fertility are considered pure soil limitations, but climate also has an

FIG. 11. Asia. Broad soil regions (after Buringh *et al.*, 1975) with potential
productivity in grain equivalents per hectare (PPGE).

influence. Normally climate and soils interact in determining the
amount of available water, seedbed preparation or the possibility of
harvesting root crops mechanically. If a clear idea is to be obtained
about the demands which the cultivation of a certain crop puts on the
land or of the extent to which land causes limitations for crop growth
then account must be taken of the land qualities and the requirements
of the land use types. Certain types of land use are determined by basic
ecological, management and conservational requirements, which in
turn affect land evaluation.

The land qualities required for good crop land may be listed as
follows (selected from Beek and Bennema, 1972):

1. Sufficient drainage to allow deep root growth.
2. Enough available water to prevent growth stagnation.
3. Enough available nutrients for the full development of the crop.

4. Suitable conditions for the preparation of a good seedbed.
5. Soil/weather conditions for growth, ripening and harvesting of crops.
6. Trafficability from farm to land and on the land.
7. Suitability for mechanised operations.
8. Resistance to erosion.

In the normal procedure of land evaluation, all qualities of each land unit are analysed, rated and compared with the requirements of land use. For our immediate purpose, however, this is not possible and, in accordance with Buringh (1980), the limitations are combined as (a) soil/land limitations and (b) water deficiency limitations. For the water deficiency limitations, calculations are made on the basis of the ratio between actual transpiration and the potential evapotranspiration, presuming that all soils have a water storage capacity of 150 mm water. This assumption is far from correct but the simplification is necessary in order to avoid complicated calculations.

For land evaluation purposes, Beek (1978) describes land in terms of land (mapping) units (LU) and compares the land qualities of these LUs with the requirements of the land utilisation types (LUTs). For the same reason Buringh distinguished his 222 physiographic broad soil regions, each region being more or less homogeneous in terms of soil and climatic conditions.

Figure 12 shows how these broad soil regions in northern America are related with the soil map. To distinguish the broad soil regions rough topographical characteristics are also taken into account. Lowlands, uplands and high mountains are indicated by A, B and C, respectively. The letter D is used for dry deserts and tundras where crop production is impossible or only possible with irrigation.

It will be clear that the broad soil regions may still include very different soils and climates but that they are homogeneous enough in both aspects on this scale to serve as a basis for calculations of the productivity.

In every broad soil region of the categories A, B and C, part of the soils are unsuitable for crop production as a result of unfavourable land qualities. They may be too steep, too shallow, too stony, too badly drained, too poor, or in permanent use for non-agricultural purposes. The area taken into urbanisation, etc. is rapidly increasing (in the USA by a rate of 1 000 000 ha year^{-1}); nearly always it is the best quality land that is used (Buringh, 1981).

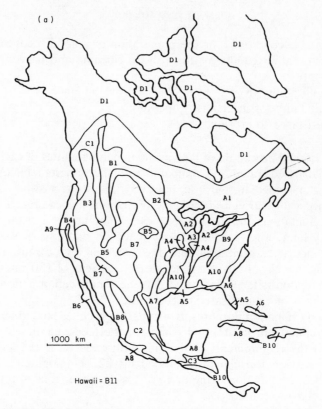

(a)

FIG. 12. (a) The broad soil regions of North and Central America (after Buringh *et al.*, 1975) compared with (b) the soil map of a part of northern America.

Key to part (b):

Zonal soils

Pz	Podzol soils
G	Grey wooded soils (Canada)
BP	Brown podzolic soils
GB	Grey-brown podzolic soils
RY	Red and yellow podzolic soils
Pr	Prairie soils
RPr	Reddish prairie soils
Cz	Chernozem soils
Cs	Chestnut soils
RCh	Reddish chestnut soils
Br	Brown soils
RBr	Reddish brown soils
NC	Non-calcic brown (Shantung brown) soils
Sz	Sierozem (grey desert) soils
RD	Red desert soils

Intrazonal soils

Pl	Planosols
Rz	Rendzina soils
So	Solonchak and solonetz soils
W	Wiesenböden, ground-water podzol and half bog soils
Bg	Bog soils

Azonal soils

L	Lithosols and shallow soils, sands, lava bed
A	Alluvial soils

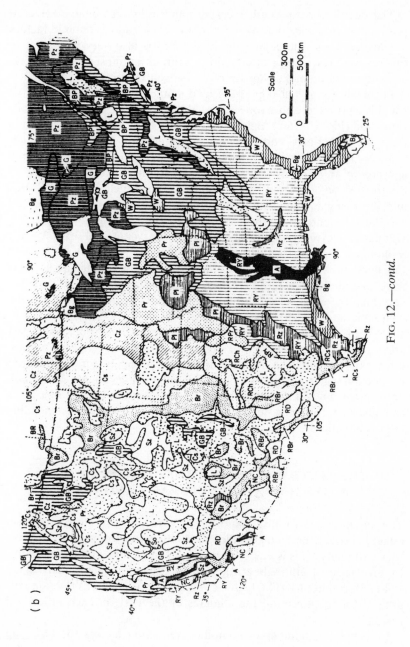

Fig. 12.—contd.

The decision as to whether certain land units are suitable for crop production is a very delicate one. Many social and economic factors are involved and the capital input required is also very important in this respect. The danger of erosion or salinisation must be assessed, as must the environmental impact of a changed landscape.

For each broad soil region the land suitable for crop production is roughly appraised and expressed as the fraction of potential agricultural land (FPAL). Very high values of 0·45–0·50, or even greater than 0·5, are sometimes encountered. South-eastern England, Holland, France and southern Germany as well as the Po valley and the chernozem areas of eastern Europe, and southern Russia inclusive of South-west Siberia show FPAL values > 0·45. Much of Ireland, Mid- and West England and southern Sweden exhibit values of 0·25–0·3 but for West Ireland, and northern Scotland the fraction is < 0·15. For Denmark, North Germany and Poland, the value is 0·30–0·35; for mountainous countries such as Spain, the value is 0·20–0·25. In Asia the flood plains of the large Chinese, Indian and Bangladesh rivers have extremely high FPALs of > 0·5. The south-eastern USA shows very high fractions, whilst in South America large areas in Venezuela, Columbia and Uruguay have FPALs of 0·35–0·4. Central and southern Africa are characterised by FPAL values of 0·30–0·35. These last areas contain huge surfaces of potential agricultural land, at present little exploited and so forming important reserves for future crop production. They also have high PPGE values (Figs 10 and 11). It will be of great interest to know the maximum possible yields these areas can sustain in order to judge if it is eventually worthwhile extending crop production.

THE MAXIMUM PRODUCTION (MPGE) OF THE POTENTIAL AGRICULTURAL LAND (PAL)

The potential agricultural land (PAL) area is not always of high quality: in fact, its land qualities in relation to crop production may vary extremely. This is due both to climate as well as to soil conditions. In the study of Buringh et al. (1975), reduction factors caused by soil/land conditions (FSC) and by water deficiency (FWD) are appraised for the soils and the climates of the PAL in each broad soil region.

In Table 6 a number of combined reduction factors for FSC and

TABLE 6

THE POTENTIAL PRODUCTIVITY IN GRAIN EQUIVALENTS (PPGE); THE FRACTION OF POTENTIAL AGRICULTURAL LAND (FPAL); THE REDUCTION FACTORS FOR SOIL/LAND CONDITIONS (FSC) AND WATER DEFICIENCIES (FWD) AND THE MAXIMUM LAND PRODUCTIVITY IN GRAIN EQUIVALENTS FOR A NUMBER OF INTERESTING BROAD SOIL REGIONS ACCORDING TO BURINGH *et al.* (1975)

Broad soil regions		PPGE	FPAL	FSC	FWD	FSC + FWD	Maximum land productivity, grain equivalents ($t\,ha^{-1}$)
West Norway	(C1)	9	0·5	0.7	1·0	0·7	6
S.E. Norway	(B1)	10	0·3	0·5	1·0	0·5	5
N. Scotland and W. Ireland	(B3)	12	0·2	0·6	1·0	0·6	7
Central Ireland and Mid Europe	(B4)	15	0·4	0·7	0·9	0·63	9
Denmark, Poland and N. Germany	(A7)	15	0·6	0·7	0·8	0·56	8
Central Russia (most)	A2	13	0·4	0·6	0·9	0·54	7
S.E. England and France	B5	17	0·6	0·8	0·9	0·72	12
Holland	A9	15	0·5	0·9	1·0	0·9	13
Chernozem Russia	A4	19	0·7	0·9	0·5	0·45	9
Po delta	A10	23	0·6	0·9	0·3 (irr.)	0·27	7
Spain	B7	29	0·5	0·6	0·3 (irr.)	0·18	6
S. Italy	B9	23	0·5	0·7	0·3	0·21	4·5
Greece	B11	28	0·2	0·7	0·3	0·21	5
S.E. Canada	A1	13	0·4	0·5	0·9	0·45	6
Chernozem Canada	B1	14	0·5	0·8	0·5	0·4	6
Cornbelt USA	A3	24	0·7	0·9	0·5	0·45	11
Florida USA	A6	30	0·6	0·6	1·0	0·6	18
N. Island	B12	23	0·5	0·7	0·9	0·63	15
Central Congo	B10	33	0·6	0·5	0·5	0·25	8
East Africa	B11	33	0·3	0·6	0·5	0·3	10
Japan	B15	20	0·4	0·7	1·0	0·7	14
Central China	A7	21	0·6	0·9	0·5	0·45	9
S. China	B7	27	0·3	0·5	0·9	0·45	12
Ganges delta	A3	34	0·6	0·9	0·7	0·63	21
Java	B10	35	0·5	0·7	0·8	0·56	20
Low Colombia	A3	34	0·5	0·7	0·7	0·49	17
Amazon area	A1	32	0·5	0·6	0·8	0·48	15
Central Brazil	B4	34	0·5	0·6	0·6	0·36	12
N. Argentine	A9	24	0·5	0·9	0·6	0·54	13

FWD are listed together with PPGE and FPAL values; in the last column the resulting maximum land productivity in grain equivalents (MPGE), calculated from PPGE and the combined reduction factor, are given. In Europe the combined reduction factors (FSC and FWD) differ greatly, as shown by some selected broad soil regions in Table 6 and on the map (Fig. 13), and lead to great differences in MPGE for

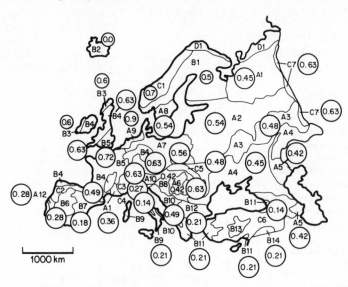

FIG. 13. Europe. The combined reduction factors for limiting soil conditions (FSC) and limiting water deficiencies (FWD) for the calculation of maximum land productivity in grain equivalents (MPGE) and of potential productivity in grain equivalents per hectare (PPGE) shown for the broad soil regions of Europe.

these regions. In south-east England and in France the combined reduction factor is 0·7 giving a MPGE of 12 t ha^{-1}. In Holland this factor is 0·9, which means agricultural land with soils of high quality (FSC = 0·9) and practically no water deficiencies (FWD = 1·0). For this reason the MPGE is 13 t ha^{-1}, somewhat higher than the value for England although the PPGE is lower. In Ireland and the English Midlands only 9 t ha^{-1} is possible, and in Denmark, Poland and northern Germany only 8 t ha^{-1}.

Although soil conditions in the chernozem areas of Russia have satisfactory FSC (i.e. 0·9) and PPGE values are not very low, water deficiencies (FWD = 0·5) reduce the combined reduction factor to

0·45, and so the MPGE is only 9 t ha^{-1}. Marked water deficiencies are also responsible for the very low reduction factors in the Po delta (0·27), Spain (0·18), southern Italy (0·21) and Greece (0·21) and result in extremely low MPGE values of 7, 6, 4·5 and 5 t ha^{-1}, respectively, unless the land is irrigated. Even in Norway, with much lower PPGEs, the MPGE is still about 5–6 t ha^{-1} due to the high rainfall.

Table 6 also shows some other important broad soil regions of the world. In Canada the MPGEs are only 6 t ha^{-1}, partly because of water deficiency (the chernozem area) and partly as a result of poor soil conditions (South-east Canada). The USA cornbelt shows a MPGE of 11 t ha^{-1} because of a higher PPGE. Values in Florida are highest (18 t ha^{-1}) because there is no lack of water and the PPGE is high. New Zealand's North Island has a relatively high MPGE (15 t ha^{-1}) due to high soil quality and favourable rainfall. In Africa, although the PPGE is high, the combined reduction factor is extremely low (0·25– 0·3), resulting in MPGEs of 8 and 10 t ha^{-1} for the Congo and East Africa, respectively. The FPAL, however, is relatively high (0·5 and 0·6, respectively), which suggests that an extension of production may be readily possible in these areas.

Japan shows a high reduction factor of 0·7 and relatively high MPGEs. Central and southern China, in contrast, exhibit lower values of 9 and 12 t ha^{-1}, respectively, attributable to water deficiencies in central China and poor soil conditions in South China. Moreover, in South China the FPAL is also very low. Very high MPGEs are found for the Ganges–Brahmaputa flood-plain and delta and for Java (21 and 20 t ha^{-1}, respectively). Both broad soil regions show excellent soil conditions and relatively low water deficiencies (reduction factors of 0·63 and 0·56, respectively). Since FPALs are also relatively high in both areas (0·6 and 0·5), these factors together explain the ability of these regions to feed an enormous population.

In the tropical parts of South America, the MPGEs are considerable, e.g. 17, 15 and 12 t ha^{-1} for Lower Columbia, the Amazon area and central Brazil, respectively. Because of the rather high FPALs, the enormous land areas and the low number of inhabitants, some of the most important land reserves for agricultural production are present in these regions. Northern Argentina, which also has a high reduction factor (0·54), shows a high MPGE.

In conclusion, the foregoing account has shown how the MPGE can be estimated for each broad soil region. More detailed work which is being performed in some research centres will provide more detailed forecasts, as soon as more information on soils, climates, crops, etc. is available. It will be especially important for land qualities to be determined more precisely. Such additional information will also clarify why actual productivities fall so far behind the maximal land productivities in many cases.

REFERENCES

Anon (1980a). Summary Description of Thailand Agricultural Model, THAM-1. Centre for World Food Studies, Res. Rep. SOW 80-2, Wageningen.

Anon (1980b). The Model of Physical Crop Production. Centre for World Food Studies, Res. Rep. SOW 80-5, Wageningen.

Beck, K. J. and Bennema, J. (1972). Land evaluation for rural purposes. Proc. Second Asian Soil Conference, Jacarta, Indonesia. Vol. 1, pp. 295–302.

Beek, K. Y. (1978). Land Evaluation for Agricultural Development. ILRI Publ. no. 23, Wageningen.

Birkeland, P. W. (1974). Pedology, Weathering and Geomorphological Research. Oxford University Press, London.

Blokhuis, W. L. (1980). Vertisols. In: Land Reclamation and Water Management. Developments, Problems and Challenges. ILRI Publ. no. 27, Wageningen, pp. 44–8.

Brinkman, R. and Smyth, A. J. (Eds) (1973). Land Evaluation for Rural Purposes. Summ. of Exp. Consult., 1972. ILRI Publ. no. 17, Wageningen.

Brinkman, R. (1980). Planosols. In: Land Reclamation and Water Management. Developments, Problems and Challenges. ILRI Publ. no. 27, Wageningen, pp. 57–61.

Bunting, B. T. (1966). The Geography of Soil. Hutch. Univ. Library, London.

Buol, S. W., Hole, E. D. and McCracken, R. J. (1973). Soil Genesis and Classification. Iowa State Univ. Press, Iowa.

Buringh, P. (1977). Food production potential of the world. World Developm. 5(5–7), 477–85.

Buringh, P. (1980). A Comparison of Three Methods for Supplying Physical Data on a Crop Production for Agricultural Development. Centre for World Food Studies, Res. Rep. SOW 80-3, Wageningen.

Buringh, P. (1981). De wereldvoedselvoorziening (world food supply). In address at the opening of the 63rd Dies Natalis of the Agricultural University, Wageningen, 9 March.

Buringh, P. and van Heemst, H. D. J. (1977). An Estimation of World Food Production Based on Labour-orientated Agriculture. Centre for World Food Market Res., Amsterdam–The Hague–Wageningen.

Buringh, P., van Heemst, H. D. J. and Staring, G. J. (1975). Computation of the Absolute Maximum Food Production of the World. Agric. Univ. Wageningen, Wageningen.

Carter, G. F. and Pendleton, R. L. (1956). The humid soil; process and time. Geogr. Rev. 46, 488–507.

de Wit, C. T. (1965). Photosynthesis of leaf canopies. *Versl. Landbk. Onderz.* (*Agr. Res. Reports*) 663.

Dokuchayev, V. V. (1886). Materialen zur Wertschätzung der Böden des Gouvernements Nishnij-Novgorod I (Russian).

Fitzpatrick, E. A. (1980). *Soils, their Formation, Classification and Distribution.* Longman Inc., London, New York.

Ganssen, R. and Hädrig, F. (1965), *Atlas zur Bodenhunde Bibliograf.* Inst. AG, Mannheim.

Knapp, B. J. (1979). *Soil Processes.* George Allen and Unwin, London.

Linnemann, H. and Buringh, P. (1981). *De wereldvoedselvoorziening.* Rede 63 e Dies Natalis Landbouw Hogeschool, Wageningen.

Marbut, C. F. (1928). A scheme for soil classification. *Proc. First Int. Congr. Soil Science 4,* pp. 1–31.

Penning de Vries, F. W. T. (1973). *Substrate Utilisation and Respiration in Relation to Growth and Maintenance in Higher Plants.* Agric. Univ. Wageningen, Wageningen.

Pons, L. J. (1977). Soil management and soil improvement in the planning of mechanized intensive kinds of agricultural land use and their requirements to land qualities. *SEFMIA Proc. Int. Sem. Soil Env. and Fert. Man in Intensive Agr.,* Tokyo, pp. 18–34.

Schlichting, E. (1964). *Einführing in die Bodenhunde.* Verlag Paul Parey, Hamburg and Berlin.

Sibirtsev, N. M. (1899). Kurze Uebersicht der wichtigsten Bodentypen. Ruszland. Die Not. der Inst. v. Nowo-Alexandria 11 (Russian).

Strahler, A. N. (1960). *Physical Geography,* 2nd edn. John Wiley and Sons, New York.

Thorpe, J. (1931). The effects of vegetation and climate upon soil profiles in northern and northwestern Wyoming. *Soil Science* **32,** 283–301.

US Dept. of Agriculture (1938). *Yearbook of Agriculture.* US Government Printing Office, Washington DC.

US Dept. of Agriculture (1975). *Soil Taxonomy. A Basic System of Soil Classification for Making and Interpreting Soil Surveys.* Agricultural Handbook no. 436. US Government Printing Office, Washington DC.

Discussion

Professor Buringh pointed out that the information which Professor Pons had given relating to potential productivity which was based on his work was now somewhat outdated. The earlier figures and diagrams had related to calculations from radiation input and temperature and attempted to predict what maximum photosynthetic yield would be if the canopy of the crop was closed throughout the whole growing season. This was clearly a wrong interpretation of data which gave an over-estimate because, even theoretically, crop yield cannot be simply the product of radiation input and growing season length. The old and more recent figures suggested that maximal productivity would be considerably lower. The interesting thing, however, was that in Holland average farm production was already approaching these revised estimates of average maximal productivity. *Professor Pons* agreed that the figures of Professor Buringh which he had quoted did imply a closed canopy. They had value for reasons of comparison, not only between different climates, but also to get an equal theoretical maximum level to start from. Potential productivity is a theoretical, but simple, level of reference on which all kinds of reduction factors may be applied to get maximum productivity for certain crops, soils and climates. *Professor Bushuk* asked whether, on the basis of current knowledge, we could begin to make decisions about certain husbandry practices which would be compatible with the long-term maintenance of soil fertility. He was thinking particularly about minimal or zero tillage. The same general point was elaborated on later in the discussion by *Dr Lake*. He drew attention to the marked changes which could take place in the ecology of the soil if inversion of the soil by the time-honoured methods of ploughing were discontinued and so-called minimal cultivation adopted. He pointed out that because of the advent of herbicides it was no longer necessary to cultivate land deeply to control weeds and that in some countries like Bangladesh, where intensive hand-weeding of crops was practised, non-inversion of the soil was a

39

practical reality. He made a plea for the preparation of maps similar to those prepared in the UK indicating on what soils non-inversion processes could be adopted. *Professor Pons*, in reply to these questions, emphasised the weather-dependent nature of seedbed preparation which must take place whether there was soil inversion or not and additionally drew attention to work in progress in Holland relating to the effect of traffic on the soil. Experiments were not complete, but should provide interesting data related to soil compaction. Generally, however, *Professor Pons* thought that not enough knowledge was really available on this point. Probably for some soils this would already be possible. But the problem was so complicated that, at the moment, no overall models for different soils could be constructed.

A general discussion took place relating to other aspects of the calculation of potential productivity. *Professor Jarvis* asked about the derivation of the grain equivalent yield and whether the factor 0·43 was based on the harvest index, to which *Professor Pons* replied that this was an average factor equal to the ratio of grain dry weight to total dry weight and had been used simply to obtain the potential productivity in grain equivalents. The factor was roughly estimated from very general data, indicating the ratio between grains and roots, stems, leaves and flowers. *Dr Landsberg* asked whether the various modification factors used in the estimation of potential production in grain equivalents had been tested against actual determinations in the field and made a plea for this. *Professor Pons* stated that virtually all the reduction factors applied related to soil conditions as affected by climatical zones. These were very difficult to estimate precisely in an independent fashion and they had associative effects on crop growth. Although rough estimates, they were of considerable importance in the evaluation of land capability. In his opinion it would never be possible to give exact values of these factors. *Professor Buringh* then mentioned the work that he is doing on the building of mathematical models based on available water, nutrient and organic matter for a specific crop growing at a specific site. These were being tested by appeal to experimentation and such work should do much to clarify the factors involved. The problem is now, however, to simplify the obtained data to make the results clear. *Sir Kenneth Blaxter* asked whether the soils of the northern temperate region would eventually mature to become senile in the same way that the soils of the subtropics and tropics had matured and what the implications of this would be in terms of their fertility. Despite the long time scales, can we envisage that the basic fertility of soils in northern Europe and the United States would slowly decline? *Professor Pons* stated that while looked at in the short-term, one could state that the northern soils were in a quasi-equilibrium state, nevertheless they were changing and deteriorating. This was already evident for some soils in the temperate areas developed on poor parent materials. These already showed very poor nutrient status, but man had also contributed to the degradation. The yearly loss, however, was so small that only minimal applications of fertilisers might counteract it. In this respect, it was doubtful whether in recent times, with all kinds of polluted rains, the leaching was yet continuing. Rubification would certainly also spread over temperate soils if the soils were given enough time (>40 000 years) to develop. *Professor Truszczynski* asked whether there were any close links between soil type, the zonal distribution of soils and soil classification with the health and well-being of animals and man and with the quality of produce. *Dr Fowden*, in reply, stated that perhaps this aspect would be dealt with later in the Symposium and that perhaps the question could be considered latèr during the course of discussions. *Professor Pons* commented that the quality of wheat was certainly partly associated with climatic factors and particularly with the water supply at different tension levels in the soil.

Professor MacKey pointed out that man had in fact tried to find solutions to problems of difficult climate and difficult soil in particular regions. He instanced the work on the Negev where there is but 50 mm of rain per annum. The soils here characteristically form a crust which gives a water run-off with little penetration, allowing water to be accumulated in depressions. Since biblical times the populations there have found this to be a solution in a difficult agricultural situation and at present Israeli practices in that line appear to be highly successful. Similarly, there are problems arising with regard to agricultural practices leading to the misuse of soil and the emergence of problems such as aluminium toxicity. Here breeding of plants tolerant to adverse conditions could be highly successful and he instanced the International Rice Research Institute programmes where some success had been obtained. He pointed out that in fact man's activities can result in a movement against the general rule of decline in soil fertility with time.

Mr Wilkinson of ADAS stated that while it was interesting to look at land capability on a global scale, the local problem is usually far more important. He instanced the blueprint approach to crop production which had resulted in considerable increases in yield through activities of those farmers who practised this approach. Here, cognisance was taken of soil and cultural factors required to overcome the known physical limitations. However, economic factors became overriding in deciding what was possible. Land capability maps are based upon a physical classification which must be dynamic and not static and climatic change or extreme variability could well result in an alteration in the capability of the land resources within a country. *Professor Pons* replied that he had chosen this small scale of generalisation in relation to the targets of the Symposium. For this reason, the land qualities could not be dealt with in detail. For greater scale problems, land qualities could be calculated in more detail, but he had always taken into account that land qualities which might limit the crop growth were nearly always dynamic combinations of climate and soil characteristics. Changes in climate may also change the characteristics of the soil, but only in the long-term. Changes in water regime however may induce short-term changes. Chernozems in eastern Europe, for example, were after 10 years of irrigation already showing marked decreases in the organic matter contents of the A_1 horizon because of accelerated microbiological decomposition under longer humid conditions when irrigated. Erosion and salinisation may also change the soil rapidly. Changes of climate will, however, change land qualities and for this reason will also change crop production. *Dr Gormley* raised questions related to elevated carbon dioxide levels in peat soils and how this influenced the growth of leafy crops but the Chairman decided that this was better left until later in the Symposium when these specific aspects would be dealt with.

Climate and Crop Distribution

A. H. BUNTING,[a] M. D. DENNETT,[b] J. ELSTON[c]
and C. B. SPEED[b]

[a] *Plant Science Laboratories,* [b] *Department of Agricultural Botany,*
University of Reading, UK

[c] *Department of Plant Sciences, University of Leeds, UK*

INTRODUCTION

Climate is the major factor determining the world distribution of crop species. The climate of a locality restricts the choice of species which can be grown. Other factors, particularly economic and social considerations and soil type, then determine which of the suitable species a farmer grows.

In this paper we shall describe the world distribution of crop species and the climates in which some species are grown. From this we can suggest the nature of the various climatic constraints on crop distribution.

CROP DISTRIBUTION

Man relies on relatively few crops for the greater part of his food supply. The estimated world output in 1978 of the major crops, other than fruits and vegetables, is shown in Table 1 using data collated by FAO (FAO, 1980). These 20 crops are those whose annual output, worldwide, is more than 10 million tonnes. The first three crops, wheat, rice and maize, account for 58% of the output of these 20 crops. The first seven account for nearly 80%. It is apparent that if so few species provide so large a part of the world food output each must include a range of types and cultivars adapted to different environmental conditions. Nevertheless, as we shall see, each species is adapted to a relatively narrow band of climatic conditions.

43

TABLE 1

WORLD PRODUCTION, AREA HARVESTED AND AVERAGE YIELD PER HECTARE OF
THE 20 MAJOR CROP SPECIES IN 1978. PRODUCTION OF ROOT AND TUBER
CROPS GIVEN AT 14% WATER CONTENT AND OF SUGAR CROPS AS TONNES OF
SUGAR. DATA FROM FAO (1980)

Crop	Production (million tonnes)	Area harvested (million ha)	Average yield (tonnes ha^{-1})
Wheat	450	266	1·90
Rice (in husk)	386	145	2·66
Maize	364	118	3·08
Barley	194	94	2·07
Soya beans	81	53	1·51
Cane sugar	76	13	5·71
Sorghum	69	52	1·31
Potatoes	54	18	2·91
Pulses	51	72	0·71
Oats	51	28	1·83
Cassava	49	14	3·54
Beet sugar	42	9	4·82
Bulrush millet	36	55	0·66
Sweet potato	34	13	2·57
Rye	32	16	1·98
Cottonseed	24	–	–
Plantain	20	–	–
Groundnut	19	19	0·97
Sunflower	13	11	1·15
Oilseed rape	11	11	0·92
Total	2 056	1 007	2·04

The main supplies of dietary energy in most parts of the world come
from two groups of plants, the cereals and the root and tuber crops
(cassava, potatoes, sweet potatoes, yams, aroids). The cereals dominate world agriculture. The four crops with the largest production are
cereals (Table 1). In 1978 approximately 757 million ha of cereals
were harvested. This was about 74% of the harvested area of all crops.
Wheat, rice and maize alone provided 49% of the harvested area. The
harvested area of root and tuber crops was 50 million ha or 5% of the
total harvested area.

The ratio of the harvested area of root and tuber crops to that of
cereals was calculated for each country (Fig. 1). The ratio was greater
than 100% in two areas only—equatorial Africa and Papua New
Guinea. In these areas the climate is generally continuously wet and

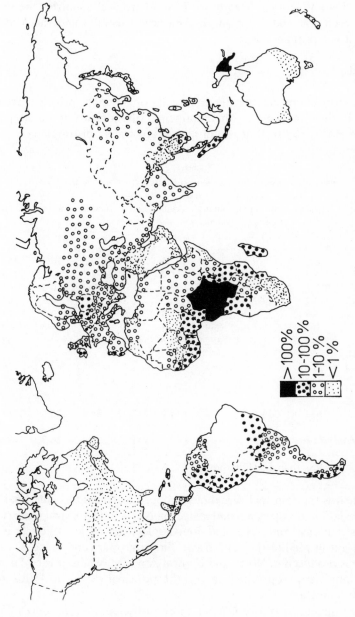

Fig. 1. The area of root and tuber crops as a percentage of the area of cereal crops for each country in 1978.

humid, which hinders the setting of grain in cereals and makes both harvesting and storage hazardous. In most tropical countries the ratio is between 1% and 10%; in N. America, Australia and the Middle East, it is less than 1%.

Cereals

The distribution among the continents of the eight principal cereal crops is given in Table 2. The continental divisions are those adopted by the FAO (1980). Wheat and maize, are widely distributed.

TABLE 2

PRODUCTION OF CEREAL SPECIES (MILLION TONNES) IN 1978

Cereal	Africa	North and Central America	South America	Asia	Europe	USSR	Oceania	World
Wheat	8·6	72·8	12·1	122·5	94·6	120·8	18·6	450·0
Rice	8·3	8·0	11·5	354·0	1·9	2·1	0·5	386·3
Maize	27·8	197·5	26·8	54·2	48·4	9·0	0·3	363·9
Barley	4·2	20·7	1·3	30·2	71·3	62·1	4·3	193·8
Sorghum	10·8	23·8	8·5	23·9	0·8	–	0·7	68·5
Oats	0·2	12·3	0·9	1·5	15·3	18·5	1·8	50·6
Rye	–	1·3	0·2	2·5	14·9	13·6	–	32·5
Bulrush millet	10·5	–	0·3	23·1	–	2·2	–	36·1
Total of above species	70·1	336·4	61·6	611·9	247·72	228·4	26·3	1581·8
Total cereals	71·6	338·3	61·7	617·5	251·2	229·4	26·3	1596·0

–, Indicates less than 100 000 tonnes.

Wheat is the principal cereal of Europe, USSR and Oceania (mainly Australia); it occupies second place in North and Central America, South America and Asia and fourth place in Africa (though it is important in Mediterranean Africa). Fifty-four per cent of the world's maize is produced in North and Central America (where it is by far the most important crop) but it is also the principal cereal in Africa and South America.

The distribution of rice is much more restricted. Asia produces 95%

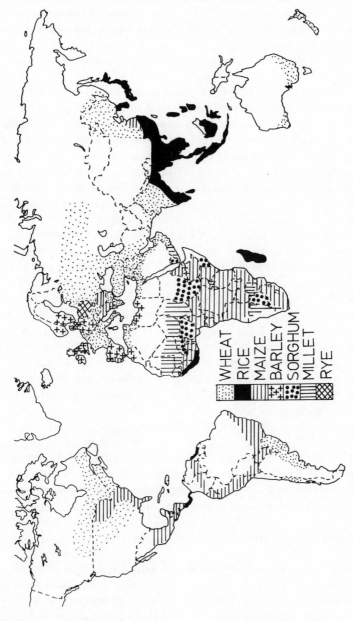

FIG. 2. The predominant cereal crop, by area occupied, for each country in 1978.

of the total output. The main areas of production of barley, oats and rye are in Europe and the USSR which together account for 69, 67 and 88%, respectively, of the world production of these species. Sorghum is produced in Asia, North and Central America and Africa and 93% of the world production of bulrush millet is in Asia and Africa.

An alternative analysis of the relative importance of cereal species can be derived from national agricultural statistics. The FAO publish estimates of the production, area harvested and yield of the main crops, country by country. We have taken the area harvested as a measure of the importance of each crop, and for each country we have ranked the cereal crops in order of decreasing importance. For each country, the first ranking cereal is shown in Fig. 2. In some countries where two cereals occupy very similar total areas, both have been shown, for example millet and sorghum in Upper Volta and Nigeria. Some large countries, such as China, India and USA, where two or more crops are almost equally important but are grown in different areas, have been subdivided. National figures provide only a rough guide to the actual areas of production of particular crops, but more detailed statistics are not easily available for most countries.

It can be seen from Fig. 2 that neighbouring countries tend to have the same principal cereal, suggesting that the major factors affecting the choice of crop operate on a large scale. Particularly noticeable are the areas of rice dominance in South-east Asia and of maize dominance in central and southern parts of America and Africa. Wheat dominates temperate latitudes but is replaced by barley where economic factors are favourable (as in the UK) or the length of growing season is too short (as in Finland, Libya). Rye is now much less important than it was 50 years ago but it remains the principal cereal in Poland. Sorghum is widespread (Table 2) but it is the principal cereal in only a few areas such as Sudan, Botswana and parts of West Africa. Bulrush millet is the principal crop only in the driest areas, particularly in West Africa and Sudan.

Root and tuber crops

An analysis of the world production of root and tuber crops by crop and continent is given in Table 3. As in Table 1, the data have been standardised at 14% water content to facilitate comparison with cereals. The total output, worldwide, at 14% water content, is less than 10% of the total output of cereals.

TABLE 3

PRODUCTION OF ROOT AND TUBER CROPS AT 14% WATER CONTENT IN 1978
(MILLION TONNES)

Crop	Africa	North and Central America	South America	Asia	Europe	USSR	Oceania	Total
Potatoes	0·9	4·0	2·0	6·6	24·0	17·0	0·2	54·7
Cassava	17·5	0·4	12·5	18·6	–	–	0·1	49·1
Sweet potato	1·5	0·4	0·6	31·7	–	–	0·2	34·4
Yams, aroids and others	6·2	0·1	–	0·6	–	–	0·2	7·1
Total roots and tubers	26·1	4·9	15·1	57·5	24·0	17·0	0·7	145·3

–, Indicates less than 100 000 tonnes.

Potatoes are the only significant root and tuber crop in Europe and the USSR, which, taken together, account for 75% of world production. Cassava is the most important root crop in Africa (17·5 Mt) and South America (12·5 Mt) but Asia also produces a substantial quantity (18·6 Mt). Sweet potatoes are produced mainly in Asia (particularly China) which accounts for 92% of world production (31·7 Mt). Similarly, yams are mainly produced in Africa, particularly West Africa (6·3 Mt, 86%) though they are locally very important in parts of Oceania and Central America. These patterns of production can be seen clearly in Fig. 3.

Distribution and origins

From Table 1 and Fig. 2 it would appear that the present day distributions of maize and rice are significantly influenced by their regions of origin in middle America and southern and eastern Asia, respectively. Since its introduction to Africa by the Portuguese early in the sixteenth century, maize has spread, and may well have displaced sorghum, throughout much of Africa, where it is the principal cereal. However, in Madagascar, which is strongly influenced ethnically and culturally by the East Indies, rice is the main cereal. Rice has made surprisingly limited inroads so far into the wetter parts of Africa. Maize is also important in many countries of Asia and Europe, and its range is extending into cooler regions. Perhaps this reflects the wide range of ecological adaptations of maize in traditional Amerindian

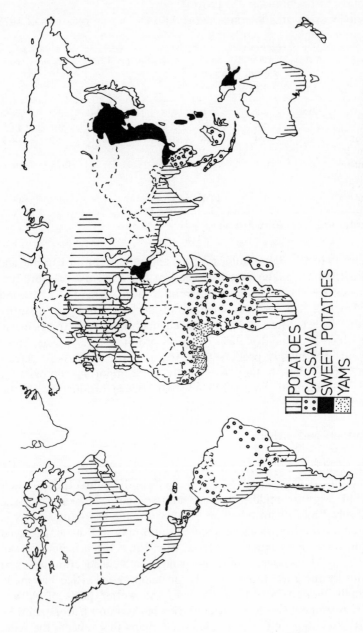

FIG. 3. The predominant root and tuber crop, by area occupied, for each country in 1978.

agriculture throughout the Americas before Columbus, aided perhaps, by its outcrossing breeding system which readily enables an unselected population of maize to generate new diversity in new environments.

Wheat ranged in early times throughout Europe, the Mediterranean basin and Asia from its original homeland in the Fertile Crescent of South-west Asia and after the 'Discovery' it was carried to the Americas and spread widely there. It may well be that wheat was originally outbreeding, and that while it was still in active genetic contact with its wild relatives it became adapted to a wide range of environments in its native region, much as in the case of maize.

Sorghum and bulrush millet are African cereals. Sorghum evolved in the seasonally arid but relatively wetter parts of the Sudan–Ethiopian region, whereas bulrush millet was probably domesticated in what is now the Sahara desert. Both crops spread to Asia, like many other African economic plants, thousands of years ago. The oldest known archaeological sorghum was in India 5000 years ago. Sorghum was carried to the Americas about 100 years ago. Barley, oats and rye have remained largely European and Russian except for the importation of barley and oats into North America by European settlers in the eighteenth and nineteenth centuries.

Of the root and tuber crops, potato is now more important in Europe and the USSR, and cassava in Africa and Asia, than in their native America. Potato comes from higher and cooler regions, and cassava from lower and warmer regions, in the Americas.

Sweet potato is generally regarded as an American cultigen, but it is today important mainly in Asia and parts of the Pacific. This distribution, and some unresolved questions about the time and manner of its appearance in the Western Pacific, would be more easily understood if it were to be found that this crop was domesticated separately in Asia and the Americas, but for this we do not have evidence at present.

Interesting as these evolutionary influences on distribution are, adaptation to climate is plainly the most significant determinant of the current and future distribution of crops.

CLIMATE AND CROP DISTRIBUTION

Though historical and evolutionary factors seem to have some influence on distribution, it is also evident that each crop is adapted to different climatic conditions. To define these, monthly means or totals

of climatic data were assembled for representative locations of production of wheat, rice, maize and bulrush millet. Usually one climatic
location was selected for each country in which the crop concerned
occupied more than 5% of total harvested area. The approximate
growing season was estimated for each crop and the mean temperature
of that season was calculated. These means have been plotted against
annual rainfall (Fig. 4). Growing season temperature was chosen

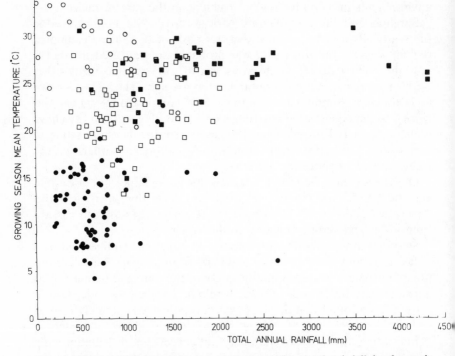

FIG. 4. Mean growing season temperatures and annual rainfall in the main
growing areas of wheat (●), rice (■), millet (○) and maize (□).

because temperatures outside the season can have no more than small
and indirect effects on the crop. Rainfall, however, can be stored in the
soil so that growing season rainfall does not necessarily indicate the
amount of water which can be used by the crop.

Countries where all the production of the crop is irrigated have been
omitted. The four crops occupy distinctive climatic domains. Wheat is

important where mean growing season temperatures are relatively cool, between 5 and 18°C. Where winter wheat is grown, mean values include the temperatures of the winter months. Nevertheless, mean temperatures in the spring and summer rarely exceed 18°C where wheat occupies more than 5% of the total harvested area. Most wheat is grown where total rainfall is between 200 and 1000 mm per year. Rice and bulrush millet are grown where mean temperatures exceed 20°C and may be as hot as 30°C (rice) or nearly 34°C (millet). Bulrush millet is the main cereal of the driest areas. It is restricted to areas of annual rainfall of less than 1000 mm, but at the drier end of the range it can be important where rainfall is less than 100 mm. In such regions specialised cultural practices based on water harvesting in natural or artificial catchments are used. Of all the main cereals bulrush millet is the best adapted to hot environments where the wet season is short. Most rice is in areas wetter than 1000 mm, and is the only important cereal in areas where there is rainfall throughout the year. Maize is important over a wider temperature range than the other cereals (from 13 to 32°C) overlapping with wheat at the cooler end. It is less well adapted than millet to dry conditions, but it is grown in much wetter ones—the range is from 500 to 2000 mm.

In a study of cropping patterns in West Africa (Dennett et al., 1981) the proportion of arable land in a country devoted to particular crops was related to the average length of the period of the year during which rainfall exceeded potential evaporation (M, in days), i.e. a crude measure of the length of the period when growth is not likely to be restricted by water shortage. In this analysis it was not possible to separate the statistics for bulrush millet and sorghum so these crops were treated as one. The fraction of arable land under bulrush millet and sorghum exceeds 0·8 when M is less than 50 days (Fig. 5a). When M exceeds 150 days the fraction under bulrush millet and sorghum is less than 0·3. The fraction of arable land under rice increases with M (Fig. 5b). The proportion of land occupied by maize, which is historically not an important crop in West Africa, does not vary so clearly with M, but Fig. 5c suggests (and agronomic experiments abundantly confirm) that the area under maize could be substantially increased in many West African countries. The converse of this is that the traditionally favoured crop, sorghum, extends in both West Africa and Sudan, deep into increasingly wetter country to which it is increasingly ill-adapted.

The preceding analysis has shown that crops occur in particular

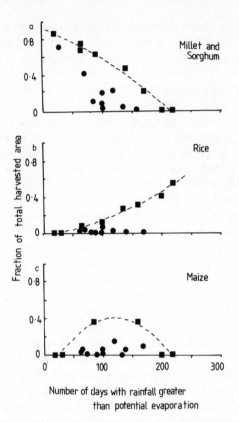

FIG. 5. The fraction of arable land of a country under (a) millet and sorghum, (b) rice and (c) maize, for countries in West Africa, plotted against the number of days in the year when mean rainfall exceeds potential evaporation (M).

climatic domains and that with the partial exception of maize the crop domains are relatively small. Though wheat is grown in many diverse parts of the world, times of sowing are such that the temperature conditions during the growth period are relatively similar. Thus in India, wheat is a winter crop. That the domains are relatively small, even though there is considerable genetic diversity within a crop, is surprising. Wheat, for example, comprises two main species, bread wheat and durum wheat. Though durum wheat is found mainly in warmer and drier areas (e.g. southern Europe) than bread wheat, the differences are small compared with the differences between the wheat and rice domains.

CLIMATIC CONSTRAINTS ON CROP DISTRIBUTION

Crops have climatic domains because different crops have different characteristic physiological adaptations and different genetic bases. We will now consider the match of crop to climate, through the physiology of the crop, in more detail. We shall use wheat as an example, though we could have used any crop that has been thoroughly studied.

For a crop to be grown successfully the following conditions must be satisfied:

1. The species must be able to germinate and grow at the prevailing temperatures. Extreme cold or warm temperatures must not destroy the crop.
2. There must be a supply of water available to the plant to meet the demand for transpiration and maintain turgidity during the period of growth. The water may come from crop-season rainfall, storage in the soil or irrigation.
3. The development pattern of the crop over time (which depends mainly on temperature and photoperiod), must be such that its growth cycle can fit into the constraints imposed by 1 and 2. If, however, development is too rapid because temperatures are warm, yield may be decreased because the crop has too little time to accumulate dry matter by assimilation. The need for particular climatic conditions for harvesting may also constrain the development pattern.
4. The climate must not favour the vigorous development of serious diseases. Humidity is often an important factor here.

We shall consider these constraints first for wheat, as an example, and then review other crops briefly.

Wheat

In order to link wheat physiology with climate we need more detail of wheat climates. The main areas of wheat production in those countries in which the harvested area of wheat is more than 5% of all arable land are shown in Fig. 6. Wheat is widely distributed but is generally restricted to areas more than 30° from the equator, except at high altitude as in Kenya.

The approximate sowing and harvesting times are also shown in Fig. 6. There are three patterns of wheat production. In the first, winter

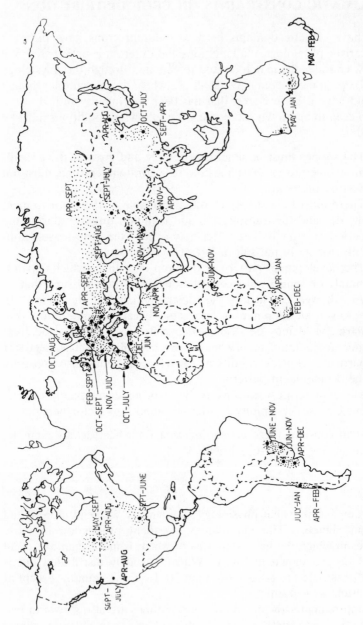

FIG. 6. The wheat growing areas of countries with more than 5% of their arable land under wheat. Climatic stations used in the analysis, and months of sowing and harvesting, are shown.

wheat, the crop is sown in the autumn, over-winters in the vegetative stage and is harvested in the following summer. This is the pattern of production in North-west Europe and the Southern Great Plains of the USA. The second pattern is spring wheat, sown in the spring and harvested later in the summer, as for example in Canada. Spring wheat is often grown where the winters are too severe for winter wheat. The third pattern of production is common in the Mediterranean area. Wheat is sown in the autumn and harvested in the spring. The plants grow continuously throughout this period. This may well be the ancestral pattern associated with the origin of the crop in the winter rainfall regions of South-west Asia.

Monthly climatic data from 71 representative locations within each of the principal growing areas were obtained (Fig. 6). Frequency diagrams of mean monthly temperatures at the times of sowing and harvesting for the three patterns of wheat production are shown in Fig. 7. The patterns are evidently similar. Monthly mean temperatures at sowing mostly range from 8 to 16°C for winter wheat, 6 to 12°C for spring wheat and 12 to 20°C for Mediterranean wheat. The range from 8 to 20°C covers sowing in most parts of the world (Fig. 7). Growth room experiments have shown that wheat germinates at a wide range of temperatures, from about 4 to 37°C, but that 'optimum' germination is obtained at 25 to 30°C (Evans *et al.*, 1975; Lomas, 1976). Evidently the mean standardised temperature used in climate studies does not indicate the actual temperature of any particular part of the environment, such as in the seedbed.

Harvesting normally occurs at warmer temperatures than sowing; 16 to 24°C for winter wheat, 10 to 24°C for spring wheat and 18 to 26°C for Mediterranean wheat (Fig. 7). Generally wheat is sown in a relatively cool season and matures under conditions of warmer temperatures and smaller rainfalls. The minimum temperature for spring wheat is cooler because some harvests are delayed to as late as possible in the autumn in order to obtain the longest possible growing season.

The mean temperatures during the growing season are shown in Fig. 8 (see also Fig. 4). In most wheat climates the mean temperature of the growing season lies between 7 and 17°C and little wheat is grown where mean temperatures exceed 18°C. Assimilation in wheat has a broad optimum range between 10 and 25°C (which does not conflict with the mean values, since assimilation can occur only during daylight hours). It decreases slightly at cooler temperatures and considerably at warmer ones (Evans *et al.*, 1975). Leaf initiation and leaf expansion

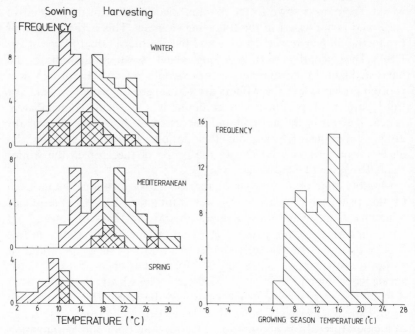

FIG. 7. Frequency distribution of mean monthly temperatures at sowing and harvesting in the main wheat growing areas of the world.

FIG. 8. Frequency distribution of mean growing season temperatures in the main wheat growing areas of the world.

continue, though slowly, until the temperature falls below about 0°C (Gallagher, 1979).

Monthly mean minimum and maximum temperatures during the growing season are shown in Fig. 9. Maximum temperatures range from 13 to 31°C but most wheat is grown in climates with maxima less than 26°C, (as would be expected from the effects of temperature on assimilation cited above). Minimum temperatures for spring and Mediterranean wheat range from 3 to 19°C but most minima are below 15°C. The minimum temperature for winter wheat is obviously colder, but no wheat is grown where monthly mean winter temperatures are below −6°C. The insulation provided by snow cover can moderate the effects of cold air temperatures and so protect against winter kill.

Mean annual rainfalls in the wheat growing areas are shown in Fig. 10. Most wheat is grown in climates in which annual rainfall lies between 200 and 800 mm. Wheat is grown in drier areas but this

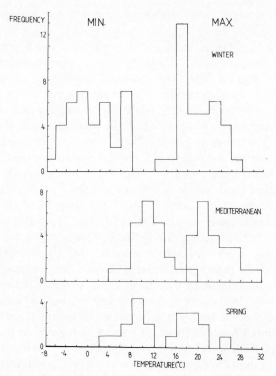

Fig. 9. Frequency distribution of mean monthly minimum and maximum temperatures in the main wheat growing areas of the world.

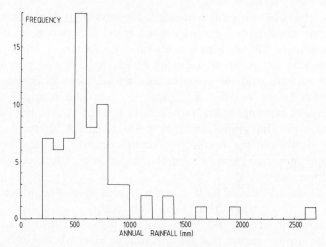

Fig. 10. Frequency distribution of annual rainfall totals in the main wheat growing areas of the world.

requires irrigation (as in India and Egypt) or a fallow system (as in parts of Australia). Little wheat is grown where rainfall exceeds 1000 mm. In regions with larger rainfall totals there is usually no significant dry season to permit satisfactory ripening of the grain.

To summarise, the frequency distributions suggest that there is an 'optimum' climatic range within which the predominance of wheat will be greatest. The range is broad, about 8 to 18°C for mean growing season temperature and 500 to 800 mm for annual rainfall. The spread of the distribution, measured for example by the standard deviation, summarises how sensitive the distribution of the crop is to the particular climatic factor. The optimum for distribution of wheat need not necessarily be the same as that for yield. This topic is dealt with by Cooper (see 'Plant Breeding for Different Climates') in this volume.

The growing season for wheat may be limited at either end by temperature or by shortage of water. Potential crop evaporation is the amount of water transpired by a short green crop completely covering the ground and freely supplied with water. A simple water balance may be calculated by subtracting estimates of potential crop evaporation from rainfall totals. This water balance is a guide to the time and duration of possible growing seasons. Actual water use by the crop will usually be less than the potential rate when crop cover is incomplete or when the crop is ripening. Water can also be stored in the soil. Water balances and temperatures of selected wheat production areas are shown in Fig. 11a–e.

In a winter wheat area (Cambridge, England, Fig. 11a) the major temperature constraint is in the autumn when it is necessary to sow and establish the crop before growth rates become very small in the winter months. Many winter cultivars of wheat have to experience a period of relative cold for vernalisation before they can flower. This ensures that flower initiation does not occur until the spring. Growth rates increase as temperature increases in the spring and the crop is harvested soon after midsummer. Soil water usually returns to field capacity throughout the profile in December, and from about April potential evaporation exceeds rainfall and the crop matures as the soil profile dries.

Swift Current (Canada) is in a spring wheat area—the winters are too cold for winter wheat (Fig. 11b). The crop is sown in May, when temperatures have risen, and the ground has thawed. The crop matures during the warm summer and is harvested in September. Throughout this period the transpiration of the crop is withdrawing water from the

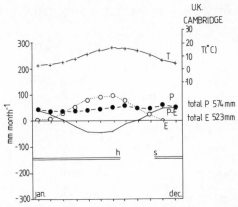

FIG. 11. Monthly temperatures (+), precipitation (●), potential evaporation (○) and precipitation minus potential evaporation for representative wheat growing locations: (a) (above) Cambridge, England.

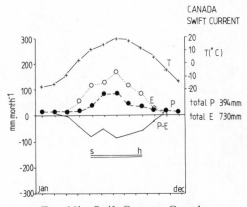

FIG. 11b. Swift Current, Canada.

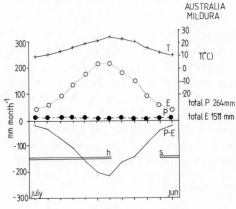

FIG. 11c. Mildura, Australia.

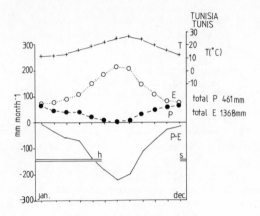

FIG. 11d. Tunis, Tunisia.

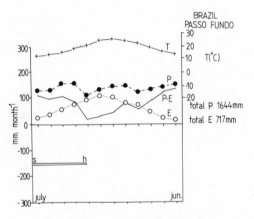

FIG. 11e. Passo Fundo, Brazil.

soil profile. Maturation may be hastened, and yield decreased, by shortage of water. The shortest growing season for spring wheats is about 90–100 days (Peterson, 1965; Bommer and Dambroth, 1974). The length of time during which temperature conditions are favourable is the major constraint on the growing of wheat at high latitudes and at increasing altitudes in the tropics.

Mildura (Australia, Fig. 11c (Nix, 1975)) has a mean annual rainfall of 260 mm. This is considerably less than the potential evaporation, and consequently cannot meet the requirements of the crop. A fallow system in therefore used, with a crop every other year. Mildura is at the dry edge of the Australian wheat belt, and even with the fallow system there is a large risk that large water deficits will develop in the latter phases of crop development. The other climatic constraint on wheat in this area is the possibility of frost damage if the ears emerge too early.

Tunisia provides a typical example of the Mediterranean wheat production system. Wheat is sown in December at the coolest time of the year and matures on an increasing soil water deficit (Fig. 11d).

The climate of the main wheat growing area of Brazil (e.g. Passo Fundo, Fig. 11e) is unlike that of other wheat areas in the world (Mota and Acosta, 1974). The crop is sown in June, the coolest month, with a mean temperature of 12·9°C and is harvested in November before early summer temperatures become excessively hot. The main feature of the climate is the positive water balance throughout the season. Drought does not therefore present difficulties for wheat in southern Brazil. The major climatic limitation is that the warm and humid conditions lead to the development of many diseases.

The examples given above show the diversity within the general climatic domain of the crop, of environments in which wheat is grown. Time of sowing is usually such that the crop passes through the main part of its vegetative period under relatively cool and moist conditions with mean temperatures around 10 to 17°C. In most parts of the world, wheat matures, flowers, and fills and ripens its grain on increasing soil moisture deficits, and usually in warm sunny conditions. Most wheats are photoperiod sensitive, requiring lengthening days for flowering. This ensures that the grain is formed and filled at a climatically favourable time of the year, that the crop matures before the soil water deficit becomes too severe, and that conditions are dry at harvest time.

Other crops

The preceding detailed analysis can be repeated for other crops, though we have not attempted to do so in this paper. We hope, however, that the methods of analysis will seem useful. A brief summary of the climatic requirements of several cereals is given in Table 4. With the exception of rice, proso millet and oats, they require relatively dry warm conditions for maturation. There is therefore a cereal crop suitable for all but the wettest and coldest climates of the world.

Several tropical cereals (rice, maize, sorghum and bulrush millet)

TABLE 4
GENERAL CLIMATE SUITABILITY OF THE PRINCIPAL CEREALS (BASED LARGELY ON KASSAM (1977))

	Cereal		Mean temperature (°C)	Range of growing season (days)	Photoperiodic response[a]	Comments
Triticum aestivum	Wheat	spring	<20	90–130	LD/DN	Cold for vernalisation
		winter	<20	180–240	LD	
Hordeum sativum	Barley	spring	<20	80–130	LD/DN	Not very hardy
		winter	<20	170–240	LD	
Avena sativa	Oats	spring	<20	90–130	LD/DN	Withstands humid conditions at harvest
		winter	<20	180–270	LD/DN	
Secale cereale	Rye	spring	<20	90–130	LD/DN	Very winter hardy
		winter	<20	200–270	LD/DN	
Oryza sativa	Rice		>20	100–180	DN/SD	Thrives in wet and warm conditions; grain often has to be dried
Zea mays	Maize		>15	120–300	SD/DN	Many forms photoperiodic, needs dry conditions for grain harvest
Sorghum bicolor	Sorghum		>20	90–280	SD/DN	Many forms photoperiodic, needs dry conditions for grain filling
Panicum miliaceum	Proso millet		>20	55–280	SD/DN	Matures in humid conditions, drought resistant
Pennisetum typhoides	Bulrush millet		>20	60–120	SD/DN	Generally matures in dry conditions

[a] LD flowering induced in lengthening days; SD flowering induced in shortening days; DN time of flowering unaffected by day length, usually flowering at a fixed leaf number.

include both short-day and day-neutral forms. The significance of this diversity has been described for sorghum and bulrush millet (and also for cowpea) in West Africa (see Bunting, 1975). In the wetter parts of the savannah regions of West Africa, both the total rainfall and the length of the growing season (the period during which precipitation exceeds evaporation) decrease from north to south. The date of the onset of the rains is unpredictable from year to year, though it is generally earlier in the south than the north. The end of the rains is much more consistent from year to year, earlier in the north and progressively later in the south.

Throughout the region sorghum is the traditional preferred cereal. If sorghum flowers before the end of the rains, the ears and the developing grains are severely damaged by insects and fungi; if it flowers later, the water stored in the soil may not be sufficient to maintain the crop for long enough to fill and mature the grain. As a result, in each locality the local population of sorghum flowers at a time precisely related to the average date of the end of the rains (defined as the date on which increasing evaporation and decreasing precipitation are equal). This delicate timing is achieved by a photoperiodic mechanism, but the price of this is that sorghum populations are closely adapted to the conditions of their native place, and that sorghum breeders have to retain this adaptation in developing improved varieties (Curtis, 1968).

In many of the wetter parts of the savannah region, bulrush millet is sown as early as possible, and before sorghum, as a sort of catch crop to shorten the hungry gap by producing an early harvest. For this purpose day neutral populations are used which flower at a small and fixed leaf number. Ecologically, they are desert ephemerals, which flower and set seed as soon as they can.

In the drier, more northerly parts of the savannah region, where the rainfall is smaller and more variable, and the dates of both the start and the end of the rains are unpredictable, photoperiodic sorghums are replaced by day-neutral types. In some drier areas, photoperiodic bulrush millets are said to be grown, but if so they too give place, in the drier areas, to day-neutral desert ephemerals.

In the wetter parts of the sorghum belt, spreading types of cowpea (*Vigna unguiculata*) are intersown into the sorghum (after it has been weeded) to protect the surface of the soil, to control late weeds, to add some nitrogen to the system, and to provide edible leaves in the earlier stages and a crop of grain at the end. The development of these cowpeas is very delicately timed so that flowers and fruits form only after the leaf area index of the sorghum has begun to decline and the risk of insect damage to the pods is diminishing. This is achieved by photoperiodic means. Further north, in drier areas, the cowpeas are non-photoperiodic desert ephemerals.

South of the main savannah belt, in wetter regions where roots and tubers begin to replace sorghum as the staple, the early sown hungry gap crop is not a bulrush millet but a cowpea (perhaps because the lack of dietary protein is more important in these diets than in cereal based diets). These cowpeas are more or less day-neutral, so that they deliver their produce as early as possible.

Rice also includes both photoperiodic and day-neutral forms, but in this crop the day-neutral adaptation appears to fit the needs of intensive multiple cropping, in which its short period of growth helps to increase the number of crops per year, for example, by permitting dry season cropping (as in Bangladesh).

Photoperiod can also interact strongly with day and night temperature. During the past 10 years these relationships have been intensively studied in cowpea, chickpea (*Cicer arietinum*) and soya (*Glycine max*) in the Plant Environment Laboratory at Reading by Summerfield and others (among more than 60 references, see Summerfield *et al.*, 1981). For maximum yield in cowpea, the total duration of the crop has to be fitted into the total time available, the genotype to be used has to be generally adapted to the temperature conditions, and the period up to the initiation of the first inflorescence has to be as long as possible (to permit as large a vegetative framework to be formed as possible) without unduly decreasing the time available for flowering and the filling of fruits on that framework. Cowpea (and apparently soya also) contains sufficient physiological diversity to allow genotypes to be selected for any tropical, subtropical or continental temperate environment.

Perhaps the most concise reflection on the spectacle of varietal diversity in crops is to say that agronomically and physiologically there is no such thing as 'the species' (Bunting, 1961) except in the very broadest sense.

CHOICE OF CROP

Information such as that in Table 4 provides the basis for choosing suitable crops to be introduced or expanded in an area. The mean temperature, the water balance, and the length of growing season and the possibilities of change in the existing systems will further narrow the choice of crops and guide the selection of genotypes or populations.

There are other, less obvious, climatic constraints on crop choice. Climate, along with soil type, can determine when it is possible to prepare the soil before planting and to weed and cultivate it afterwards. Cultivation may not be possible because of lack of rain, as in the seasonally arid tropics, because of excess rain, as in the autumn on heavy soils in North-west Europe or because the ground is frozen. Comparable constraints may apply at harvest time. Humid wet conditions lead to difficulties with disease and insect pests in cereals and may make harvesting and drying difficult. In wet soils it may be difficult or impossible to harvest root crops.

Any crop that is grown must fit in with the other crops on the farm. In most temperate agriculture this is mainly a question of timing the harvest and the preparation of land for the next crop. In tropical agriculture much of the cropping is mixed or sequential, often for climatic and environmental reasons. In a seasonally arid climate with a short rainy season, early sowing of a sole crop and timely weeding are essential, to capture as much as possible of the soluble nitrogen in the soil before it is leached by intense rainfalls, and to minimise the amount that is captured by weeds.

Climatic hazards can also affect crop choice. For example, 85% of cultivated land in Mauritius is under sugar cane. This is primarily because of historical factors, but an important reason for the dominance of sugar cane is that it is capable of recovering from cyclone damage. The risk of frost is a major constraint on the location of high value crops such as citrus and coffee.

Other climatic constraints operate through effects on pests and diseases and on crop quality. These are dealt with later in this volume.

We have so far in this paper taken climate as being a fixed property of an area. In reality, climate is weather averaged over a lengthy period. An assessment of the agricultural climate of the area must include assessment of the variability from year to year. It is important that a crop provides a reasonable return in most years and since weather varies from year to year it is necessary for the crop to be able to respond flexibly to fluctuations in weather.

In marginal areas, and particularly in areas near the margins of deserts, weather fluctuations from year to year may lead to disasters where governments are not able to manage the agricultural and human consequences. The United States can take a series of dry years in the south-west in its stride. The country is large, the communications are efficient, and government can offset shortages in one area by withdrawals from storage and by purchasing and moving produce from other parts of the country or from abroad. The government of a small, poor, landlocked country in the Sahelian zone may be quite unable to resolve within the national frontiers the consequences of a 200 km fluctuation in the summer position of the intertropical convergence zone; and there is very little agronomy can do to help except through storage of food, feed or water, all of which are costly and may be administratively and politically difficult into the bargain.

The longer term fluctuations and trends in climate which can be deduced from climatic records are relatively small. It is said that in the 1960s and 1970s the growing season in the UK decreased by about 10 days in length (Lamb, 1973). Plant breeding, crop protection and farming practice ensured that yield and output increased continuously over this period. What may have been a drying cycle in the Sahel over the same period, superimposed on what may be a much longer term drying trend, may well accelerate the depopulation of the more marginal parts of the region.

In spite of 30 years of enthusiasm and effort, we do not yet seem to be within sight of human control of climate. We shall surely continue to offset dry conditions, where water is available, by irrigation. But otherwise we shall evidently have to accept climate more or less as it is, and make the best of it over the critical century ahead until the human population of the world reaches its expected plateau or peak.

POSSIBILITIES FOR CHANGE

Changes in crop distribution have certainly occurred in the past. Often these result from economic or social factors and represent changes that were already climatically possible, e.g. the change from oats to barley in England and Wales resulting from the replacement of horses by tractors, and the remarkable growth of soya bean production in Brazil, which is now the second largest producer in the world.

In a number of crops, plant breeding has widened the limits within which they can be grown successfully, and has often helped to extend them to areas which were previously marginal. An example from northern Europe is the increase in the northward extent of maize cultivation. Maize is now quite widely grown for grain in France as far north as the Loire (total about 10 Mt a year). Further north and in much of southern England, it is grown for silage. In central and southern France 300 000–400 000 tonnes of grain sorghum is produced each year. Increased winter hardiness in oilseed rape has led to a great increase in the area of the winter crop in northern Europe. However, the main effect of the production of new varieties has been to increase the yield of crops in locations where they were previously grown, rather than to widen the distribution of the crop.

Changes in crop distribution may be needed for several reasons. They might help to meet the increasing demand for agricultural products, they might help farmers and nations to make more productive use of agricultural resources, and they might replace less nutritious crops by more nutritious ones in areas where the compositions of diets are thought to be unsatisfactory.

The present population of the world is about 4500 million people. By the year 2000 it may be around 6200 million, and 100 years hence it may have reached a plateau of perhaps 12 000 million humans. Most of the increases will be recorded in the developing countries, which contain about 74% of mankind now and may contain 79% in 20 years time, of whom 46% will probably live in towns and cities. If modest assumptions are made about increases in the effective demand of these populations, output may have to be increased by more than half over the next 20 years and perhaps quadrupled during the next century. Technically there are reasons for sober confidence about the first of these tasks, and the second is probably feasible. At least we have a century in which to try.

Over the next 20 years it seems likely that, with some exceptions, most of the increased output will come from the crops we have now, grown where they are grown now, and more through increases in yield per harvest and number of harvests per hectare per year, than through increases in arable area. The contributions of additional crops are likely to be limited.

However, it seems evident that more rice could be produced in the humid tropical environments of Africa and the Americas, provided the rather substantial energy inputs required for field production (from human and animal muscles or from internal combustion engines) and for drying (from rice straw or timber) can be met. It is no accident that most rice is produced in the most densely populated parts of the developing world and that relatively little is produced in the sparsely populated humid tropics of Africa and the Americas. But as the population of Africa increases from 470 million now to 830 million 20 years hence, in a continent where there are at present few economic alternatives to agriculture, this may change. Though the population of Latin America is expected to grow from 368 to 608 million, there are important non-agricultural alternatives.

We may also expect the areas of maize and of soya bean to increase, particularly where (in spite of energy costs) mechanisation is technically and managerially, as well as economically, feasible. Maize may well occupy more land in areas of Latin America and in Africa to which it is already adapted, and where unused land is available. As we learn how to make fuller use of the adaptation to cool temperatures of the high Andean types of maize and the breeding materials derived from them, the crop may spread into cooler regions, as it did in Kenya 20 years ago. Soya bean (for feeding animals rather than humans) may well spread to new areas in Africa which are climatically similar to those of Brazil in which it has been so dramatically successful in recent years.

During the next 80 years, we may expect important advances in the distribution of maize, particularly in cooler regions, probably at the expense of other cereals. This is because its potential yield per hectare (already 6–7 tonnes on average in the United States) is larger than that of its competitors (wheat yields only $2 \cdot 2$ tonnes ha^{-1} in the United States). Sorghum, which like maize is a C_4 plant, may spread in drier regions—at present it yields 4 tonnes ha^{-1} in the United States. We may also expect considerable increases in the area of irrigated rice in poorer countries of Africa and the Americas, and probably of soya bean also.

In respect of use of productive resources, the main changes in distribution which can be imagined are related to increases in the number of harvests per hectare per year. Perhaps short season grain legume crops, filling gaps in the production cycle, will become more important in some countries.

From the nutritional point of view, the replacement of root and tuber crops in the humid tropics by rice or maize is attractive to many observers. However, to many producers who are not accustomed to cereals, the extra requirements of support energy, particularly labour, and the difficulty of storing grain safely in warm and wet conditions, may be at least as important. Cassava, which is able to produce a return on land too poor for maize, is said to have been gaining ground at the expense of cereals in Africa for many years, and if this is so there are bound to be good reasons for the change. We may expect the trend to continue so long as labour and plant nutrients are in short supply.

It is, of course, possible that entirely new crops, such as triticale, may enter the scene on a considerable scale, as sugar beet did about 150 years ago, but one may be forgiven for doubting whether any new crop can have any major impact, on a world scale, in the 20 years ahead.

It does not seem useful to attempt to assess the effects on crop distribution of the large-scale production of plant biomass for conversion by fermentation or otherwise to alcohol to fuel internal combustion engines, mainly because so far as can be foreseen at present the very special conditions in which this could succeed on a significant scale exist in very few countries. It is not likely to happen in India or China, but it could happen in Brazil and perhaps in the United States, Argentina and Sudan. The crop species in question so far are sugar cane, cassava, sweet stemmed sorghum and perhaps sweet potato.

Perhaps a little less unlikely are substantial increases in the production of plant oils for diesel engines, which might lead to substantial changes in the distribution of oil palm.

All such developments will tend to divert agricultural resources away from the production of food, fibre and other necessary farm products. In a hungry world, the consequences of such shifts must be very cautiously assessed. Although the range of technical possibilities agricultural science can offer is vast, none can be achieved without access to considerable resources.

ACKNOWLEDGEMENT

The support of the Overseas Development Administration is gratefully acknowledged.

REFERENCES

Bommer, D. and Dambroth, M. (1974). Climate and wheat production in the world. In: *Agrometeorology of the Wheat Crop. Proc. World Meteorological Organisation Symposium*, Braunschweig, 1973, pp. 1–18.

Bunting, A. H. (1961). Some problems of agricultural climatology in tropical Africa. *Geography* **46**, 283–94.

Bunting, A. H. (1975). Time, phenology and the yields of crops. *Weather* **30**, 312–25.

Curtis, D. L. (1968). The relation between the date of heading of Nigerian sorghums and the duration of the growing season. *J. appl. Ecol.* **5**, 215–26.

Dennett, M. D., Elston, J. and Speed, C. B. (1981). Climate and cropping systems in West Africa. *Geoforum* (in press).

Evans, L. T., Wardlaw, I. F. and Fischer, R. A. (1975). Wheat. In: *Crop Physiology* (Ed. L. T. Evans). Cambridge University Press, London, p. 101.

FAO (1980). *Production Yearbook 1979*, Vol. 33. FAO, Rome.

Gallagher, J. N. (1979). Field studies of cereal leaf growth. I. Initiation and expansion in relation to temperature and ontogeny. *J. expt. Bot.* **30**, 625–36.

Kassam, A. H. (1977). Agroclimatic suitability assessment of rainfed crops in Africa by growing period zones. *Agro-ecological Zones Project Report Vol. 1. Methodology and Results for Africa. World Soil Resources Report 48.* FAO, Rome.

Lamb, H. H. (1973). Climatic change and foresight in agriculture: the possibilities of long-term weather advice. *Outlook on Agriculture* **7**, 203–10.

Lomas, J. (1976). Meteorological requirements of the wheat crop. In: *Agrometeorology of the Wheat Crop (Supplement). Proc. World Meteorological Organisation Symposium*, Braunschweig, 1973, pp. 1–29.

Mota, F. S. da and Acosta, M. J. C. (1974). Agrometeorology of the wheat crop in Brazil. In: *Agrometeorology of the Wheat Crop. Proc. World Meteorological Organisation Symposium*, Braunschweig, 1973, pp. 19–40.

Nix, H. A. (1975). The Australian climate and its effects on grain yield and quality. In: *Australian Field Crops, Vol. 1: Wheat and Other Temperate Cereals* (Eds A. Lazenby and E. M. Matheson). Angus and Robertson, Sydney and London, pp. 183–226.

Peterson, R. F. (1965). *Wheat: Botany, Cultivation, and Utilization.* World Crops Books Series, Leonard Hill, London.

Summerfield, R. J., Minchin, F. R., Roberts, E. H. and Hadley, P. (1981). Cowpea (*Vigna unguiculata* (L.) Walp.). In: *Potential Productivity of Field Crops under Different Environments* (Ed. S. Yoshida). IRRI, Los Banos, Philippines.

In addition the following sources have been consulted:

Climatological measurements

Arakawa, H. (Ed.) (1969). *Climates of Northern and Eastern Asia. World Survey of Climatology, Volume 8.* Elsevier, Amsterdam.

Griffiths, J. F. (Ed.) (1972). *Climates of Africa. World Survey of Climatology, Volume 10.* Elsevier, Amsterdam.

Schwerdtfeger, W. (Ed.) (1976). *Climates of Central and South America. World Survey of Climatology, Volume 12.* Elsevier, Amsterdam.

Smith, L. P. (1976). *The Agricultural Climate of England and Wales.* Ministry of Agriculture, Fisheries and Food Technical Bulletin 35. HMSO, London.

Thran, P. and Broekhuisen, S. (1965). *Agro-ecological Atlas of Cereal Growing in Europe*. Agroclimatic Atlas of Europe, Vol. 1. Pudoc, Wageningen.

World Meteorological Organisation (1971). *Climatological Normals (CLINO) for CLIMAT and CLIMAT Ship Stations for the Period 1931–1960*. WMO/OMM No. 117. TP. 52, Geneva.

Crop distribution

Berger, J. (1962). *Maize Production and the Manuring of Maize*. Centre de l'Etude de l'Azote, Geneva.

Brichambaut, G. P. de and Wallen, C. C. (1963). *A Study of Agroclimatology in Semi-Arid and Arid Zones of the Near East*. Technical Note No. 56, World Meteorological Organisation, Geneva.

Brown, L. H. and Cochemé, J. (1973). *A Study of the Agroclimatology of the Highlands of Eastern Africa*. Technical Note No. 125, World Meteorological Organisation, Geneva.

Cochemé, J. and Franquin, P. (1967). *An Agroclimatology Survey of a Semi-arid Area in Africa South of the Sahara*. Technical Note No. 86, World Meteorological Organisation, Geneva.

Cole, J. P. and German, F. C. (1970). *A Geography of the USSR*. Butterworths, London.

Davies, H. R. J. (1973). *Tropical Africa: An Atlas for Rural Development*. University of Wales Press, Cardiff.

Fremlin, G. (Ed.) (1974). *The National Atlas of Canada*. Macmillan, Ottawa.

Hanna, L. W. (1971). Climate and crop-potential in Uganda. In: *Studies in East African Geography and Development* (Ed. S. H. Ominde). Heinemann, London.

International Rice Research Institute (1977). *Proc. Symp. on Cropping Systems Research and Development for the Asian Rice Farmer*, 21–24 September 1976. IRRI, Los Banos, Philippines.

International Rice Research Institute (1978). *Rice Research and Production in China: An IRRI Team's View*. IRRI, Los Banos, Philippines.

Kalesnik, J. A. and Pavlenko, V. F. (Eds) (1976) *The Soviet Union–A Geographical Survey*. Progress Press, Moscow.

Kowal, J. M. and Kassam, A. H. (1978). *Agricultural Ecology of Savanna: A Study of West Africa*. Oxford University Press, London.

Leakey, C. L. A. and Wills, J. B. (Eds) (1977). *Food Crops of the Lowland Tropics*. Oxford University Press, London.

Oxford University Press (1972). *Oxford Economic Atlas of the World*. 4th edn. Oxford University Press, London.

Patterson, S. H. (1979). *North America*. Oxford University Press, London.

Singh, J. (1974). *An Agricultural Atlas of India: A Geographical Analysis*. Vishal Publications, Kurukshetra University Press, India.

Sprague, G. F. (1975). Agriculture in China. *Science* **188,** 549–55.

Thran, P. and Broekhuisen, S. (1969). *Agro-ecological Atlas of Cereal Growing in Europe*. Atlas of Cereal Growing Areas in Europe, Vol. 2. Pudoc, Wageningen.

Times Newspapers (1973). *The Times Atlas of the World*. Times Newspapers, London.

Van Royen, W. (1954). *The Agricultural Resources of the World.* Atlas of the World's Resources, Vol. 1. Prentice-Hall, New York.

Wadham, S. M. and Wood, G. L. (1950). The wheat industry. In: *Land Utilization in Australia.* Melbourne University Press, Melbourne.

Wilsie, C. P. (1962). *Crop Adaptation and Distribution.* W. H. Freeman & Co., San Francisco and London.

Yoshida, S. (1977). Rice. In: *Ecophysiology of Tropical Crops* (Eds P. de T. Alvim and T. T. Kozlowski). Academic Press, New York, pp. 57–87.

Yoshida, S. (1978). *Tropical Climate and its Influence on Rice.* IRRI, Los Banos, Philippines.

Discussion

Mr Oram commented on the future role of maize and sorghum in Latin America where sorghum was expanding very fast. He therefore doubted whether Professor Bunting's general comment on maize was correct for that region. He pointed out that high altitude adaptations of sorghum existed as well as of maize. He also commented about the lack of success that had been achieved in the introduction of soya into developing countries other than Brazil. There were certainly a series of problems related to crop substitution potential and the expansion of acreages of crops. For example, a considerable increase in the acreage of cassava was taking place in Thailand with the animal feed market in view and cassava cultivation was attractive on low-income farms. With respect to wheat, it was now one of the world crops, consumption of which was growing fastest in developing countries. In Bangladesh, for example, its acreage had increased from 300 000 to 2 million ha in the course of but a few years. However, in many tropical countries where wheat consumption was expanding, wheat production was not possible because of climatic limitations and imports were rising rapidly. Some of these changes in world cropping policies and consumption patterns should perhaps be viewed with caution. In reply, *Professor Bunting* stated that sorghum certainly had one advantage, that it was deeper rooting than maize and was better able to withstand drought. However, maize was certainly more resistant to bird damage, which could be very severe in Africa, and moreover, at the present stage of crop improvement, the varieties available would give larger yields per hectare. Admittedly, in the United States where breeding of sorghum is more advanced, a national average yield of 4 tonnes ha^{-1} had been attained. Perhaps as sorghum breeding developed in Africa, sorghum might well overtake maize. With respect to cassava, *Professor Bunting* stated that he was not particularly concerned about the small content of protein. In the quantities of sorghum which Americans like to eat, it could provide an appreciable supply of protein, about one-sixth of what is regarded as the safe allowance for man; and in any event it was usually supplemented by other foods with larger contents of protein. The market in Thailand was mainly for cassava chips for export, but in Africa cassava is an essential source of dietary energy at the domestic level. He went even further by stating that the advent of the Malthusian spectre was probably being delayed in Africa by the cassava crop! As far as soya was concerned, the limit to the development of this crop in many countries was the absence of a market. A further difficulty in many areas was the need to inoculate the seed with *Rhizobium japonicum*, though certain Indonesian varieties could nodulate successfully with indigenous cowpea *Rhizobium* in some African soils. A third problem was that outside China and Japan few people knew how to prepare soya as a food, though African women in northern Nigeria have indeed found ways of making acceptable dishes from soya. On wheat, *Professor Bunting* continued that the 'high-yielding' varieties of wheat had been one of the great successes of the Green Revolution. Provided that appropriate varieties are available, it was possible to extend the acreage in climatically suitable parts of the developing world. He wondered, however, for how long it would be possible to continue to grow wheat in Australia at relatively small yields per hectare as energy costs increased, even though the nitrogen was obtained cheaply by biological nitrogen fixation. *Professor Morton* asked whether the opaque and floury genes introduced into the maize crop would have some nutritional advantage in the less developed countries, to which *Professor Bunting* replied that the limitation at the moment, which did not seem likely to be overcome readily, was that the yields of cultivars containing these genes was considerably less than those of more conventional types. *Professor Heide* pointed out that root crops were possibly subjected to fewer climatic constraints than a number of other crops and are also less specific in their soil requirements. The climatic range of possibility for them was quite considerable and they were efficient crops in terms of the total photosynthate stored. He also remarked that work in Norway had shown that several perennial grasses and certain winter cereal varieties did not require vernalisation but rather reacted to short day length. These were similar reactions to those noted by Professor Cooper with *Lolium*. *Professor Bunting*, in reply, said that he felt that since the total production of roots in the world was equivalent to no more than 10% of the output of cereals, it would be necessary in the next few years to concentrate on cereal crops to meet the demands of mankind. He emphasised the multiplication problems which are involved. The International Institute of Tropical Agriculture at Ibadan had bred a series of disease resistant, large yielding cassavas, and had issued as many as 2 m planting pieces a year, but up to 2 years ago the Nigerian national programme had devoted only a few hectares to multiplying them. To improve crops in the developing countries it is necessary to overcome the serious limitation presented by the absence of plant breeding industries. *Mr Jackson* returned to the root cereal argument and stated that, usually speaking, the argument is an economic one concerned with the very considerable labour inputs into the crop. He further commented on the energy inputs for cereals and raised questions about the desirability of self-sufficiency. Was it indeed reasonable to encourage a country to produce cassava for export to maintain the animal production industries of Europe? *Professor Bunting* stated that it was quite evident that certainly West African peoples and possibly many others wished to eat wheat bread and that it was necessary to take account of this, no matter what one might think 'ought' to be done. If the world's requirement of cereals in the year 2000 is about 3000 million tonnes, which corresponds to about 480 kg per head, this will require substantial increases in yields per hectare in all regions, but particularly in those already able to produce large yields. In the poorer countries, the physical infrastructure to support development and output would have to be increased. During the next 20 years we shall concentrate particularly on doing those things that we can already do effectively. He thought that all world tendencies over that period would make it difficult for poorer countries to achieve self-sufficiency however much they might wish to do so. *Professor Britton* asked what were the implications of Professor Bunting's analyses for future trade in agricultural crops. Broadly speaking, two attitudes were adopted by policy makers, one that the trade is a risky business to be avoided if possible, and the other that countries should take advantage of differentials in economic capability and extend interdependency. He asked whether Professor Bunting thought that the agronomic differentials between countries would widen, because if so it seemed that self-sufficiency policies might reduce rather than improve the world food situation. *Professor Bunting* stated that among the many reasons for the relatively slow advance of agriculture in many LDCs might well be the weakness of their agricultural knowledge systems (including education, training and extension, as well as research) and the lack of infrastructure for agricultural improvement.

Though for these reasons and others many LDCs would not advance much towards self-sufficiency within the next 20 years, he thought that within the next century there would be a tendency for greater self-sufficiency as the knowledge structure and physical infrastructure advanced and government policies and management practices became more effective in the poorer countries. *Dr Darling* pointed out that the discussion had rather ignored barley which was an excellent crop for the drier areas and very little attention had been directed towards its improvement except for brewing and distilling type industries. He again returned to the problem of the cereal grains versus the roots as food sources. He pointed out that wheat was really a convenience food in one sense of this term insofar that cassava roots and roots generally had to undergo considerable preparation before cooking. Urbanisation in the less developed countries had led to a requirement for more package-type of foods of the convenience type and in many parts the loaf of bread was much preferable to the cassava root. *Professor Bunting*, in reply, stated that this was very true but it did not exclude cassava. For example, in West Africa, a woman has to expend as much labour in preparing a tonne of cassava for eating as she does in growing it. However, the gari fermentation process gives an acceptable food which is easy to store and transport and also to prepare for eating.

Plant Breeding for Different Climates

J. P. COOPER

Welsh Plant Breeding Station, Aberystwyth, UK

INTRODUCTION

Crop production can be regarded as the conversion of environmental inputs into economic end products, which may consist of human or animal foodstuffs or industrial raw materials. One of the most important climatic inputs is the seasonal distribution of solar radiation, which provides both the energy used for the growth of the crop and that fixed in the final end product. The growing season during which the crop can make use of this energy, however, is usually limited by the other climatic factors of temperature and water supply as well as by the requirements of particular farming rotations. The aim of the plant breeder is to develop varieties which provide the most effective conversion of light energy within the possible growing season. He therefore needs to identify the major climatic inputs and constraints in his particular environment, those features of the crop which determine the effective response to them and the amount of genetic variation available for selection and breeding (Wallace *et al.*, 1972; Evans, 1975; Cooper, 1981*a*; Wilson, 1981).

CLIMATIC INPUTS AND CONSTRAINTS

The seasonal input of light energy varies with latitude and cloud cover, being comparatively uniform through the year in equatorial regions, often with $1600-2000 \, \mathrm{J \, cm^{-2} \, d^{-1}}$ but with increasing seasonal amplitude with increasing latitude. The highest energy inputs of over

$710 \text{ kJ cm}^{-2} \text{ year}^{-1}$ are found in subtropical areas with little cloud cover, but this high input is usually associated with marked water shortage, i.e. high evaporative demand and low rainfall. North temperate regions have a comparatively low annual input, about $400 \text{ kJ cm}^{-2} \text{ year}^{-1}$, but can reach daily inputs of over 2000 J cm^{-2} in midsummer, equivalent to those of tropical regions.

The length of the potential growing season can, however, be limited by temperature, by water supply or by the requirements of particular farming systems. In north temperate or continental regions, for instance, it is markedly limited by winter cold, which may prevent the survival of certain crops, or require a degree of winter hardiness, often associated with dormancy. A more important limitation in many regions is water shortage, since this usually coincides with periods of high insolation and hence high potential production. In Mediterranean climates, for instance, the active growing season begins with the autumn rains, continues during winter and early spring and ceases at the beginning of the dry season in early summer, whilst in savanna regions crop production usually depends on a short and often unreliable rainy season (Bunting *et al.*, this volume).

The particular temperature threshold which delimits the growing season will depend on the crop since species and even varieties differ in their critical and optimum temperatures. The limits set by water supply are usually estimated from water balance calculations; though the limiting soil-water deficit will again differ with the crop and the stage of growth. Potential evapotranspiration for instance is often used as a convenient measure of radiation input and hence of potential crop production, whilst actual evapotranspiration takes into account the effects of seasonal moisture stress. Finally, fluctuations in both temperature and water supply from year to year must be taken into account in quantifying these environmental constraints.

CROP STRATEGIES

In order to make the most effective use of the possible growing season, a crop needs to produce and maintain an active photosynthetic cover for as long as possible during that growing season, and to allocate the maximum amount of assimilates to the economic end product.

Photosynthetic productivity

The net photosynthetic productivity of the crop canopy will depend on the photosynthetic activity of the individual leaves, their arrangement in relation to light interception, and the extent of respiratory losses.

Individual leaf photosynthesis

The photosynthetic response of the individual leaf to light and temperature is well documented (Troughton, 1975; Cooper, 1976). At low light intensities, limitations are primarily photochemical and the leaf can fix up to 10% of the total incoming radiation (i.e. up to 20% of the photosynthetically active radiation (PhAR)), but as the light intensity increases the availability of CO_2 becomes more important, and eventually when CO_2 becomes limiting, light saturation and the maximum photosynthetic rate are reached.

Considerable variation exists between different crops in their ability to make use of high light energy inputs. A major distinction is between those, including most temperate crops and such tropical crops as rice and cassava, which possess the more usual C_3 photosynthetic pathway, and those including maize, sugar cane and many tropical grasses, which have developed the modified C_4 pathway. In C_3 species, light saturation is reached at comparatively low light intensities, say half of full summer daylight, with a maximum photosynthetic rate of some 50–100 ng CO_2 cm^{-2} s^{-1}, corresponding to 2% fixation of PhAR. On the other hand, in those tropical and subtropical species with the C_4 pathway, light saturation is rarely attained even in full summer sunlight, and maximum photosynthetic rates of 200–250 ng CO_2 cm^2 s^{-1} can be achieved, i.e. 4–5% fixation of PhAR. These higher values for C_4 species are based to a large extent on the absence of photorespiration, which in C_3 species can result in the loss of 30–40% of the gross photosynthesis. C_4 species are thus well adapted to high insolation environments, while their greater stomatal resistances to water vapour transfer results in greater water use efficiency under conditions of water stress (Hatch *et al.*, 1971; Troughton, 1975).

Even so, marked varietal or genotypic differences in maximum photosynthetic rates per unit leaf area have been reported in both C_3 crops including rice, barley, soya bean, lucerne, and C_4 crops such as sugar cane and maize (Wallace *et al.*, 1972; Wilson, 1981). In few cases, however, were these differences associated with total or economic yields, suggesting that in the material examined total assimilation of the crop was limited by factors other than the photosynthetic rate of the individual leaf, or perhaps that as in wheat and rye grass, a high rate per unit area of leaf was associated with smaller leaves (Evans and Dunstone, 1970).

Since the greater efficiency of the C_4 over the C_3 photosynthetic system is associated with a lack of photorespiration, attempts have been made to select for decreased photorespiration in C_3 species in the hope of increasing their maximum photosynthetic rate (Zelitch, 1976). Variation in photorespiratory activity has been reported for certain C_3 species, including tobacco and rye grass, in some cases with favourable effects on net photosynthesis (Wilson, 1972; Zelitch, 1976).

Crop species also vary markedly in their photosynthetic response to the other limiting climatic factors of temperature and water supply. Most temperate C_3 crops, for instance, have optimum temperatures around 20°C; photosynthesis is considerably reduced below 10°C and may cease around 5°C. Most subtropical and tropical species, on the other hand, including both C_3 crops (tobacco, cotton) and C_4 (maize and sugar cane) have optimum temperatures of some 30–35°C and photosynthesis and indeed chlorophyll development may be inhibited below about 15°C (Bauer *et al.*, 1975; Cooper, 1976; McWilliam, 1978). Even within species, however, locally adaptive varieties or ecotypes may differ in their temperature sensitivity. In tall fescue, for instance, ecotypes from the eastern Mediterranean show higher optimum temperatures for photosynthesis than those from North-west Europe, whilst in sorghum genotypic differences in photosynthesis at high temperatures have been reported (Sullivan and Ross, 1979).

The effect of water shortage on photosynthesis operates initially through stomatal closure, though as discussed later, the leaf water potential at which such closure occurs will differ with the species (Turner, 1979). At a later stage, water stress may have more direct effects on the rest of the photosynthetic system (Slavik, 1975). Little is known of the extent of genetic variation in photosynthetic response to the varying aspects of water stress, though genotypic differences have been reported in wheat (Townley-Smith and Hurd, 1979) and in sorghum (Blum, 1979).

Considerable variation thus exists for various components of individual leaf photosynthesis in many crop species, though apart from the major distinction between C_3 and C_4 crops, its significance in terms of crop yield is still far from clear

Canopy structure and light interception

In a closed crop canopy, in contrast to the individual leaf, incoming radiation is distributed over a considerable leaf area with consequent increase in its utilisation by photosynthesis. Potential crop photosynthesis, however, is influenced greatly by the arrangement of leaves in the canopy which determines the degree of penetration of light down the crop, and the area of leaf surface which can be illuminated (Saeki, 1975; Ludlow, 1978). During early establishment, most leaves will be fully exposed to light, and crop photosynthesis will be limited by the amount of light which can be intercepted. As the leaf area increases, however, not only is more of the incoming light energy intercepted, but it is transmitted and reflected over a larger leaf area, up to a leaf area index of 4–10 or more (i.e. 4–10 cm^2 of leaf per cm^2 of ground). Light saturation is rarely reached in a complete crop canopy, even in C_3 species, and the photosynthetic rate usually increases up to the stage when light interception is complete. The maximum photosynthetic rate of the whole crop is thus considerably higher than that of the individual leaf. In temperate C_3 crops, for instance, values of 200–300 ng CO_2 cm^{-2} (of ground surface) s^{-1} are commonly obtained, which, taking into account respiratory losses, correspond to crop growth rates during the main growing season of some 20–30 g m^{-2} d^{-1} (i.e. the fixation of some 3–4% of PhAR). In C_4 species such as maize and Sudan grass with high insolation, even higher values have been reported, corresponding to crop growth rates of over 50 g m^{-2} d^{-1} (i.e. a fixation of over 5% of PhAR). At lower temperatures (say below 20°C) and lower light inputs, however, the crop growth rates achieved by C_4 crops may be no greater than those of C_3 species (Loomis and Gerakis, 1975; Cooper, 1976).

The leaf area over which the incoming light can be distributed (and hence potential crop photosynthesis) is markedly influenced by the arrangement of leaves in the canopy. In crops with flat horizontal leaves, such as many forage or grain legumes, most of the light will be spread over a comparatively small leaf area index of some 3–4 while in cereals and grasses with longer more erect leaves, it can be distributed over a much larger leaf area index of 7–8 or more, with correspondingly higher potential canopy photosynthesis.

Varietal and genotypic differences in leaf arrangement and canopy structure has been reported in many crops including maize, rice, soya beans and forage grasses, with in some cases significant effects on crop growth rate and crop photosynthesis (Wallace *et al.*, 1972; Wilson, 1981).

Respiratory use of assimilates

Crop photosynthesis provides both the energy required for the growth of the crop and that accumulated in the final dry matter, and some 50% of the assimilates initially fixed may be required as a source of energy by the plant (Robson, 1973; Biscoe *et al.*, 1975). Most of these will be needed for active growth and production of new tissue, but there is also a requirement for the maintenance of existing tissue, which will be greatest at the later stages of crop growth, with a large standing biomass (McCree, 1970; Penning de Vries, 1974). Variation in this 'maintenance' requirement, as measured by the dark respiration of mature tissue has been reported in several crop species including sorghum, rye grass and barley, suggesting the possibility of breeding for reduced 'maintenance' respiration and so making more assimilates available for dry matter yield. A negative correlation between such maintenance respiration and crop growth rate has been reported for certain of the above species (Wilson, 1981), and in perennial rye grass, selection for low maintenance respiration has resulted in an increase in crop growth rate particularly at high summer temperatures (Wilson, 1975*b*; 1976).

Duration of crop canopy

The annual or seasonal photosynthetic production of the crop canopy will be influenced markedly by its possible duration. For a range of crops in the UK, for instance, Monteith (1977) found a close relation between total dry matter production and intercepted solar radiation of about 1.4 g MJ^{-1}, corresponding to 2·4% fixation of total radiation (i.e. about 5% of PhAR). Indeed, for perennial crops, such as forest trees or forage grasses which can maintain a crop canopy for the whole year, an annual yield of over $20 \text{ tonnes ha}^{-1}$ of dry matter (corresponding to 2–3% conversion of PhAR) has been reported for temperate regions and over $60 \text{ tonnes ha}^{-1}$ (i.e. 4–5% conversion) in the tropics or subtropics (Cooper, 1975; Loomis and Gerakis, 1975).

For most crops or environments, however, the potential growing season, i.e. the possible duration of the leaf canopy, is limited by seasonal constraints of temperature or water supply. These climatic limitations often pose two conflicting requirements for the crop, (i) the ability to initiate and continue active leaf growth and photosynthesis under moderate temperature or water stress, and (ii) survival of more extreme conditions, either by means of a degree of dormancy, or by a life cycle which avoids the period of extreme stress.

Temperature stress

The ability to germinate and expand leaf surface actively at moderately low temperatures and/or to survive frost damage or low temperature chill are important characteristics determining the possible sowing or planting date of a crop. In north temperate and continental regions, for instance, such ability is valuable in extending the growing season of spring planted crops such as sugar beet and potatoes, making possible more effective use of increasing light inputs in spring and early summer (Wareing and Allen, 1977). They can also determine the geographical limits of the crop, as in the attempted introduction of such subtropical species as maize and soya beans to more northerly latitudes (Duncan, 1975; Shibles et al., 1975).

The temperature requirements for both active growth and survival are usually related to the climatic origin of the crop (Cooper, 1976; McWilliam, 1978). The optimum temperature for germination and leaf growth of most temperate crops, for instance, is around 20°C with considerable reduction below 10°C, and growth may cease between 0 and 5°C. Many tropical and subtropical crops, both C_3 and C_4, on the other hand, show optimum temperatures of 35–40°C, and temperatures below 10–15°C may seriously limit growth or even survival. Conversely in some tropical environments, as for maize in Nigeria, high temperatures may seriously limit germination and active leaf growth during the seedling stage.

Even so, considerable variation exists in these temperature responses within many crops, usually related to past climatic selection. In the temperate forage grasses (*Lolium*, *Dactylis* and *Festuca*) for instance, populations from Mediterranean climates where winter is the active growing season can grow actively at temperatures of 0–5°C, but are rather frost susceptible, whereas populations from northern and continental climates become dormant at moderately low temperatures, but show considerable cold hardiness (Cooper, 1964). Similar variation in temperature response between locally adapted populations has also been reported for the tropical grasses *Setaria* and *Paspalum* (McWilliam, 1978). Again, in the small grain cereals, selection for improved winter hardiness has allowed autumn rather than spring planting, providing a closed photosynthetic cover to take advantage of increasing light energy in the early spring, whilst in the subtropical *Phaseolus* and maize, variation in temperature response has made possible the extension of the crop to cooler environments.

Water stress

In many environments, shortage of water is a major factor limiting the possible growing season. Germination and successful establishment of the crop requires adequate water supply, but its subsequent growth or even survival can be limited by a combination of high evaporative demand and/or lack of soil water within the root range of the crop.

Several crop strategies have been developed which allow continued growth and photosynthesis under conditions of water shortage. In the first place, the crop may limit water loss by stomatal control. The leaf water potential at which stomata close varies with the crop, ranging from about -8 bars for field bean to about -28 bars for cotton, though the absolute value differs with the growth history of the plant. The extent of genetic variation in the critical leaf water potential is not yet clear, though varietal differences have been reported in sorghum (Turner, 1979). The more efficient use of water of species with the C_4 photosynthetic system, which have a higher stomatal resistance to water vapour transfer, has already been mentioned, whilst a more extreme strategy is shown by species such as pineapple with the CAM (crassulacean acid metabolism) photosynthetic system in which CO_2 is taken in and fixed into organic acids during the night making it possible for the stomata to close completely during the high evaporative demand of the day (Downton, 1971; Troughton, 1975).

Quite apart from a complete closure of the stomata (which, of course, also prevents CO_2 exchange) variation in such leaf characteristics as stomatal size and frequency, or surface ridging of the leaf have been reported as leading to reduced water loss as in barley, *Panicum* and rye grass (Wilson, 1981). Perennial rye grass lines selected for smaller or fewer stomata appear able to continue leaf growth more actively under moderate water stress (Wilson, 1975a).

In yet other crops, including sunflower and soya bean, the ability to adjust leaf osmotic potential and so maintain cell turgor at low leaf water potentials can be important, though little is known of the extent of genetic variation in this characteristic (Turner, 1979).

The availability of water to the crop will be influenced by the extent of its root range. Much of the success of sorghum compared with maize under dry conditions is associated with its greater root range, whilst in upland rice, varietal differences in resistance to seedling drought are closely correlated with the proportion of deep roots (O'Toole and Chang, 1979).

The above mechanisms may serve to improve water use efficiency and growth of the crop during periods of moderate water shortage, but in many environments as in Mediterranean and savanna climates, long and regular periods of drought occur, and yet other strategies are required. One of the most usual is to tailor the life cycle of the crop to the period when water is likely to be available. In a Mediterranean climate, for instance, winter annual crops including the small grain cereals and such forage species as Wimmera rye grass and subterranean clover, germinate with the autumn rains, grow actively through the winter and flower and produce seed before drought begins in the spring. In these winter annuals, the time of flowering and seed production, i.e. the length of the life cycle, is determined by genetically controlled responses to vernalisation and photoperiod and is usually closely related to the potential growing season as limited by water supply (Cooper, 1964). Similarly, in savanna climates, the life cycle of locally adapted varieties of sorghum closely fits the season of water availability (Bunting *et al.*, this volume).

On the other hand, perennial species such as shrubs and perennial grasses in these environments often survive the drought period by the onset of dormancy, often associated with the development of a deep rooting system (McWilliam, 1978; Turner, 1979).

Considerable variation clearly exists both between and within crop species for those environmental responses which allow the crop to cope effectively with the climatic limitations of temperature and water stress. It must be remembered, however, that the duration of the growing season can also be limited by the rotational requirements of particular farming systems, i.e. by the availability of land for sowing following a previous crop, or the optimum time of harvesting in relation to subsequent cropping. Indeed, in many tropical environments multiple cropping systems, with several short or overlapping growing seasons, may provide a greater total or economic yield than does a longer duration single crop (Chang and Vergara, 1972).

Allocation of assimilates

Although total dry matter production depends largely on the duration and photosynthetic activity of the crop canopy, crops are grown to provide an economic end product, which may consist of seeds, fruits or

vegetative storage organs, such as roots or tubers. The relative allocation of assimilates to this end product, i.e. the harvest index, is thus an
important determinant of economic yield (Evans, 1975).

In certain crops, the economic yield consists of the leaf canopy itself
as in short-duration leaf vegetables or forage crops grown either with a
restricted growing season or under multiple or sequential cropping. In
such crops, with a harvest index approaching 80–90%, the rapid
establishment of a closed photosynthetic surface after sowing is particularly important. On the other hand, where climatic or farming
requirements allow, perennial forage crops may be grown, to be
utilised by successive harvests, either by grazing or cutting. In such
perennial crops, whilst rapid initial establishment is clearly of value,
even more important are regrowth and persistence over a series of
harvests. These features will be greatly influenced by the relative
partition of assimilates between harvested yield and the residual leaf
area or reserves left after defoliation (Cooper, 1981b).

However, many important crops, particularly the staple cereals in
which the grain is the economic end product, have a determinate habit
of growth with a limited life cycle. There is a well defined separation of
the allocation of assimilates between the vegetative and the reproductive phase, and the harvest index consequently rarely rises above 50%.
In such crops, the timing of flowering and seed production is usually
under the control of developmental responses to vernalisation and
photoperiod, and locally adapted varieties have usually been selected
for those responses which fit their life cycles most effectively into the
growing season. Furthermore, in the small grain cereals, much of the
dry matter of the grain is produced from current assimilation after
anthesis, although some assimilates can be translocated from the stem,
and climatic conditions (including light energy input) during flowering
and grain filling are particularly important (Evans *et al.*, 1975; Austin
and Jones, 1976). In maize, on the other hand, a greater proportion of
assimilates are usually transferred from the stem, and the length of the
effective assimilation period is therefore longer (Duncan, 1975). In
these crops the plant breeder, whilst aiming for a life cycle which fits
into the possible growing season, also needs to ensure the maximum
allocation of material to the grain.

In contrast, many other important crops including potato, cassava,
sugar beet or sugar cane, have an indeterminate habit of growth.
Concurrent leaf growth and transfer of assimilates to the appropriate
vegetative sink can thus continue almost indefinitely, giving a possible

harvest index to root or tuber of some 70–80%. A major breeding objective is the continuation of an active photosynthetic surface for as long as possible, together with the maximum allocation of assimilates to the economic end product (Moorby and Milthorpe, 1975). In the potato, for instance, considerable variation exists in the onset and rate of tuberisation often under the control of photoperiod or temperature. Most of the original South American potatoes were short-day in their tuberisation response and the development of varieties for more northerly latitudes has involved selection for the ability to initiate tubers rapidly under long-day conditions (Mendoza and Estrada, 1979).

Clearly, for the same length of growing season the potential yield of an indeterminate crop, such as the potato, with a harvest index of 80% is considerably greater than that of a determinate cereal with a harvest index of only 50%. Even so, a far greater proportion of the edible energy in the world is derived from grain rather than tuber crops, possibly because of the adaptation of cereals to a wider range of climatic environments (particularly those involving a degree of water stress), their lower labour requirements for harvesting and ease of transport and storage (Bunting et al., this volume).

In yet a further group of crops such as field bean, soya bean and cotton, with an indeterminate habit of growth, the allocation of assimilates to vegetative growth and to flowering and seed production can continue simultaneously. Whilst this provides flexibility in response to fluctuating environmental conditions the resultant competition for assimilates often results in low and unpredictable economic yield. In such species the introduction of the determinate habit, as is now possible for the field bean, may be a valuable breeding objective (Shibles et al., 1975).

It will be clear from the above discussion that a wide variety of strategies have been developed by crop plants to allow an effective response to different climatic inputs and constraints. These strategies involve both those morphological and physiological features which determine total crop photosynthesis and also those developmental responses which control the duration of the life cycle and the allocation of assimilates to particular end products. Furthermore, considerable genetic variation exists even within individual crops for many of these features, often related to past climatic or agronomic selection. Such variation can provide valuable raw material for the plant breeder to use in developing improved varieties adapted to different climatic environments and management systems.

BREEDING FOR CLIMATIC ADAPTATION

The objectives of the plant breeder are to improve the yield, reliability and quality of his crop, and in so doing adaptability to different climatic environments or management systems are important features. To achieve this end he needs to identify the most promising sources of genetic variation of the characters required in his crop and to devise the most appropriate selection and breeding procedures for their incorporation into improved varieties (Wallace *et al.*, 1972; Cooper, 1981*a*).

Sources of genetic variation

The first step in any breeding programme is the collection, survey and characterisation of the available genetic variation in the crop and its wild relatives. The present pattern of variation of any crop is a complex of its past evolutionary history modified by more recent human activity (Simmonds, 1976). A primary source of variation for many valuable characters is often provided by the centre or centres of diversity, possibly corresponding to early areas of domestication. In historic times, however, extensive migration of crops has occurred including the temperate cereals and many forage crops from Eurasia to North and South America, and conversely such species as maize, potato and tomato from the Americas to other parts of the world. Again in Australia, which has no indigenous cultivated species, all the present crops have been introduced from elsewhere, including the small grain cereals and forage crops into temperate and Mediterranean climates and such tropical species as sugar cane and banana into the higher rainfall tropical areas.

The wide distribution of many important crop species has been associated with the development of a range of local varieties, adapted to local climates and farming systems, which provide a valuable source of variation for the plant breeder. In attempting to make use of such variation, however, the breeder must remember that such locally adapted varieties, particularly under subsistence farming systems, may well have been selected primarily for survival and reliability of yield under fairly low inputs of water and fertilisers and often with appreciable weed competition. Changes in the intensity of management including irrigation, higher fertiliser inputs and more effective weed control may well change the characteristics required in the crop, particularly those which contribute to improved yield potential.

Furthermore, the breeder often wishes to extend the climatic range of a crop to a new environment where no locally adapted material may be available, as with the current interest in developing varieties of such subtropical species as maize, soya beans or *Phaseolus* for more northerly latitudes. Whilst making full use of locally adapted varieties, it is therefore usually desirable to collect potential breeding material from a wider range of environments, and also to include related wild species which may carry genes for adaptation to temperature or water stress (in addition to such important features as disease and pest resistance).

Such wide collection and conservation of genetic material both of the crop plants themselves and of related wild species is of increasing importance in view of the activities of the plant breeder himself in developing new uniform high yielding varieties which in many parts of the world are replacing the more varied locally adapted populations. Furthermore, although many plant breeding programmes already involve the collection of potential breeding material from a range of environments, the plant breeder is naturally interested in those which appear to be most useful in his own programme, and may well discard those which have no apparent immediate value. The International Board for Plant Genetic Resources which was set up in 1964 is therefore playing an increasingly important role in encouraging the collection, conservation and characterisation of genetic resources of crop species and their wild relatives in many climatic environments throughout the world (IBPGR, 1975).

Selection procedures

Having obtained the necessary range of genetic variation the plant breeder needs to decide on the most appropriate selection criteria procedures. In terms of climatic adaptation, he is particularly concerned with those characteristics which allow the most effective use of the possible growing season as limited by temperature, water supply or farming requirement, though these must, of course, be combined with other important features such as disease and pest resistance and nutritive quality.

The extent of variation in many of these characteristics has already been discussed. The ability to germinate and expand leaf area more actively at low temperatures, for instance, together with cold tolerance, may allow the extension of the growing season as with the potato and sugar beet, or the introduction of such crops as maize and soya bean to the more northerly latitudes. Similarly, more efficient water use can be achieved both by extending the root range and by modifying those leaf characteristics which control evaporative loss, whilst the timing of the life cycle to fit into the available growing season, as in the cereals, often involves selection for appropriate responses to vernalisation and photoperiod. The use of photoperiodically insensitive forms of wheat and rice, for instance, has made an important contribution to the spread of improved varieties to a wide range of latitudes (Chang and Vergara, 1972). Similarly, the sensitivity to photoperiod and temperature of the onset and rate of tuberisation in tuber crops such as the potato is an important feature in developing varieties adapted to different climatic regions (Mendoza and Estrada, 1979).

Many of the characteristics responsible for climatic adaptation, such as length of life cycle, harvest index and response to seasonal variations in temperature and water supply can be effectively assessed in the breeding nursery, though it is important that such assessment should be made in the environments and under the managements in which the variety will be used in practice. The additional use of a wider range of environments in the initial screening programme, however, makes it possible to assess breeding material for more general climatic adaptability, and statistical techniques, such as those developed by Finlay and Wilkinson (1963) for barley varieties in South Australia, allow the estimation of the extent of genotype–environment interaction, and the degree of general or specific adaptation of different genotypes of selection lines.

For certain of these characteristics which determine climatic adaptation, however, it may be possible and indeed valuable to develop rapid early screening techniques under more controlled conditions in the glasshouse or growth room (as indeed is already common in disease screening) (Cooper, 1981a). For effective use in a breeding programme such tests must show a definite advantage over field selection procedures and their results must correlate well with subsequent field performance. They should, for instance, be able to handle large numbers of individuals rapidly and reliably, preferably early in the life cycle and at any time of the year. Such techniques are likely to be especially useful in assessing response to such climatic stresses as low temperature and water shortage where field assessment is often restricted to a particular season of the year and may be made difficult by large year to year fluctuations in the particular stress factor. Screening tests for cold hardiness and growth at low temperatures have already been developed for many crops including potatoes, cereals and forage grasses (Gusta and Fowler, 1979). Direct methods for screening for response to water stress in the young seedling stage have been used effectively in rice (O'Toole and Chang, 1979) and for sorghum (Blum, 1979) and indirect techniques such as selection for smaller or fewer stomata have led to improved water use efficiency in some species such as rye grass (Wilson, 1975a, 1981).

Similarly, those developmental responses to temperature and photoperiod which control the onset of flowering or tuberisation and hence the partitioning of assimilates, can often be measured rapidly under controlled conditions, although any advantage over field assessment at a single location is more doubtful. Even so, such screening may be of value in predicting the behaviour of the material in other climatic environments.

The possibility and indeed the value of rapid screening for the various components of crop photosynthesis is less certain. Although variation has been reported in such features as maximum photosynthetic rate of the individual leaf, leaf arrangement in relation to light interception and the extent of photorespiration and other respiratory losses, their relative importance in determining total or economic yield is far from clear (Wallace *et al.*, 1972; Evans, 1975). Even so, in certain species, selection for low dark respiration or for leaf characteristics which influence light interception, have been able to increase total dry matter production appreciably. Features determining the establishment and duration of the crop canopy and the allocation of assimilates to the economic end product, i.e. a greater harvest index, appears to be even more important in determining both yield and climatic adaptation (Evans, 1975).

Achievements and potential

Plant breeding has already provided varieties with improved yield and climatic adaptation in many crops. In most developed countries, as in north-western Europe, North America and Australia, with long established programmes in plant breeding, a steady advance over many years has been achieved in both public and private sector breeding. In the UK, for instance, national average yields of wheat increased slowly over the first 50 years of this century from about 2·1 to 3·0 tonnes ha^{-1} but have since advanced more rapidly to 5·7 tonnes ha^{-1} in 1980. This increase has been associated largely with an increase in harvest index rather than in total biomass (Bingham, 1981). Similarly, in the Corn Belt of the USA, maize yields have trebled in 45 years, about half of this increase being attributable to new varieties.

In the developing world, however, much of the advance is comparatively recent, with an important role being played by the International Agricultural Research Centres, which now have extensive programmes on the breeding and improvement of most major crops in the tropics and subtropics (Jennings; 1976; Bunting, 1981). The first two centres, the International Rice Research Institute (IRRI) in the Philippines and the International Centre for Maize and Wheat Improvement (CIM-MYT) in Mexico, were established by the Rockefeller and Ford Foundations to undertake intensive research and training on these three major staple cereals, including a strong plant breeding component, in cooperation with national and regional organisations in this field. Subsequently, these two Foundations set up the International Centre of Tropical Agriculture (CIAT) in Columbia to work on farming systems for humid tropical Latin America, including cassava and *Phaseolus* beans, and in 1968 the International Institute for Tropical Agriculture (IITA) in Nigeria, with special interest in cowpeas, sweet potatoes, yams and aroids worldwide, and in cassava, maize, rice and soya beans for the African tropics. In 1971 responsibility for these endeavours passed to the Consultative Group on International Agricultural Research, a consortium of national donors and international agencies, and since that time nine new institutes have been added including the International Potato Centre (CIP) in Peru, the International Crops Research Institute for Semi-Arid Tropics (ICRISAT) in Hyderabad and the International Centre for Agricultural Research in Dry Areas (ICARDA) in Syria and Lebanon.

All these centres have accumulated large collections of plant genetic resources, nearly 200 000 accessions in all, which are used extensively to produce improved broad-based populations with improved yield, response to irrigation and improved management, and better adaptation to climatic and soil characteristics, together with continuing resistance to pests and diseases. These improved breeding materials are then fed into national testing and breeding services.

Considerable improvement has already been achieved in the staple cereals (Jennings, 1976; Arnold, 1980). In the decade from 1966–76, for instance, wheat production in India rose from 10·4 million tonnes to 28·3 million tonnes, with an increase in average yield from 940 kg ha^{-1} to 1410 kg ha^{-1} associated with the use of more productive varieties. Similarly, the use of varieties produced by CIAT in Columbia increased the yield of irrigated crops of rice from 3 tonnes ha^{-1} in 1966 to 5·4 tonnes ha^{-1} in 1974.

These increased crop yields are often associated with improvements in management such as increased fertiliser inputs, irrigation and improved disease and weed control as well as with the use of improved varieties. In some cases the comparison of older and newer varieties under standard conditions has allowed the relative contribution of variety and management to be assessed (Austin et al., 1980). For cereals in the UK, for instance, of the considerable advance in yield between 1947 and 1975, the contribution of improved varieties accounted for 60% of the increase in wheat and 48% in spring barley (Silvey, 1978). Similarly, in Iowa, USA a critical comparison under standard managements of maize varieties produced in the 1970s showed an overall increase of 57% over those of the 1930s.

Although disease and pest resistance has been an important breeding objective in most crops, much of the improvement in yield has been based on features which enable the crop to make most effective use of the available climatic inputs by fitting its life cycle to the possible growing season and/or by increasing its harvest index (Evans, 1975, Bingham 1981). In wheat, for instance, the use of the Norin semi-dwarfing genes, originally from Japan, together with the introduction of the day-neutral habit has provided varieties for low latitude countries, which could respond to irrigation and fertilisers without lodging, and furthermore could extend the practice and advantages of multiple cropping. Similarly, in rice the development of semi-dwarf varieties of day-neutral type with a reduction of the life cycle from about 180 to about 100 days has greatly increased production in irrigated areas in Thailand, North India and Sri Lanka, though improvement has not been so great in rain fed areas where water supply is less predictable. Conversely in maize, the development of varieties capable of growing at lower temperatures and adapted to longer photoperiods for flowering has made possible the extension of the crop northwards in both North America and North-west Europe.

Even so, for many crops, particularly in the tropics and subtropics, yields are still well below those which might be expected on the basis of theoretical models of crop growth photosynthesis (Monteith, 1972; 1977). Continued improvement in fitting the life cycle to the possible growing season and in increasing the harvest index should be possible. In developed countries, however, with a long record of varietal improvement the maximum yields may already be close to those predicted on theoretical grounds and other features of the crop may require consideration. For winter wheat in the UK, for instance, a yield of over $10\ \text{tonnes ha}^{-1}$ which can be obtained from modern short-strawed varieties with a high harvest index is now approaching the predicted maximum of $12–14\ \text{tonnes ha}^{-1}$ (Austin, 1978) and it has been suggested that improvement of the basic efficiency of photosynthesis of the individual leaf may be an important future breeding objective (Bingham, 1981).

Furthermore, the present discussion has been concerned primarily with the efficient use of such climatic inputs as light energy and water supply. In future the plant breeder may need increasingly to consider the efficient use of other possible limiting inputs, including the major soil nutrients, N, P and K, and the support energy required for cultivation, harvesting and processing.

SUMMARY

In terms of climatic adaptation a major contribution made by the plant breeder is to produce varieties whose life cycles fit the particular constraints of the climatic environment, and make the most effective use of the incoming light energy during the available growing season. In most crops, considerable genetic variation exists for many of the characteristics which determine the possible duration of the crop canopy in relation to limitations of temperature or water supply, its photosynthetic production and the allocation of assimilates to the economic end product. Effective breeding programmes must depend on the collection and characterisation of this genetic variation and on the development and use of appropriate selection procedures both in the field and under controlled conditions. For this purpose the plant breeder requires a sound knowledge of the range of genetic variation available in his crop, and also the relative importance of the various characteristics which determine efficient adaptation and yield under the particular range of climatic conditions.

REFERENCES

Arnold, M. H. (1980). Plant breeding. In: *Perspectives in World Agriculture.* Commonwealth Agricultural Bureaux, Farnham Royal, UK, pp. 67–89.

Austin, R. B. (1978). Actual and potential yields of wheat and barley in the United Kingdom. *ADAS Quart. Rev.* **29**, 76–87.

Austin, R. B. and Jones, R. B. (1976). The physiology of wheat. Cambridge Pl. Breed. Inst. Rep. for 1975, pp. 20–73.

Austin, R. B., Bingham, J., Blackwell, R. D., Evans, L. T., Ford, M. A., Morgan, C. L. and Taylor, M. (1980). Genetic improvements in winter wheat yields since 1900 and associated physiological changes. *J. agric. Sci., Camb.* **94**, 675–89.

Bauer, H., Larcher, W. and Walker, R. B. (1975). Influence of temperature stress on CO_2 gas exchange. In: *Photosynthesis and Productivity in Different Environments* (Ed. J. P. Cooper). Cambridge Univ. Press, London, pp. 557–86.

Bingham, J. (1981). The achievements of conventional breeding. *Phil. Trans. Roy. Soc. B London* **292**, 441–54.

Biscoe, P. V., Scott, R. K. and Monteith, J. L. (1975). Barley and its environment. III. Carbon budget of the stand. *J. appl. Ecol.* **12**, 269–93.

Blum, A. (1979). Genetic improvement of drought resistance in crop plants: A case for sorghum. In: *Stress Physiology in Crop Plants* (Eds H. Mussell and R. C. Staples). John Wiley and Sons, New York.

Bunting, A. H. (1981). CGIAR: the first ten years. *Span* **24**, 3–4.

Chang, T. T. and Vergara, B. S. (1972). Ecological and genetic information on adaptability and yielding ability in tropical rice varieties. In: *Rice Breeding.* Intern. Rice Res. Inst., Los Banos, Philippines, pp. 431–52.

Cooper, J. P. (1964). Climatic variation in forage grasses. I. Leaf development in climatic races of *Lolium* and *Dactylis. J. appl. Ecol.* **1**, 45–61.

Cooper, J. P. (Ed.) (1975). Control of photosynthetic production in different environments. In: *Photosynthesis and Productivity in Different Environments.* Cambridge Univ. Press, London, pp. 593–621.

Cooper, J. P. (1976). Photosynthetic efficiency of the whole plant. In: *Food Production and Consumption : The Efficiency of Human Food Chains and Nutrient Cycles* (Eds A. N. Duckham, J. G. W. Jones and E. H. Roberts). North-Holland Publishing Company, Amsterdam, pp. 107–26.

Cooper, J. P. (1981a). Physiological constraints to varietal improvement. *Phil. Trans. Roy. Soc. B London* **292**, 431–40.

Cooper, J. P. (1981b). Physiological and morphological advances for forage improvement. *Proc. XIV Int. Grassld Congr.* (in press).

Downton, W. J. S. (1971). Adaptive and evolutionary aspects of C_4 photosynthesis. In: *Photosynthesis and Respiration* (Eds M. D. Hatch, C. B. Osmond and R. O. Slatyer). Wiley Interscience, New York, pp. 3–17.

Duncan, W. G. (1975). Maize. In: *Crop Physiology : Some Case Histories* (Ed L. T. Evans). Cambridge Univ. Press, London, pp. 23–50.

Evans, L. T. (1975). The physiological basis of crop yield. In: *Crop*

Physiology: *Some Case Histories* (ed. L. T. Evans). Cambridge Univ. Press, London, pp. 327–55.

Evans, L. T. and Dunstone, R. L. (1970). Some physiological aspects of evolution in wheat. *Aust. J. Biol. Sci.* **23**, 725–41.

Evans, L. T., Wardlaw, I. F. and Fischer, R. A. (1975). Wheat. In: *Crop Physiology*: *Some Case Histories* (Ed. L. T. Evans). Cambridge Univ. Press, London. pp. 101–49.

Finlay, K. W. and Wilkinson, G. N. (1963). An analysis of adaptation in a plant breeding programme. *Aust. J. agric. Res.* **14**, 742–54.

Gusta, L. V. and Fowler, D. B. (1979). Cold resistance and injury in winter cereals. In: *Stress Physiology in Crop Plants* (Eds H. Mussell and R. C. Staples). John Wiley and Sons, New York.

Hatch, M. D., Osmond, C. B. and Slatyer, R. O. (Eds) (1971). *Photosynthesis and Photorespiration*. Wiley Interscience, New York.

IBPGR (1975). *The Conservation of Crop Genetic Resources*. IBPGR, Rome.

Jennings, P. R. (1976). The amplification of agricultural production. In: *Food and Agriculture*. Scientific American Inc., Freeman & Co., San Francisco, pp. 125–30.

Loomis, R. S. and Gerakis, P. A. (1975). Productivity of agricultural ecosystems. In: *Photosynthesis and Productivity in Different Environments*. (Ed. J. P. Cooper) Cambridge Univ. Press, London, pp. 145–72.

Ludlow, M. M. (1978). Light relations of pasture plants. In: *Plant Relations in Pastures* (Ed. J. R. Wilson). CSIRO, Melbourne, Australia, pp. 35–49.

McCree, K. J. (1970). An equation for the rate of respiration of white clover plants grown under controlled conditions. In: *Prediction and Measurement of Photosynthetic Productivity* (Ed. I. Setlik). Centre for Agricultural Publishing and Documentation, Wageningen, pp. 221–30.

McWilliam, J. R. (1978). Response of pasture plants to temperature. In: *Plant Relations in Pastures* (Ed. J. R. Wilson). CSIRO, Melbourne, Australia, pp. 17–34.

Mendoza, H. A. and Estrada, R. N. (1979). Breeding potatoes for tolerance to stress: Heat and frost. In: *Stress Physiology in Crop Plants* (Eds H. Mussell and R. C. Staples). John Wiley and Sons, New York, pp. 228–62.

Monteith, J. L. (1972). Solar radiation and productivity in tropical ecosystems. *J. appl. Ecol.* **9**, 747–66.

Monteith, J. L. (1977). Climate and the efficiency of crop production in Britain. *Phil. Trans. Roy. Soc. B London* **281**, 277–94.

Moorby, J. and Milthorpe, F. L. (1975). Potato. In: *Crop Physiology*: *Some Case Histories* (Ed. L. T. Evans). Cambridge Univ. Press, London, pp. 225–57.

O'Toole, J. C. and Chang, T. T. (1979). Drought resistance in cereals—rice: a case study. In: *Stress Physiology in Crop Plants* (Eds. H. Mussell and R. C. Staples). John Wiley and Sons, New York, pp. 374–405.

Penning de Vries, F. W. T. (1974). Substrate utilization and respiration in relation to growth and maintenance in higher plants. *Neth. J. Agr. Sci.* **22**, 40–4.

Robson, M. (1973). The growth and development of simulated swards of perennial rye grass. II. Carbon assimilation and respiration in a seedling sward. *Ann. Bot.* **37,** 501–18.

Saeki, T. (1975). Distribution of radiant energy and CO_2 in terrestrial communities. In: *Photosynthesis and Productivity in Different Environments* (Ed. J. P. Cooper). Cambridge Univ. Press, London, pp. 297–322.

Shibles, R. M., Anderson, I. C. and Gibson, A. H. (1975). Soybean. In: *Crop Physiology: Some Case Histories* (Ed L. T. Evans). Cambridge Univ. Press, London, pp. 151–89.

Silvey, V. (1978). The contribution of new varieties to increasing cereal yield in England and Wales. *J. natn. Inst. agric. Bot.* **14,** 367–84.

Simmonds, N. W. (Ed.) (1976). *Evolution of Crop Plants.* Longman, London and New York.

Slavik, B. (1975). Water stress, photosynthesis and the use of photosynthates. In: *Photosynthesis and Productivity in Different Environments* (Ed. J. P. Cooper). Cambridge Univ. Press, London, pp. 511–36.

Sullivan, C. Y. and Ross, W. M. (1979). Selecting for drought and heat resistance in sorghum. In: *Stress Physiology in Crop Plants* (Eds H. Mussell and R. C. Staples). John Wiley and Sons, New York, pp. 263–82.

Townley-Smith, T. F. and Hurd, E. A. (1979). Testing and selecting for drought resistance in wheat. In: *Stress Physiology in Crop Plants* (Eds H. Mussell and R. C. Staples). John Wiley and Sons, New York, pp. 447–64.

Troughton, J. H. (1975). Photosynthetic mechanisms in higher plants. In: *Photosynthesis and Productivity in Different Environments* (Ed. J. P. Cooper). Cambridge Univ. Press, London, pp. 357–91.

Turner, N. C. (1979). Drought resistance and adaptation to water deficits in crop plants. In: *Stress Physiology in Crop Plants* (Eds H. Mussell and R. C. Staples). John Wiley and Sons, New York, pp. 344–72.

Wallace, D. H., Ozbun, J. L. and Munger, H. M. (1972). Physiological genetics of crop yield. *Adv. Agron.* **24,** 97–146.

Wareing, P. F. and Allen, E. J. (1977) Physiological aspects of crop choice. *Phil. Trans. Roy. Soc. B London* **281,** 107–19.

Wilson, D. (1972). Variation in photorespiration in *Lolium. J. exp. Bot.* **23,** 517–24.

Wilson, D. (1975a). Leaf growth, stomatal diffusion resistances and photosynthesis during droughting of *Lolium perenne* populations selected for contrasting stomatal length and frequency. *Ann. appl. Biol.* **79,** 67–82.

Wilson, D. (1975b). Variation in leaf respiration in relation to growth and photosynthesis of *Lolium. Ann. appl. Biol.* **80,** 323–28.

Wilson, D. (1976). Physiological and morphological selection criteria in grasses. In: *Breeding Methods and Variety Testing in Forage Plants* (Ed. B. Dennis). Proc. Fodder Crops Section, Eucarpia, Roskilde, Denmark, p. 9–18.

Wilson, D. (1981). Breeding for morphological and physiological traits. In: *Plant Breeding Symposium II* (Ed. K. J. Frey) Iowa State Univ. Press, Iowa.

Zelitch, I. (1976). Biochemical and genetic control of photorespiration. In: CO_2 *Metabolism and Plant Productivity* (Eds R. H. Burris and C. C. Black). University Park Press, Baltimore, pp. 343–58.

Discussion

Professor Bushuk asked whether the 'multiline' approach to variety development was a method to be adopted to develop plants with a wider range of tolerance to climatic and moisture stress, to which *Professor Cooper* replied that this approach had been quite successful in dealing with disease build-up and it was interesting and worth consideration to apply it to environmental stresses. Alternative approaches of assessing material for its general or specific adaptability had, however, also been successful. The statistical approach of Finlay and Wilkinson in South Australia, for instance, based on the performance of barley varieties grown in a range of environments, made it possible to make selections both for general and specific adaptability. *Dr Lake* raised questions relating to the problem of selection of physiological types suitable under both natural ecosystems and in monoculture. The required attributes of a plant under the one were not necessarily the best in other situations. For example, a plant which could economise in water through poor conductivity during the spring would be at a disadvantage in an open ecosystem, but in monoculture this attribute might well be helpful. Improved photosynthesis and a low maintenance requirement would obviously be of benefit in both and it seemed sensible to think in terms of the fundamental process as a beginning. Another example was light interception—cereal varieties with long stems might well be advantageous in a natural environment, but not necessarily so in a monoculture. *Professor Cooper* agreed with this concept pointing out that water shortage in a mixed sward containing rye grass and white clover had a preferential adverse effect on the white clover in which wilting occurred. Under the same presumptive conditions of soil moisture, however, a monoculture of white clover continued to grow actively. The implications in terms of sources of genetic material for the plant breeder were quite considerable. Many local varieties of crops have been selected under conditions of low nutrient input and considerable competition in terms of weeds, and were usually rather heterogeneous. The attributes required in a crop growing as a mixed population with low nutrient inputs were not necessarily those required of a plant growing in monoculture with high inputs. *Professor MacKey* raised the question of the relationship between the root and the shoot. Before flowering, the correlation between dry weight of root and shoot in spring wheat is very high at 0·87. Tall plants will tend to give deep roots and well tillered plants many roots. An ideotype model entirely based on the capacity of the shoot will not work, and the correlated pattern between shoot and root will complicate the decisions of the plant breeder even more. The wheat plant has adapted to a thick stand, i.e. low tillering and low number of crown roots, by developing more seminal roots. *Professor Cooper* stated that presumably selection for other attributes might well modify root–shoot relationships, but this had not been a deliberate step on the part of the plant breeder. The fact that one can manipulate separately the root system is of considerable interest, and it raises the question of how far breeders could set up ideotypes of crop plants, that is to say combinations of morphogenetic features which would be likely to maximise yield. His opinion was that in trying to set up such an ideotype it might be desirable to consider its value in responding to the potential variation from year to year with climatic factors such as water stress. *Professor MacKey* continued the discussion on this aspect saying that he had enlarged the size of glumes in wheat in the knowledge that a large proportion of the photosynthate was translocated from the head to the grain. As an effect, tillering decreased due to the increased dominating role of the main shoot as the sink. We have to understand all these correlated consequences before we can more definitely improve yield.

Professor Wareing pointed out that in Britain we have a potentially long growing season, but because of the maritime influence we tend to have a long cool spring, in which the rise in temperature lags behind the improvement in solar radiation. Consequently crop growth is limited by temperature and the ability to utilise assimilates in leaf growth, rather than by photosynthesis. There appears to be considerable genetic variation in the ability to grow at cool temperatures, as has been shown for grasses and potatoes, so that it should be possible to obtain improved early growth by breeding. Very little is known about the physiological characteristics which determine the ability to grow at cool temperatures. We need to know to what extent it is 'sink' determined, through effects on cell division and cell extension, or whether it involves differences in metabolism, including photosynthesis and respiration. *Dr Scott*, on the same point, stated from experience with sugar beet one can select for the ability to produce leaves at low temperature; however, such improvements are only useful if they are not at the expense of other temperature-dependent attributes, notably bolting resistance. Unfortunately there is evidence that this is not so.

Dr Landsberg pointed out that there are significant differences in the efficiency with which plants grow in terms of nitrogen utilisation and requirements. He was not sure whether these differences are present between cultivars but suggested that, since nitrogen is an important environmental variable, breeding for nitrogen requirement should be considered. *Professor Cooper* stated that while he had concentrated on response to climate, there were a number of reports of important genetic differences in soil nutrient utilisation. Comparatively little work had been done on variation in response to soil nutrients, presumably because of the cheapness of artificial sources of nitrogen. It was important to consider the uptake of such nutrients in relation to the nutritional requirements of the consumer. Timothy (*Phleum pratense*) for instance, has aerial parts which are very low in sodium whatever the sodium status of the soils and there appears to be a block in transport from roots to shoots. Indeed the shoots are so low in sodium that they do not provide sufficient of the element for the milking cow. *Professor Wareing* continued the discussion on these lines. Forest trees do show differences between species regarding their demand for nitrogen. Broadly, they can be divided into nitrogen demanding and less demanding species. The birch relocates nitrogen, and is thus less demanding whereas the sycamore does not do so and under nitrogen-limiting conditions the clones with a low nitrogen requirement indulge in less nitrogen recirculation. *Dr Lake* stated that while it might be thought that considerations of the nitrogen supply were somewhat irrelevant to those of climate, it is of some interest that the specific uptake of nitrogen by the root for different species is much the same at say 18°C root temperature, but when the temperature reduces to 8°C the uptake rate drops to 50% for the temperate species, barley and oilseed rape, but with maize drops to zero. *Professor Cooper* stated that these species differences were obviously very interesting but for the plant breeder it would be more important to look at any varietal differences as in the high altitude maizes which had, of necessity, to deal with low temperature. *Professor Jarvis* asked the speaker how he thought a plant breeder should make use of the information on crop properties provided by the crop physiologist and assign priorities to them in his breeding work. Much is now known of relevant physiological properties, but in the past, as the speaker pointed out, this information has not been consciously used. *Professor Cooper* replied that for the plant breeder it is not quite sufficient simply to show that a particular process or character is important in the physiology of the plant; it is also necessary to show that it could usefully improve yield. In some instances, selection for physiological features has been unsuccessful. For example, in perennial rye grass selection for increased photosynthetic rate on a leaf area basis gave no increase in dry matter production, largely because high photosynthetic rate was correlated with small leaf size and particularly small mesophyll cell size. In contrast, selection for lowered dark respiration of mature tissue did give rise to an increase in seedling and total canopy yield and the improved cultivars so obtained are now being multiplied for official testing. Similarly, selection of plants with fewer stomata has given rise to cultivars which in field plots have shown increased dry matter yield under limitation of water supply. It is thus not sufficient to set up a physiological model of the crop plant which on theoretical grounds should give improved yield, it is necessary to isolate cultivars with these contrasting physiological features and to show that they have advantages under field conditions.

Climate and the Availability and Nutritive Value of Food

I. D. MORTON

Queen Elizabeth College, University of London, UK

INTRODUCTION

During the past few decades, consideration has been given to the effect of climate on the growth and breeding of plants but little attention seems to have been given to the actual nutritive value of the food so produced. Bryson and Murray (1977) have reviewed the effect of climate on food production but did not deal in any detail with the quality of the food. The recent book *Food, Climate and Man* edited by Biswas and Biswas (1979) treats food production in some detail. In the foreword to this book, Mostafa Kamal Tolba points out that there are 10 considerations which must be borne in mind for increased food production. These are:

1. Expansion of the area under agriculture
2. Transfer of technology
3. Relation between the input of energy and output of food
4. The use of fertilisers
5. The use of pesticides
6. The inter-relationship of weather and climate on crop production
7. Prevention of the loss of food stocks
8. Irrigation
9. Distribution of food
10. Development of strategies to solve the world food problems

I have listed these in detail as I think they do have something to offer us in considering the value of food produced in different areas of the world and under different climates. In this book a chapter by A. K.

Biswas entitled 'Climate, agriculture and economic development', reviews the effect of climate and economic development on food production but the author unfortunately does not deal with the actual nutritive value of the food.

THE EFFECTS OF CLIMATE ON CROP COMPOSITION AND QUALITY

It is well known that wheats grown in different areas of the world under different climates have different compositions. We teach students that there is a distinction between winter wheat and spring sown wheat and that there are strong and weak flours. If we look more closely at this, we find that these characteristics are related to the percentages of protein and starch in the flour. The over-wintered wheat produces grains which, when milled, produce flour with a lower percentage of protein and a higher percentage of starch. The spring sown wheat has, however, a higher percentage of protein and less starch. We may also be well aware that the vegetable oils produced from the legume crops such as soya bean or peanut possess different triglycerides depending on which part of the world they are grown in. Admittedly the differences are small but clearly fatty acid compositions are related to climate.

Kefford (1979) reviewed the impact of climatic variability on food processing. He pointed out that climate can have an effect on the quality of raw materials and on their subsequent processing.

In discussing this topic I should like to deal with the effects of climate on the major food components such as proteins, carbohydrates and fats and then deal with the effect of climate on the minor constituents of food such as vitamins. Flavour itself is also an important aspect of food acceptability and I would like to make some small mention of this. I appreciate that flavour may not necessarily be related to the nutrient value of food but it is an important factor in food consumption.

COMPOSITION OF OIL SEEDS

Brown et al. (1975), reviewing the fatty acid composition of peanuts grown at different latitudes in the United States, concluded that the changes in composition encountered in crops from different locations probably reflected temperature induced effects. Mono-unsaturated acids in the triglycerides increased and poly-unsaturated fatty acids decreased with increasing ambient growth temperature. The percentage of the mono-unsaturated fatty acids appeared to be governed not only by the availability of oxygen and the rate of oxygen diffusion into the actively metabolising cells but also by the higher metabolic rate recorded at elevated temperatures. Peanuts grown in southern Texas normally set and mature in July and August and are harvested in August or September when the surface soil temperatures rise to 40°C or even higher. Peanuts, however, grown in the northern parts of the United States normally set fruit in September. They are harvested in late October when the maximum surface soil temperature is probably between 20 and 35°C. The possibility that differences in photoperiod, degree of maturity and seed sources may have been responsible for the differences in lipid composition seems unlikely. Photoperiodicity and maturity cannot be completely excluded but the fact that the lipids are synthesised below the soil level argues strongly against a photoperiodic explanation. An interesting suggestion is that the decreased or increased carbohydrate supplies might significantly alter the energy balance within the seed. Lotti *et al.* (1977) reviewed the composition of the oils from 17 varieties of peanuts grown in various localities between 31° parallel south and 39° north and compared this data with that for the same varieties grown in Pisa. Their results clearly indicated that seed weight increased for the crops grown in warmer climates whilst percentage composition of the fatty acids indicated higher quantities of linoleic acid and lower quantities of oleic acid present in the crops from colder climates. Interestingly enough these authors also investigated the chemical nature and relative amounts of sterols. There was an increase of β-sitosterol and a decrease in campesterol and stigmasterol in the oils from crops grown in cooler climates.

Lotti *et al.* (1976), studying the effect of climate on the composition of rapeseed, showed that low erucic acid varieties grown in a warm climate have a higher erucic acid concentration and a lower oleic acid concentration than those grown in a cooler climate. The reverse is true for the high erucic acid varieties of rapeseed.

Marquard *et al.* (1977) reviewed the composition of the oil produced from linseed grown in Finland, Canada, Morocco, New Zealand and other countries. They concluded that the differences due to location of growth were much greater than those due to any difference in variety of linseed. The tocopherol content of the linseed oil was affected mainly by climate, a combination of photoperiodicity, humidity and temperature. Temperature and day length also have an effect on the fatty acid composition of summer rapeseed oil. The palmitic and oleic acid contents of the oil increase with increasing temperature irrespective of day length while the linoleic and linolenic acid contents decrease with increasing temperature and day length (van Hal and van Baarsel, 1974). Considerable interest has been shown in some eastern European countries such as Poland in the composition and quality of safflower, sunflower and mustard oils from different areas. Szyrmer (1974) has pointed out that in general climatic conditions of growth and particularly for sunflowers, the variety often has a greater effect on the oil content and composition than has fertiliser. Even milk fat produced by cattle is not exempt from changes due to the temperature of the animal's environment. Studies from Russia by Kurkova (1973) have shown that the content of saturated fatty acids with high melting point decreases in the northern parts whilst the content of unsaturated fatty acids in the butter fat increases. Is this a reflection of the food consumed or not?

The chemical composition of soya bean seed grown in the USSR is altered under different climatic conditions (Al'bert et al., 1976); the effects of weather and soil are less marked than those of climate. Under conditions leading to an increase in the protein content of seeds, lysine and methionine contents tend to decrease. However, when the oil content of the seeds is increased then the concentration of oleic acid is markedly increased and linoleic acid decreased. Williamson (1974) in Queensland has shown that climatic conditions during the growing season have a major influence on plant populations and yield of soya beans. When the plant population increased there was an increase in seed yield provided moisture was adequate, but yield decreased when moisture stress continued throughout growth. In his summary he indicates the most suitable plant population for Queensland conditions.

The soya bean work is confirmed by other work from Germany; Marquard et al. (1980) showed that high linoleic and linolenic acid concentrations are always associated with low temperature and incomplete maturity of the seed. There was a significant negative correlation between oleic and linoleic or linolenic acids present in the soya bean oil and the degree of maturity. High concentrations of more unsaturated acids were associated with lower temperatures and incomplete maturity.

Climate also influences the possible contaminants of oils such as aflatoxin. Giridhar and Krishamurthy (1977) in India have shown that peanut oil produced from a rainy season crop contains a much higher concentration of aflatoxin when compared with the oil produced from seed grown in the winter season. Dry area crops contained much less aflatoxin. Pistachio nuts have been investigated and here the contamination by aflatoxin is correlated directly with the amount of rainfall in the growing area after ripening and before harvest (Mojtahedi *et al.*, 1980). Danesh *et al.* (1979) have established the correlation between rainfall data and the aflatoxin contamination of such foods as nuts imported into the United States.

THE COMPOSITION OF FRUITS

Some interesting surveys in California (Nauer *et al.*, 1974; 1975) and in Israel (Cohen *et al.*, 1972) indicate that citrus fruits such as clementines, lemons, grapefruit and oranges grown in the coastal regions have a higher ascorbic acid content than fruit grown in interior desert-type locations. Warmer climatic zones, of course, do produce larger fruit and the percentage of juice is higher in grapefruit and lemons grown in the interior. With mandarins and oranges grown in the hot desert, however, the fruit was coarser in texture and the juice the lowest by actual weight. Cooler coastal zones are preferable if citrus fruits with a higher ascorbic acid content are required. Climate also affects the picking quality of Corsican clementines (Sanchez *et al.*, 1978). Citrus fruits are important as contributors of ascorbic acid in the diet.

The quality of wine depends on the variety of grape from which it is produced but climate–variety interaction can be important. Rain, fog, hail, wind and late autumn and early spring frosts are important aspects of climate. Perhaps the most important requirement is warmth from the sun (Webb, 1981). Over many years grapes grown at different locations in Switzerland (Vautier *et al.*, 1978) show a higher malic acid and total acid content when fruit is ripened in the sun. Grapes ripened in the shade have much lower concentration of total acids. There was, however, little effect of direct sun on the total sugar content or on the tartaric acid concentration. Climate has an effect on the sugar content and the acid content in Tokai grape varieties (Jenco, 1977). The sugar content varies inversely with the acid content and a survey over a number of years in south-eastern Europe indicates clearly that the climate has marked effects. Cold regions tend to produce grapes of high total acid content with malic acid predominating, while warm viticultural regions produce grapes of low total acidity and a relatively higher percentage of tartaric acid (Webb, 1981). Research in Italy has indicated that meteorological factors are important in influencing the mineral and sugar content of Chianti wine (Sabatelli and Stella, 1976).

The problems of wine making in regions with a hot climate are well known. The activity of the yeasts and the rate of the fermentation vary markedly with temperature. A high fermentation temperature adversely affects the quality of the wine (Ambrois, 1976). The essential oils in the grapes, which contribute much of the fruity aroma of wines, are changed markedly during fermentation under adverse climatic conditions, particularly at high temperatures (Bezzubov et al., 1973); the content of esters and alcohols increases and the wine often has a stronger bouquet but the trace flavour constituents can largely be lost. In one Swiss report, the content of tartaric acid appears to be quite independent of climatic conditions (Wejnar, 1974).

THE SUGAR-PRODUCING CROPS

In the UK and the rest of Europe we obtain a considerable proportion of our sugar from sugar beet. Adverse climatic conditions during the growing period produce a low quality juice from beet and consequently a lower yield of sugar (Osvald et al., 1977). The duration of sunshine and the sum of the ambient daily temperatures are positively correlated with the development of polarisation in sugar beet crops (Trzeciak, 1976). Should there be high rainfall during the growing season with beet, a considerable amount of invert sugar may be formed due to high invertase activity (Januszewicz et al., 1976). American work (Ryser, 1975) shows clearly that the percentage of sugar from sugar beet depends significantly on the temperature distribution of the growing crop and not so much on the actual root yield as such.

Sugar cane (which is the crop grown in the Central Americas, India and other tropical areas) behaves somewhat differently. In India, it has been shown that the high sugar accumulation in the cane was favoured by a cool night temperature of 12–16°C and a daytime temperature of 22–26°C with low relative humidity (Venugopal et al., 1974).

This brings me to the mention of C_3 and C_4 plants in their given environments. C_4 plants tend to be tropical and subtropical whilst the temperate plants are almost exclusively C_3. The benefit from the C_4

character shows up under high light intensity and at high temperatures. Fowden (1980) has indicated that the C_4 mechanism for photosynthesis shows to advantage at temperatures above 25°C. The difference between the two systems is that with the C_3 plants two molecules of 3-phosphoglyceric acid are the photosynthetic products of a reaction between carbon dioxide and a C_5 compound. An alternative mechanism in which carbon dioxide combines with a C_3 organic acid to yield C_4 dicarboxylic acids occurs in the C_4 plants. Examples of C_4 plants are tropical and semitropical species such as sugar cane and maize which produce dry matter rapidly at high light intensities. If we are to make use of these observations, clearly the nature of the plant and its photosynthetic process must be known. Fowden (1980) has commented that sugar is just an energy-containing compound and that if we are looking to photosynthesis as a source of energy products then should we not be seeking to harness plant photosynthetic processes to produce hydrogen?

CEREAL CROPS

Wheat

Olifer (1973) has shown that climatic conditions play a greater role in determining the chemical composition of wheat than does the fertiliser or other factors. Rainfall during the harvest can lead to deterioration of the grain and under Australian conditions Moos et al. (1972) have shown that there is germination in the ear following heavy rainfall which leads to wheat with marked α-amylase activity and susceptibility of the starch to attack by this enzyme. This clearly would have far reaching effects on the quality of the wheat.

Wheat grows best in a climate with between 229 and 762 mm (9–30 in.) rainfall per year. High temperature will inhibit the growth, particularly when associated with high humidity (Kent, 1975). This means that the tropics are not suitable areas for the growth of wheat, except at high altitudes. The plants prefer a period with the temperature between 6 and 13°C and 80 days suitable weather. The wheat plants are inhibited by autumn rain, frost or summer drought (Oram, this volume). The winter soil temperature determines the time of sowing and hence the type of wheat grown. In soils which are not continuously frozen during winter, autumn sowing is practised—the so-called 'winter wheat' which has a high yield and usually a lower protein content. In soils which are frozen, the wheat is sown in the spring. It has a shorter growing season, a lower yield and a relatively higher protein percentage. Wheat is most successful when grown as a cool temperature crop with a long growing season and abundant rainfall through to maturity. A late high temperature can lead to premature ripening and shrivelled grain with a high protein content.

Regional trends within the UK have been tabulated and discussed by Leitch and Boyne (1976). They reviewed both oats and wheat and showed that with 13 varieties of oats from 17 different stations ranging from Seale Hayne in the South-west to Aberdeen in Scotland, the Scottish station grain had lower nitrogen contents than the English but higher oil contents. This inverse relationship was present over several years. There were, however, significant differences between varieties. To obtain oats with a high nitrogen content consistently, the correct variety and growing location would have to be chosen with care. The variety 'Forward' is low both in nitrogen and oil while 'Castleton Potato' is well above average in nitrogen and the highest of all in oil.

The average protein content for each class of wheat from different countries is summarised in Table 1.

The influence of climate upon the quality of wheat cannot be over-emphasised and was clearly shown in a tri-state experiment in the

TABLE 1

PROTEIN CONTENT FOR DIFFERENT CLASSES OF WHEAT (ADAPTED FROM COLE-MAN (1930))

Country of origin	Hard Red winter wheat	Hard Red spring wheat	Soft Red winter wheat	White	Durum
Argentine (export)	11·7	–	10·8	8·3	10·7
Australia	10·1	13·1	11·5	10·3	16·2
Canada (export)	14·5	13·2	–	12·1	11·8
England	–	9·7	9·5	9·0	–
Germany	–	13·8	10·2	–	–
India	10·0	14·0	9·7	10·2	10·0
Italy	–	–	11·2	10·3	11·4
Russia	13·0	14·5	12·4	10·6	15·3
USA (export)	10·9	12·8	10·3	11·0	12·0

United States (Swanson, 1938). Three sets of experiments were designed. Soil from two states was shipped to the third state and wheat grown on the three plots. The same wheat seed was used and the experiment lasted several years. Soil from Kansas and California was shipped to Maryland and soil from Maryland was likewise shipped to Kansas and California. The results are summarised in Table 2. The kernels in the state of Kansas were all smaller than in the other states and the protein content was uniformly high. Climate clearly has a greater influence than soil but this experiment has been criticised as the nutrients could have come from deeper layers in the soil.

TABLE 2

EFFECT OF CLIMATE ON THE QUALITY OF WHEAT (TRI-STATE EXPERIMENT) (ADAPTED FROM SWANSON (1938))

	Wheat grown in Cal. soil from			Wheat grown in Kan. soil from			Wheat grown in Md. soil from		
	Cal.	Kan.	Md.	Cal.	Kan.	Md.	Cal.	Kan.	Md.
g/100 Kernels	32·0	25·1	23·6	20·3	19·1	18·0	23·2	27·4	23·6
% Protein content	13·2	11·3	14·8	17·5	19·3	19·7	11·8	12·5	12·9

Cal. = California; Kan. = Kansas; Md. = Maryland.

It should be remembered that in wheat the vitamin B_1 content can also vary with location of growth and season as well as variety. There appears to be a positive correlation between the protein and the thiamin contents (Greer et al., 1952b). Iron present in wheat grain is strongly influenced by the locality and appears also to be positively correlated with the protein content (Greer et al., 1952a). An examination of Manitoba and English wheats has shown that the Canadian wheat contains more protein, fat, magnesium, iron and zinc than the English wheat. The English wheat had higher carbohydrate, potassium, calcium and copper values. The values for fibre, thiamin, riboflavin, sodium, phosphorus and chlorine were similar. These relationships applied also to the flours (McCance et al., 1945).

The value of wheaten flour protein as a source of amino acids was strikingly demonstrated in the studies by Widdowson and McCance (1954) with the trials of undernourished children at Duisburg. Wheat proteins are capable of maintaining high rates of growth although lysine is the limiting amino acid. In the normal mixed diet, this relative deficiency of lysine is made good by lysine supplementation from other constituents in the diet. The flour protein has less basic amino acids, arginine and lysine, but more glutamic acid and proline than whole grain protein. In the milling process, the aleurone layer is normally removed to form part of the bran and germ, both of which are poor in storage protein but rich in protein with higher contents of the basic amino acids. The use of fertilisers can increase the ratio of storage to salt-soluble types of protein and hence cause a shift in the amino acid composition. In wheat grain from different climates small differences occur in the ratio of storage proteins to aleurone layer proteins.

Considerable work has been carried out in Russia looking at the differences in quality of spring and autumn sown wheats. If spring wheat is exposed to frost during maturing there is a dramatic reduction in nutrient accumulation into the grain, affecting principally proteins, starches and lipids (Bolotova *et al.*, 1977). The hot summer of 1976 in Europe during the latter stages of the growth and harvest with wheat yielded grain and flour of exceptional baking quality (Calvel, 1976). Wheat from such harvests is strong with a high gluten content and during the milling only small amounts of improver are necessary with a short maturing period. A survey in France following the 1976 harvest showed that the protein content of hard wheats varied from 13·1 to 17·9%, considerably higher than in the previous harvest (Nuret, 1976).

Rye

Experimental work with rye has indicated that climatic conditions markedly influence the protein content and also the quality of the protein. The globulin, gliadin and glutenin content are not altered but the 'filling' protein (albumen type) is affected markedly (Subda, 1976*a*, *b*, *c*).

Barley

Barley is often grown for use in beer production or for animal feedstuffs. With barley, the protein content varies according to the location of growth. English barley has a mean protein content of 9·16%, Canadian 13·0% and American 12·12% (Kent, 1943). In a hot dry climate, the protein content of barley grain is raised although the percentage of full grains in the ears is likely to be low. Barley grown in Ethiopia (Alkaemper, 1974) at higher altitudes has a reduced protein content. At 1800 m the protein content is 16·5% and at 2800 m the protein content is only 9%. These reduced protein contents are advantageous for malting barley but not for ensuring a proper protein supply for the population. Alkaemper found similar results with wheat in which at 1700 m the protein was 16·8% and at 2400 m only 9%.

A survey made in France from 1944 to 1965 to check the quality of the barley grown during that period indicated that climatic factors had a clear influence on the content and composition of proteins and also on the starch reserve (Scriban *et al.*, 1977). A high environmental temperature during growth increases the protein content of barley grain. The hot dry summer weather of 1976 in Europe produced barley with an unusually high protein content but the percentage of full grains was low (Mangstl and Reiner, 1976).

Rice

Rice is a cereal that is essentially a swamp plant with a high water requirement. A temperature between 18 and 38°C is essential during the growth period of 4 to 6 months. These requirements can be met over large areas of tropical and subtropical regions, even at relatively high altitudes in high rainfall regions. There are two agriculturally distinct types of rice, the lowland or wetland rice and the upland or dryland rice. The International Rice Research Institute is currently developing new improved varieties. The protein content for rice varies from 11% in brown rice to 9·1% in paddy rice, polished rice being in between at 9·8%. The polished rice has the highest carbohydrate content of 88·9%, with brown rice 83·2% and paddy rice only 71·2% (Kent, 1975). Climatic factors clearly can influence the nutritional value of the rice grain.

Maize

Maize is inadequate as a source of protein for growth. The grain protein content is low and the amino acid pattern is unbalanced. Zein, the storage protein is deficient in lysine and tryptophan. Recent breeding work has now produced the opaque-2 and floury-2 varieties in which the endosperm protein has nearly 70% more lysine and 20% more tryptophan. Maize as a crop requires adequate moisture and temperatures around 20 to 30°C for satisfactory growth. As the newer improved varieties are grown and used around the world, we should be able to estimate more clearly the climatic effects on the nutritive value. There will be some, as we know in this country to our cost—so often the summer is just not warm enough for the maize cobs to develop and ripen. Some recent American work (Jurgens *et al.*, 1978) with maize indicates that withholding water gives fewer kernels to the ear and the kernels, although having a higher protein content of 11% contrasted with 8·3%, have a lower oil content (3·1% content contrasted with 3·8%).

Sorghum and millet

Sorghum is the basic food in many parts of Africa and Asia and the millets are likewise a major source of energy and protein for many people in Asia and Africa. New hybrids have been developed for both cereals in the past few years, particularly using the hl gene in sorghum. Both plants can tolerate and survive under conditions of continuous or intermittent drought. Both species are relatively good sources of protein although lysine is the first limiting amino acid. The protein percentage for each is of the order of 11; analyses from Africa indicate a range of 9·7 to 13·7% and India 7·8 to 21·0% for sorghum. Figures for the millets range from 6·7 to 13·6% for African samples and 7·2 to 11·4% for Indian samples. Occasional analyses have been reported with extraordinarily high protein values for both species (Hulse *et al.*, 1980). More work needs to be done in studying the effect of climate upon yield and nutritive value of both sorghum and millet grown under normal and ideal conditions in many parts of the world. It is evident that in the coming years, we can expect improvement in the utilisation of new varieties of both plants.

Triticale

Triticale is a man-made cross between wheat and rye but the nutritive value is limited because of the relatively low content of certain amino acids inherited from both parents. Varieties are being developed which are insensitive to day length so that the crop can be grown in lower latitudes. The protein content is generally high, of the order of 20%, and is high in lysine. Some recent Indian work indicates that triticale varieties can be used satisfactorily for baking (Bakshi *et al.*, 1978). These workers also found a significant difference in grain quality characteristics depending on the location of growth and the climate. It will be interesting to see whether this work can be expanded and studies made on plants grown in different regions.

OTHER FOOD CROPS

Onions are a useful crop contributing to the carbohydrate and ascorbic acid intake of many peoples. Climatic factors can affect the nutrient content and composition of onions (Doruchowski and Bakowski, 1978). Cranberries are a fruit which contribute markedly to the ascorbic acid intake especially when taken in the form of drinks. Climate affects the vitamin C and sugar content of these fruits (Schmid, 1977). We should not forget ordinary potatoes which will grow at quite high altitudes and in many different parts of the world. A survey of some 30 year trials of potato varieties (Seppaenen, 1977) indicates that the tuber yield is strongly dependent on how early the crop is planted but the starch percentage in the tuber is related to the effective accumulated temperature and rainfall after the onset of the flowering. The total yield of starch is related to the same factors as tuber yield. Potatoes are also a valuable source of ascorbic acid.

If apple trees are subjected to stress during the period of blossom setting or later in the summer season, they can produce fruit which do not keep well and readily suffer storage injury (Stoll, 1977). To obtain apples with good sugar content, day temperature as well as the hour of picking has to be watched (Battaglini and Battaglini, 1975). Research in progress at East Malling (personal communication) indicates that the flavour of apples can be influenced by intensive growing. When the apple trees are planted almost too closely and intensively cropped, there are indications that the flavour is not so well developed as that of apples grown on trees with the usual spacing. I look forward to reading the reports of this work because so often the flavour of a food has been neglected yet the micro-climate around an apple tree clearly may be very important. Climate also can determine which varieties of apples can be grown in which region. The failure of the Cox's Orange in North America is an example.

Tea is a drink which is enjoyed by many people. The flavour of tea is related to the presence of carotenoids, alkaloids and certain terpenes and aldehydes in the processed black tea. Variation in the content of these compounds is related to carbon dioxide fixation and the extent of intra- as compared with extra-chloroplastic reactions. Extra-chloroplastic biogenesis of terpenoid compounds leads to development of tea flavour while intra-chloroplastic fixation of carbon dioxide and the consequent biogenesis of different terpenoids results in teas without flavour. The content of the flavour compounds is related to climatic conditions and has recently been reviewed by Wickremasinghe (1974).

Hops which are used to flavour different types of beer contain humulones and α-acids. The content of these compounds can be closely associated with the mean air temperature during the months of August and September when the hop flowers are setting (Connaughton, 1977). This is clearly an effect of the micro-climate on the plant constituents.

CONCLUDING REMARKS

In discussing this topic, I have endeavoured to look at the effect of the major climatic differences upon our food crops and in some cases, at the effect of the micro-climate. I have concentrated on cereals as they are the most important staple foodstuff worldwide and we still do not fully understand or know all the effects of climate on their nutrient composition. The newer varieties with improved lysine and tryptophan content offer hope for the future. Let us not, however, forget that people eat food because they like it and it appeals to them. So often the flavour of a food has been neglected. Clearly we should understand why food grown under one set of climatic conditions can be so much more pleasant to eat than the same food grown under an adverse set of climatic conditions.

ACKNOWLEDGEMENTS

I should like to express my thanks to various colleagues for their advice and particularly to Dr N. L. Kent for his advice on cereals.

REFERENCES

Al'bert, V. E., Krasil'nikov, V. N., Kyuz, E. P., Gorshkova, E. I. and Stoikova, V. Ya. (1976). Chemical composition of soybean seeds and variations induced by weather, soil and climatic conditions. *Prikladnaya Biokhimiya i Mikrobiologiya* **12**(2) 186.

Alkaemper, J. (1974). The influence of altitude on yield and quality of cereals in Ethiopia. *Zeit. fuer Acker-u. Pflanzenbau* **140**(3), 184.

Ambrois, U. (1976). Alcoholic fermentation in regions with a Mediterranean climate. *Industrie delle Berande* **5**(2), 82.

Bakshi, A. K., Sekhon, K. S., Sandhu, G. S. and Gill, K. S. (1978). Baking performance of triticales as affected by locations and irrigation conditions. *Indian Miller* **9**(3), 19.

Battaglini, M. and Battaglini, M. (1975). Variations in the sugar contents of nectar from *Pirus malus* L. and *Prunus domestica* L. as a function of some biological and microclimatic factors. *Annali Facotta Agraria, Univ. Studi Perugia* **30,** 207.

Bezzubov, A. A., Egorov, I. A., Rodopulo, A. K. and Skuin, K. P. (1973). Essential oils in grapes and wine. *Proc. 2nd Conf. Biochem. Grapes and Wine*, p. 82.

Biswas, M. R. and Biswas, A. K. (Eds) (1979). *Food, Climate and Man.* John Wiley and Sons, New York.

Bolotova, M. N., Nikolaenko, O. I., Baiko, V. G. and Nechaev, A. P. (1977). Biochemical characteristics of spring wheat grain exposed to night frost during maturing. *Izvestiya Vysshikh Uchebnykh Zavedenii, Pishchevaya Teknol.* (6), 29.

Brown, D. F., Cater, C. M., Mattil, K. F. and Darroch, J. G. (1975). Effect of variety, growing location and their interaction on the fatty acid composition of peanuts. *J. Food Sci.* **40,** 1055.

Bryson, R. A. and Murray, T. J. (1977). *Climates of Hunger: Mankind and the World's Changing Weather.* Univ. of Wisconsin Press, Madison.

Calvel, R. (1976). The quality of wheat and flours of the 1976/77 harvest. *Bull. Anciens Eleves de l'Ecole Francaise de Meunerie* (276), 294.

Cohen, A., Lomas, J. and Rassis, A. (1972). Climatic effects on fruit shape and peel thickness in 'Marsh seedless' grapefruit. *J. Amer. Soc. Hort. Sci.* **97**(6), 768.

Coleman, D. A. (1930). USDA Technical Bulletin No. 193.

Connaughton, M. J. (1977). Weather influences on the α-acid content of seedless hops. *J. Dept. Agric. Fish. Irish Rep.* **74,** 5.

Danesh, D., Mojtahedi, H., Barnett, R. and Campbell, A. (1979). Correlation between climatic data and aflatoxin contamination of Iranian pistachio nuts. *Phytopathol.* **69**(7) 715.

Doruchowski, R. W. and Bakowski, J. (1978). Nutritional value of onions. *Zywienie Czlowieka* **5**(3), 197.

Fowden, L. (1980). A chemist among plants. *J. Roy. Soc. Arts* **129**(5293), 50.

Giridhar, N. and Krishamurthy, G. V. (1977). Studies on aflatoxin content of groundnut oil in Andhra Pradesh with reference to climatic conditions and seasonal variations. *J. Fd. Sc. & Tech. India* **14**(2), 84.

Greer, E. N., Pringle, W. J. S. and Kent, N. L. (1952a) The composition of British-grown winter wheat. II. Iron and manganese contents. *J. Sci. Fd Agric.* **3**(1) 16.

Greer, E. N., Ridyard, H. N. and Kent, N. L. (1952b). The composition of British-grown winter wheat. I. Vitamin B_1 content. *J. Sci. Fd Agric.* **3**(1), 12.

van Hal, J. G. and van Baarsel, H. M. (1974). Influence of temperature and day length on the fatty acid composition of summer rapeseed (*Brassica napus*). *Proc. Internationaler Rapskongress*, p. 243.

Hulse, J. H., Laing, E. M. and Pearson, O. E. (1980). *Sorghum and the Millets: Their Composition and Nutritive Value.* Academic Press, London.

Januszewicz, I., Mossakowska, K., Korolczuk, E. and Zelazny, K. (1976). Determination of the effect of temperature and rainfall conditions on the activity of beet invertase during the 1974/75 campaign. *Gazeta Cukrownicza* **84**(3), 59.

Jenco, M. (1977). Effect of climatic factors on the quality of musts from Tokai grape varieties. *Vinohrad* **15**(11), 243.

Jurgens, S. K., Johnson, R. R. and Boyer, J. S. (1978). Dry matter production and translocation in maize subjected to drought during grain fill. *Agron. J.* **70**(4), 678.

Kefford, J. F. (1979). Impact of climate variability on food processing. *CSIRO Food Res. Quarterly Austr.* **39**(1), 1.

Kent, N. L. (1943). Some characteristics of barley. *Milling* **101**, 240.

Kent, N. L. (1975). *Technology of Cereals*, 2nd edn. Pergamon Press, Oxford, pp. 44, 75, 97.

Kurkova, M. F. (1973). Effect of climatic conditions on the fatty acid composition of milk fat. *Izvestiya Vysshikh Uchebnykh Zavedenii Pishchevaya Teknol.* (3), 20.

Leitch, I. and Boyne, A. W. (1976). *The Nutrient Requirements of Farm Livestock. No. 4. Composition of British Feedingstuffs, Technical Review and Tables.* Agric. Res. Council, London.

Lotti, G., Baragli, S. and Izzo, R. (1976). Effects of climate on the composition of rape seed oil. *Riv. della Soc. Ital. Sci. dell' Aliment.* **5**(9), 293.

Lotti, G., Baragli, S. and Gentili, M. (1977). Acid and sterol composition of groundnut oil in relation to climate. *Riv. Ital. delle Sost. Grasse* **54**(12), 506.

Mangstl, A. and Reiner, L. (1976). Effects of the high environmental temperature on the protein content of barley. *Brauwelt* **116**(30), 971.

Marquard, R., Schuster, W. and Hornarnejad, R. J. (1980). Productivity and quality of oil and protein of six soybean varieties in cultivation studies at two German locations. *Fette Seifen Anstrichm.* **82**(3), 89.

Marquard, R., Schuster, W. and Iran-Nejad, H. (1977). Studies on tocopherol and thiamin content of linseed from world-wide cultivation and from phytotron under defined climatic conditions. *Fette Seifen Anstrichm.* **79**(7), 265.

McCance, R. A., Widdowson, E. M., Moran, T., Pringle, W. J. S. and Macrae, T. F. (1945). The chemical composition of wheat and rye and of flours derived therefrom. *Biochem. J.* **39**(2), 213.

Mojtahedi, H., Danesh, D., Hughighi, B. and Barnett, R. (1980). Secondary and subsequent postharvest mycotoxin contamination of Iranian pistachio nuts. *XII Internat. Congr. Microbiol.*

Moos, H. J., Derera, N. F. and Balaam, L. N. (1972). Effect of preharvest rain on germination in the ear and α-amylase activity of Australian wheat. *Austr. J. Agric. Res.* **23**(5), 769.

Nauer, E. M., Goodale, J. H., Summers, L. L. and Reuther, W. (1974). Climate effects on mandarins and Valencia oranges. *California Agriculture* **28**(4), 8.

Nauer, E. M., Goodale, J. H., Summers, L. L. and Reuther, W. (1975). Climate effects on grapefruit and lemons. *California Agriculture* **29**(3), 8.

Nuret, H. (1976). Characteristics of wheats of the 1976/77 harvest. *Bull. Anciens Eleves de l'Ecole Francaise de Meunerie* (276), 285.

Olifer, V. A. (1973). Biological productivity and cycle of nutrients in crops of spring wheat grown in chernozem soils in the Altai region. *Agrokhimiya* (11), 60.

Osvald, R., Frankova, M. and Capelak, J. (1977). Composition of sugar beet and juices in the 1976/77 campaign. *Listy Cukrovarnicke* **93**(18), 181.

Ryser, G. K. (1975). A weather index method and temperature distribution applied to sugar beet yields and sugar percentage. *J. Amer. Sugar Beet Technologists* **18**(4), 312.

Sabatelli, M. P. and Stella, C. (1976). Effect of meteorological factors on ash composition of true Chianti. *Rivista di Viticultura e di Enologia* **29**(10), 406.

Sanchez, C. D., Blondel, L. and Cassin, J. (1978). Effect of climate on the quality of Corsican clementines. *Fruits* **33**(12) 811.

Schmid, P. (1977). Long term investigation with regard to the constituents of various cranberry varieties (*Vaccinium macrocarpoa Ait*). *Acta Horticultura* (61), 241.

Scriban, R., Hermant, J-J., Scriban, A. and Oudin, J. (1977). The influence of agricultural climatology factors on the Aurore barley variety cultivated by Secobra from 1944–1965. *Bios* **8**(11), 11.

Seppaenen, E. (1977). Influence of weather conditions and late blight on the yields of potatoes in Finland. *Diss. Abstr. Intern.* C**37**(3), 529.

Stoll, K. (1977). The causes of storage injury to apples. *Schw. Zeit. Obst-Weinbau* **113**(11), 240.

Subda, A. (1976a). Changes in protein quantity and quality and in some baking characteristics of varieties and strains of rye grown under different environmental conditions. I. Changes in contents of 4 protein fractions of rye varieties and strains grown under different environmental conditions, *Hodowla Roslin, Aklimat. i. Nasiennicto* **20**(2), 211.

Subda, H. (1976b). Changes in protein quantity and quality and in some baking characteristics of varieties and strains of rye grown under different environmental conditions. II. Quantitative and qualitative changes in electrophoretic protein fractions of rye varieties and strains grown under different environmental conditions. *Idem* **20**(2), 225.

Subda, H. (1976c). Changes in protein quantity and quality and in some baking characteristics of varieties and strains of rye grown under different environmental conditions. III. Evaluation of rye varieties and strains grown under different environmental conditions on the basis of some baking characteristics. *Idem* **20**(3), 251.

Swanson, C. O. (1938). *Wheat and Flour Quality*. Burgess Publishing Co., Minneapolis, Ch. IX, X and XI.

Szyrmer, J. (1974). Effect of growth conditions and NPK fertilisation on yield, and on oil content and quality of white mustard, safflower and sunflower. *Hodowla Roslin, Aklimat. i Nasiennicto* **18**(5), 389.

Trzeciak, S. (1976). Tests on definition of effect of major meteorological factors on sugar content of sugar beet at two developmental stages. *Zeszyty Naukowe Akad. Rolnicza w Szczecinie* (53) (Rolnictwo XIV), 285.

Vautier, P., Simon, J.-L., Gnaegi, F., Koblet, W., Zanier, C. and Tanner, H. (1978). Maturation of grapes exposed to direct sunlight and those shaded by foliage. *Revue Suisse de Viticulture, Aboriculture, Horticulture* **10**(1), 7.

Venugopal, R., Palaniappan, S. P., Morachan, Y. B., Murugesan, M. M. and Santha, R. (1974). Effect of climate on sugar cane yield and sugar recovery percentage. *Indian Sugar* **24**(5), 423 and 429.

Webb, A. D. (1981). The biochemistry of growing grapes and making wine. *Trends in Biochemical Sciences* **6**(3), III.

Wejnar, R. (1974). Studies of the malic and tartaric acid contents of ripe grapes in relation to climatic factors. *Mitteilungen, Rebe, Wein, Obstbau u. Fruechteverwertung* **24**(2/3), 123.

Wickremasinghe, R. L. (1974). The mechanism of operation of climatic factors in the biogenesis of tea flavour. *Phytochem.* **13**(10) 2057.

Widdowson, E. M. and McCance, R. A. (1954). *Med. Res. Coun. Spec. Rep. Ser. No. 287*. HMSO, London.

Williamson, A. J. P. (1974). The effects of various plant populations on agronomic characters of several varieties of soybean under rain-grown conditions in Southern Queensland. *Queensland J. Agric. and Animal Sci.* **31**(3), 285.

Discussion

Dr Hatch responded to questions on the effect of climatic factors on sugar cane yields and C_4 plant growth as follows. At least in Australia where sugar cane is an annual crop the major period of sugar accumulation corresponds to the winter period when reduced temperature and water supply reduces vegetative growth.

Compared with C_3 plants, C_4 plant photosynthesis and growth is particularly responsive to increasing light. C_4 plant photosynthesis may also be substantially greater than C_3 plant photosynthesis in the light limited region, particularly in the higher temperature range. The reason that C_4 plants are more efficient at higher temperatures is that their quantum yield is unaffected by increasing temperature. Quantum yield in C_3 plants declines with increasing temperature.

Dr Slack referred to the possible effect of temperature on the proportion of the different unsaturated fatty acids in triglycerides and the idea that the effect lay at the level of oxygen tension in relation to desaturation. The concentration of oxygen which is saturating for the oleate and linoleate desaturases is probably about 2% and it may well be that the factor is not oxygen tension but rather the differential effect of temperature on the rate of synthesis of oleate and on the rates of oleate and linoleate desaturation. Even so, it is possible that diffusion processes in the seed coat may result in very low oxygen tensions sufficient to account for the phenomenon. *Mr Jackson* asked about the variation in protein content and quality of cereals in Europe generally—the concept of a specification of quality in wheats was given definition by the Intervention Agencies in European countries. *Dr Bushuk* pointed out that the association between protein content of grain and temperature could be related to the overall growth of the plant and seed development. Higher protein content is often associated with a lower kernel weight and factors which inhibited kernel weight resulted in higher protein content. It seemed more sensible to regard the increase in protein content as a consequence of the decrease in the

123

amount of storage carbohydrate, a conclusion with which *Professor Morton* agreed. *Professor MacKey* mentioned that in developed countries we are not quite so dependent on protein quantity, since there are possibilities to compensate for baking performance by improving gluten quality. The Manitoba variety, Marquis, grown in Sweden and having a higher protein content, does not show the same loaf volume as the best Swedish spring wheats. *Professor MacKey* then went on to suggest that one way to regard crop plants in relation to their overall efficiency was to express their productivity in terms of glucose equivalent. One gram of glucose was, on this basis, equivalent to 0·83 g of storage polysaccharide, 0·40 g protein and 0·33 g fat. This approach seemed to be a reasonable way of assessing crops, or rather seed crops, in terms of their biological efficiency and gave the very interesting result that winter rape and winter wheat produced in seed the same weight of glucose equivalent. Leguminous crops show low efficiency. *Dr Austin* continued the discussion on protein content of wheat stating that while a major factor in accounting for the differences in bread-making quality between wheats from different parts of the world was probably climatic, the type of protein was at least as important as the total amount and was under strong genetic control. The exploitation of genetic differences in the protein composition should enable plant breeders to select varieties with improved baking quality to be grown in Britain, which has a climate previously thought unsuitable for the production of bread-making wheat. *Mr Smith* also pointed out that it was often much easier to relate variation of the weather to variation in quality than it was to relate it to variation in quantity and he gave several examples. *Dr Cooke* asked about consumer needs in relation to agricultural practice. He commented on one of the tables presented by Professor Morton relating to the performance of the same variety of wheat grown on three different soils which had been transported to three different situations. Other work in the mid-West of the USA had related yield and protein content of grain to water and nitrate content of soil. High protein was achieved when soil moisture deficit increased during growth and there was a large reserve of nitrate in the subsoil. These factors were likely to be responsible for high protein in the wheat in Kansas. The effects of altitude on the protein content of barley grown in Ethiopia were likely to be influenced by differences in rainfall, nature of soil, and nitrogen supply, related to altitude. There was too little information or concern about the effects of agricultural conditions and practices on the composition of crops, which affected their quality. Recent nutritional surveys by MAFF mentioned only calcium and iron among the mineral nutrients and suggested that iron supplies may be deficient in members of large families. There was a need for such nutritional factors to be related to the argicultural conditions under which food was produced. *Dr Cooke* asked who should be responsible for such investigations at the interface between agricultural science and food science. *Professor Morton*, in reply, indicated that very little was known about this situation and there was a real need for proper investigational work. *Sir Kenneth Blaxter* stated that he thought that certainly in western Europe diets were sufficiently varied such that man would hardly be affected by the relatively small variations in the nutritive value of cereal grains. With pigs fed on barley as the main energy source, however, the lysine content of the grain and its total protein were of considerable importance and cognizance was taken of this in advising the farming community from season to season for the lysine and protein contents did indeed vary with the weather. In the 1979–80 season, the barley crop in Scotland had been rather poor with very low bushel weights and again cognizance had to be taken of this in designing animal rations. *Dr Curtis* emphasised two different aspects of the situation with regard to the provision of food. Increasingly, food processing and food production had to be considered together. The food processing industry needed to be able to manipulate the input to a considerable extent and this was often made difficult by climatic effects producing uncontrollable changes in the quality of the inputs. He suggested also that insufficient attention had been given to climatic effects on the nutritionally undesirable compounds present in some crops. He instanced the potato variety, Lenape, in the USA. In more northern latitudes the content of glyco-alkaloids in this cultivar was unexpectedly increased and the variety was hurriedly withdrawn. In another example he quoted work of the Scottish Plant Breeding Station examining new cultivars with improved eelworm resistance which were derived from *Solanum vernei*. The crosses made using this genetic material were tested in different latitudes and very much higher glyco-alkaloid concentrations were found in climatic conditions associated with the higher latitudes. *Professor Morton* stated that while he had only mentioned the aflatoxins in his lecture, he was very well aware of other undesirables and pointed out that the amounts of alkaloids in potatoes are only slightly less than those which would constitute a toxic dose. *Professor Kaufman* pointed out that the high variation in the protein content of other nutrients in foods from different locations caused a certain amount of anxiety about the calculation of human nutrient intakes from food tables. He wondered whether any differences in geographical incidence of disease could in fact be associated with geographical variations of food composition. *Professor Morton* stated that food tables were known to vary in their intrinsic accuracy and were certainly averages. Many of the figures published up to the early 1970s were certainly open to some doubt, but he quite realised that there were specific problems relating to nutrient deficiencies and excesses which would not be revealed from consultation of average food tables. An obvious instance was the incidence of cancer in certain races in East Africa.

Weather and Yield Variation
of Crops

J. L. MONTEITH

University of Nottingham School of Agriculture,
Sutton Bonington, Loughborough, Leics., UK

R. K. SCOTT

Broom's Barn Experimental Station,
Higham, Bury St. Edmunds, Suffolk, UK

COMPLEXITY OF THE SYSTEM

'Climate determines what crops the farmer can grow; weather influences the annual yield, and hence the farmer's profit, and most
important, especially in underdeveloped and overpopulated countries,
how much food there is to eat'.

This final sentence of a review by Watson (1963) links the discussion
of climate and food production by previous contributors to our own
concern with the impact of weather on the fluctuations of yield which
occur season after season in all agricultural systems. For most crops,
the relation between weather and yield is extremely complex but three
main facets can be distinguished in principle, if not always in practice
(Penman, 1962). First, individual elements such as light and temperature have a direct effect on physiological processes such as photosynthesis and leaf expansion. Second, weather controls the spread of
fungal diseases, insects, pests and weeds which can restrict crop
growth. In terms of yield, these 'indirect' effects of weather are often
more significant than the 'direct' effects but they are also much harder
to quantify, to analyse and to predict. Third, weather governs the
farmer's day-to-day programme by setting capricious limits to field
operations. These limits too are difficult to quantify but are of special
importance when weather is erratic during preparation of the seedbed
or at harvest.

Year by year fluctuations of yield of the type analysed by Dennett (1980) are a consequence of the interaction of all three sources of yield variation. Many attempts have been made to correlate long series of yield measurements with corresponding weather, usually expressed in terms of the monthly averages of temperature, rainfall, and radiation (or sunshine) during the growing season. The pioneering work of Lawes (1880) on rainfall and the wheat yields from Broadbalk inspired several later studies on records from the same site, but after almost a century of effort, Yates (1969) was pessimistic: 'The results that have emerged from this immense amount of arithmetic... are therefore somewhat meagre'.

The main reason for this lack of progress is the complexity of the dynamic interaction between crops and their environment. Even when the growth of a crop is not limited by disease or by problems of husbandry, the response of physiological processes to weather changes throughout the growing season as plants age and as they react and adapt to periods of stress.

How should this complexity be handled when attempts are made to describe how yields are likely to depend on individual elements of weather? We decided that a review of purely statistical conclusions would contribute little to this meeting: they bypass mechanisms which we know are fundamental to crop–weather relationships, even though we cannot express them in exact quantitative terms. At the other extreme, we were able to make little progress by appealing to elaborate computer models of crop growth which *do* incorporate comprehensive mathematical descriptions of physiological mechanisms. Unfortunately, comprehensiveness carries a penalty—the introduction of many disposable constants and arbitrary functions. In consequence, little confidence can be placed on predictions from a computer model of the relation between crop yield and a specific element of weather.

Attempting to steer a middle course, we shall describe the performance of a crop in terms of the simple but fundamental distinction between its rate of growth and the duration of the growing season. We then consider how rates and duration of growth may depend on weather.

A SCHEME FOR ANALYSIS

For a start, we believe it is essential to distinguish clearly between the length of the *growing season*, as determined by the climate of a site, and the duration of the *growth period* for a specific crop growing on that site. In temperate climates, the length of the growing season is often identified as the average length of the period without frost. Even for crops which can survive frost, growth in winter is severely inhibited by low temperature, lack of light or a combination of both unfavourable factors. In the semi-arid tropics, the length of the growing season is determined by the balance between rainfall and evaporation.

Cereal crops and potatoes, growing in western Europe, mature and die for genetic and physiological reasons before the end of the growing season. The growth period for these crops is shorter than the growing season. In contrast, the growth of maize in North America is sometimes abruptly curtailed by frost. In such cases, the growth period and the growing season finish together and are of equal length for a crop which starts to grow at the beginning of the growing season. Later we shall show that the distinction between growth period and growing season is particularly important for understanding how crop yields are related to temperature.

Within the growth period, the rate of crop growth C (in units such as $g\,m^{-2}\,day^{-1}$ or $kg\,ha^{-1}\,day^{-1}$) usually increases while the canopy is closing, achieves an almost constant maximum value C_m for several weeks during the 'grand period of growth', and then decreases to zero during a final senescent phase. (In some mathematical treatments, growth is expressed as a sinusoidal function of time, i.e. there is a smooth transition from an initial phase of increasing C to a final phase of decreasing C. This behaviour is characteristic of crops suffering from drought or disease and is *not* an appropriate starting point for an attempt to relate crop growth to weather.) A representative mean value of the maximum growth rate C_m can usually be determined by examining a record of standing dry weight measured at regular intervals during the growing season although definition of the period of maximum growth rate is necessarily somewhat subjective. We therefore relate the dry weight of a crop at harvest (W_m) to the length of the growth period from germination to harvest (t_g) by writing

$$W_m = C_m(t_g - t_l)$$

where $t_g - t_l$ is the *effective* length of the growth period and t_l is the time lost as a consequence of incomplete light interception at the beginning of growth and of senescence in the period before harvest (Fig. 1).

For a well-managed crop, the value of C_m will correspond to almost complete light interception and can be calculated from one of many

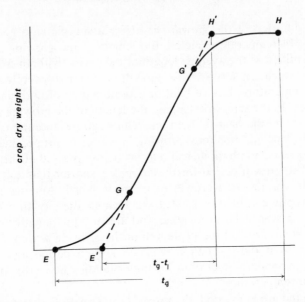

Fig. 1. Formal representation of increase in crop dry weight with time. The crop emerges at E and the formation of a complete canopy at G is followed by the 'grand period of growth' GG' in which the crop growth rate has a maximum and effectively constant value C_m given by the slope of GG'. The crop is harvested at H.

The same amount of dry matter would be produced by a crop growing at rate C_m between E' and H' as shown by the dashed line extrapolating GG'. The growth period from emergence to harvest (t_g) is therefore effectively reduced by the time lost when the canopy is incomplete (EE') and when the photosynthesis rate is reduced by senescence $(H'H)$.

models of crop photosynthesis (e.g. Charles-Edwards, 1978; Goudriaan and van Laar, 1978; Monteith, 1981a). When a sowing is too thin or when establishment is poor, C_m may be substantially smaller than the value that would be obtained with a dense stand but should nevertheless reach a stable value during the main growth phase.

In principle, this treatment can be extended to incorporate the effects of shortage of water or of nutrients, disease, etc. (see Fig. 4, p. 141). Singly or together, these stresses can reduce the rate of growth at any stage of development (and may also interfere with development). However, if C_m is assigned some standard value characteristics of a healthy crop, the effect of stress can be expressed as a reduction in the effective length of the growing season. In some circumstances t_g will be shorter (e.g. premature senescence) and in others t_l will be longer (e.g. slower closing of the canopy).

Using this framework, we shall now consider the influence of environmental factors on the separate terms C_m, t_g and t_l.

C_m and light

In Britain, in Holland, and presumably over much of western Europe, C_m lies between 15 and $20\,\mathrm{g\,m^{-2}\,day^{-1}}$ for a wide range of arable crops and vegetables growing during the summer if unstressed by drought or disease (Sibma, 1968; Greenwood *et al.*, 1977). This conservatism suggests that the best crop yields should be strongly correlated with the length of the growth period, a deduction difficult to test because the time from germination to harvest is rarely recorded in reports of agronomic experiments. However, the world record yields for a number of temperate and tropical crops, tabulated by Cooper (1975), are indeed strongly correlated with the growth period (Fig. 2) and reveal a clear distinction between C_3 and C_4 species (Monteith, 1978). For C_3 crops, the mean growth rate was $13\cdot0\pm1\cdot6\,\mathrm{g\,m^{-2}\,day^{-1}}$ and the corresponding C_4 rate was $22\cdot0\pm3\cdot6\,\mathrm{g\,m^{-2}\,day^{-1}}$.

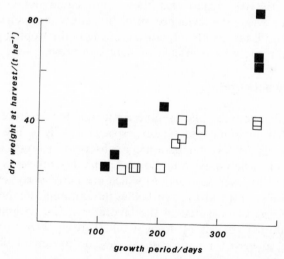

FIG. 2. Total dry weight at harvest for very high yielding crops in relation to growth period. ■ C_4 plants; □ C_3 plants (after Cooper (1975) and Monteith (1978)).

The lack of variation in C_m may seem difficult to reconcile with what we know about the dependence of photosynthesis rate on solar irradiance and about the great variability of irradiance from day to day. Two points help to resolve the paradox. First, C_m is a mean rate for a period usually extending over 4 to 8 weeks. Even in Britain, the standard deviation of insolation from year to year is only about ±10% in a given month and ±6% over a period of 2 to 3 months in summer. Second, even for a fractional difference of ±10% in sunlight, the corresponding change of photosynthesis in C_3 plants is smaller by a factor of two to three because of the effects of light saturation prevailing during periods of bright sunshine (Monteith, 1981b). Taking both effects together, values of C_m for the same (C_3) variety should not change from one season to another by more than a few per cent, and differences will usually be obscured by errors of measurement.

There are, however, several situations in which crop growth rate would be expected to be almost proportional to irradiance. First, for C_3 crops during spring and autumn in temperate latitudes, leaves will rarely be light saturated. Second, for highly efficient C_3 crops, light saturation may be unimportant even during summer. (We have found consistent reports of short-term growth rates up to $30 \, \mathrm{g \, m^{-2} \, day^{-1}}$ for potatoes and sugar beet in England and calculations from a model (Monteith, 1981a) suggest that these rates could not be achieved unless there was little evidence of light saturation even in strong sunlight.) Third, for healthy C_4 crops growing in the tropics, photosynthesis should rarely be restricted by light saturation.

C_m and temperature

The relation between photosynthesis rate and temperature is moderated by other environmental factors, especially by light. The maximum response to changes of temperature is observed in bright light when the supply of carbon dioxide to the sites of photosynthesis is limited by diffusion and by enzyme reactions which are particularly temperature sensitive. Most crops are grown below the optimum temperature for photosynthesis as measured in the laboratory. The optimum can be exceeded during periods of drought but there appears to have been little work, at least for temperate species, on the interaction of heat and water stress on gas exchange.

The effect of temperature on leaf photosynthesis has been clearly demonstrated for tropical (C_4) grasses and tropical (C_3) legumes (Ludlow and Wilson, 1971) but the evidence for temperate species is less consistent. Specifically, the literature shows positive temperature responses for perennial rye grass (Sheehy et al., 1980) and for barley (Littleton, 1971). Approximate figures are $+6\%$ $°C^{-1}$ at around 10°C and $+3\%$ $°C^{-1}$ at around 15°C. The photosynthesis of wheat leaves appears to be much less sensitive to temperature (de Vos, 1977).

To place these values in context, the standard deviation of mean monthly temperature over the June to August period is of the order of ± 1 to 2°C. In Britain the temperature of plant tissue is almost always below the optimum for metabolic processes—approximately 25°C. Above 25°C, in a range which prevailed for long periods in 1976, both photosynthesis rate and duration of development respond adversely to increasing temperature. The relative significance of these two components is discussed later.

The temperature history of leaves can affect photosynthesis in so far as leaves developing in high temperatures are usually thinner and capable of less photosynthesis per unit leaf area (Woledge and Jewiss, 1969). Outdoors and in a canopy, this response is unlikely to have a major influence on growth because light transmitted through thinner leaves will be intercepted by other foliage. Senescence is accelerated at higher temperatures and this too is considered later.

In short-term laboratory experiments, the respiration of an individual organ, or of a whole plant, increases with temperature but the fraction of a given quantity of assimilate which is subsequently respired appears to be much less sensitive to temperature (Ryle et al., 1976). Presumably, respiration over periods of several weeks must be limited by the assimilate supply (Breeze and Elston, 1978). Measurements on wheat by Winzeler et al., (1976) showed little dependence of the respiration:photosynthesis ratio on temperature until the final senescent stage of growth.

To summarise, in most systems of agriculture, leaf photosynthesis is not sensitive to differences in temperature from one year to another during the growth period and neither is respiration because it is coupled to photosynthesis. Moreover, differences in temperature for a specific month are confined to a few degrees Centigrade at most sites. Only in extreme climates will yields be significantly affected by the influence of anomalously high or low temperatures on the photosynthesis rate. In Iceland, the yield of hay is known to be highly correlated with temperature over the range 0 to 10°C. In the semi-arid tropics, the photosynthesis of seedlings growing through a dry soil may be inhibited by a high surface temperature if not by a shortage of water. We have not been able to find measurements which either support or contradict this suggestion but the phenomenon may be one of the main factors responsible for poor crop establishment in dry areas. The maximum fraction of incident light intercepted by such crops falls far short of the figure of 90 to 95% common in temperate agriculture.

C_m and water stress

Cell division and cell expansion are the first processes affected during a period of drought, but with increasing stress, photosynthesis is restricted partly as a result of stomatal closure and partly because of increased mesophyll resistance. For some species, there is evidence that stomatal closure is a response to an increase of mesophyll resistance operating in such a way that the intercellular concentration of CO_2 is stabilised (Takeda et al., 1978). If the internal concentration were effectively independent of the stomatal resistance, at least during daylight, then the rate of assimilation by a leaf would be approximately proportional to its transpiration rate divided by the mean saturation deficit of the surrounding air (Monteith, 1981b). This deduction is consistent with the evidence for crop dry matter production reviewed by Bierhuizen and Slatyer (1965).

The reduction in crop growth rate associated with water stress is a consequence of the decrease in free energy of cellular water, a quantity often monitored in physiological experiments. But for practical purposes, and particularly for assessing the irrigation requirements of a crop, shortage of water is usually expressed as a soil-water deficit—the amount of water needed to restore the soil to field capacity expressed in the same units as rainfall. Experiments with perennial rye grass at Hurley showed that leaf expansion is progressively affected by deficits greater than 12·5 mm and that growth rate is reduced by 10% when the deficit reaches 25 mm (Stiles and Williams, 1965). For sugar beet, Draycott and Messem (private communication) found that growth was checked in June when the deficit increased beyond 35 mm.

To avoid the difficulty of describing in detail the progressive and manifold effects of drought on growth, Penman (1971) analysed the results of irrigation experiments at Woburn and at Rothamsted in terms of a 'limiting deficit' (D_l)—the amount of soil-water lost from the profile up to the point where growth effectively stops (see Fig. 4, p. 141). French and Legg (1979) concluded that the values of D_l for a range of crops were about 2·5 times greater in clay at Rothamsted than in sand at Woburn, a ratio consistent with the relative water holding capacities ($-0·1$ to -15 bars) of the two profiles.

In principle, the limiting deficit must increase during the growing season as roots penetrate to greater depths and Draycott and Messem showed that the deficit for sugar beet was 35, 50, 75 and 125 mm in June, July, August and September, respectively. In temperate climates with a transpiration rate of 2 to 4 mm day^{-1}, the penetration of the root system by an arable crop, once it is established, will usually keep pace with the demand for water until the roots are impeded mechanically or stop growing at an appropriate point in the developmental time-table. In either case, it is appropriate to quote a single limiting deficit describing the response to water for a particular crop on a particular site. In regions where transpiration rate is 4 to 8 mm day^{-1}, the concept of a single limiting deficit will be less useful, particularly in light soil when the downward penetration of the root system cannot keep pace with the demand for water.

Climatologically, it is the difference between rainfall and evaporation which determines the rate of change of soil-water content and in all parts of the world where crops are grown, the variability of rainfall in time and space is much greater than the corresponding variability in evaporation. In most of Britain for example, crop evaporation during summer proceeds at a mean rate of 2·5 to 3 mm day^{-1} and annual potential evaporation lies between 450 and 500 mm with little year-to-year variation. In contrast, the amount of rain falling on a site during any month can change by an order of magnitude from one year to the next. In summer, spells of persistent rain or persistent drought are both common. The rainfall in any month may exceed the rate of potential evaporation (so that the soil is always wet) or may be confined to occasional light showers equivalent to the water lost by evaporation in a few days. From west to east, rainfall decreases much more rapidly than evaporation increases so that the probability of crop growth being checked by drought changes from close to zero in parts of the west, and particularly in the hills, to about 100% on parts of the east coast. Unlike light and temperature which are difficult to modify extensively, it is possible to increase water supply by irrigation where and when the exercise is likely to be profitable.

To summarise again, there are fundamental physiological reasons why the amount of dry matter produced by a crop should be strongly correlated with the amount of water lost by transpiration. In many climates, water loss is limited by the amount held in the root zone, supplemented by rainfall and by irrigation where it is available. Soil-water deficit is therefore a useful quantity to correlate with crop growth and in temperate climates it is possible to define a limiting deficit, characteristic of crop and soil, at which growth effectively ceases. A shortage of water can therefore be translated into a loss of time for growth rather than a reduction in growth rate and this point will be taken up in the next section.

PHENOLOGICAL RELATIONS

Duration of growth (t_g)

When the development of a crop from germination to maturity is limited physiologically rather than by bad weather, the length of the growth period is simply the sum of time spent in each developmental phase. Much evidence from the laboratory and from the field demonstrates that the reciprocal of time in each phase (a measure of development rate) is a linear function of temperature below an optimum T_o. For germination or for seedling growth when the growing point is below the soil surface, soil temperature at the appropriate depth appears to determine the development rate. With a vegetative or reproductive apex above the soil surface, development rate depends on the temperature of the apical tissue which is usually close to the air temperature (Peacock, 1975).

By extrapolating the linear relation between a measured rate of development r and a corresponding temperature T, it is possible to determine a base temperature T_b at which development would stop (Fig. 3). When a rate of development is expressed as the reciprocal of the time for a complete developmental phase, i.e. $r = 1/t$, the change of temperature per unit change of rate or $(\partial R/\partial T)^{-1}$ is the 'thermal time' or 'accumulated temperature' required for the completion of the phase. In calculating this requirement, it is essential to use the appropriate base temperature. An arbitrary figure of 6°C (42°F), which has no special physiological significance, slipped into the literature over a century ago and has been widely used by climatologists unaware of its origins and defects (Monteith, 1981b). Angus et al. (1980) have recently shown that a wide range of crops grown in Australia have base

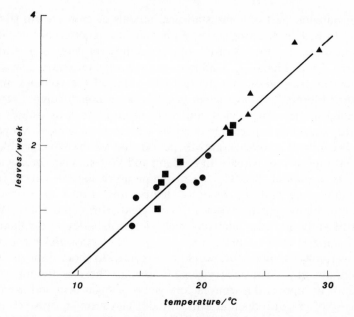

Fɪɢ. 3. Rate of leaf emergence for a maize hybrid grown at three altitudes in Kenya as a function of weekly mean temperature at each site. ●, Elgon (2250 m); ■, Kitale (1890 m); ▲, Chemelil (1268 m). The regression line gives a base temperature of $T_b = 9.5°C$ (after Cooper, 1979).

temperatures distributed in two main groups with modal values of 3 and 11°C but with no species between 5 and 7°C.

In general, temperate crops have base temperatures in the range from 0 to 10°C and tropical crops from 10 to 20°C. There appears to be a corresponding range in optimum temperatures, i.e. about 22 to 27°C for temperate species and 32 to 37°C for tropical species. Little systematic work has been done on the response of development to temperatures above the optimum which are rarely significant in temperate agriculture. In the tropics, it is likely that the temperature of germinating seeds and of the leaf meristem after germination will often be above the optimum or even above the limiting temperature at which organised metabolism stops.

Even for temperate crops, relatively few attempts have been made to relate the developmental timetable to weather in general or to temperature in particular but the classic studies of Nuttonsen (1955) are a notable exception and accumulated temperature or 'heat units' are an integral part of some statistical models of crop growth (Baier, 1973). In Britain, the long series of phenological records collected over 50 years ago by the Ministry of Agriculture provide a wealth of material from which an assiduous student might extract consistent temperature responses, but the fact that some of the volumes in the Ministry Library still have uncut pages is not a hopeful sign!

Taking a very simple view, the yield of crops such as cereals and potatoes would be expected to decrease with increasing mean temperature because of a shorter growth period and we have been able to demonstrate this for cereals. In England and Wales, mean cereal yields decrease by about 5% $°C^{-1}$ mean temperature for the period from May until July and the recorded temperature range of $±1·5°C$ is therefore equivalent to about ±8% in yield. Kirby and Ellis (1980) have recently ascribed relatively high yields of barley in Scotland to lower summer temperatures, at least in part. For grass and sugar beet, however, lower temperature would be expected to shorten the growing season, thereby decreasing yields. In Britain there is (unpublished) evidence to support this from factory yields of sugar beet and from the decrease of grass production with altitude. The strong positive correlation between hay yields in Iceland and summer temperature has already been referred to.

Lost time (t_1)

During canopy closure

In Britain, perceptible growth of overwintering crops usually begins late in March and progresses from a canopy intercepting 50% of incident light or less, to 90% in 3 to 6 weeks depending mainly on temperature. Spring-sown cereals form a complete canopy about 1 month later than winter crops; potatoes reach this stage sometime in June depending on seed tuber management, but sugar beet usually not until early July (Watson, 1971). With spring-sown crops, any restriction on rate of emergence imposed by shortage of water is usually trivial compared with the control exerted by temperature. However, seedlings can be killed either by too dry or too wet conditions when these occur at particularly sensitive stages (Longden, 1972).

For most crops and irrespective of climate, a leaf area index (LAI) of 4 to 6 is sufficient to intercept more than 90% of photosynthetically active radiation and to ensure that a maximum growth rate is achieved. For sugar beet the rate of leaf production and expansion increases linearly with temperature over the range of 5 to 20°C (Milford and Riley, 1980). Temperature affects final leaf size of sugar beet and potatoes, individual leaves becoming larger and thinner as temperature increases. After exceptionally cold periods, leaf size of potatoes can be so restricted that the canopy of very early plantings never closes. An important step is to check whether measurements made in controlled conditions can predict behaviour in the field. One such exercise for sugar beet (Scott and Jaggard, 1978) accurately described the expansion of leaf area in a season when temperatures were near average and predicted that if weekly temperatures were consistently 1°C below average from April until July, without a corresponding difference of incident radiation, then the *interception* of radiation would be 10% less over the growing season. This difference can be set against the fact that April and May temperatures in England range from 2°C below to 2°C above the long-term mean.

For cereals, provided the soil-water deficit is less than 50 mm in a clay soil and transpiration is less than about $0·5$ mm h^{-1} (i.e. during winter and much of spring in Britain) the rate of expansion of the leaf surface is governed largely by temperature. Later in the season, however, usually during the afternoon on days with long periods of bright sunshine, the normal relationship between temperature and leaf extension rate breaks down as water stress increases (Biscoe and Gallagher, 1977). It is not certain whether periods of water stress limit the final size of individual leaves.

The grass crop is a special case for it is harvested sequentially and productivity is determined by the speed of regrowth after grazing or cutting. This is partly determined by weather, but internal factors, partly related to previous management, modify the weather response. If growth during the preceding phase has been rapid and defoliation severe, there is a pronounced lag phase, with the depletion of reserves in the stubble leading to a prolonged negative carbon balance and it may be 5 weeks before a full canopy is regained (Leafe *et al.*, 1974). The photosynthesis of the individual leaves in the re-established sward is less light-responsive than during the first spring growth phase, apparently because the exposure to dim light during the early growth phase permanently impairs performance.

By senescence

In flowering crops, leaf production is usually complete by anthesis and thereafter photosynthesis depends on the persistence of existing leaves. The major arable crops display a range of determinism: barley and winter wheat produce only about 9 to 13 leaves on the main stem if sown at normal dates; potatoes produce few branches and leaves if grown from physiologically old seed but many more when the seed is physiologically young; sugar beet continues to produce leaves until the end of the season. Although the extent of photosynthesis from the cessation of leaf production onwards can be critically important in determining yield, there is little direct evidence about the effects of weather conditions during this period. Comparisons made in the East Midlands between crops growing in the cool, damp July–September period of 1972 with those grown in 1970 and 1971, when weather was warmer and brighter, clearly show the extent to which the cooler conditions delayed senescence (Gallagher and Biscoe, 1978; Scott and Wilcockson, 1978). The leaf area duration of barley after anthesis was halved in 1970 compared with 1972 and senescence of the potato haulm occurred at the same rate but was about 4 weeks earlier in 1971 than in 1972.

There is some evidence from experiments in controlled environments that when plants are maintained with a minimum of water stress, increasing temperature has a marked effect on senescence (Ford *et al.*, 1976). In the field, senescence is almost invariably hastened by the combination of high temperature and water stress and there is a need for studies to separate the two factors.

By water stress

The analysis of irrigation work at Woburn and Rothamsted already referred to can be presented as a method for assessing the amount of growth time lost as a result of water stress, although it was not originally derived in these terms (Monteith, 1981*b*). The analysis includes the concept of a maximum soil-water deficit (D_m) which would be achieved if transpiration continued at a potential rate throughout the growing season. In the model developed by Penman (1971), growth stops when the deficit exceeds its limiting value for growth (D_l) (determined experimentally) and does not start again until the deficit reaches D_m, thereafter decreasing because rainfall exceeds evaporation (Fig. 4). The time lost is the amount of water notionally transpired when the deficit increases from D_1 to D_m (or $D_m - D_l$) divided by the corresponding mean rate of potential evaporation. The success of this analysis depends on the very close relation between growth rate and transpiration rate already discussed.

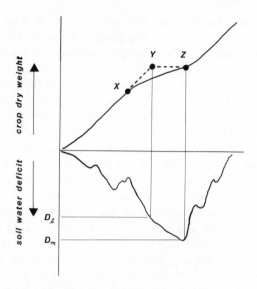

FIG. 4. Increase of crop dry weight with time (above x axis) and corresponding change of soil-water deficit (below x axis), estimated from the *potential* rate of evaporation. Growth is slowed at X as a result of soil-water stress but continues at its maximum rate after Z when rainfall exceeds evaporation so that the soil-water deficit decreases. In effect, the crop continues to grow at a maximum rate to the point Y as shown by the dashed extrapolation of the growth curve and growth is zero from Y to Z. In the sense of Fig. 1, YZ is the time lost by drought.

The positions of Y and Z determine the values of the limiting and maximum deficits D_1 and D_m and from the geometry of the figure, YZ is given by $(D_m - D_1)$ divided by the mean potential evaporation during the period when the deficit increases from D_1 to D_m.

HARVEST INDEX

In the analysis to this point, we were concerned mainly with the total amount of dry matter produced by a crop before it is harvested rather than the economic yield. We complete the story by considering the relation between yield and dry matter and the extent to which this is sensitive to differences of weather from season to season.

It is often convenient to express the economic yield of a crop simply as a fraction of total dry matter—the harvest index (H)—but there are several reasons why consistent measurements of this quantity are difficult to obtain. Most, if not all, crops lose foliage before harvest and failure to account for this can introduce errors both in the harvest index and in the estimation of the length of time over which C_m is likely to be maintained. Where comparisons are made between crops which mature at different rates, different amounts of dry matter can be lost in leaf fall. By combining records of potato growth from Rothamsted and Sutton Bonington, Allen and Scott (1980) estimated that some 5% by weight of foliage material fell from the plant before the end of linear bulking. Thereafter, the amount increased considerably until haulm death and differences in rates of maturation complicated comparisons of growth within and between seasons. For sugar beet, grown with standard cultivation in 1980, estimates of weight loss due to leaf fall before a November harvest range from 12 to 20%.

Compared with some other aspects of plant and crop growth, systematic information about the effects of weather on H is difficult to obtain. To illustrate the extent of our understanding of the subject, we shall compare three crops—sugar beet, barley and oil seed rape. In its first vegetative year of growth, the sugar beet crop does not pass through the distinct developmental phases experienced by barley and oil seed rape and there is an allometric relationship between growth of tops and storage root.

Records from 27 crops included comparisons between two sites, three seasons, different durations of the growing period, with and without irrigation, and given nil or optimal dressings of nitrogen. Total dry matter yields, ranging from 10 to 20 tonnes ha^{-1}, were well fitted by a line representing $H = 0.50$ (in this case the ratio of sugar to total dry weight). Small differences between treatments could be ascribed to lack of nitrogen or water stress late in the season tending to increase H. Draycott and Webb (1971) showed that, with extreme agronomic treatments, the range of H was 0.47–0.57. Thus, compared with the changes in total dry weight for which weather is responsible, changes in H are of minor importance in determining sugar yield.

For barley, the three components of grain yield (ear number, grain number per ear and individual grain weight) are determined during specific phases of the developmental timetable. The conditions favouring a large yield component are those which maximise the amount of assimilate available per unit of thermal time and per relevant organic unit, i.e. per plant during the time stem number is being determined, per ear when the number of grains per ear is fixed, and per grain during the grain filling period (see Hawkins and Cooper (1981) for a recent example from maize). Does it follow that if conditions were cool and bright so that development was delayed but growth was prolific when the number of grains per ear was determined, then a large harvest index would follow? Conversely, if conditions for assimilation during grain growth were unfavourable, would harvest index be depressed? For some crops, the answer must be 'no'. It is clear from the literature (Biscoe and Gallagher, 1977) that variation in H of the barley variety Proctor is slight and there is little tendency for it to change systematically with yield. Thus changes in H are trivial in determining grain yield compared with changes in total dry matter production, which reflects the time over which C_m is maintained.

Day *et al.* (1978) imposed drought by protecting Julia barley from rain for different developmental periods, including the whole of the life cycle. Despite a two-fold range of total dry matter production between treatments, H was remarkably conservative in the range from 0·41 to 0·46.

It is clear from measurements on wheat that when the weather is very hot and dry during grain growth, H can be affected to some extent. In 1976, for example, H for Maris Huntsman grown in England fell from the usual value of 0·45 to 0·37, but this is a small response considering how extreme the weather was (Gallagher *et al.*, 1976).

Why is H not more variable? Because of the lack of variation in C_m, there is a limit to how much a positive response associated with favourable weather in one developmental period can be sustained in the succeeding one. If many potential grain sites are created in favourable conditions, the plant then aborts many so that it can support those whose growth is maintained beyond the most juvenile stage. In general, final grain number in many cereals appears to be related to the weight of the plant at anthesis, which is a measure of the plant's ability to fill the grains. A further feature of the growth of barley, and some other cereals, tends to stabilise H. At least some varieties seem able to buffer themselves against adverse conditions during grain growth by translocating material previously stored in the stem. For all these reasons, the effects of weather on grain yield in cereals are usually determined by changes in total dry matter production and therefore by the length of the growth period rather than by changes in H.

For oil seed rape, Table 1 indicates that in successive and admittedly extreme seasons, H (here the ratio between dry seed yield and total dry weight) changed two-fold. The rape plant is structurally more

TABLE 1

HARVEST INDEX OF OIL SEED RAPE CROPS GROWN AT THE
UNIVERSITY OF NOTTINGHAM SCHOOL OF AGRICULTURE IN
CONTRASTING SEASONS AND WITH THREE SOWING DATES

Sowing	August	September	October
1975–76	0·15	0·24	0·28
1976–77	0·24	0·25	0·35

plastic than barley. Thus, response to favourable weather conditions in terms of potential pod and seed number can be very marked. This must place an extreme strain on the ability to fill the seeds which are present, and we have found no evidence that the plant has the ability to compensate by translocation for unfavourable conditions during seed growth. In 1976, the early sown crop grew prolifically until flowering to produce many pods, but because of constraints imposed first by C_m and then by drought, many seeds aborted. Those retained had their growth severely curtailed by drought and high temperatures so that the weight of individual seeds and the value of H were the smallest in the 7 year series of experiments. In 1977 there was a prolonged, predominantly cool period during the time seed retention and seed filling were in progress and the particularly large H of the late sown crop resulted from the combination of moderate growth up until anthesis followed by favourable conditions for seed retention and growth (Mendham *et al.*, 1981). Thus, it seems that for crops with growth characteristics which resemble oil seed rape, weather effects on harvest index may be more pronounced than for potatoes, sugar beet or cereals.

CONCLUSION

To simplify the presentation of a complex topic, we have taken refuge in many generalisations and approximations. In particular, we ignored the interaction of weather elements although we recognise that they are central to the impact of weather on yield. However, we believe that the simple scheme we have proposed can be developed to take account of at least some of these interactions and a recent paper by Smith and Harris (1981) contains a good example. The work is essentially a stochastic analysis of rainfall and temperature in a Mediterranean climate and represents a very satisfying compromise between the two contrasting methods of attacking the crop–weather problem discussed in our introduction.

Using weather records for Aleppo in northern Syria, Smith and Harris calculated the maximum length of the growing season for a series of 14 years from the distribution of rainfall. For each of these seasons, they evaluated the corresponding thermal time for comparison with the duration of thermal time needed for a particular variety of wheat to reach maturity. Dry matter production and yield were then estimated from the radiation regime (determining photosynthesis rate) and from the length of the growth period as determined by rainfall in the driest years and otherwise by temperature. This information is contained in Fig. 5 which shows the predicted frequency distribution of yield for three varieties, one maturing early, one late and one combining the best features of both.

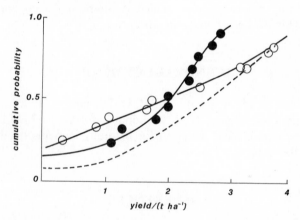

FIG. 5. Probability distributions for the yield of wheat at Aleppo, Syria, predicted from records of rainfall and temperature (1961–74). In wetter years, a late maturing wheat (○) would give higher yields than an early maturing variety (●) but the early variety would yield more in dry years. The dashed line illustrates the response of an ideotype or ideal variety producing some seed in a short season but with the capacity to produce more grain in a wet season (after Smith and Harris, 1981).

Finally, we believe it may be helpful to summarise the scheme discussed in this paper with the help of Table 2. For completeness, we have included photoperiod, not strictly an element of the weather, but a component of the environment which interacts strongly with temperature in determining the rate of developmental processes. In a very

TABLE 2

RELATIVE IMPORTANCE OF ENVIRONMENTAL FACTORS IN RELATION TO RATE
AND DURATION OF CROP GROWTH AND HARVEST INDEX

	Light	Photoperiod	Temperature	Rainfall
C_m (maximum growth rate)	**		*	***₌
t_g (length of growing season)		*	*** (temperate)	*** (tropical)
t_1 (lost time)	*		***	***
H (harvest index)	*	*	*	**

arbitrary system of rating, three stars indicate a response which is usually strong, two a response which is often significant and one a response which is occasionally significant.

ACKNOWLEDGEMENTS

We thank E. J. Allen, P. V. Biscoe, M. D. Dennett, A. P. Draycott, K. W. Jaggard, E. L. Leafe, N. J. Mendham and G. F. J. Milford for contributing unpublished data and for helpful comments on the ideas on which this review is based.

REFERENCES

Allen, E. J. and Scott, R. K. (1980). An analysis of growth of the potato crop. *J. Agric. Sci. Camb.* **94**, 583–606.

Angus, J. F., Cunningham, R. B., Moncur, M. W., and MacKenzie, D. H. (1980). Phasic development in field crops. I. Thermal response in the seedling phase. *Field Crops Res.* **3**(4), 365–78.

Baier, W. (1973). Crop–weather analysis model. *J. Appl. Meteorol.* **12**, 937–47.

Bierhuizen, J. F. and Slatyer, R. O. (1965). Effect of atmospheric concentration of water vapour and CO_2 in determining the transpiration–photosynthesis relationship of cotton leaves. *Agric. Meteorol.* **2**, 259–70.

Biscoe, P. V. and Gallagher, J. N. (1977). Weather, dry matter production and yield. In: *Environmental Effects on Crop Physiology* (Eds J. J. Landsberg and C. V. Cutting). Academic Press, London.

Breeze, V. and Elston, J. (1978). Some effects of temperature and substrate content upon respiration and the carbon balance of field beans. *Ann. Bot.* **42**, 863–76.

Charles-Edwards, D. (1978). An analysis of the photosynthesis and productivity of vegetative crops in the United Kingdom. *Ann. Bot.* **42**, 713–31.

Cooper, J. P. (1975). Control of photosynthesis production in terrestrial systems. In: *Photosynthesis and Productivity in Different Environments* (Ed. J. P. Cooper). Cambridge University Press, London.

Cooper, P. J. M. (1979). The association between altitude, environmental variables, maize growth and yields in Kenya. *J. Agric. Sci. Camb.* **93**, 635–49.

Day, W., Legg, B. J., French, B. K., Johnston, A. E., Lawlor, D. W. and Jeffers, W. de C. (1978). A drought experiment using mobile shelters. *J. Agric. Sci. Camb.* **91**, 599–623.

Dennett, M. D. (1980). Variability of annual wheat yields in England and Wales. *Agric. Meteorol.* **22**, 109–11.

Draycott, A. P. and Webb, D. J. (1971). Effects of nitrogen fertiliser, plant population and irrigation on sugar beet. Part 1, Yields. *J. Agric. Sci.* **76**, 261–7.

Ford, M. A., Pearman, I. and Thorne, G. N. (1976). Effects of variation in ear temperature on growth and yield of spring wheat. *Ann. Appl. Biol.* **82**, 317–33.

French, B. K. and Legg, B. J. (1979). Rothamsted irrigation 1964–76. *J. Agric. Sci. Camb.* **92**, 15–37.

Gallagher, J. N. and Biscoe, P. V. (1978). Radiation absorption, growth and yield of cereals. *J. Agric. Sci. Camb.* **91**, 47–60.

Gallagher, J. N., Biscoe, P. V., and Hunter, B. (1976). Effects of drought on grain growth. *Nature*, **264**, 541–2.

Goudriaan, J. and van Laar, H. H. (1978). Calculation of daily totals of the gross assimilation of leaf canopies. *Neth. J. Agric. Sci.* **26**, 373–82.

Greenwood, D. J., Cleaver, T. J., Loquens, S. M. H. and Niendorf, K. B. (1977). Relationship between plant weight and growing period for vegetable crops in the U.K. *Ann. Bot.* **41**, 987–97.

Hawkins, R. C. and Cooper, P. J. M. (1981). Growth, development and grain yield of maize. *Expl. Agric.* **17**, 203–7.

Kirby, E. J. M. and Ellis, R. P. (1980). A comparison of spring barley grown in England and Scotland. 2. Yield and its components. *J. Agric. Sci. Camb.* **95**, 111–16.

Lawes, J. B. (1880). Our climate and our wheat crops. *J. Roy. Agric. Soc. England. Ser. 2.* **16**, 173–210.

Leafe, E. L., Stiles, W. and Dickinson, S. E. (1974). Physiological processes influencing the pattern of productivity of the intensively managed grass sward. *Proc. 12th International Grassland Congress*, pp. 442–57.

Littleton, J. (1971). The gas exchange of barley leaves and ears. Ph.D. Thesis, University of Nottingham.

Longden, P. C. (1972). Effect of some soil conditions on sugar beet seedling emergence. *J. Agric. Sci. Camb.* **79**, 543–5.

Ludlow, M. M. and Wilson, G. L. (1971). Photosynthesis of tropical pasture plants. *Aust. J. Biol. Sci.* **24**, 449–70.

Mendham, N. J., Shipway, P. A. and Scott, R. K. (1981). The effects of delayed sowing and weather on growth, development and yield of winter oil-seed rape. *J. Agric. Sci. Camb.* **96**, 389–416.

Milford, G. F. J. and Riley, J. (1980). The effects of temperature on leaf growth of sugar beet varieties. *Ann. Appl. Biol.* **94**, 431–43.

Monteith, J. L. (1978). Reassessment of maximum growth rates for C_3 and C_4 crops. *Expl. Agric.* **14**, 1–5.

Monteith, J. L. (1981a). Does light limit crop production? In: *Physiological Processes Limiting Plant Productivity* (Ed. C. B. Johnson). Butterworths, London.

Monteith, J. L. (1981b). Climatic variation and the growth of crops. *Quart. J. R. Met. Soc.* **107** (in press).

Nuttonsen, M. Y. (1955). *Wheat–Climate Relationships and the use of Phenology in Ascertaining the Thermal and Photo-thermal Requirements of Wheat.* American Institute of Crop Ecology, Washington, DC.

Peacock, J. (1975). Temperature and leaf growth in *Lolium perenne*. II. The site of temperature perception. *J. Appl. Ecol.* **12**, 115–24.

Penman, H. L. (1962). Weather and crops. *Quart. J. R. Met. Soc.* **88**, 209–19.

Penman, H. L. (1971). *Irrigation at Woburn, VII.* Report of Rothamsted Experimental Station for 1970. Part 2.

Ryle, C. J. A., Cobby, J. M. and Powell, C. E. (1976). Synthetic and maintenance respiration losses of $^{14}CO_2$ in uniculm barley and maize. *Ann. Bot.* **40**, 571–86.

Scott, R. K., and Jaggard, K. W. (1978). Theoretical criteria for maximum yield. *Proc. of the 41st Winter Congress of the International Institute of Sugar Beet Research* (IIRB), pp. 179–198.

Scott, R. K. and Wilcockson, S. J. (1978). Application of physiological and agronomic principles to the development of the potato industry. In: *The Potato Crop: the Scientific Basis for Improvement* (Ed. P. M. Harris). Chapman and Hall, London.

Sheehy, J. E., Cobby, J. M. and Ryle, G. J. A. (1980). The use of a model to investigate the influence of some environmental factors on the growth of perennial rye grass. *Ann. Bot.* **46**, 343–65.

Sibma, L. (1968). Growth of closed green crop surfaces in The Netherlands. *Neth. J. Agric. Sci.* **16**, 211–16.

Smith, R. C. G. and Harris, H. C. (1981). Environmental resources and restraints to agricultural production in a Mediterranean-type environment. In: *Soil-water and Nitrogen in Mediterranean-type Environments* (Eds J. L. Monteith and C. Webb). Nijhoff and Junk, The Hague.

Stiles, W. and Williams, T. E. (1965). The response of rye grass/white clover sward to various irrigation regimes. *J. Agric. Sci. Camb.* **65**, 351–64.

Takeda, S., Sugimoto, H., and Agata, W. (1978). Water and crop production. I. The relationship between photosynthesis and transpiration in corn leaf. *Japan Jour. Crop Sci.* **47**, 82–9.

de Vos, N. M. (1977). *Crop Photosynthesis.* Agricultural Research Report. Publication 25, CABO, Wageningen.

Watson, D. J. (1963). Climate, weather and plant yield. In: *Environmental Control of Plant Growth* (Ed. L. T. Evans). Academic Press, New York.

Watson, D. J. (1971). Size, structure and activity of the productive system of crops. In: *Potential Crop Production* (Eds P. F. Wareing and J. P. Cooper). Heinemann, London.

Winzeler, H., Hunt, L. A. and Mahon, J. D. (1976). Ontogenetic changes in respiration and photosynthesis of uniculm barley. *Crop Sci.* **16,** 786–90.

Woledge, J. and Jewiss, O. R. (1969). The effect of temperature during growth on the subsequent rate of photosynthesis in leaves of Tall Fescue. *Ann. Bot.* **33,** 879–913.

Yates, F. (1969). *Investigation into the Effects of Weather on Yields.* Report of Rothamsted Experimental Station for 1968. Part 2, pp. 46–49.

Discussion

Professor Hawthorn congratulated the speakers on developing a very interesting scheme and asked whether it was possible to use this to look at those aspects discussed in a previous session by Professor Morton relating attributes of weather to the quality of food. Certainly, there was every indication that fast growth gave rise to poor flavour in a number of crops. *Professor Monteith* remarked that in preparing information for an ARC review he and his co-author had found little relevant information on weather and quality. Certainly, temperature and water relationships needed systematic examination in relation to aspects of quality. *Dr Thompson* wondered whether the reduction of the effective growth period caused by water stress could be calculated solely from the raised crop temperature caused by reduced transpiration, to which *Professor Monteith* replied that he thought that the simplification they had undertaken in the scheme had probably gone far enough. He went on to discuss certain aspects of the effect of water stress and temperature inter-relationships pointing out that slight stress was associated with a small increase in developmental rate whereas severe stress slowed developmental rate. *Dr Landsberg* quoted older work on the effect of temperature on the types of carbohydrates in crops. Cool seasons led to increases in sucrose content. The high quality of English apples was probably accounted for by the relatively cool climate. *Sir Kenneth Blaxter* asked how far capacitances should be built into the scheme and asked whether Professor Monteith thought that the simplification might constrain thinking at some later time. *Professor Monteith* replied that he regarded the scheme as a scheme and not a precise model and admittedly there were a number of capacitances to be considered, one of which was the storage component implicit in the harvest index for cereals. *Professor Webster* asked about the variation of maximal yield and how far it was really correct to state that the second variable of importance in determining this was temperature. Was not a contributing one total day length, if not accumulated radiation? *Professor Monteith* replied that at Sutton Bonington there had been no obvious correlation of yield with radiation, indeed over the growth period for arable crops there is not much variation in radiation input in the UK from year to year or from north to south. Temperature does not influence C_m much but appears to be the most important weather element after light. *Professor Bunting* asked about the extent to which the harvest index term might be affected by environment and time. He pointed out that many crops produce economic yield as a result of virtually exclusively vegetative growth, so that they always have a 100% harvest index. At the other extreme, cereals and other crops whose economic product arises from a terminal, usually reproductive phase, have to enter and complete that phase or else they can have no harvest index at all. In between are the historically indeterminate crops, like most grain legumes, in which vegetative and reproductive growth are contemporaneous and increasingly competitive, so that harvest index increases with time. *Dr Scott* replying stated that the scheme focused attention on the need for precise measurements of harvest index. There were a number of complex inter-relationships not yet fully understood which were concerned with its determination. Obviously, Professor Bunting was correct in these respects. He gave examples from sugar beet which showed that when experiments were conducted in which comparisons could be made relating to time of sowing or temperature, it appeared that despite large differences in the environmental conditions during the growing season the root–shoot ratio seemed virtually preset. Furthermore, the percentage of sucrose in the dry matter appears to be different from the earliest time at which measurements were made. Of the crops in Dr Scott's experience, oil seed rape would be most similar to some of the grain legumes. With oil seed rape, the figures which had been given in the published paper relating to the summers of 1976 and 1977 showed how the sequence of weather experienced during the developmental phases when individual components of yield were fixed, determined the harvest index, notably the production of a framework of the plant on which to 'hang' the seed, the process of seed setting and retention, and the final process of seed filling. Conditions in the two years gave very different relationships in two at least of these factors. *Mr Wilkinson* of ADAS stated that he was delighted to see that the proposed scheme of Professor Monteith did in fact incorporate two factors used to assess the climatic limitations involved in land capability classification, notably thermal time and moisture deficit. He described certain aspects of this land classification scheme which gave considerable weight to the crop yields and the flexibility of cropping of the land as it relates to climate, soil and topography. *Dr Lake* posed the question of how plant breeders should react. Should they breed crops to match the climate understanding that climate was an average of a variety of weathers, or should they think in terms of breeding robustness or resistance to the variable weather? Again, what lessons were to be learned from the scheme about the ways in which new crops were to be introduced and plant breeding programmes instituted to make them more suited to new conditions. *Dr Scott* replied that one could visualise that yields in cereals could be increased by breeding programmes which in effect increased the time dimension, that is late maturing characteristics could be introduced. There were, however, a whole number of additional problems which should perhaps be considered. There is a reluctance on the part of farmers to adopt varieties which would make it difficult for them to deal with the short period for farm operation between harvest and a subsequent sowing. He thought that the scheme would be useful in terms of breaking down conceptually the mode of possible attack. It would enable a focus to be made on those aspects of growth and development which appeared central to selection programmes. *Professor Buringh* emphasised that the harvest index was in fact a variable which was dependent upon many other interacting things. It was under consideration in his own laboratories using a mathematical model to introduce various factors related to the harvest index of a specific crop growing at a specific site. It was important to know at which stage of crop development a drought period occurred, as this also could influence a harvest index.

Climate, Pests and Disease

L. P. SMITH

2 Greenway, Berkhamsted, Herts, UK

If it is assumed that the statements listed below are basically true, then it is clear that searches for weather/pathogen relationships should form an important part of any programme designed to increase food production.

1. Considerable losses due to pests and diseases are incurred throughout the processes of food production
2. Control measures are becoming increasingly available to minimise such losses if applied at the correct time
3. The incidence and intensity of pest and disease attacks are influenced by weather conditions, past, present and future

If the weather is ignored, a campaign against these losses can be based on a system which demands the application of protective measures on a certain pre-arranged date and at intervals thereafter, reinforced by curative measures as and when necessary. An improvement to this is to take action on dates determined phenologically, by reference to crop stages and animal age, rather than by the Gregorian calendar. In areas where attacks occur every year with some degree of regularity, this system has obvious advantages, if only to the manufacturers of the treatment materials and equipment.

There are, however, areas in which the time of onset and the intensity of pest and disease attacks vary considerably from year to year, and where some form of advisory forecasting can be of the greatest assistance. There may be years when protective measures are a waste of money. If they are to be used, correct timing is essential because for control to be effective it must be established at an early stage; late applications can be futile. Any forecast system must be able to identify the years of major and minor incidence and intensity, or in other words, the extremes. In this respect it differs from a meteorological forecast which concentrates on the occurrence of a phenomenon and is least reliable in regard to intensity and duration.

To understand the complexity of the influence of weather, it is helpful to examine the life cycle of a pathogen, stage by stage:

1. Survival during the 'off-period', possibly involving an intermediate host, which ensures the existence of initial foci for subsequent resurgence
2. Attainment of maturity at the end of the off-period
3. Emergence, release or eviction, and the method of mobility
4. Transfer over varying distances from very short to very long airborne trajectories
5. Survival during transfer
6. Deposition or attachment to new host
7. Infection and subsequent incubation
8. A further cycle leading to secondary infection and later to epidemic spread

From the point of view of the selfish gene of the pathogen, the weather must be favourable at each and every stage of the sequence. A break in the chain will halt progress, or at very least slow it down. A succession of cycles, all under favourable weather conditions and without check, will soon lead to an epidemic.

The specific nature of these favourable conditions is a function of the pathogen, but whatever the required conditions may be, many of them may occur frequently or reliably enough to provide no appreciable obstruction to pest or disease progress. At one or more points in the chain, however, the weather requirements may be very specific indeed, and it is at such a stage that the whole sequence becomes very weather sensitive, and if these stages can be identified, a single critical weather factor can be deduced.

If this can be done, and if the occurrence of this significant weather can be derived from standard meteorological observations which are readily available, then a pest/disease forecast system can be envisaged. For example, air temperature and humidity reports can be used to identify possible infection periods for potato blight; soil temperatures in March will indicate the timing in April or May of the emergence of nematodes which cause nemato-diriasis; knowledge of measured rainfall and calculated transpiration can lead to an estimate of wet grass conditions suitable for the intermediate snail host of the liver-fluke parasite.

The time lag between the significant weather and the pest/disease incidence may be short or long. In the examples given above, the advance notice provided by the accurate interpretation of the previous weather would be of the order of 1–2 weeks for potato blight, 4–6 weeks for nemato-diriasis, and 4–6 months for liver-fluke. Even longer warnings are possible if contamination of stored forage crops such as hay or silage is involved. Mouldy hay, harvested in a wet June or July could be fed to a cow bulled at the end of the year, causing mycotic abortion of a calf due the next autumn. In some human diseases, the weather effect can be traced back a long way to previous events. The respiratory disease, farmer's lung, is the result of inhalation of spores from mouldy hay; Balkan nephritis, a killer disease of the Danube valleys, appears to depend on the occurrence of a mycotoxin in stored maize in peasant communities. It seems quite possible that other weather-induced mycotoxins await discovery, for if a fungus is involved, the weather conditions are likely to be critical at one or other stage from the start of germination to the end of storage.

Critical weather with an almost direct effect on links in the chain is not the only subject of interest. In some instances, especially in animal diseases, it is the indirect effect of weather which may be important. This may be termed 'exposure' or environmental stress.

As an example, pregnancy toxaemia or 'twin-lamb' disease of ewes seems to be closely linked to weather stress, chiefly cold rain and wind. This is a cumulative effect, but some results of cold stress exposure may be more immediate, especially when very young animals are involved. Lamb losses of up to 30% have been encountered on a farm near Reading (hardly an extreme example of an adverse climate) which were associated with environmental conditions in the days just after birth.

A cold stress, producing a temporary lowering of the body temperature, may also facilitate infection by pathogens. Examination of the sites of calf-houses with a bad record of losses due to pneumonia indicate that almost always they were in pronounced frost hollows, possibly because the planning authorities recommended that they should be kept out of sight to avoid spoiling the countryside.

Examination of records of human diseases tends to confirm that low temperatures on a winter morning are significant in regard to the incidence of the common cold and of influenza. A very close simulation of the morbidity of acute bronchitis over a seven-year period can be constructed by the use of humidity and minimum temperature records alone, the only reference to disease being the morbidity at the start of the series. Such external conditions should be interpreted as an additional stress, not a direct cause and effect, and this leads to the hypothesis that in many diseases, it is a combination of stresses, a coincidence in time and place, which should be sought as a potential explanation.

Moving further along this line of thought, and making use of evidence from several epidemics, it seems likely that a series of multiple stresses, separated in time by a period of time equal to the incubation or latent time of the disease, will lead to a rapid increase in incidence. In other words, if the adverse weather factor occurs repeatedly at times which are critical in the disease sequence, what was originally an isolated outbreak will grow quickly into an epidemic.

It should be stressed that in all the examples so far quoted, no forecasting of weather is involved, but only the correct interpretation of the effects of past weather. This is an immense advantage. No simple weather-based criterion can be the whole truth, a working accuracy of some 80% being usually sought. Weather forecasts are also subject to the possibility of error, and if they were to be used in conjunction with a weather-based disease forecast there would be a combination of errors, a process of multiplication, not addition, which can easily lead to an unacceptable level of inaccuracy.

The only real test of a pest or disease forecast is whether or not it offers a real help to the primary producer. It is not always necessary, although obviously preferable, to know exactly why it is successful. For example, forecasts of the incidence intensity of swayback, a copper deficiency disease of sheep, can be based on the number of days with snow cover. The reason behind this is debatable, but adequate results are obtained.

If simple weather criteria do not give satisfactory results, additional complexities have to be introduced, but, if only to avoid problems of data acquisition, simplicity is always to be preferred. In recent years, possibly encouraged by the increased availability and use of computers, a trend towards comprehensive models, attempting to quantify all stages of pest or disease development, has become more popular. In theory this is a long-awaited advance towards a higher standard of accuracy, but model-making must not become an end in itself. Most important of all, a computer must never become a substitute for thought, but an efficient, rapid, auxiliary designed to obviate time-consuming data handling. Making the most use of available facilities is only common sense, but overplaying one's hand is a sure road to catastrophe.

Returning to the problem of finding a critical weather factor, the first need is for reliable data. A supply of meteorological data is usually available on a regular and accurate basis. It may not be exactly in the form required, but it often can be manipulated into a suitable derived form. Comparable pest and disease data of an equivalent standard are often very difficult to find, but considerable use can be made of limited information in the early stages of an investigation. For example, accurate long-term records of liver-fluke in Anglesey, compiled by one veterinary surgeon in Ruthin, provided sufficient evidence to deduce a weather–disease incidence relationship, which was subsequently successfully applied to the whole of the British Isles and also to other European countries such as France and Norway. A relationship between day maximum temperatures and hyperthermia in pigs was established because one gatekeeper at a London abattoir kept accurate daily records of the pigs which were dead on arrival or which later died in the holding pens.

Once a tentative relationship is put forward, it must go through a trial period before it can become fully operational. If during this 'private' trial period it shows signs of promise, the much needed pest and disease data will become more readily available, sometimes leading to modifications or regional adjustments in the method of forecasting. Once confidence has been established, it is ready to 'go public', and a local, regional or national advisory system can be set up, coupled with an increased flow of educational material. In the early stages, the correct forecast of a severe outbreak can do wonders in increasing the confidence of the consumer.

Several plant and animal diseases are now forecast in Britain in such a manner. Meteorological data are passed, with varying degrees of sophistication, to the decision-making pathologists or veterinary authorities. The resulting forecasts are often included in the special farming weather forecasts, such as that given on Sundays on BBC television. The responsibility for these forecasts remains with the Ministry of Agriculture, not with the Meteorological Office.

Other countries have different systems, geared to their own communication facilities, their present state of knowledge regarding their own particular problems, and to the operational demand. There is little doubt that further extension of such types of scientifically based advice, always provided that it is reliable, can do much to reduce present production losses.

Methods which work in one region are specially designed to work reliably within the climate of that region; they cannot always be transferred without modification for application elsewhere. The principles remain, but the details are different. The particular expression of the critical weather factors change as the climate changes, but everywhere there are weather criteria awaiting identification and subsequent use. Many publications of the World Meteorological Organization, Geneva, contain numerous examples of the state of our present knowledge (see list of references).

Working relationships may have to be established on a regional basis, but the problem is international. Airborne pests and diseases pass through no passport control, and they ignore land frontiers or even oceans. A coffee rust disease may have travelled from Africa to South America by wind, rather than by boat or airplane. A rice disease (hoja blanca) may have moved from Cuba to Florida, and in the reverse direction, more than once by an airborne route. Wheat rusts can travel very long distances by air, and even locusts have been known to have been carried from North Africa to the British Isles. There are more pollutants in the air than noxious chemicals, and there is a limit to the efficiency of ground quarantine regulations, excellent though they may be. It has been rightly said 'Now is the time to look at the invisible'.

Despite the advances which should and could be made, the problem is likely to increase rather than diminish. Disease resistance is easier to talk about than to acquire on a permanent basis. Monoculture encourages the spread of an attack, and a pesticide which kills 99% of known germs will tend to encourage the prevalence of the small resistant minority. Pests and diseases have a disconcerting ability to alter in their characteristics so as to 'change the rules', and what is referred to as the shift and drift of viruses is a constant threat to any complacency.

Be that as it may, the challenge is one that cannot be ignored, and active collaboration between scientists, planners, advisors and farmers is essential if we are to overcome the threat to survival. Some of the worst historical incidences of disease, such as the Black Death and on a smaller scale, the Irish potato famine, have followed a period of over-population, under-nourishment, and a subsequent heavy mortality when a new pathogen against which there is no natural resistance invades the scene. An American professor, McNeill (1977) has pointed out that historians have often ignored the effects of disease on the downfall of civilizations. Few of the modern generation know that the Spanish Lady, the influenza epidemic of 1918–1919 killed more people than the 1914–18 World War. We have little defence to offer against a completely new bacteria or virus. Even the best of intentions may go astray when it is realised that one of the unforeseen results of new irrigation schemes in Africa has been an increased spread of diseases such as bilharzia.

Mistakes have been made in the past, both of omission and commission, but with the intelligent application of modern knowledge and techniques, it is not too much to at least hope that our future actions will produce a better track record. The prize is our very existence.

BIBLIOGRAPHY

McNeill, W. H. (1977). *Plagues and Peoples*. Blackwell, Oxford, 369 pp.

World Meteorological Technical Notes, in chronological order:
Bourke, P. M. A. (1955). The forecasting from weather data of potato blight and other plant diseases and pests. Tech. Note 10, WMO, Geneva, 48 pp.
De Villiers G. D. B. (Ed.) (1963). The effect of weather and climate upon the keeping quality of fruit. Tech. Note 53, WMO, Geneva, 180 pp.
Rainey, R.C. (1963). Meteorology and the migration of desert locusts. Tech. Note 54, WMO, Geneva, 115 pp.
Post, J. J. (Ed.) (1963). The influence of weather conditions on the occurrence of apple scab. Tech. Note 55, WMO, Geneva, 41 pp.
Hogg, W. H. (Ed.) (1969). Meteorological factors affecting the epidemiology of wheat rusts. Tech. Note 99, WMO, Geneva, 143 pp.
Smith, C. V. (1969). Meteorology and grain storage. Tech. Note 101, WMO, Geneva, 65 pp.
Smith, L. P. (1970). Weather and animal diseases. Tech. Note 113, WMO, Geneva, 49 pp.
Hurst, G. W. (1975). Meteorology and the Colorado potato beetle. Tech. Note 137, WMO, Geneva, 51 pp.
Gibson, T. E. (Ed.) (1978). Weather and parasitic animal disease. Tech. Note 159, WMO, Geneva, 174 pp.
Omar, M.H. (Ed.) (1980). Meteorological factors affecting the epidemiology of the cotton leaf worm and the pink bollworm. Tech. Note 167, WMO, Geneva, 46 pp.

Discussion

Professor Gregory pointed to the problems of dealing with both climate and weather. In hydrology one required operational forecasting to predict flooding and this was on a restricted time base. Water engineers in planning hydrological schemes, however, needed to have much longer time periods to consider and in fact could be stated to deal with climate. He asked whether one could use long-term climatic modelling in decision processes relevant to agriculture. *Professor Monteith* emphasised that the model that he had produced was a deterministic one and in this sense could be contrasted with the correlation type analysis based on associations, many of which were non-linear and many of which hid underlying relationships. However, simple deterministic models could become the basis of stochastic models of yield and climate as Smith and Harris had shown and this was likely to be an important trend. *Dr Thompson* stated that it had been found possible to develop an operational prediction model of potato blight which, while simple, incorporated all the important stages within each cycle of infection, but at the same time was designed to be run with standard meteorological data: he cautioned against the development of too many models which had no prospect of simplification for operational use. He also indicated how our knowledge of disease processes can sometimes advance quite inadvertently, citing the recent outbreak of foot and mouth disease which indicated hitherto unsuspected distances over which this virus can travel and then infect. *Professor Webster* gave an example of the problems associated with correlation type analysis when looking at calf pneumonia. Firstly, there was clear experimental evidence that there was no effect of a specific cold stress on the incidence of pneumonia in calves in a given infective environment. The statistical association that had been noted with respect to incidence of calf pneumonia did not provide any basis for giving advice. The chain of events was somewhat complex: because of the effect of cold on livestock they are housed in winter and when weather becomes very cold, it is common practice to reduce the ventilation in the building to prevent heat loss by air movement. Humidity builds up and air velocity is reduced, the number of bacteria-carrying aerosols increases and their size is altered so that organisms enter the lung and lower trachea rather than being trapped at a higher level of the respiratory tract. Admittedly, there is a statistical association, but action taken on this could be quite wrong. *Mr Jackson* stated that while the bad weather conditions for the harvest of 1976 led to an 18% drop in UK cereal output, there was by no means so marked an effect on farm incomes and one should not forget the complex inter-relationships of yield variation and the economic climate. *Dr Woodhead* mentioned the incidences of long range transport of pathogens from West Africa, notably of coffee rust to Brazil and banana rust to the Caribbean. Referring to Professor Monteith's paper, he noted that humidity and vapour pressure deficit did not appear explicitly in the Monteith–Scott scheme. *Professor Monteith* stated that one can include dimensions of humidity in terms of the concept of lost time. He went on to ask Mr Smith if he could give any examples of how micrometeorological methods, as distinct from empirical analysis, had been used to explore the relation between weather and disease and asked how this information could indeed be used usefully in predictive situations. *Mr Smith* stated that the simplistic approach was obviously only a beginning and a way of solving urgent problems and giving immediate solutions, but that the micrometeorological approach would certainly give more reliable information. *Professor Hirst* continued on the problem of distinguishing between generalisations and detailed understanding. He pointed out that in dealing with diseases on plants too little attention had been given to the effects of diseases. The cereal disease, *Rhynchosporium* killed patches of leaves. Mildew disturbs the metabolism of the plant while net blotch appears to have a fairly specific toxic action. Apple scab, codling moth damage and potato scab have but cosmetic effects. Pathologists have in the past appeared to have had a fixation on the extent of the damage done and its effect on yield, but what is really required is to look at the physiological processes of the diseased plant. One should consider not what was lost but what the effects were on future productivity. He continued regarding the limitations which were placed on forecasting activities, but thought that we were now entering an era of hope when the older methods of analysis of numerical data could be replaced by microprocessors which would give information in real time. *Professor*

MacKey stated that if one looked at the time-related aspects of the severity of infection one could discern two quite different effects. In specific resistance, the whole progress curve will be delayed due to an initial decrease of effective inoculum. In non-specific resistance, which acts on the efficiency and speed of the reproduction cycle of the pathogen, the shape of the curve becomes flattened. With the two effects cooperating, this flattening will be exaggerated. A correct interpretation has to acknowledge this interaction. *Professor Truszczynski* made a similar set of remarks related to human and animal pathogens emphasing the importance of the type and virulence of the organism on the effect of meteorological factors.

Climate and Food from Fish: The Longer Term Effects of Climate on Marine Life

R. JONES

DAFS Marine Laboratory, Aberdeen, UK

INTRODUCTION

According to Crisp (1965), 'climate' describes the prevailing meteorological variables and may be expressed as average seasonal values together with their range of variation. He uses the word 'weather' to refer to the day-to-day units which together, constitute the climate.

In this paper, emphasis has been given to the longer term effects of climatic variations on marine life. Climatic variations have influenced the ocean, and been accompanied by fairly well documented changes in sea temperature and sea ice (Beverton and Lee, 1965). This is discussed in general, along with details of particular instances in which there have been changes in the marine fauna associated with climatic change.

WORLD FISH CATCHES AND LEVELS OF PRODUCTION

World catches

The development of world fish catches from 1938–1977 is shown in Table 1. Immediately before (1938) and after (1945) the Second World War, catches amounted to about 20×10^6 tonnes. During the following decades, catches increased and by 1970 had attained 69×10^6 tonnes. During the 1970s, catches continued to increase, but at a declining rate and by 1977 appeared to be levelling off at about

167

TABLE 1

WORLD CATCHES OF FISH (MILLIONS OF
TONNES) (FROM FAO STATISTICS)

Year	Catch
1938	21
1948	20
1955	29
1960	40
1965	54
1970	70
1976	72
1977	71[a]
1978	72

[a] In 1977, 10×10^6 tonnes came from
freshwaters and 60×10^6 tonnes from
the sea.

74–75×10^6 tonnes. Some idea of the proportions coming from freshwater and from the sea is shown using the 1977 statistics. Of the
71×10^6 tonnes landed in 1977, 10×10^6 tonnes came from freshwaters
and 60×10^6 tonnes from marine fisheries.

Distribution of world catches and distribution of primary and secondary production

The distribution of world marine fish catches is shown in Table 2.
Although captured throughout the world oceans, the major proportion
is found to come from the coastal and continental shelf regions of the
major land masses. There is a clear relationship between the major

TABLE 2

DIVISION OF THE OCEAN INTO REGIONS OF DIFFERENT PRODUCTIVITY (FROM
RYTHER, 1969)

Region	Percentage of ocean	Primary production $(gC\,m^{-2}\,y^{-1})$	Harvesting level[a]	Percentage of total fish production
Open ocean	9·0	50	5	<1%
Coastal zone	9·9	100	3	50
Upwelling areas	0·1	300	1–2	50

[a] Number of trophic steps from primary production to harvesting by man.

concentrations of fish catches and the major centres of primary and secondary production.

The potential for fish production

Given an idea of the distribution of fish catches, and its dependence on the distribution of fish production, it is appropriate to consider the factors that determine the level of production in any particular area. Of these, one of the most important is the trophic level at which a particular species feeds. The situation is summarised in Table 3, where it is shown that different fish species may, conveniently, be divided into three groups.

TABLE 3

SOME CHARACTERISTICS OF FISH GROUPED ACCORDING TO TROPHIC LEVEL

Group	Trophic level[a]	Kind of species	Potential production	Market value	Examples
1	Phyto-plankton	Pelagic	High	Low	Sardine, anchovy
2	Zooplankton	Pelagic	Medium	Low	Herring, mackerel
3	Small fish and benthos	Pelagic and demersal	Low	High	Cod, haddock

Trophic level at which principal food is obtained.

Group 1 comprises species that feed at a relatively low level in the food chain. Sardines and anchovies for example, which exploit both phyto- and zooplankton are important examples of this group.

Group 2 comprises species which feed further up the food chain. The herring, which feeds on zooplankton, is an important example of this group.

Group 3 comprises species which feed either on small fish, which themselves feed on zooplankton, or on benthic animals. Demersal fish species and some pelagic fish species are important members of this group.

Each group exploits food at a progressively higher level in the food chain and each link in the food chain is associated with a loss of potential food energy. In general therefore, it is to be expected that the potential for production will be greatest in group 1 species and least in

group 3. Group 1 species are characterised by high production potential, low market value and a tendency towards instability of stock size
when subject to exploitation. At the other extreme, species in group 3
tend to have a low production potential, a relatively higher market
value, and a greater capacity to withstand exploitation. In general
therefore, marine fish production comes mainly from coastal regions,
and is dependent on the level of primary production and harvesting
level.

EFFECTS OF CLIMATE

Fish production is not constant but tends to vary, due to a variety of
factors, some of which are influenced by climate and the ways in which
this interacts with ocean currents and influences temperature. It is
appropriate therefore to consider the role of ocean currents and
changes in temperature.

Ocean currents

In both the Atlantic and the Pacific oceans, the current circulation is
dominated by anti-cyclonic systems situated north and south of the
equator. Figure 1 shows the situation in diagrammatic form. North of

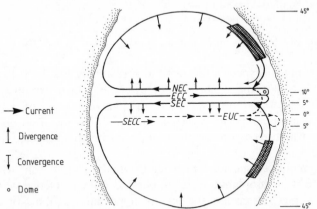

Eastern boundary upwelling area   *NEC* - North equatorial current   *SEC* - South
equatorial current   *SECC* - South equatorial countercurrent   *ECC* - Equatorial countercurrent
EUC - Equatorial undercurrent

Fig. 1. Diagram of the distribution of upwelling in an eastern boundary
current (from Cushing, 1969).

the equator the current is clockwise leading to a north equatorial current flowing westerly. South of the equator the circulation is anti-clockwise leading to a south equatorial current also flowing to the west. On the eastern side of the oceans there are currents approximately parallel to the coast, south flowing north of the equator and north flowing south of the equator.

Temperatures

A large part of the solar energy budget is mediated through the surface of the oceans and it is well established that the interaction between the sea, the sea currents and the atmosphere has important meteorological consequences and may also have direct or indirect effects on fisheries (Southward *et al.*, 1975). Periodic variations in temperature are known to have recurred during the past 100 years or so, and there are several examples of changes in fish stocks and marine life that appear to be associated with these changes. The mode of temperature change, which extends throughout the top 250 m, and involves corresponding salinity changes in the north-east Atlantic, is interpreted as resulting from shifts in the North Atlantic current system (Fig. 2). For example the Gulf stream constitutes part of an anti-cyclonic vortex in the North Atlantic. According to Iselin (1940),

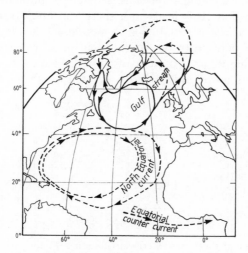

Fig. 2. General circulation of the Atlantic Ocean in January (from Tchernia, 1980).

based on theoretical considerations, the warm surface layer of the vortex should have a maximum thickness near its centre (which in this case is the Sargasso Sea). It is suggested that wind-induced increases in the transport of the North Atlantic gyre are accompanied by a radial shrinkage of the current system and that this leads to a deepening of the thermocline in the Sargasso Sea. This in turn should tend to raise the equilibrium temperature of the ocean surface slightly, because the water at the surface would be less influenced by mixing with cold deep water. The radial shrinkage of the current system and the deepening of the thermocline would be associated with a withdrawal of warm surface water from the north. Conversely a weakening of the transport of the North Atlantic gyre would be associated with a raising of the thermocline in the Sargasso Sea, and the excess of warm water would force the current system radially outward and further northwards, possibly discharging quantities of warmer near-surface water to high latitudes. Taylor (1978) considers that processes such as these have been a characteristic feature of changes in the North Atlantic current system throughout the last 100 years.

Temperature changes tend to be inversely related to the strength of the trade and westerly winds, and these are associated with weather patterns characterised by well defined stationary surface high pressure or low pressure systems. For example if there is a high pressure region, the westerly air flow in the upper troposphere is split into two branches around the region. This leads to a sharp transition from the normal zonal flow in a west-east direction to meridional flow in a north-south direction (or south-north direction). High pressure regions therefore lead to blocking weather patterns usually defined as those which exist for 10 days or more and extend over at least 45° of latitude (Burroughs, 1979).

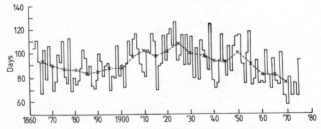

FIG. 3. Number of days of westerly circulation over the British Isles, 1861–1974. The dashed line shows 10 year means plotted at 5 year intervals (from Lamb, 1972).

Figure 3 shows the numbers of days of westerly circulation over the British Isles from 1861–1974. The figure shows that westerly circulation was at a minimum about 1890. It increased until about 1925 and then decreased again.

Changes in air temperature

Figure 4 shows deviations from the global mean surface air temperature between 1880–1884 and 1965–1969. From a minimum at the end of the 19th century, air temperature rose by about 0·5°C by the mid-1940s. After that it began to decline again. According to Crisp (1965) the climatic change which has occurred between about 1870 and the present day has been most marked in high latitudes. In Britain for example, the change in mean temperature has been of the order of only a fraction of a degree. In Stockholm the rise has been nearly 1°C, and in West Greenland and Spitzbergen 4–5°C.

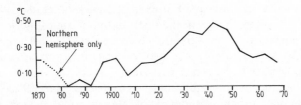

FIG. 4. Deviations from the global mean surface air temperature between 1880–1884 and 1965–1969 (from Cushing and Dickson, 1976).

Changes in sea temperature

During the previous century, there were three rather short, warm periods in the North Atlantic area (i.e. 1810–1823, 1840–1850 and about 1873–1882) while in the present century a longer warm period first became noticeable about 1915 (Taning, 1953). The magnitudes of these changes have tended to be more noticeable at high latitudes than at low latitudes. For example, in the Davis Strait and between Iceland and Shetland there was an increase of 0·4–0·8°C reaching a maximum between 1950 and 1960. In general, maximum temperatures appear to have been reached somewhere between 1945 and 1960 (Beverton and Lee, 1965). Beverton and Lee (1965) quoting Prahm (1958), state that on the Great Fisher Bank in the North Sea, summer temperatures on the seabed rose by 0·3–0·4°C between 1906–1915 and 1921–1939. In 1946–1955 they had fallen back again by 0·8°C in May, but by only 0·3°C in July–August. On the Fladen ground there was a rise but of no more than 0·25°C between 1906–1915 and 1921–1939. Temperatures then remained at the same value throughout 1946–1955. According to Southward (1960), bottom temperatures off Plymouth showed an over-all rise of 0·25°C over 40 years with most of the rise in the August–January period. The data show that the late 1940s and the late 1950s were the warmest periods. These changes are relatively small, compared with seasonal changes in the same areas. For example, in the southern North Sea, the seasonal variation in temperature is from about 4°C in February–March to 16°C in August, an annual range of 12°C (Laevastu, 1963). At the end of the last century, and the beginning of this century, the fall in temperature from 1876–1880 to 1906–1920 was between 0·5 and 1°C (Beverton and Lee, 1965).

Indications are that since about 1950, temperatures have started to decline again, and that this can be associated with meteorological changes in more recent years. For example, Dickson *et al.* (1975) have described a marked change in the distribution of atmospheric pressure over the northern North Atlantic which occurred in 1970–1971 and lasted until at least 1974. An area of high pressure anomaly over Greenland, which had been a persistent feature of winters since the early 1950s, declined abruptly and was replaced from 1970–1974 by an area of low pressure anomaly of almost equal magnitude. The results have been almost a reversal of wind direction from generally north-east until 1969 to west or south-west between 1971 and 1974, implying an increase in the strength of the westerlies. It is interesting to note that the winter of 1962–1963 was one of the coldest for about 70 years. Thus in general, over most of the North Atlantic, the present century began with a relatively cool period followed, during the 1920s, by a warming, which with some fluctuations has been largely maintained until about the 1950s.

Changes in ice cover

Associated with changes in temperature, have been changes in ice cover.

Beverton and Lee (1965) refer to Lamb and Johnson (1959) and Schell (1961), with reference to changes in ice cover in the Greenland and Iceland areas. According to these authors the frequency of ice in the 1965–1974 period was 12–16 weeks per year. Since 1920 however, it has been as low as 1–1·5 weeks per year, as in the 1840–1854 period. Changes in ice cover along the west coast of Greenland since 1820 have been similar to those in Iceland. In the Barents Sea, the mean ice limit for all months between April and August was much further to the north-east during the period 1929–1938 than during the period 1898–1922, an improvement that began in the Barents and Kara Seas in 1920. Thus during the present century there has been a marked improvement in ice conditions at Greenland, Iceland, and in the Barents Sea.

EFFECTS OF TEMPERATURE ON THE FAUNA

One meteorological variable, namely temperature, necessarily exercises a major influence. Humidity, rainfall and sunshine are of lesser importance because they can only influence the upper part of the water column except in certain land-locked seas such as the Baltic. Here salinity as much as temperature determines faunal distribution. Some useful remarks on the effect of temperature on the marine ecosystem have been made by Crisp (1965) and most of the observations below derive from his work.

Faunal changes that have occurred and that may be associated with the increase in sea temperature at high latitudes, include the northward extension of the cod fisheries at West Greenland, an increase in warm-water species of the bottom fauna of western Spitzbergen (Blacker, 1957), and the greater penetration of Atlantic invertebrates and fish in the Baltic associated with increasing quantities of salt water inflow.

According to Hutchins (1947), for some species the northern limits might be set by the temperature being too cold, either in summer for breeding or in winter for survival. For example, the Portuguese oyster can live in British oyster beds but does not breed there. Other species, such as the conger eel, cannot survive low temperatures in winter. Similarly, southern limits may be set by summer temperatures which are too high for survival (e.g. for the common mussel on the east coast of the United States) or by temperatures which are too high for breeding (this may be true for the common shore barnacle in the latitude of Plymouth).

The direct influence of temperature is clearest when temperatures approach the lower lethal limits. Woodhead and Woodhead (1959) for example have shown that certain physiological processes in cod, particularly osmoregulation, are disturbed below 2°C, a temperature which corresponds roughly to the transition between waters of Atlantic and Arctic origin and constitutes an effective limit to the northerly distribution of this and other boreal species. Death of cod has been observed when they become trapped in cold water of Arctic origin, (Templeman, 1965). The cold winters of 1946–1947 and 1962–1963 caused death in a number of species in the North Sea, particularly sole (Beverton and Lee, 1965).

Crisp (1965) refers to Darwin who repeatedly emphasised that the distribution of species could only be explained in terms of the distribution of their prey, predators or competing species. Such biotic relationships are thought to stabilise communities against the direct impact of physical variables. For example, where the northern boundary of one species abuts on the southern boundary of another, the territory of each is restricted by biological competition. The physical barriers which might operate, are in fact replaced by biological ones and therefore the climate may not directly control such boundaries, although it may cause them to shift. In Crisp's view, probably the majority of species in temperate latitudes are only indirectly controlled by temperature. He suggests that this is why they do not show a perfect correspondence between their distribution and the distribution of any particular isotherm. It would also explain why they are not necessarily influenced by temperature extremes. Their abundance,and distribution would be influenced by changes in the climate but only to a limited extent.

Examples of faunal changes that may be associated with changes in temperature

Particular examples of faunal changes that may be associated with changes in temperature may be found in the Greenland cod fishery, the distribution of some intertidal invertebrates, the abundance of certain species in the English Channel, and in the Peruvian anchovy fishery.

The Greenland cod fishery

Taning (1953) and Beverton and Lee (1965) summarise changes in temperature and cod catches in the West Greenland cod fishery.

During the last century, in the warm period of 1810–1823, cod is said to have been particularly numerous around West Greenland in the entire coastal region from Julianehab to Disko Bay. This coincided with a period that must have been generally mild in the North Atlantic ocean since some southern species of fish were observed at Iceland about that time. By the beginning of this century however, corresponding with a cold period, the Greenland cod stock was at a low level and up to 1917 there were only small local fjord populations of cod in Greenland. Then, in the early 1920s, sea temperatures rose abruptly by more than 1°C (Fig. 5) and large numbers of adult fish appeared off

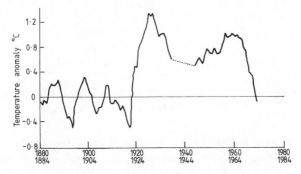

FIG. 5. Sea surface temperature anomalies in West Greenland waters during 1876–1970 (from Malmberg, 1979–1980).

the south-west coast and penetrated as far north as latitude 72°N. The build-up of cod is demonstrated by the increase in catch of Greenland cod between about 1920 and 1960 and over this period the catch increased from a negligible level to 400×10^3 tonnes per year (Fig. 6). During the 1930s a permanent spawning stock was established in Greenland, although some fish on the southern banks were temporary migrants from Iceland. By the 1950s the interchange of cod with Iceland had declined considerably and this coincided with a reduction in the flow of the Irminger current, in which larvae would otherwise have been carried to Greenland from the Icelandic spawning grounds. After 1960, there was a decrease in both the temperature and the catches. At Iceland the warming was just as great as at Greenland but no major change in the cod population can be demonstrated. Spawning became more widespread but appears to have been at the expense of, rather than in addition to, the main spawning centre in the south-west. It did not lead to an increase in abundance.

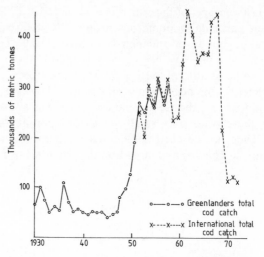

FIG. 6. Catches in the West Greenland cod fishery 1930–1974 (from Beverton and Lee, 1965).

An interesting feature of the growth of the Greenland cod stock is that this was due to some exceptionally good year classes, rather than to the result of gradual change. These good year classes occurred during a relatively small number of warm years starting in 1924, as illustrated by the good correlation between bottom temperatures in June on Fyllas Bank off West Greenland, and the year class strength of cod in Greenland waters, over a temperature range up to 3°C.

Changes in intertidal invertebrates

Around the British Isles, Southward and Crisp (1954), have demonstrated how, between 1934 and 1951, the arctic-boreal form of the common barnacle all but disappeared, and its place was taken by an increase in the more southern species, *Chthalmus*. They associated this change with the steadily rising sea and air temperatures, and pointed out that in the intertidal zone it may be assumed that the changes in sea temperature would be similar to those recorded on land.

Crisp (1965) pointed out that the most marked changes in intertidal species are to be observed near their boundaries. During the extremely cold conditions of 1963 some extreme temperatures were reached in the south-east, particularly on the coasts of Dorset, Hampshire, the

Bristol Channel and Caernarvonshire. The large top shell *Monodonta* is a slow moving species unable to migrate rapidly downshore in cold weather, and in some areas, populations of this species were destroyed by the sudden onset of severe frosts. By contrast the southern species of barnacle *Chthalmus* was almost unaffected, suggesting that the northern limit of its distribution may be only indirectly controlled by temperature. From general considerations, Crisp concluded that the range of distribution of intertidal forms does not fluctuate widely with variations in weather and climate because of various stabilising forces. Thus biotic interactions may prevent organisms from occupying territory in which the extremes of physical conditions may regularly cause mortality. Additionally, topographical features in the environment may create barriers, the positions of which are independent of the prevailing isotherms. He suggested that gradual changes in the climate over a number of years, by altering the balance between species, are more effective in modifying the general pattern of distribution than short periods of severe weather. The latter can cause very heavy mortalities but does not necessarily have a noticeable effect on over-all distribution.

Changes in the English Channel and the Russell Cycle

The Russell Cycle refers to certain changes that have taken place in the western English Channel and the following observations are taken from Russell (1973), Southward *et al.* (1975), Cushing (1978) and Colebrook *et al.* (1978). In general, the period of warming this century has been associated with a change in species composition in the English Channel, various cold-water species having a tendency to decline and warm-water species to increase (Fig. 7).

For example, in the western English Channel, the abundance of young fish, excluding clupeids, dropped sharply to a low level in the 1930s, and remained at a low level until about 1965. At the same time there was a marked decrease in zooplankton abundance, including medusae. Also the indicator species *Sagitta elegans* was replaced by *Sagitta setosa*. Among the clupeids, some species declined. For example between 1925 and 1935 recruitment to the Plymouth herring started to decline, due to the failure of the 1925 year class. Other species increased; in 1926, pilchard eggs were recorded in unusually high numbers in July and by 1935 pilchards were abundant throughout the summer and replaced the herring in the western English Channel.

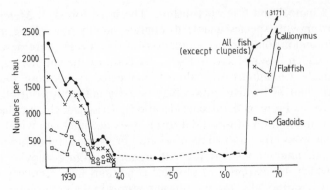

FIG. 7. The Russell Cycle, showing catches of the planktonic stages of various
fish species between 1924–1971 (from Russell, 1973).

Associated with these changes is the fact that maximum winter phosphate levels decreased fairly rapidly at the end of the 1920s, from about $0·67$ μg litre^{-1} to about $0·47$ μg litre^{-1}.

Since 1963 there has been a progressive change in the water mass off Plymouth and since 1970 a return to the conditions of the 1920s and early 1930s. As in the 1920s, the fauna characterising the period 1970–1974 contained fewer warmer water species while a number of colder water, lower salinity, north-western indicator species, became common. For example, in 1965 the numbers of spring spawned larvae increased by about an order of magnitude and the species composition of the young fish populations at present is not significantly different from that of the previous period of abundance; gadoid, flatfish, sandeels and *Callionymus* species making up the greater proportion of the catches. In 1970–1971 the macroplankton returned to the level of the 1920s. In the following year the winter phosphorus concentration rose to the pre-1930 level and the summer-spawned fish larvae recovered. In the summer of 1972 *Sagitta elegans* returned for the first time since the 1930s and by 1973 it was again abundant. It is likely that the pilchards declined in numbers towards the end of the 1970s. According to Southward (1962) most of the changes off Plymouth may be confined to the northern side of the English Channel. Thus the Russell Cycle passed through its pilchard, low phosphorus, low macroplankton condition during the period of warming that peaked in 1945. The cycle was reversed during the period 1965–1975.

In conclusion, these changes in the English Channel can be linked with temperature changes, but are not thought to be due to the effect of temperature directly. They are more likely to be due to the more widespread environmental changes that occurred contemporaneously.

The Peruvian anchovy and the El Niño phenomenon

Off the coast of Peru is a very important fishery based on the stock of anchoveta there. The fortunes of the stock appear to be associated with the upwelling off the coast of Peru and its variation in connection with a phenomenon known as El Niño.

The following account of the meteorological and hydrographic conditions associated with this phenomenon are taken from Craig (1974). The eastern tropical Pacific is dominated by anti-cyclonic systems on each side of the equator. The combination of these, i.e. a clockwise circulation to the north and an anti-clockwise one to the south, gives westerly moving airstreams along the line of the equator while the southern system gives winds that blow north-west along the coast of Peru.

Since the upper water transport is directed to the right of the wind in the northern hemisphere and to the left in the southern, these winds induce transport away from the coast of Peru and lead to upwelling in a coastal strip roughly 10 km wide. They also induce divergent flows at the equator and hence upwelling at this latitude also. During an inter-Niño, the cold waters of the Peru upwelling are continuous with the equatorial upwelling giving a cold streak in the tropical Pacific following the coast of Chile and Peru and extending along the equator by the Galapagos Islands. This is about 10 000 km long and 300–1000 km wide.

The long term picture is thus of an unstable regime, with an asymmetrical form and variable periodicity. Approximately one year in every seven the cold streak disappears leaving only a strip of reduced coastal upwelling south of Callao. Warm oceanic waters flood back to the equator and approach more closely to the coast of Peru. For example, Fig. 8 shows changes in sea surface temperature in the tropical Pacific and their association with El Niño occurrences in 1957, 1965, 1969, 1972–73 and 1976 (Newell, 1979).

According to one estimate, the supply of nutrients due to upwelling is reduced to about one-third or less during an El Niño and is confined largely to the southern half of the coast of Peru. Where there is an invasion of equatorial water, upwelling may be practically zero, and plant production may become negligible.

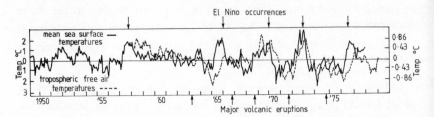

FIG. 8. Changes in sea surface temperature in the tropical Pacific and association with El Niño occurrences (from Newell, 1979).

The anchoveta

The following account is based largely on information from Valdivia (1978), Anon (1974), and unpublished data provided by the Instituto del Mar del Peru. During an El Niño period, the effect on the anchoveta is to reduce the area of distribution of the fish with a concentration of fish in those spots where plant production can continue. The shoals tend to occur at a greater depth than normal (up to 200 m) with some displacement to the south of the normal locality. There is no evidence of an increase in the adult mortality rate but the rate of reproduction is reduced due to a failure of the maturation cycle and probably also due to poor survival of larvae. These changes in the anchoveta population and its accessibility, result in heavy mortality among the Guano bird population (Craig, 1974). For example, Fig. 9 shows variations in the population of Guano birds and the catch of anchoveta.

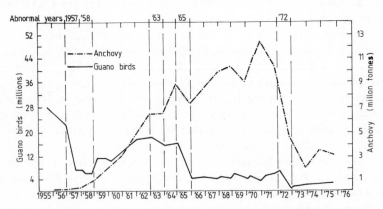

FIG. 9. Variations in the population of Guano birds and the catch of anchoveta (from Valdivia, 1978).

In the 1950s, catches of anchoveta were relatively small but during the 1960s there was a gradual increase in catches to reach a peak of about 12×10^6 tonnes in 1970. This was followed by a relatively rapid decline to a level of about 2×10^6 tonnes. Currently, catches are restricted by quota to about 1×10^6 tonnes or less.

In the period between 1965 and 1970 fishing was intensive. The annual recruitment of young fish to the fishable stock was high, however, and the spawning stock was maintained at an intermediate level of about 15×10^6 tonnes compared to that of about 25×10^6 tonnes before the fishery began.

With the approach of the 1972 El Niño conditions, however, the situation suddenly changed. Recruitment from spawnings in 1971 and 1972 was poor in both years, and much lower than any previous recruitment observed during the period of the fishery. At the end of 1971, the fat content of the mature-sized individuals was exceptionally high for the time of year. It may be that these fish laid down fat rather than gonads as a survival adaptation at that time. The 1972 failure was associated with a low spawning stock and with El Niño conditions from before the spawning period until after recruitment and might reasonably be ascribed to environmental conditions, or to reduced adult stock size, or to the two acting in combination. In addition, the fish became concentrated in an area close to the coast and the catch per unit effort remained high in relation to the abundance of fish. Fishing therefore continued to be profitable even when the total stock had been reduced very considerably. The result of the combination of poor recruitment and intense fishing on the highly concentrated adult stock was that the amount of fish left to form a spawning stock at the end of 1972 was only about 2×10^6 tonnes.

During the first half of the 1970s, there was a slow build-up in the stock aided by favourable recruitment in 1975 and this led to an increase in the stock to a level of $10–12 \times 10^6$ tonnes by the beginning of 1976. Another El Niño in 1976, however, led to the appearance of warm water along the coast during a large part of the year causing the fish to concentrate once more in a narrow area close to the coast where feeding conditions appeared to be unfavourable since the normal diatom/zooplankton assemblage was scarce and dinoflagellates were unusually abundant. The growth of the fish was below normal and the fish were very lean and with a low fat content.

The result was that the stock available at the beginning of 1977 was lower than ever before at the beginning of any year, and a catch of

about 1×10^6 tonnes which was taken in the first half of 1977, must
have decreased the stock still further. Thus, although conditions during
1976 were different from the classical El Niño years of 1972 and 1957,
the effect on the fishery was still disastrous.

The El Niño phenomenon has been known for a considerable time
in Peru and has been principally associated with the mortality of sea
birds. At times when there are hydrographic and meteorological indications of an El Niño, there have been numbers of bird carcasses
strewn along the beaches. These usually die in emaciated conditions
and since their chief food is the anchoveta the implication is that they
have died from a lack of this species. During the 1957–1958 El Niño
for example, when the fishery was only just beginning, the number of
birds fell from 28×10^6 to 6×10^6 (Fig. 9). There was a partial recovery
in the 1960s, but during the 1970s the bird population fell to a very
low level presumably due to the disastrous decline in the anchoveta
stock.

The decline in the birds is not merely due to the death of adults
observed on the beaches. Eggs and young in nesting areas are frequently abandoned. It appears that the displacement in the anchovy
distribution into deeper water to the south, takes them away from the
grounds in which the birds normally fish and makes them inaccessible.
The shift is beyond the birds' point of no return, and this frequently
leads to futile and senseless migrations away from the nesting areas,
leading to the abandonment of the eggs and young. Some birds are
reported as having reached as far as the east coast of South America.
Thus directly among the adults, and indirectly among the juveniles, the
fall in the bird population is primarily due to the change in the
distribution of the anchovy and its inaccessibility.

The history of the Peruvian anchovy fishery provides an extreme
example of the influence of meteorological and hydrographic conditions on a fishery. It is particularly unfortunate that, at times when the
fishery has been declining due to recruitment failure, the adults should
be concentrated so close to the coast as to make them extremely
vulnerable to fishing. Control of fishing tends to be difficult, since, even
though other species such as sardine and mackerel are available for
capture further offshore, the boats must steam for longer distances
offshore, ignoring the relatively good anchovy fishing close to the
coast. In practice the enforcement problem has tended to be such that
although quotas have been imposed, it has not always been possible to
restrict the fishing for anchoveta effectively.

SUMMARY AND CONCLUSIONS

This paper considered the main factors that determine the level of fish production and ways in which fish production and faunal biomass may have been influenced by climatic change. The principal conclusions are:

1. Fish production in the sea is most important on the continental shelves and coastal regions throughout the world oceans. The level of production is principally dependent on the level of primary production and on the harvesting level.

2. As far as a climatic variation is concerned, temperature changes appear to have been particularly important. There have been a number of warm periods during the last century and a period in this century in which there was a general warming of the North Atlantic from about 1920 to about 1950. There are a number of examples of changes in the marine fauna that appear to be associated with these temperature changes, either directly or indirectly. Some examples are:

   (a) The Greenland cod fishery. Associated with an increase in temperature in the 1920s there was a build-up of the Greenland stock due to a number of good year classes, which caused the fishery to increase until about 1960. Since then there has been a decline in both temperature and in catches.

   (b) Around Britain, there has been a change in the relative distribution of two species of barnacles. This is demonstrated by a northward shift in the southern limit of the common barnacle, a cold-adapted species. At the same time there has been a northerly shift of the northern limit of *Chthalmus*, a warm-adapted species.

   (c) In the English Channel, during the warm period from about 1930–1960, there has been a decline in some species and an increase in others. Since about the middle of the 1960s there has been a return to the conditions of the pre-1920s.

3. Off the the coast of Peru there is a fishery for anchovy which is influenced by variations in the hydrography of the eastern Pacific. In particular, there is an irregular oscillation of the local hydrographic conditions such that about once every seven years there is a reduction in the degree of coastal upwelling and this is associated with a considerable drop in the productivity of the

region. These periods have been associated with the mortality of the birds that feed on anchovy, due to a change in the accessibility of the anchovy at these times. Since about 1972, two of these periods have coincided with heavy fishing, and this has resulted in a reduction in the stock to an exceptionally low level, and to the virtual collapse of the fishery.

REFERENCES

Anon (1974). Report of the fourth session of the panel of experts on stock assessment of Peruvian anchoveta. *Instututo del Mar del Pery* **2**(10), 603–723.

Beverton, R. J. H. and Lee, A. J. (1965). Hydrographic fluctuations in the North Atlantic Ocean and some biological consequences. In: *Symposia of Institute of Biology, No 14. Biological Significance of Climatic Change in Britain* (Eds C. G. Johnston and L. P. Smith). Proceedings of a symposium held at the Royal Geographical Society, London, 29–30 October 1964. pp. 79–107.

Blacker, R. W. (1957). Benthic animals as indicators of hydrographic conditions and climatic changes in Svalbard waters. *Fish. Invest. Lond. Ser. 2* **20**(10), 49.

Burroughs, W. (1979). Cold spells, heat waves and blocking anti-cyclones. *New Scientist* **81**(1142), 492–4.

Colebrook, J. M., Reid, P. C. and Coombs, S. H. (1978). Continuous plankton records: the change in the plankton of the southern North Sea between 1970 and 1972. *Mar. Biol.* **45**, 209–13.

Craig, R. E. (1974). El Niño and Peru's fishing waters. *Fishing News International* October.

Crisp, D. J. (1965). Observations on the effects of climate and weather on marine communities. In: *Symposia of Institute of Biology, No 14. Biological Significance of Climatic Change in Britain* (Eds C. G. Johnston and L. P. Smith). Proceedings of a symposium held at the Royal Geographical Society, London, 29–30 October 1964. pp 63–77.

Cushing, D. H. (1969). *Upwelling and Fish Production.* FAO Fisheries Technical Paper no. 84 FRs/T84. FAO, Geneva, 40 pp.

Cushing, D. H. (1978). Biological effects of climatic change. *Rapp. P.-v. Cons. int. Explor. Mer* **173**, 107–16.

Cushing, D. H. and Dickson, R. R. (1976). The biological response in the sea to climatic changes. *Adv. Mar. Biol.* **14**, 1–122.

Dickson, R. R., Lamb, H. H., Malmberg, S. A. and Colebrook, J. M. (1975). Climatic reversal in northern North Atlantic. *Nature, London* **256**, 479–82.

Groen, P. (1967). *The Waters of the Sea.* Van Nostrand Co Ltd, London, 328 pp.

Hutchins, L. W. (1947). The bases for temperature zonation in geographical distribution. *Ecol. Managr* **11**(3), 325–35.

Iselin, C. O. D. (1940). Preliminary report on long-period variations in the transport of the Gulf Stream system. *Papers Phys. Oceanogr. Met.* 8.

Laevastu, T. (1963). Surface water types of the North Sea and their characteristics. *Serial Atlas of the Marine Environment.* Am. Geog. Soc., Washington D.C.

Lamb, H. H. (1972). *Climate, Past, Present and Future. I. Fundamentals and Climate Now.* Methuen, London, 613 pp.

Lamb, H. H. and Johnson, A. I. (1959). Climatic variation and observed changes in the general circulation. *Geogr. Ann., Stockholm* **41**, 94.

Malmberg, S. A. (1979–1980). *Astand sjavar og fiskstofna vid islands 1–4*, 25 pp. English summaries.

Newell, R. E. (1979). Climate and the ocean. *Am. Scientists* **67**(4), 405–16.

Prahm, G. (1958). Summer bottom temperature in two selected areas of the Central North Sea in the years 1900–1956. *Annls, biol., Copenh,* **13**, 78–9.

Reid, P. C. (1977). Continuous planktonic records: changes in the composition and abundance of the phytoplankton of the north-eastern Atlantic Ocean and North Sea, 1958–1974. *Mar. Biol.* **40**, 337–9.

Russell, F. S. (1973). Summary of the observations on the occurrence of the planktonic stages of the fish off Plymouth, 1924–1972. *J. Mar. Biol. Ass.* **53**, 347–55.

Ryther, J. H. (1969). Photosynthesis and fish production in the sea. *Science* **166**(3901), 72–76; *Geogr. Annls.* **41**, 94–134.

Schell, I. I. (1961). The ice off Iceland and the climates during the last 1,200 years approximately. *Geogr. Annls.* **43**, 354–62.

Southward, A. J. (1960). On changes of sea temperature in the English Channel. *J. Mar. Biol. Ass. UK* **39**, 449–58.

Southward, A. J. (1962). The distribution of some planktonic animals in the English Channel and approaches. II. Surveys with the Gulf III high-speed sampler, 1958–1960. *J. Mar. Biol. Ass. UK* **42**, 275–375.

Southward, A. J. and Crisp, D. J. (1954). Recent changes in the distribution of the intertidal barnacles *Chthalmus stellatus* (Poli) and *Balanus balanoides* (L.) in the British Isles. *J. Anim. Ecol.* **3**, 163–77.

Southward, A. J. Butler, E. I. and Pennycuick, L. (1975). Recent cyclic changes in climate and in abundance of marine life. *Nature, London* **253**, 714–17.

Taning, A. V. (1953). Long-term changes in hydrography and fluctuations in fish stocks. *ICNAF Annual Proceedings, Vol. 3 (1952–1953)*, pp. 69–77.

Taylor, A. H. (1978). Long-term changes in the North Atlantic current system and their biological implications. *Proc. Roy. Soc. Edinburgh* **76B**, 223–43.

Tchernia, P. (1980). *Descriptive Regional Oceanography.* Pergamon Press, London.

Templeman, W. (1965). Mass mortalities of marine fishes in the Newfoundland area, presumably due to low temperature. ICNAF Spec. Publ. No. 6. 137–48.

Valdivia, J. E. (1978). The anchoveta and El Niño. *Rapp. Proc. Verb. Reun.* **173**, 196–202.

Woodhead, P. M. J. and Woodhead, A. D. (1959). The effects of low temperatures on the physiology and distribution of the cod, *Gadus morhua* L., in the Barents Sea. *Proc. Zool. Soc. London* **133**, 181–99.

Climate and Food from Fish: Climate and Fish Cultivation

C. B. COWEY

Institute of Marine Biochemistry, St. Fittick's Road, Aberdeen, UK

Although fish cultivation, albeit in primitive form, was first practised over 2000 years ago, only a small fraction of the fish consumed by man is derived from this source. Thus over the period 1974–1984 the total annual protein harvest from world fisheries is expected to increase from 9.3×10^6 tonnes to 14×10^6 tonnes. Over the same period protein production from aquaculture is expected to rise from 0.84×10^6 tonnes to 1.7×10^6 tonnes (Kinne and Rosenthal, 1977). Despite the large percentage increase in protein obtained from aquaculture the harvest would still only represent about 1.0% of global protein production by 1984.

Fish cultivation probably originated with freshwater species and the greater part of current aquaculture production is from fresh and brackish waters. The most important climatic elements affecting fish cultivation are temperature, light and (because of the emphasis on fresh and brackish water species) rainfall. The cardinal significance of temperature is recognised by the general division of cultivated fish into warm water and cold water species although the thermal tolerance of certain species is such that they may be grown in either environment.

Animal protein production by terrestrial animals is based predominantly on the use of herbivores (cattle, sheep) and omnivores (poultry, pigs). Herbivorous species of fish that feed near the base of the photosynthetic food chain, with a direct and efficient conversion of plant matter to animal flesh are found mainly among tropical or warm water species (carp, mullet, *Tilapia*, milkfish). By virtue of this, and the more favourable temperature conditions favouring year round growth, the tropics offer greater potential for fish culture than do temperate regions. The availability of a number of species of different food habits that occupy different ecological niches lends itself to the practice of

189

polyculture wherein several species with complementary requirements (bottom feeders, pelagic feeders, plankton eaters, leaf eaters) are stocked together so that the entire water column is used with enhanced overall productivity. Polyculture may be particularly useful when natural food chains are created in ponds by fertilisation of the water with nitrates, phosphates, urea or manure (only supplementary feedings of pelleted diets would then be necessary).

Fish cultivation in temperate regions is largely based on carnivorous species (salmonids, eels) with a high dietary protein requirement. Some of the wholly marine species have a requirement for living food in the larval stages. This is expensive to raise and less convenient to handle than dry feed. The suitability of coastal areas for cultivation of marine species is difficult to assess; climatic factors (particularly wind in conjunction with wave action and tides) are important here in that only well protected areas can be used. As such zones comprise less than 3% of the total sea surface area, the area practically available for marine cultivation is much less than certain optimistic predictions have indicated.

Very few species of fish can as yet be bred and reared under controlled culture conditions and thus be amenable to genetic stock improvement. So, by contrast with agriculture many cultured species consist of wild populations or populations in which wild characteristics predominate. In cases where animals cannot yet be bred under controlled conditions they must be obtained from the field. Unpredictable changes in abundance, ecological dynamics and weather contribute to a considerable degree of uncertainty in field collections of culture materials.

TEMPERATURE ACCLIMATION AND COMPENSATION

In the natural environment fish live at temperatures ranging from less than 0°C to greater than 40°C. Studies on a number of species have shown that body temperature is normally within a degree or so of water temperature; the exchange of respiratory gases in the gills leads also to complete thermal equilibration and because thermal diffusion is more rapid than molecular diffusion there are, in most aquatic poikilotherms, no temperature gradients.

No single species of fish can survive over the entire temperature range mentioned and many species display both upper and lower critical temperatures within this range. The effects of a rise in temperature on temperate species, particularly in their young stages, is well illustrated by studies of McCormick *et al.* (1972) on brook trout (*Salvelinus fontinalis*). There is an immediate increase in growth rate (at maximum food ration) until a peak (optimum) value is reached after which, with further increase in temperature, growth rate falls rapidly and mortalities ensue. Values illustrating marked differences in optimum temperature for growth of a number of cultivated species are shown in Table 1. Thermal tolerance diagrams relating acclimation

TABLE 1
OPTIMUM TEMPERATURE FOR GROWTH OF CERTAIN FISH SPECIES GIVEN A HIGH
RATION

Species	Size (g)	Optimum temperature (°C)	Reference
Salmo trutta	10–300	12·8	Elliott (1975a)
Oncorhynchus nerka	6–20	15	Brett *et al.* (1969)
Salmo gairdneri	0·3–3	17·2	Hokanson *et al.* (1977)
Ictalurus punctatus	4	30	Andrews and Stickney (1972)

temperature to critical temperature for growth, feeding and survival have been constructed for a number of species and reveal a gradation from stenothermal to eurythermal habits (Elliott, 1981). The area of the tolerance zone (expressed as °C^2) obtained from such diagrams serves as an index of thermal tolerance; values given in Table 2

TABLE 2
CRITICAL TEMPERATURES AND THERMAL TOLERANCE FOR CERTAIN SALMONIDS
AND CYPRINIDS (DATA FROM ELLIOTT, 1981)

Species	Lower critical range (°C)	Upper critical range (°C)	Upper incipient lethal temperature (°C)	Thermal tolerance (°C^2)
Oncorhynchus nerka	0–7	22–28	24·4	505
Salmo gairdneri	0–9	19–30	26·2	583
Rutilus rutilus	0–12	25–38	33·5	770
Carrassius auratus	0–17	27–42	41·0	1 220

indicate that salmonids have much a much lower range than do cyprinids. Thermal limits for survival, feeding and growth narrow progressively.

Adaptation to temperature is seen as involving both acclimation and compensation, the former process being a 'non-genetic reversible response of the organism to environmental change', the latter 'an evolved adaptation permitting higher (or lower) metabolic rates at extremes of polar (or tropical) environments which could not be predicted from studies conducted in one or other of the normal habitats' (Brett, 1970). Several studies relating standard metabolic rate† to water temperature for fish from different climates have apparently demonstrated a metabolic compensation, particularly on the part of polar species, to very low temperatures. Studies of Scholander *et al.* (1953) and Wohlschlag (1960) show that polar species maintain a higher metabolic rate at low temperatures than would be expected from studies on temperate species (Fig. 1). These data have, however, been severely criticised by Holeton (1974) who pointed out that Krogh's 'standard curve' (Ege and Krogh, 1914) obtained from data on goldfish, *Carrasius auratus* (labelled 'temperate' in Fig. 1) is certainly inaccurate at its lower end (0–5°C) where Q_{10} values reach 10·9 and that other values are also too high by comparison with data obtained on the same species by Beamish and Mookherji (1964). Holeton (1974) questioned the data of Scholander *et al.* (1953) and Wohlschlag (1960) because of the very short acclimation times and the probability that elevated metabolic rates, resulting from capture and handling, were measured. Holeton's studies, which avoided these pitfalls, showed some variation between the Arctic species examined. Values for Arctic cod, *Boreogadus saida* ($70 \, \text{mg} \, O_2 \, \text{kg}^{-1} \, \text{h}^{-1}$ at $-1·5°C$) were not inconsistent with previous values for Arctic fish, values for five species of Arctic cottids were much lower at this temperature ($38 \, \text{mg} \, O_2 \, \text{kg}^{-1} \, \text{h}^{-1}$) while values for five other species (three *Zoarcidae* and two *Cyclopteridae*) were uncompensated.

The balance of the evidence is that much of the data relating to Antarctic fish (upper — · — line in Fig. 1) is not valid evidence for temperature compensation; among Arctic fish there is some variation and temperature compensation is not common to all species, several certainly lack this characteristic.

† The term 'standard metabolic rate' is applied because of the problems involved in measuring resting or basal metabolic rate, standard metabolism describes the minimum observed rates (Brett and Groves, 1979).

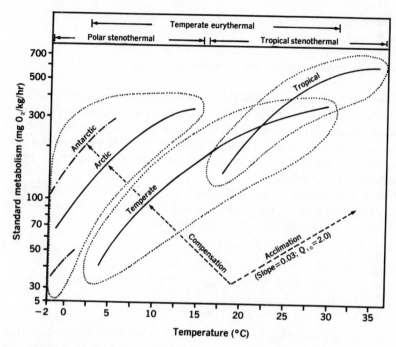

FIG. 1. Relationship between temperature and standard metabolic rate in marine fish from different climatic zones. · · · · ·, Indicates range of variability within each zone. – – –, Direction of metabolic compensation between species and metabolic compensation within species (reproduced with permission from Brett (1970)).

The curve for tropical species in Fig. 1 shows little downward compensatory displacement by comparison with the curve for temperate species and only limited metabolic compensation seems to occur, the fish functioning at high maintenance levels. Thus Brett and Groves (1979) show that the minimum energy expenditure of tropical species is some 70% higher than that of temperate species at the mid-point of their temperature range. Values for standard metabolic rate quoted by these authors are $0.2 \, \text{kcal kg}^{-1} \text{h}^{-1}$ for Arctic species at $-1.5°C$, $0.3 \, \text{kcal kg}^{-1} \text{h}^{-1}$ for temperate species at $15°C$ and $0.5 \, \text{kcal kg}^{-1} \text{h}^{-1}$ for tropical species at $26°C$. Finally Brett and Groves (1979) show that the data relating standard metabolism to temperature for goldfish is almost linearised by an exponential transformation, giving a Q_{10} of 2.3 over the temperature range 10–$30°C$. A similar value is obtained for a number of other temperate species over their tolerable temperature range.

Evidence from studies on protein synthesis

Protein synthesis involves the turnover and replacement of a large number of enzymes and probably comprises a significant proportion of maintenance metabolism. Studies in mammals suggest that rates of protein synthesis bear a constant ratio to basal metabolic rates and account for about 20% of energy consumption (Garlick *et al.*, 1976; Nicholas *et al.*, 1977).

Protein synthetic activity measured *in vivo* in livers of toad fish (a eurythermal species) over a wide range of temperatures (Mathews and Haschemeyer, 1978) fell into three ranges:

1. At 17–30°C the Q_{10} value was 2·5, close to that stated for standard metabolic rates of temperate species
2. Over the range 7–17°C Q_{10} values were elevated to approximately 5
3. Below 7°C protein synthesis was inhibited

Results obtained on a number of other species (Smith and Haschemeyer, 1980) showed that the average liver protein synthetic rate in Antarctic fish is about double that expected on the basis of the $Q_{10} = 2·5$ line. In white muscle the protein synthetic rates of Antarctic fish were about three times those anticipated. Interestingly, values for rainbow trout white muscle were also elevated. The results support the view that in both Antarctic fish and rainbow trout (*Salmo gairdneri*) significant adaptation of muscle protein synthesis occurs.

ADAPTATION AT THE CELLULAR LEVEL

Enzymes

Although certain physical properties of solutes such as viscosity and diffusion (which do affect metabolic processes) are temperature dependent, metabolic adaptation to temperature is exercised in large measure via enzymatic processes.

Immediate adaptation of enzyme activity to a fall in temperature may occur, at least in part, as a consequence of an increase in enzyme–substrate affinity, that is the decrease in Michaelis constant, K_m, defined as that substrate concentration at which half maximal velocity is attained. Longer term adaptation to temperature (acclimation) may involve (i) turnover number, (ii) increase in enzyme concentration, (iii) formation of isoenzymes with different properties.

Within the body few enzymes function in the presence of saturating substrate concentrations; rates of activity are normally less, perhaps considerably less, than V_{max}. Such a system provides for metabolic responsiveness and control. Should an enhanced rate of enzymic activity be necessary, this might be achieved either by an increase in substrate concentration (control by K_m) or in response to the presence of regulating ligands (modulators). The system also provides a possible means of reducing the temperature sensitivity of enzyme reactions. Many enzymes from fish tissues show a direct relationship between K_m and assay temperature, K_m decreasing as assay temperature falls, so that when substrate concentrations are limiting the enzyme reaches a higher saturation state at lower temperatures and the fall in catalytic rate is less than would occur at nonlimiting substrate concentrations.

Direct effects of temperature on the substrate kinetics of glyceraldehyde-3-phosphate dehydrogenase from cod (*Gadus morhua*) muscle and of serine aminotransferase from rainbow trout liver are shown in Table 3. Many fish enzymes behave similarly over much of their ambient temperature range (Hazel and Prosser, 1974). As a

TABLE 3

THE VARIATION WITH TEMPERATURE OF K_m PHOSPHATE OF GLYCERALDEHYDE-3-PHOSPHATE DEHYDROGENASE FROM COD AND RABBIT MUSCLE AND OF K_m SERINE AND K_m PYRUVATE OF SERINE AMINOTRANSFERASE FROM RAINBOW TROUT LIVER

Temperature (°C)	K_m (mM^{-1})			
	Glyceraldehyde phosphate dehydrogenase		Serine aminotransferase	
	Cod	Rabbit	Serine	Pyruvate
5	0·71	0·18	2·4	0·14
10	–	–	6·1	0·16
15	1·25	0·54	8·1	0·21
25	2·77	2·17	10·0	0·28
30	–	–	17·5	0·59
35	4·50	3·33	–	–

result of this relationship, when enzyme reactions are measured at physiological substrate concentrations the decreased rate of catalysis at low temperatures is partially counteracted by the apparently enhanced affinity of enzyme for substrate. Thus the Q_5^{15} of the reaction catalysed by serine aminotransferase fell from 2·14 at 10 mM serine to 1·10 at 0·66 mM serine.

The temperature–K_m relationship ('positive thermal modulation') will be affected by the manner in which other parameters change, in particular

1. An increase in substrate concentration with temperature, if it occurs, will limit positive thermal modulation
2. Variations in intracellular pH that may occur with temperature, may also limit the change in K_m

Thus the observed alteration in K_m pyruvate of skeletal muscle lactate dehydrogenase from teleost fishes, a freshwater elasmobranch and rabbit measured at pH 7·4 were considerably dampened when the pH of the assays was varied in accordance with the normal variation of intracellular pH and body temperature of each species (Somero, 1978a).

The general applicability and importance of positive thermal modulation is uncertain at the present time, but it seems likely that some immediate compensation of metabolic rates to changing temperatures may be achieved through variations in K_m values. Two further points should be noted. First, if low temperature compensation via K_m proceeded to an extent that enzymic rates, especially those of regulatory enzymes, closely approached or reached V_{max}, the loss of regulatory sensitivity incurred would offset the advantages gained—K_m values, at least of regulatory enzymes, must be maintained within the range where regulation is effective (Somero, 1978b). Second, the temperature–K_m relationship is not unique to fish or even poikilotherms but is common to enzymes from homeotherms.

In a number of instances it has been shown that allosteric modulation of some enzyme reactions is affected by temperature change. Behrisch and Hochachka (1969) showed that K_i for AMP (adenosine monophosphate) inhibition of fructose diphosphatase from trout liver fell by a factor of 30 when assay temperature was reduced from 25 to 0°C, leading to a reduction of Q_{10} because the enzyme was not inhibited at the lower temperature. Sensitivity of enzyme–modulator interaction to temperature thereby provides a means of compensation;

at present such sensitivity appears to extend to only relatively few enzymes and appears not to have general applicability.

Modification of turnover number is currently regarded by several workers (e.g. Somero, 1978a,b) as the main factor in temperature acclimation (turnover number being moles product formed per minute per active centre in the enzyme molecule). The pattern of catalytic efficiency of homologous enzymes from warm- and cold-blooded animals is shown in Table 4. The V_{max} values for homologues are in inverse proportion to the functional temperature of the animal. Thus in the case of halibut (*Hippoglossus stenolepis*) and tuna (*Thunnus thynnus*) muscle lactate dehydrogenases, the V_{max} values at 5°C are almost three times those of the rabbit enzyme. At 35°C, the differences are much smaller due to the larger activation enthalpy of the rabbit muscle lactate dehydrogenase. Much the same applies to the data on glyceraldehyde-3-phosphate dehydrogenase (Cowey, 1967). Data of this type are also said to hold good for enzymes from cold-blooded animals adapted to different temperatures (Somero, 1978b).

TABLE 4

VALUES OF $V_{max}{}^a$ FOR ALDEHYDE OXIDATION BY GLYCERALDEHYDE-3-PHOSPHATE DEHYDROGENASE AND FOR PYRUVATE REDUCTION BY MUSCLE (M4) LACTATE DEHYDROGENASE OF DIFFERENT VERTEBRATES

Temperature (°C)	Glyceraldehyde-3-phosphate dehydrogenase		Muscle (M4) lactate dehydrogenase[b]			
	Rabbit	Cod	Halibut	Tuna	Chicken	Rabbit
5	6	19	355	355	168	95
15	22	50	–	–	–	–
25	88	118	–	–	–	–
35	180	225	1 826	1 846	1 184	958

[a] $V_{max} = \mu$moles substrate converted per minute per milligram of enzyme protein.
[b] Lactate dehydrogenase data are from Somero (1978a).

Modification of catalytic efficiency is bound to necessitate amino acid substitutions in the protein; these are unlikely to occur within an individual during a period of temperature acclimation. It is noticeable that differences in catalytic efficiency are present in virtually all comparisons of homologous enzymes between species. There is generally an identity of amino acid sequence around the active site of interspecific homologues, consequently amino acid substitution at other positions would seem capable of altering catalytic efficiency.

Somero (1978a,b) lists thermodynamic activation parameters of a number of homologous enzymes from different thermally adapted vertebrates. Activation free energy (ΔG) is lower for enzymes of the cold adapted species and a lowering of this free energy barrier would lead to an increase in reaction rate. Non-active site rate enhancement is seen by Somero as involving the formation and breakage of weak bonds (between amino acid side chains and peptide backbone linkages or between protein groups and water) during catalysis. According to Somero (1978a) 'these rate enhancing weak bonds need not occur at or near the active site to promote a reduction in ΔG'.

Although differences in catalytic efficiency are clearly important in temperature adaptation, a great deal more data on turnover numbers of homologous enzymes from different species is necessary before the general applicability of this mechanism can be evaluated.

Perhaps one of the most obvious ways in which an animal might adapt to change in body temperature is by increasing or decreasing cellular enzyme concentration. Unless an enzyme is equipped to function efficiently over a wide temperature range, however, there might be little to gain by increasing the concentration of enzymes (other than the formation of different isoenzymes) as a temperature compensating mechanism.

Several examples have now been identified of cold enzyme variants, induced in fish subjected to reduced environmental temperatures, of enzymes that were present in only small amounts (or even absent) in the warm acclimated state. Specific isoenzymes, with well defined thermal limits, in rainbow trout include, from brain, acetylcholine esterase (Baldwin and Hochachla, 1970) and, from liver, pyruvate kinase (Somero and Hochachka, 1968), citrate synthase (Hochachka and Lewis, 1970) and isocitrate dehydrogenase (Moon and Hochachka, 1972). Many of these enzymes exhibit a 'U'-shaped K_m–temperature curve, the minimum K_m corresponding to that environmental temperature at which that isoenzyme is quantitatively predominant. K_m values increase sharply both above and below the minimum K_m so that the enzyme functions only over a restricted temperature range corresponding approximately to the shallow horizontal part of the 'U'. Thus warm variants would not be effective in the cold and vice versa, and different isoenzymes would be required at different acclimation temperatures.

The behaviour of these isoenzymes is thus quite different from that of enzymes showing a linear dependence of K_m on assay temperature such as glyceraldehyde-3-phosphate dehydrogenase and serine aminotransferase mentioned earlier. The use of thermal enzyme variants would seem to be only one of a number of mechanisms used by eurythermal fish in temperature adaptation for, if this strategy were used over an extensive metabolic range, it would involve a wholesale biochemical restructuring of the animal to ensure that the 'correct' isoenzymes were present following changes in environmental temperature.

COMPOSITION OF MEMBRANE LIPIDS

Although a number of physiological changes occur in fish in response to alteration in environmental temperature, the only structural changes known to occur are in the fatty acid composition of lipids and especially of membrane lipids. Many data have established that there is an inverse relationship between the degree of unsaturation of membrane fatty acids and the environmental temperature at which the fish lives.

The functional integrity of biomembranes is related to the maintenance of an appropriate fluidity permitting, among other things, the movement of protein molecules within the lipid phase and this is dependent upon the existence of a particular liquid–crystalline phase. A fall in ambient temperature will tend to bring about a phase transition from liquid crystalline to gel leading to a loss of fluidity. Such changes would have serious consequences for the animal affecting many features of cellular activity (transport processes, activity of membrane-bound enzymes, oxidative phosphorylation and so on). The organism responds by increasing the proportion of unsaturated fatty acids present in the membrane thereby reducing the mesomeric transition temperature.

Temperature dependent changes in fatty acid composition of goldfish tissues have been described by many authors including Johnston and Roots (1964), Knipprath and Mead (1968), Kemp and Smith (1970), Miller *et al.* (1976). The most recent data is that of Hazel (1979) who examined the quantities of different phospholipids and the composition of fatty acids esterified to them in livers of rainbow trout acclimatised at 5 and 20°C. Hazel showed that there was an increase in size of the polyunsaturated fatty acid fraction of all types of phospholipid except lysolecithin in the 5°C trout; at the same time, amounts of saturated fatty acids decreased. The increase was mainly due to changes in $20:5(n-3)$, $20:3(n-3)$, $20:4(n-6)$ and $22:6(n-3)$; smaller amounts of $(n-9)$ fatty acids were found in the 5°C trout (Table 5).

TABLE 5

PROPORTIONS OF CERTAIN FATTY ACIDS (PER CENT BY WEIGHT) IN SOME LIVER PHOSPHATIDES OF RAINBOW TROUT ACCLIMATED TO 5 AND 20°C (DATA OF HAZEL, 1979)

Fatty acid	Total phospholipid		Phosphatidyl-choline		Phosphatidyl-ethanolamine	
	5°C	20°C	5°C	20°C	5°C	20°C
$18:1\,(n-9)$	12·75	14·67	12·39	14·26	18·01	18·74
$20:3\,(n-3)$	3·01	1·87	2·11	1·11	2·52	2·55
$20:4\,(n-6)$	3·24	2·63	0·99	0·93	4·31	3·54
$20:4\,(n-3)$	0·37	0·36	0·50	0·47	0·40	0·17
$20:5\,(n-3)$	4·06	2·24	3·35	2·72	8·46	2·34
$22:6\,(n-3)$	35·20	33·43	40·95	32·83	32·90	32·41

There was a marked positional distinction between fatty acids esterified in the phosphoglycerides. In both choline and ethanolamine phosphatides, over 95% of the polyunsaturated fatty acids are esterified in the 2-position; in phosphatidyl ethanolamine, saturated fatty acids, monoenes and most of the dienes are esterified at position 1; significant quantities of monoenes and dienes occurred in position 2 in phosphatidyl choline.

Neither cholesterol content nor phospholipid:cholesterol ratio were altered during temperature acclimation in rainbow trout.

The ability of fish to modify their membrane lipids in this way depends basically on an adequate supply of essential fatty acids in the diet either prior to or at the time of acclimation. For most fish this means a dietary source of $(n-3)$ fatty acids (Castell, 1979), and this requirement may be more demanding at lower temperatures. Some species, including salmonids, can themselves elongate the chain of and desaturate 18-carbon fatty acids such as linolenic acid to give polyunsaturated fatty acids such as $20:5(n-3)$ and $22:6(n-3)$. Other species, including many marine ones, lack this capacity (Owen et al., 1975; Cowey et al., 1976a,b) and long chain highly unsaturated fatty acids must be supplied preformed in the diet.

Conversely, warm water fish seem unlikely to be so demanding in their requirement for polyunsaturated fatty acids. Support for this thesis is evident in the findings of Stickney and Andrews (1972). They obtained very good growth of channel catfish at 30°C with diets containing 10% beef tallow as the sole source of lipid. This diet supplied high levels of saturated and monoenoic acids but only 0·2% of $18:2(n-6)$ and no $(n-3)$ acids.

TEMPERATURE AND GROWTH

Apart from food intake, to which growth rate is closely linked, the independent variables which bear heavily on growth rate are temperature and fish size. Consequently two of the principal studies at the whole animal level concerned with the effect of temperature on the growth of temperate water fish have done so by examining its influence on the relation between growth and ration (Brett *et al.*, 1969; Elliott, 1975*a,b*). A graph of this relation for sockeye salmon, *Oncorhynchus nerka* (Brett *et al.*, 1969) is shown in Fig. 2. From zero food intake and a negative growth rate the curve rises sharply with increasing food intake, the tangent to the curve drawn from the origin (zero food intake; zero ration) corresponds to the maximal ratio of growth to food consumption, i.e. the point at which gross conversion efficiency is highest and this has been termed the optimal ration. Maximum ration is obtained from the asymptote at which growth rate reaches a plateau. It may be noted that optimum ration is well below maximum ration.

The effect of temperature on this curve has been examined (Brett *et al.*, 1969) for small (13 g) sockeye salmon over the range 1–24°C (Fig. 3). At low temperatures (5°C) the curve is far to the left and compressed with relatively low weight loss in the absence of food, a small maintenance requirement and a growth plateau is attained at a low maximal weight gain. At 10°C (approaching the optimum for this species) the curve is markedly extended and has moved to the right with a large increase in maximum growth rate and an increased maintenance requirement. At temperatures (e.g. 20°C) above the optimum, maintenance requirements increase sharply while maximum growth rate declines, the curve takes on a sigmoid shape because fish that are underfed at this relatively high temperature expend energy searching for food giving a convex shape to the curve at low food intakes (Brett *et al.*, 1969).

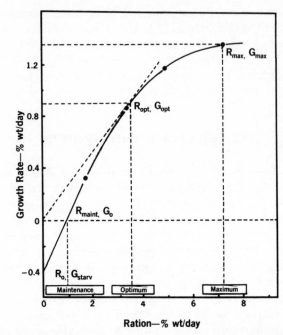

FIG. 2. Relationship between growth rate (G) and rate of food uptake (R) in young sockeye salmon (mean weight 13 g) at 10°C. The main parameters of the GR curve, with abbreviations are shown (reproduced with permission from Brett (1979)).

Thus the optimal temperature for growth is related to the food available. The effects of a reduction in ration level on the growth rate of brown trout (*Salmo trutta*) were determined by Elliott (1981) and are shown in Fig. 4; this species exhibits positive growth in the temperature range 4–19°C and the optimum temperature for growth (maximum ration) is about 13°C. As ration level is increased there is a corresponding increase both in the temperature range over which growth occurs and in the optimum temperature for maximum growth. Meaningful statements on optimum temperature should therefore specify ration size.

The relationships between maximal, optimal and maintenance rations and temperature for small (13 g) sockeye salmon (Brett *et al.*, 1969) are shown in Fig. 5. Maximal food intake increased from 3% body weight day^{-1} at 1°C to 8% body weight day^{-1} at 20°C, the rate of increase decreased with temperature, and a rapid decline occurred

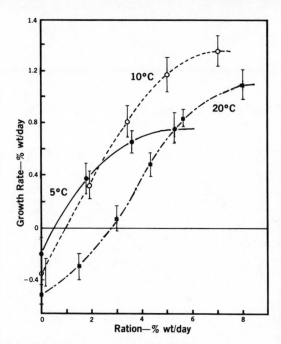

FIG. 3. Effect of temperature on the growth–ration curve for young sockeye salmon (mean weight 13 g); limits shown as ±2 S.E. Maintenance requirements occur at the point of intersection of each curve with the baseline for zero growth. The highest ration at each temperature approximates maximum ration providing a measure of the maximum growth rate (reproduced with permission from Brett (1979)).

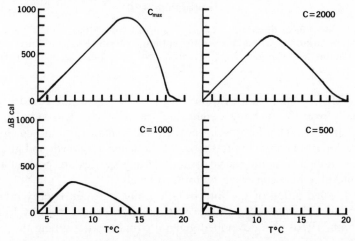

FIG. 4. Relationship between growth rate (increase in energy content (ΔB cal day^{-1})) and water temperature (T) for 50 g trout on maximum rations (C_{max} cal day^{-1}) and ration levels of 2000, 1000 and 500 cal day^{-1} (reproduced with permission from Elliott (1981)).

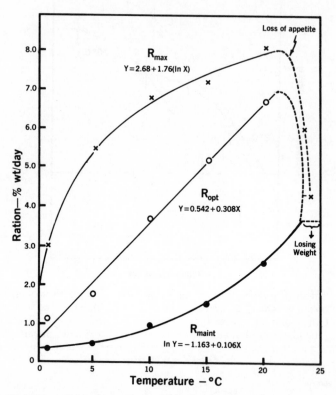

Fig. 5. Relation of different levels of ration to temperature. Upper curve for maximum ration (R_{max}) middle line for optimum ration (R_{opt}) and lower curve for maintenance ration (R_{maint}) (reproduced with permission from Brett (1979)).

above 20°C. Maintenance ration, on the other hand, increased exponentially from 0·3% body weight day^{-1} at 1°C to 3·7% body weight day^{-1} at 23°C. The difference between maintenance ration and maximal ration has been taken to represent *the scope for growth* and growth rates obtained over the thermal range of any species are governed by the interplay between these two ration levels.

A detailed study of the inter-relationships between energy intake, body size and water temperature was made on brown trout by Elliott (1975*a,b*; 1976) who developed general equations describing the relationship

$$Y = a W^{b_1 b_2 T}$$

where Y is either maximal energy intake (cal day^{-1}) or maintenance energy intake, W is live weight of fish (g), T is water temperature (°C) and a, b_1 and b_2 are constants over certain temperature ranges. From this equation Elliott (1981) was able to estimate maximum and maintenance energy intakes and thus the scope for growth of brown trout of 5–300 g in the temperature range 4–19°C. Some of Elliott's data is shown in Fig. 6 which shows that scope for growth increases with

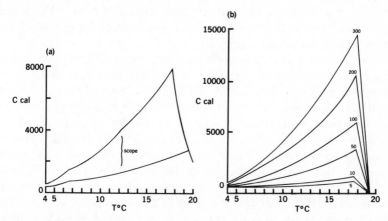

Fig. 6. (a) Relation between maximal food energy intake (upper curve), maintenance food energy intake (lower curve), scope for growth and temperature in brown trout of 100 g live weight. (b) Relationship between growth scope (C cal day^{-1}) and temperature for trout of different live weights (weight in grams) (reproduced with permission from Elliott (1981)).

temperature to a peak at about 18°C and then rapidly decreases. This optimum for growth scope differs from the optimal temperature for growth mainly because metabolic requirements and energy losses in waste products are also affected by temperature. In salmonids energy losses in faeces and excretory products respond in different ways to changes in temperature and energy intake so that there is less variation in overall energy lost than in either of its components. Thus as faecal energy losses increase as temperature decreases they also increase as the level of energy intake is increased; energy losses in excretory products (when expressed as a percentage of energy intake) increase with temperature and also increase when the level of energy intake decreases (Elliott, 1981).

Studies aimed at quantifying the partition of ingested energy have been carried out on a number of species of fish. Data obtained on carnivores given rations well above maintenance have been collected by Brett and Groves (1979) and gave an investment in growth of 29%. The overall mean values for the energy budget were

$$100I = (44 \pm 7)M + (29 \pm 6)G + (27 \pm 3)E$$

where I is energy ingested, M is metabolism, G growth and E excretion. Data from one of the most complete studies (Elliott, 1976) showed that most energy was available for growth at 13°C which corresponds precisely with the optimum temperature for growth of this species given maximum rations.

It was noted earlier that optimum ration (highest gross conversion efficiency) is well below maximum ration. The studies of Brett *et al.* (1969) on sockeye salmon and of Elliott (1975*a,b*; 1976) on brown trout have demonstrated that in both species the optimum temperature for gross conversion efficiency is less than that for maximal growth on maximal rations. In the case of sockeye salmon, maximal growth occurs at 15°C while gross conversion efficiency is highest in the range 11–12°C; the corresponding figures for brown trout are 13°C and 8–11°C. Thus in rearing temperate water fish a number of options concerning ration level and operating temperature are open and the choice depends on whether the aim is most rapid growth or most efficient growth.

LIGHT

Not only is sunlight essential for primary production in those cultivation systems that make use of natural food chains by nutrient fertilisation of pond water, but also the growth rate of fish may be affected by changes in quality, quantity or periodicity of light. In temperate regions light intensity and photoperiod change continuously as the seasons advance and the cycle of photoperiod occurs more or less in unison with temperature changes. Consequently, the effects of light on growth rates in nature may not easily be separated from those of temperature and season; experimentally the latter factors may modify effects obtained from different light regimes.

Several observations have indicated an effect of changing day length on growth rate in fish. Swift (1955) noted that the growth rate of brown trout increased in spring while water temperatures were still low, conversely, growth rate tended to decrease in autumn before any marked fall occurred in water temperature. Later Swift (1961) emphasised the distinction between the effect of day-to-day changes in day length and the effect of a constant daily photoperiod.

The importance of this distinction was verified by Gross *et al.* (1965) who examined the effect of photoperiod on growth of green sunfish held at constant temperature. A stimulating effect of increasing day length and an inhibitory effect of decreasing day length was demonstrated. A close correlation between seasonal changes in growth rate and day length was also found by Hogman (1968) in experiments with coregonids in which water temperature was partially controlled.

More recent studies on Pacific salmon fry (Clarke *et al.*, 1978) have shown that direction and rate of change of day length are the aspects of photoperiod that most affect growth. Good growth was obtained when the rate of change of day length approximated that occurring at the time of the equinox (at 50°N) but a rapidly accelerated increase in day length reduced weight gain; both constant long (20 h) photoperiod and decreasing day length were also conducive to rapid growth. The sensitivity of fry to photoperiod varied seasonally. Temperature interacted with photoperiod in such a way that the size of the fish at the end of the experimental photoperiod treatment was affected by the mean level of temperature over the course of the experiment rather than by the pattern of temperature used. Thus changes in growth rate resulting from particular photoperiod treatments were apparent sooner at higher temperatures, temperature directing the rate of physiological response.

Subsequent experiments have been directed toward exploiting sensitivity to photoperiod regime to accelerate growth and advance the time of smolting (Clarke, *et al.*, 1981). Species differed in their sensitivity to photoperiod adjustment and although hypo-osmoregulatory ability in sea water of coho salmon, *Oncorhynchus kisutch* (a species in which growth rate responds to a changing photoperiod) was influenced by photoperiod, none of the regimes used led to optimum osmoregulatory capacity being realised.

Other facets of fish physiology are affected by photoperiod, a case in point being gonad maturation. Functional maturity is sensitive to the light regime applied over a period of time prior to normal maturation. This sensitivity has been exploited by inducing off-season spawning in pink salmon (*O. gorbuscha*) through the application of particular photoperiod regimes in the early life history (MacQuarrie *et al.*, 1979).

Thus fertilised eggs are available several times a year—a significant advance in the cultivation of this species.

CONCLUDING REMARKS

Herbivorous animals are preferred subjects for cultivation because they utilise the primary production (vegetation) directly. In fish cultivation they offer the further advantage that they may be combined with other omnivorous and even carnivorous species in polyculture systems, thus utilising all the water column and occupying several ecological niches. As most of the known herbivorous species are warm water fish the tropics and subtropics are potentially the most promising areas for fish cultivation, even there herbivores seem mainly restricted to freshwater fish.

Although certain omnivorous species, e.g. carp, have a wide temperature tolerance and can be grown in temperate waters, these regions (especially the sea waters) are characteristically inhabited by carnivorous fish. Studies on oxygen consumption and properties of tissue enzymes indicate that these species are well adapted to their environment. The main structural demand for life in colder waters appears to be a high degree of unsaturation in membrane fatty acids. In dealing with the principal climatic factor affecting fish growth, namely temperature, strategies should be adopted that optimise desired features of performance. Temperature and ration size interact in a way that leave a number of options concerning ration level and temperatures open, and regimes may be adopted that will give either most rapid or most efficient growth. Finally, the neuroendocrine mechanisms that respond to photoperiod and mediate gonad maturation, growth and (in salmonids) smolting response may be exploited to promote cultivation of fish.

REFERENCES

Andrews, J. W. and Stickney, R. R. (1972). Interactions of feeding rates and environmental temperature on growth, food conversion and body composition of channel catfish. *Trans. Am. Fish. Soc.* **101,** 94–99.

Baldwin, J. and Hochachka, P. W. (1970). Functional significance of isozymes in thermal acclimation—acetylcholinesterase from trout brain. *Biochem. J.* **116,** 883–7.

Beamish, F. W. H. and Mookherji, P. S. (1964). Respiration of fishes with special emphasis on standard oxygen consumption. I. Influence of weight and temperature on respiration of goldfish, *Carrasius auratus* L. *Can. J. Zool.* **42,** 161–75.

Behrisch, H. W. and Hochachka, P. W. (1969). Temperature and the regulation of enzyme activity in poikilotherms—properties of rainbow trout fructose diphosphatase. *Biochem. J.* **115,** 287–93.

Brett, J. R. (1970). Temperature, fishes. In: *Marine Ecology*, Vol. 1, Part 1 (Ed. O. Kinne). John Wiley & Sons, New York, pp. 515–616.

Brett, J. R. (1979). Environmental factors and growth. In: *Fish Physiology. Vol. VIII, Bioenergetics and Growth* (Eds. W. S. Hoar, D. J. Randall and J. R. Brett). Academic Press, New York.

Brett, J. R. and Groves, T. D. D. (1979). Physiological energetics. In: *Fish Physiology, Vol. VIII, Bioenergetics and Growth* (Eds W. S. Hoar, D. J. Randall and J. R. Brett). Academic Press, New York, pp. 279–352.

Brett, J. R., Shelbourn, J. E. and Shoop, C. T. (1969). Growth rate and body composition of fingerling sockeye salmon, *Oncorhynchus nerka*, in relation to temperature and ration size. *J. Fish Res. Bd Canada* **26,** 2363–94.

Castell, J. D. (1979). Review of lipid requirements of finfish. In: *Finfish Nutrition and Fishfeed Technology*, Vol. 1 (Eds J. E. Halver and K. Tiews). H. Heenemann, GmbH & Co., Berlin, pp. 59–84.

Clarke, W. C., Shelbourn, J. E. and Brett, J. R. (1978). Growth and adaptation to seawater in underyearling sockeye (*Oncorhynchus nerka*) and coho (*O. kisutch*) salmon subjected to regimes of constant or changing temperature and daylength. *Can. J. Zool.* **56,** 2413–21.

Clarke, W. C., Shelbourn, J. E. and Brett, J. R. (1981). Effect of artificial photoperiod cycles, temperature and salinity on growth and smolting in underyearling coho (*Oncorhynchus kisutch*), chinook (*O. tshawytscha*) and sockeye (*O. nerka*) salmon. *Aquaculture* **22,** 105–16.

Cowey, C. B. (1967). Comparative studies on the activity of D-glyceraldehyde-3-phosphate dehydrogenase from cold- and warm-blooded animals with reference to temperature. *Comp. Biochem. Physiol.* **23,** 969–76.

Cowey, C. B., Adron, J. W., Owen, J. M. and Roberts, R. J. (1976a). The effect of different oils on tissue fatty acids and tissue pathology in turbot, *Scophthalmus maximus*. *Comp. Biochem. Physiol.* **53B,** 399–403.

Cowey, C. B., Owen, J. M., Adron, J. W. and Middleton, C. (1976b). Studies on the nutrition of marine flatfish. The effect of different dietary fatty acids on the growth and fatty acid composition of turbot (*Scophthalmus maximus*). *Br. J. Nutr.* **38,** 479–86.

Ege, R. and Krogh, A. (1914). On the relation between the temperature and the respiratory exchange in fishes. *Int. Rev. Gesamten Hydrobiologie Hydrog.* **1,** 48–55.

Elliott, J. M. (1975a). The growth rate of brown trout, *Salmo trutta* L., fed on maximum rations. *J. Animal Ecol.* **44,** 805–21.

Elliott, J. M. (1975b). The growth rate of brown trout (*Salmo trutta* L.) fed on reduced rations, *J. Animal Ecol.* **44,** 823–42.

Elliott, J. M. (1976). The energetics of feeding, metabolism and growth of brown trout (*Salmo trutta* L.) in relation to body weight, water temperature and ration size, *J. Animal Ecol.* **45,** 923–48.

Elliott, J. M. (1981). The effects of temperature and ration size on the growth and energetics of salmonids in captivity. *Comp. Biochem. Physiol.* In press.

Garlick, P. J., Burk, T. L. and Swick, R. W. (1976). Protein synthesis and RNA in tissues of the pig. *Am. J. Physiol.* **230**, 1108–12.

Gross, W. L., Roelofs, E. W. and Fromm, P. O. (1965). Influence of photoperiod on growth of green sunfish, *Lepomis cyanellus*. *J. Fish Res. Bd Canada* **22**, 1379–86.

Hazel, J. R. (1979). Influence of thermal acclimation on membrane lipid composition of rainbow trout liver. *Am. J. Physiol.* **236**, R91–R101.

Hazel, J. and Prosser, C. L. (1974). Molecular mechanisms of temperature compensation in poikilotherms. *Physiol. Rev.* **54**, 620–77.

Hochachka, P. W. and Lewis, J. K. (1970). Enzyme variants in thermal acclimation—trout liver citrate synthases. *J. biol. Chem.* **245**, 6567–73.

Hogman, W. J. (1968). Annulus formation on scales of four species of coregonids reared under artificial conditions. *J. Fish Res. Bd Canada* **25**, 2111–2.

Hokanson, K. E. F., Kleiner, C. F. and Thorsland, T. W. (1977). Effects of constant temperature and diet fluctuation on growth, mortality and yield of juvenile rainbow trout, *Salmo gairdneri* (Richardson). *J. Fish Res. Bd Canada* **34**, 639–48.

Holeton, G. F. (1974). Metabolic adaptation of polar fish: fact or artefact? *Physiol. Zool.* **47**, 137–52.

Johnston, P. V. and Roots, B. I. (1964). Brain lipid fatty acids and temperature acclimation. *Comp. Biochem. Physiol.* **11**, 303–9.

Kemp, P. and Smith, M. W. (1970). Effect of temperature acclimatization on the fatty acid composition of goldfish intestinal lipids. *Biochem. J.* **117**, 9–15.

Kinne, O. and Rosenthal, H. (1977). Cultivation of animals, commercial cultivation (aquaculture). In: *Marine Ecology*, Vol. 3, Part 3 (Ed. O. Kinne). John Wiley and Sons, New York, pp. 1321–97.

Knipprath, W. G. and Mead, J. F. (1968). The effect of environmental temperature on the fatty acid composition and on the *in vivo* incorporation of [1-¹⁴C] acetate in goldfish (*Carrasius auratus*). *Lipids* **3**, 121–8.

MacQuarrie, D. W., Vanstone, W. E. and Markert, J. R. (1979). Photoperiod induced off-season spawning of pink salmon (*Oncorhynchus gorbuscha*). *Aquaculture* **18**, 289–302.

Mathews, R. W. and Haschemeyer, A. E. V. (1978). Temperature dependency of protein synthesis in toadfish liver *in vivo*. *Comp. Biochem. Physiol.* **61B**, 479–84.

McCormick, J. H., Hokanson, K. E. F. and Jones, B. R. (1972). Effects of temperature on growth and survival of young brook trout *Salvelinus fontinalis*. *J. Fish Res. Bd Canada.* **29**, 1107–12.

Miller, N. G. A., Hill, M. W. and Smith, M. W. (1976). Positional and species analysis of membrane phospholipids extracted from goldfish adapted to different environmental temperatures. *Biochim. Biophys. Acta* **455**, 644–54.

Moon, T. W. and Hochachka, P. W. (1972). Temperature and enzyme activity in poikilotherms: isocitrate dehydrogenases in rainbow trout liver. *Biochem. J.* **123**, 695–705.

Nicholas, G. A., Lobley, G. E. and Harris, C. I. (1977). Use of the constant infusion technique for measuring rates of protein synthesis in the New Zealand white rabbit. *Br. J. Nutr.* **38**, 1–17.

Owen, J. M., Adron, J. W., Middleton, C. and Cowey, C. B. (1975). Elongation and desaturation of dietary fatty acids in turbot (*Scophthalmus maximus*) and rainbow trout (*Salmo gairdneri*). *Lipids* **10**, 528–31.

Scholander, P. F., Flagg, W., Walters, V. and Irving, L. (1953). Climatic adaptation in Arctic and tropical poikilotherms. *Physiol. Zool.* **26.** 67–92.

Smith, M. A. K. and Haschemeyer, A. E. V. (1980). Protein metabolism and cold adaptation in Antarctic fishes. *Physiol. Zool.* **53,** 373–82.

Somero, G. N. (1978*a*). Interacting effects of temperature and pressure on enzyme function and evolution in marine organisms. In: *Biochemical and Biophysical Perspectives in Marine Biology*, Vol. 4 (Eds D. C. Malins and J. R. Sargent). Academic Press, New York, pp. 1–27.

Somero, G. N. (1978*b*). Temperature adaptation of enzymes: biological optimization through structure–function compromises. *Ann. Rev. Ecol. Syst.* **9,** 1–29.

Somero, G. N. and Hochachka, P. W. (1968). The effect of temperature on the catalytic and regulatory functions of pyruvate kinases of the rainbow trout and the Antarctic fish, *Trematomus bernachii. Biochem. J.* **110,** 395–401.

Stickney, R. R. and Andrews, J. W. (1972). Effects of dietary lipids on growth, feed conversion, lipid and fatty acid composition of channel catfish. *J. Nutr.* **102,** 249–58.

Swift, D. R. (1955). Seasonal variations in the growth rate, thyroid gland activity and food reserves of brown trout (*Salmo trutta* L.) *J. Exp. Biol.* **32,** 751–64.

Swift, D. R. (1961). The annual growth rate cycle in brown trout (*Salmo trutta* L.) and its cause. *J. Exp. Biol.* **38,** 595–604.

Wohlschlag, D. E. (1960). Metabolism of the Antarctic fish and the phenomenon of cold adaptation. *Ecology* **41,** 287–92.

Discussion on Papers by R. Jones
and C. B. Cowey

Professor Taylor asked why there was such a very large increase in the catch of fish in the two decades between 1950 and 1970 and particularly what the geographical distribution of this was, to which *Mr Jones* replied that the increase in catch was simply a reflection of the increased size of the fishing fleets and technical changes in fishing methods and the discovery of new fishing grounds. By the 1970s all, or nearly all, major stocks of fish appeared to be fully exploited. *Professor Hawthorn* asked about the increased food needed to support the Iceland/Greenland cod, considering the relatively small differences in mean temperature. Was this a result of changes in the phytoplankton? *Mr Jones* observed that the cod was a species relatively high in the food chain and that there was no evidence that changes in phytoplankton were involved. The increase in the stock was primarily due to survival of the larvae that drifted towards Greenland. Most of the increase in stock took place at Greenland and the increased food needed to support these fish as adults would have had to come from Greenland waters.

Professor Heide asked whether anything was known about the photoperiodic response of fish with respect to spectral sensitivity to which *Mr Cowey* said that as far as he was aware no information was available on the special sensitivity of the fish used in the experiment, quoted. *Sir Kenneth Blaxter* asked why it was that it appeared that the chain lengths of fatty acids in the phospholipids increased as well as the unsaturation of the fatty acids of the phospholipids. One would expect an increase in melting point with chain elongation and a decrease with unsaturation. *Mr Cowey* stated that the major effect was an increase in unsaturation index and this would certainly lead to a decrease in melting point. Continuing, *Professor Morton* asked whether there were similar changes in fatty acid composition with respect to the depot fats,

213

to which *Mr Cowey* replied that there are some changes taking place in the depot fats but these are less striking than those taking place in the membrane phospholipids. There is a tendency to deplete the neutral lipids of highly unsaturated fatty acids and maintain the level in phospholipids when there is a fall in temperature or a decrease in dietary intake.

Effects of Climate on the Heat Exchanges of Man and Farm Animals

L. E. MOUNT

*ARC Institute of Animal Physiology, Babraham,
Cambridge, UK*

Man and his farm animals—cattle, sheep, pigs and poultry—are homeotherms. Homeothermy implies that when there are fluctuations in the thermal environment, the rate of metabolic heat production and the overall thermal insulation vary in such a way that the deep body temperature is regulated and tends to remain constant. In the cold, a homeotherm's metabolic rate increases, but in the poikilothermic animal, such as fish and reptiles, there is no cold-induced increase and body temperature falls, although behavioural responses diminish the effect. Homeotherms have much higher rates of heat production than poikilotherms, even when the body temperatures are equal. In the hot desert at 37°C, a mammal weighing 10 g would produce 3·5 times as much heat as a 10 g lizard, and a 10 kg mammal would produce nearly seven times as much heat as a 10 kg lizard, although in each case there is the same body temperature of 37°C (Templeton, 1970).

In northern temperate regions, thermoregulation is brought into play more usually as a result of cool conditions rather than of warm conditions, with environmental fluctuations leading to a varying demand for heat production that is additional to the minimal metabolic heat production that occurs under conditions of thermal neutrality. The zone of thermal neutrality is the range of environmental temperature throughout which heat production is at a minimum; this is a practical definition that has some limitations (Mount, 1974). The zone varies from species to species, and, within species, it varies mainly with plane of nutrition, body size and thermal insulation. The lower end of the zone is termed the critical temperature (*CT*); *CT* occupies a position of central importance in the animal's responses to its thermal

215

environment. When the environmental temperature falls below *CT*, the rate of metabolic heat production must increase if the deep body temperature is to be maintained. The upper end of the thermoneutral zone is termed the hyperthermic point; at environmental temperatures higher than this, heat dissipation, primarily by evaporative means through panting or sweating, is not sufficient to prevent a progressive rise in deep body temperature.

The implication of homeothermy for man and farm animals is that a certain quantity of food, usually a considerable amount, is required for maintenance. Growth rate in man is relatively slow, so that the maintenance requirement is a large part of the food intake even in children. Growth rates in young farm animals are high, compared with man, so that the maintenance requirement is a smaller part of the total food intake. Under cold conditions, below *CT*, heat loss (*H*) and the maintenance requirement increase, and the consequence is that the fraction of the metabolisable energy intake (*ME*) that is available for energy retention (*ER*) and growth is diminished, since $ME = H + ER$ (Mount, 1980). Man meets such conditions by increasing clothing and using shelter, but farm animals often have only limited possibilities available for avoiding harsh conditions. However, a high plane of nutrition and a coat of high thermal insulation together confer a marked degree of resistance to cold by effectively lowering *CT*, although in the absence of these factors farm animals are as susceptible as man to environmental fluctuations.

The rate at which metabolic heat is produced is therefore important in determining the use that is made of food for growth and consequently for animal production. This paper is concerned with factors in the animal and in its climatic environment that influence the metabolic rate, and with the effects of interactions between these factors. A more detailed and comprehensive account is given elsewhere (Mount, 1979).

FACTORS THAT INFLUENCE METABOLIC HEAT PRODUCTION

The principal factors that influence the metabolic rate in the healthy homeotherm are the plane of nutrition, environmental temperature, thermal insulation, physical activity, body size, age and 24-h periodicity. Initially, it is convenient to consider the climatic environment only in terms of the environmental temperature of a standardised environment; the several environmental components that in fact contribute to the thermal impact of climate, and the assessment of thermal environment, will be discussed later.

The inter-relations between metabolic rate, plane of nutrition, environmental temperature and thermal insulation are illustrated in Fig. 1, where the resulting variations in CT of a resting animal are shown diagrammatically. For a poorly insulated animal with thermal insulation R_1, CT is C_1 on a plane of nutrition PN_1. When PN_1 is increased to PN_2, CT falls to C_2. When the insulation increases from R_1 to R_2, and the animal is fed at PN_1, CT falls from C_1 to C_3. When PN_1 is then increased to PN_2, CT falls still further to C_4.

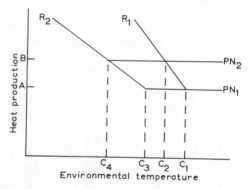

FIG. 1. Diagram of heat production against environmental temperature for a homeothermic animal of low (R_1) or high (R_2) thermal insulation, on a low (PN_1) or high (PN_2) plane of nutrition. C_1, C_2, C_3 and C_4 are the corresponding critical temperatures (Mount, 1976, by permission of Pitman).

The particular combination of plane of nutrition and thermal insulation thus determines both the metabolic rate and the temperature at which the resting animal begins to be affected by cold. In the cold, the metabolic heat flow that is required to maintain deep body temperature is inversely proportional to the animal's thermal insulation, which comprises both internal (tissue) and external insulations. CT can be lowered by increasing either the plane of nutrition or the thermal insulation. Raising the food intake from PN_1 to PN_2 gives an increment of heat production equal to AB which substitutes for what would otherwise be necessary thermoregulatory heat production if the food intake remained at PN_1 and the environmental temperature fell from C_1 to C_2.

The higher the plane of nutrition the lower is CT (Graham et al. 1959; Close and Mount, 1978), so that an animal on a high rather than a low food intake can be exposed to a greater fall in environmental temperature without raising its heat production, with a resulting diminution in cold stress. Thus the rate of metabolic heat production in the resting animal is determined primarily by the plane of nutrition in the zone of thermal neutrality and by the environmental temperature when this is less than CT. Group size affects CT by modifying the impact that the thermal environment makes on the individual animal; for the housed solitary pig fed 500 kJ kg^{-1} day^{-1} CT is 20°C, but it is 10°C for a housed group of nine pigs fed 620 kJ kg^{-1} day^{-1} (body weight 35 kg).

Raising the plane of nutrition also lowers the temperature of the hyperthermic point (Fig. 2) so that the zone of minimal metabolism

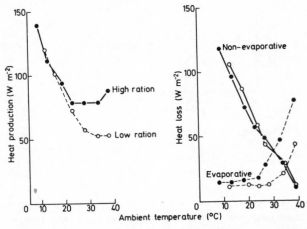

FIG. 2. Heat production and heat loss at various environmental temperatures in one closely clipped sheep during periods on a high ration (●) and a low ration (○) (reproduced from Alexander, 1974).

itself is shifted downwards along the temperature axis as the plane of nutrition increases. This means that a temperature that is within the thermoneutral zone for a given level of feeding may be either above or below the zone when the level is changed. One result of this, for animal production, is that animals on high planes of nutrition approach maximum productivity at temperatures below the optimal temperatures needed by animals on low planes. Keeping animals on high food intakes at high temperatures makes it difficult for the extra heat produced to be dissipated and may lead to a tendency to hyperthermia.

The animal indicates its preferences for a lower environmental temperature when the plane of nutrition is high. When pigs kept at 10°C were trained to switch on a bank of infra-red heaters for a short period at a time, so that they could control their thermal environment, they chose to receive 300 periods of heating per hour when they were given 400 g food per day. However, when they were fed 900 g food per day they took only 200 periods of heat per hour (Baldwin and Ingram, 1968).

The actual temperatures that apply vary widely with species and body size. The lower temperature limits in still air that can be met by metabolic response and the upper limits that can be met by heat dissipation, together with critical temperatures, are given in Table 1 for

TABLE 1

CRITICAL TEMPERATURES AND APPROXIMATE COLD AND HOT ENVIRONMENTAL LIMITS FOR THERMOREGULATION, UNDER STILL AIR CONDITIONS, FOR THE NEWBORN AND MATURE OF UNCLOTHED MAN, PIG AND LONG-HAIRED SHEEP (AFTER MOUNT, 1979)

	Critical temperature (°C)	Cold limit	Hot limit
Man			
newborn	33	27	37
mature	28	14	43
Pig			
newborn	34	0	36
mature	10	−50	30
Sheep			
newborn	30	−100	40
mature	−20	−200	40

man, pig and sheep, both newborn and mature. These species illustrate a remarkable range in cold limit, from +27°C for the human infant to a calculated value of −200°C (or even lower) for the mature long-haired sheep; even the almost hairless newborn pig has a cold limit as low as 0°C. The thermoneutral zone above 28°C for nude man typifies him as a tropical animal, whereas thermal neutrality for the sheep includes the temperatures of most habitable areas of the earth, in accordance with the widespread distribution of that species. However, these temperatures refer to still-air conditions; wind and precipitation raise CT considerably, an aspect that is discussed later. The hot limits for the three species are much closer together; the exceptional value is the relatively low hot limit for the mature pig, which is due to that animal's inability to sweat or pant effectively.

Non-shivering thermogenesis

The regulation of body temperature in the cold requires heat production additional to that from resting metabolism in a thermoneutral environment. The additional heat can be derived from muscular work, shivering, or non-shivering thermogenesis (NST). NST is the liberation of metabolic heat by processes that do not involve muscular contraction. It is of great significance for the newborn mammal, reaching a level of two to three times the minimal metabolism; it declines as the animal grows older. NST is associated with the calorigenic action of noradrenaline, and is more pronounced in smaller animals than in larger ones (Heldmaier, 1971). Adaptation to cold in small mammals appears to depend considerably on NST, requiring increased food consumption. Larger animals adapt to cold by increasing the insulation of the coat, an adaptation that is not so effective in the smaller animal. The effect of plane of nutrition on heat production is also by definition a form of NST, often discussed as diet-induced thermogenesis.

Brown fat is recognised as an important source of NST, although NST also occurs in other tissues, particularly skeletal muscle. About two-thirds of NST can arise in brown fat in the newborn rabbit, for example, where the temperature of the site of heat production in brown adipose tissue may be 2–3°C higher than colonic temperature (Hull, 1973; Jansky, 1973).

Physical activity

Heat produced by exercise substitutes for thermoregulatory heat that is produced by shivering and NST in the cold, although exercise decreases thermal insulation through movement and consequently loses some of its thermoregulatory value.

Very high levels of metabolic rate are achieved by activity, as in running mammals and flying birds, sometimes over short periods, and then the requirement is for heat dissipation rather than conservation. Taylor (1974) has calculated the metabolic rates of animals running at their top speeds. He finds that, for the short periods that the maximum effort is made, both small animals (such as mice) and large animals (horses and elephants) can increase their metabolism up to 20 times, whereas animals of intermediate size (dog, cheetah and gazelle) can increase their resting metabolic rate by a remarkable 40- to 60-fold. The cheetah achieves a calculated 54-fold increase in heat production, albeit for only a short time, when pursuing its prey. The energy cost of running in man is high compared with the cost in mammals of corresponding body size.

Body size

The relation of metabolic rate to body size has been the subject of diverse interpretations and much controversy. Following the postulation by Sarrus and Rameaux (1839) that an animal's metabolic rate is proportional to its surface area, the use of surface area as the metabolic reference base for body size became widespread, because the rate expressed per square metre gave a very much less variable quantity for animals of different species ranging widely in body weight than when the rate was expressed per kilogram (Voit, 1901). Later, empirical relations between metabolic rate (M) and body weight (W) were examined using the allometric equation $M = aW^b$ (Huxley, 1932), which has the merit that in its log–log form the linear slope gives the exponent b and the intercept the coefficient a. Following the extensive series of species studied by Benedict (1938), both Brody (1945) and Kleiber (1932, 1975) pursued the question of a generally applicable value that could be given to the exponent b, and reached 0·73 and 0·75 respectively. The exponent appropriate to the 'surface area law' is 0·67, at least for animals of similar shape, and the variation is such that it is often difficult to attach significance to deviations between 0·67 and 0·75, with correspondingly less distinction between 0·73 and 0·75.

The general conclusion is that metabolic rate is usually proportional to body weight raised to a power less than unity when several species of animals are pooled in the same investigation, and the interspecific value now most often used is 0·75. Kleiber (1975) gives 3·4 W kg$^{-0.75}$

as the mean value for fasting metabolic rate derived from a number of species. Fasting metabolism has been measured as $2 \cdot 7 \text{ W kg}^{-0 \cdot 75}$ in wether sheep (Blaxter, 1967), $4 \cdot 2 \text{ W kg}^{-0 \cdot 75}$ in cattle (Blaxter and Wainman, 1966) and $4 \cdot 4 \text{ W kg}^{-0 \cdot 75}$ in pigs (Close and Mount, 1975). In the pig, metabolism rises to $7–12 \text{ W kg}^{-0 \cdot 75}$ in fed animals depending on the plane of nutrition (Close and Mount, 1978). As a general approximation for fed animals, metabolic rates are $5 \text{ W kg}^{-0 \cdot 75}$ in sheep, $6 \text{ W kg}^{-0 \cdot 75}$ in cattle and $7 \text{ W kg}^{-0 \cdot 75}$ in pigs.

The expression W^b is termed the metabolic body size, and appropriate choice of b for a given set of results leads to proportionality of metabolic rate to this function of body weight. Since b is usually less than unity, the ratio of metabolic rate to body weight usually falls as body weight increases. The value to be given to b for investigations within one species is not necessarily the interspecific value $0 \cdot 75$, although this is sometimes used. The effect of plane of nutrition on metabolic rate could be incorporated in the coefficient a, which would be higher on a higher plane of nutrition but would leave the exponent b unchanged. An alternative approach is to relate metabolic rate to the sum of separate effects due to plane of nutrition and body weight.

Age

A large part of the effect of age on metabolic rate is due to the effects of increasing body size that is consequent on growth. Metabolic rate per kilogram declines as the animal becomes larger, although the exponent b of the metabolic body size is closer to unity in the newborn than it is in the older animal. The smaller thermal insulation of the young animal, with less subcutaneous fat and coat, coupled with the smaller body size, leads to a relatively high value for CT in the young.

However, there are effects of age on metabolic rate, distinct from the effects of body size, that are discernible in the newborn and in the elderly. In the newborn pig, for example, the thermoneutral metabolic rate rises during the first postnatal day, and corresponding effects have been demonstrated in all those mammalian species where it has been sought (Mount, 1979). In the elderly subject, metabolic rate is lower than in younger people, regardless of how it is expressed (e.g. per kilogram or per square metre), and this contributes to the tendency to hypothermia that is evident amongst older people (Kleiber, 1975; Fox et al., 1973).

24-Hourly variation

A diurnal mammal like a pig or a man has a higher metabolic rate, body temperature and activity during daylight than during the night; the resting pig's daytime metabolic rate maximum is about 30% higher than the minimum rate at night. For nocturnal mammals, such as the mouse, these quantities reach their maxima during the night. 24-Hourly variations are important in the estimation of an animal's heat production, because short-term measurements of metabolic rate made over 1 or 2 h may not only be unrepresentative of the mean 24-h value but may also, if made at different times of day, suggest differences that may be thought of as due to experimental treatment when they are instead due to 24-h variation.

In experiments on energy balance, full 24-h determinations of heat production are obviously essential. Heat storage effects due to changes in body temperature are minimised by measurements of 24-h duration, not only because any given heat storage, when expressed as a rate over a period, becomes progressively smaller as the duration of measurement increases, but also because both the beginning and end of the measurement period are in the same phase of the 24-h cycle of the animal's metabolism and body temperature.

ENVIRONMENTAL FACTORS THAT INFLUENCE METABOLIC HEAT PRODUCTION

Air temperature, wind, humidity, mean radiant temperature and solar radiation are the principal factors that affect the heat balance that is struck between an animal's heat production and its loss of heat to the environment. The balance is accomplished by heat transfer through the four channels of radiation, convection, conduction and evaporation, the characteristics of which are given in Table 2. The combination of non-evaporative and evaporative heat losses that match heat production is shown in Fig. 3; at lower temperatures, non-evaporative heat loss dominates, whereas above CT evaporative heat loss becomes increasingly important.

Under cool conditions, the net heat flow is from the animal through each channel, but under warmer conditions there may be a heat gain by the animal through one or more channels (e.g. by radiation at high radiant temperatures, or by convection at high air temperatures)

TABLE 2

FACTORS THAT INFLUENCE THE DIFFERENT MODES OF HEAT TRANSFER BETWEEN ORGANISM AND ENVIRONMENT (AFTER INGRAM AND MOUNT, 1975; COURTESY OF SPRINGER-VERLAG)

Mode of transfer	Animal characteristics	Environmental characteristics
Radiant	Mean radiant temperature of surface; effective radiating area; reflectivity and emissivity	Mean radiant temperature; solar radiation and reflectivity of surroundings
Convective	Surface temperature; effective convective area; radius of curvature and surface type	Air temperature; air velocity and direction
Conductive	Surface temperature; effective contact area	Floor temperature; thermal conductivity and thermal capacity of solid material
Evaporative	Surface temperature; percentage wetted area; site of evaporation relative to skin surface	Humidity; air velocity and direction

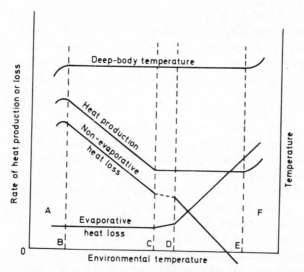

FIG. 3. Diagrammatic representation of relations between heat production, evaporative and non-evaporative heat loss and deep-body temperature in a homeothermic animal. A, zone of hypothermia; B, temperature of summit metabolism and incipient hypothermia; C, critical temperature, CT; D, temperature of marked increase in evaporative loss; E, temperature of incipient hyperthermal rise; F, zone of hyperthermia; CD, zone of least thermoregulatory effort; CE, zone of minimal metabolism; BE, thermoregulatory range (after Mount, 1974).

counter-balanced by an evaporative heat loss that is increased by the dissipation of the additional environment heat load. The quantities in Table 2 can be incorporated into heat transfer coefficients that give heat transfer rates per unit temperature difference or vapour pressure difference between animal and environment. The contribution made by each channel to heat exchange can be considered separately; more extensive accounts than the following are given elsewhere (Monteith, 1973; Mount, 1979).

Radiation

The Stefan–Boltzmann Law for total radiation from a perfectly black body is given by

$$H_r = \sigma A T^4$$

where H_r = heat transfer rate by radiation; σ = the Stefan–Boltzmann constant, $5 \cdot 67 \times 10^{-8} \, \text{W m}^{-2} \, \text{K}^{-4}$; $A =$ effective radiating area of the body; and $T =$ absolute temperature of the radiating surface. This is the one-way radiation from a given body; what is required in practice is the net radiant exchange, which is the difference between the radiant energy leaving the body and the radiant energy entering it from the environment.

Before formulating an equation to give the net radiant exchange, account must be taken of the deviation of radiating surfaces from the perfectly black body referred to in stating the Stefan–Boltzmann Law. This is done by introducing into the equation values for the emissivities of the exchanging surfaces. Emissivity has a maximum value of unity, and this is the value for a perfectly black opaque body, which reflects none of the incident radiation but absorbs all of it. A perfectly opaque reflector, on the other hand, has an emissivity of zero; it reflects all incident radiation and absorbs none of it.

Emissivity varies with the wavelength of the radiation used. For short-wave solar radiation many surfaces, including white paint and pale-coloured animal coats, have a high reflectance. For long-wave radiation (of wavelength greater than $3 \, \mu\text{m}$), however, most surfaces, including white paint, white coats and pale skin, have an emissivity that approaches unity. Thus for short-wave radiation the reflectance is dependent on colour, whereas for long-wave it is independent of colour.

When the emissivity (ε) is taken into account, the statement for total radiation from a body becomes

$$H_r = \varepsilon \sigma A T^4$$

and H_{rnet} (the radiant heat exchange resulting from the algebraic summation of incoming and outgoing radiation) is given by

$$H_{\text{rnet}} = \sigma A (\varepsilon_1 T_1^4 - \varepsilon_2 T_2^4)$$

where subscript 1 refers to the body and subscript 2 to the surroundings. This expression has been reformulated in various ways for practical use (Jakob, 1957). For a given situation, $H_{\text{rnet}} = F \sigma A_1 (T_1^4 - T_2^4)$ can be used, where F is termed the radiative interchange factor which takes account of both the configuration and the emissivities of the surfaces.

For small differences of temperature, the fourth-power relation of the Stefan–Boltzmann Law can be replaced by a first-power law as an approximation. The heat transfer coefficients for long-wave exchange,

K_R, is then given by $4\sigma T^3$, where σ is the Stefan–Boltzmann constant $(5\cdot67\times10^{-8}\,\mathrm{W\,m^{-2}\,K^{-4}})$ and T is the mean absolute temperature (Kleiber, 1975). From this, when $T = 295\,\mathrm{K}$ $(22°C)$, $K_R = 5\cdot8\,\mathrm{W\,m^{-2}°C^{-1}}$; and at $305\,K$, $K_R = 6\cdot4\,\mathrm{W\,m^{-2}°C^{-1}}$. For a mean radiant environmental temperature of 15–20°C, and a surface (skin or coat) temperature of 30–35°C, K_R is thus close to $6\,\mathrm{W\,m^{-2}°C^{-1}}$. The temperatures for this purpose are the black-body temperatures.

The animal out of doors receives short-wave radiant energy in three ways: directly from the sun, as a diffuse solar radiation due to scattering in the atmosphere, and by reflection from the ground surface. In bright sunlight, the solar radiation intercepted by an animal may be several times the metabolic heat production. White coats reflect more than half the incident solar radiation, and dark coats absorb most of it, so that differences in reflectance can have large effects on the size of the environmental heat load that an animal has to bear. Radiation falling on the coat may be reflected, absorbed, or transmitted by forward scatter towards the skin; radiation penetration is greater in white than in dark coats, and depends on the density of the coat (Cena and Monteith, 1976).

The long-wave radiant energy exchange of an animal out of doors is with the ground, surrounding objects and the atmosphere. When the mean radiant temperature differs from the air temperature, that part of the radiant heat exchange that is associated with the difference is termed the effective radiant flux (ERF). ERF is given by the product of the radiation heat transfer coefficient and the difference between the mean radiant and air temperatures; it is a measure of the thermal effect due to the difference between these two temperatures (Gagge, 1970).

Convection

The convective movement of air around an object, and the consequent transfer of heat, is either primarily forced, as when the air is moved by a fan, or natural, when it is due to a temperature difference between the air and the object that produces air movement as the result of density changes in the air.

Forced convection dominates when wind impinges on a body; natural convection dominates in still air or at low wind speeds. Kerslake (1972) comments that for man forced convective heat transfer predominates at wind speeds above $0\cdot2\,\mathrm{m\,s^{-1}}$, and natural convection at lower wind speeds. The position is similar for the pig, where for animals of 4–60 kg, forced convection dominates above $0{\cdot}2\,\mathrm{m\,s^{-1}}$ and natural convection below $0{\cdot}1\,\mathrm{m\,s^{-1}}$, with a regimen of mixed convection between $0{\cdot}1$ and $0{\cdot}2\,\mathrm{m\,s^{-1}}$. The forced convection coefficient at a wind speed of $0{\cdot}2\,\mathrm{m\,s^{-1}}$ is $3\,\mathrm{W\,m^{-2}\,^{\circ}C^{-1}}$ for the 60-kg pig and $5\,\mathrm{W\,m^{-2}\,^{\circ}C^{-1}}$ for the 4-kg pig, increasing to 5 and $8\,\mathrm{W\,m^{-2}\,^{\circ}C^{-1}}$ at a wind speed of $0{\cdot}5\,\mathrm{m\,s^{-1}}$. The natural convection coefficients are approximately $3\text{--}4\,\mathrm{W\,m^{-2}\,^{\circ}C^{-1}}$ at environmental temperatures of 20–30°C (Mount, 1977).

The convection coefficients are therefore of the same order of magnitude as the $6\,\mathrm{W\,m^{-2}\,^{\circ}C^{-1}}$ that is often taken as the mean value for the radiation coefficient. For an environment where the air and mean radiant temperatures are equal to each other, this implies that the heat transfer rates by convection and radiation are approximately equal, when conditions are those of still air or low wind speed. Measurements made on pigs bear this out (Mount, 1964).

Conduction

Although heat transfer by conduction through contact with solid surfaces is not usually important for man, it can assume considerable proportions for animals that lie on the ground or on the floors of buildings and enclosures, depending on the thermal diffusivity of the floor.

Heat loss from the pig to an insulated floor is often about equivalent per unit area to that lost from the free surface by radiation and convection (Mount, 1968). A sheep living on cold, poorly insulated ground may dissipate up to 30% of its minimum heat production by conduction (Gatenby, 1977), which is comparable with the heat loss per unit area from the free surface even under these conditions.

Evaporation

Evaporative cooling takes place either on the skin or on the mucosal surface of the upper respiratory tract. The preponderance of the site of cooling varies with species, but in both cases vaporisation of water on the surface leads to cooling of the blood flowing in the immediately underlying tissue, whether sweating or panting is involved. The water that evaporates on the skin comes from sweat secreted by the sweat glands in the skin, or sometimes, as in the pig, from the surroundings.

Man can sweat at a higher rate than any other mammal, and so through evaporative cooling can maintain a normal body temperature in hot environments (Ingram and Mount, 1975).

Panting consists of shallow, rapid respiratory movements that greatly increase the movement of air to and fro in the upper respiratory tract, leading to a corresponding increase in evaporative cooling. The tidal air is small; the importance of this lies in the small effect that panting has on pulmonary ventilation, so that there is no excessive loss of carbon dioxide and consequently little effect on the acid–base equilibrium in the form of a respiratory alkalosis (Hales, 1976). Pigs and sheep show increased respiratory frequency under hot conditions; cattle also show this response although they are more capable of sweating than sheep. The increases in the respiratory minute volume during panting range from 10-fold in the ox to 12-fold in the sheep, 15-fold in the rabbit, and to 23-fold in the dog. Some birds also pant and flutter the gular pouch at resonant frequencies. In birds, as in mammals, the increase in respiratory rate during panting is accompanied by a reduction in tidal volume (Richards, 1970). The tendency is for panting to occur in animals that have relatively low sweating capabilities (Bianca, 1968).

ANIMAL–ENVIRONMENT INTERACTIONS THAT INFLUENCE METABOLIC HEAT PRODUCTION

The impact of variations in climatic components out of doors is readily apparent from the effects of wind, rain and sun; the effect of wind on the thermal insulation of sheep is shown in Fig. 4. Rain increases heat production in both sheep and cattle, with greater effects on those animals with short coats or short fleeces (Blaxter et al., 1964). The behaviour of man and animals in orientating themselves in relation to the sun, and in adopting various postures, produces a considerable variation in the incident load of solar radiation. The projected areas for male and female subjects exposed to the sun range from 5 to 25% of the total body surface area, depending on the altitude and direction of the sun (Underwood and Ward, 1966).

The extent to which different combinations of the several components of the thermal environment influence an animal's heat loss is illustrated by variations in the critical air temperature for livestock exposed to different sets of conditions. A well fed beef cow in dry,

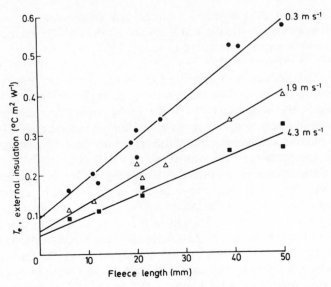

Fig. 4. The effect of wind speed on the external insulation of sheep with different fleece lengths (reproduced from Alexander, 1974, by permission of Butterworths).

calm weather with sunshine has a critical air temperature of $-21°C$, whereas when it is exposed to overcast conditions, rain and a wind of $4·5 \, m \, s^{-1}$, the critical temperature is $+2°C$ (Webster, 1974). For sheep with 100 mm fleece depth, Alexander (1974) has calculated that the critical temperature is about 0°C in still air, rising to about 23°C in a wind of $7 \, m \, s^{-1}$. The critical temperature is affected by the type of floor and bedding; in a group of 40-kg pigs it is $11·5–13°C$ on straw, $14–15°C$ on asphalt and $19–20°C$ on concrete slats (Verstegen and van der Hel, 1974). These figures give some measure of the increase in air temperature that is required to compensate for increased heat loss through evaporation, convection and conduction.

Effects of weather on livestock

The effects of weather on farm livestock can be considered in terms of the acute responses that animals make to acute changes in atmospheric conditions either acting directly on the animals or affecting the houses in which they live. In the UK, the main concern is with the effects of cold, which under field conditions is nearly always associated with a relative lack of food, added to which the greatest direct effect of low temperature is to increase the energy requirement that must be met in the food intake (Blaxter, 1962). Livestock production in the UK is rarely affected by very hot weather.

The exposure of animals to weather demands rapidly occurring physiological and behavioural responses to fluctuations in air temperature, wind, radiation and precipitation that may occur from minute to minute and may be of considerable magnitude. The implication of the exposure of an animal to fluctuations in its thermal environment is that short-term thermoregulatory responses are called into play, for example due to wind and rain or variations in solar radiation. The degree to which such responses occur, including peripheral vasoconstriction, pilo-erection, sweating, panting and behavioural responses, varies mainly with the size and thermal insulation of the animal. Large, well insulated animals, such as cattle, are relatively indifferent to thermal environment over a wide range; small, poorly insulated animals, such as the newborn pig, are highly susceptible to thermal variations and show correspondingly greater physiological, metabolic and behavioural responses. Climate, as distinct from weather, provides the long-term baseline of metabolic, insulative and morphological adaptations (Mount, 1979). Livestock are adapted to climate, but they have to respond to short-term variations in weather.

The direct impact of weather on farm animals depends on whether they are housed or not; cattle and sheep are usually out of doors, pigs and poultry are indoors. Knowledge of the responses of animals that live wholly or partly out of doors allows the determination of limiting conditions and indicates when shelter must be provided. When animals are housed, and particularly when they are given bedding, their own metabolic heat production can lead to a considerable warming of their micro-environment. Both cattle and sheep can tolerate both hot and cold conditions, although the newborn are more susceptible to cold and the sheep is cold-exposed following shearing. Whereas cattle and sheep are resistant to cold, goats tend to be cold-sensitive (Jessen, 1977).

Cattle

Cattle live in many different climates, but they are essentially cold-tolerant animals, a characteristic that is shared by both the mature and to some degree the newborn (Webster, 1974; 1978). However, under Canadian winter conditions Milligan and Christison (1974) have found that daily weight gain is adversely affected even when bedding and shelter are available. None the less, pregnant beef cows can be wintered satisfactorily in the far north (Pringle and Tsukamoto, 1974), although the digestibility of food is reduced in calves and steers exposed to low winter temperatures (Christopherson, 1976). In some parts of the UK, cattle are kept in yards to avoid poaching of pasture rather than to shield them from low temperatures (Duckham, 1963).

In veal calves, neither the growth rate nor the metabolic heat production is affected by air temperature in the range 5 to 20°C. The animals adapt to their environments mainly through variations in evaporative heat loss from the skin and respiratory tract (Webster *et al.*, 1976). Beef and dairy type calves receive less food, produce less heat and are less cold-tolerant than veal calves, but the critical temperature is still as low as 8 to 10°C (Webster *et al.*, 1978). From measurements of oxygen consumption under conditions of variable wind speed and simulated rain, it can be concluded that the heat production of young calves is increased both by wind and by rain, with an additive effect (Holmes and McLean, 1975).

In a temperate climate, the newborn unfed calf is more likely to be exposed to conditions corresponding to those below rather than in its zone of thermal neutrality, in which its metabolic rate would be at a minimum. The lactating cow fed on a high plane of nutrition is more likely to be above thermal neutrality, although in dry air thermal neutrality in cattle can extend to the level of the body temperature. Investigations into the thermal relations of cattle have been the subject of several reviews, e.g. McDowell (1972), Brown and Hutchinson (1973), Webster (1974; 1978) and Thompson (1979).

Sheep

In sheep, the combination of the high thermal insulation of the fleece ($0 \cdot 023$°C m^2 W^{-1} per millimetre depth in the Merino (Bennett and Hutchinson, 1964)) and a high cold-induced metabolic rate (Bennett, 1972) produces considerable resistance to cold. Calculated environmental temperatures at which heat loss would equal maximum metabolic rate are as low as -100°C for long-coated lambs in still air (maximum metabolism 20 W kg^{-1}), and even -120°C for mature sheep with 100 mm fleece in a wind of 7 m s^{-1} (Alexander, 1974).

Although the high insulation of the fleece normally leads to a low critical temperature, this can rise to about 28°C when the sheep is shorn to a fleece length of 7 mm, making the shorn sheep cold-susceptible (Alexander, 1974). At 15°C, the heat production of a shorn sheep is increased by 50%, whereas the heat production of a sheep with a 10 cm fleece is not measurably affected by temperatures down to 12°C (Blaxter et al., 1957; Blaxter, 1958). The environmental demand for heat production by a sheep with a 10 mm fleece exposed under dry conditions to a wind of $0.3\,\mathrm{m\,s}^{-1}$ at 10°C is less than half the demand imposed by rain and a wind of $4.5\,\mathrm{m\,s}^{-1}$ at 0°C (Blaxter, 1964). Animals that are in poor condition are particularly susceptible to the cold exposure produced by shearing, and they may die (Brown and Hutchinson, 1973). The rise in metabolic rate due to the removal of insulation by shearing in cold weather can lead to negative energy balance, although shorn sheep take in more food than unshorn sheep for each hour of grazing (Arnold and Birrell, 1977). Shorn sheep exposed to cold develop acclimatisation that takes the form of increased resistance to cooling and increased skin temperature on the extremities (Slee, 1974; Donnelly et al., 1974).

The mortality of lambs on British farms varies from 1 to 20% in moderate seasons, rising to over 40% on hill farms in severe conditions, with total annual losses in Britain probably ranging from 1·5 to 4 million. Behavioural and nutritional factors are important in addition to weather, and there are variations between breeds in their resistance to hypothermia due to rain, wind and cold (Wiener et al., 1973; Slee, 1979). In the newborn lamb exposed to cold, the fall in rectal temperature that occurs is related to the breed: Scottish Blackface, Cheviot and Soay lambs show only small falls, whereas Merino and Finnish Landrace show more marked falls soon after birth (Sykes et al., 1976; Slee, 1978). High rates of heat loss that can lead to the death of newborn lambs are due to low air temperature, wind and wetting of the coat. Of these factors, wetting of the coat can have the most dramatic effects on heat loss, being equivalent to a fall in temperature of up to 20°C. Under tranquil conditions, temperatures must be below -10°C if dry lambs are to be exposed to hazard; however, wet lambs may be in danger in winds of $4.5\,\mathrm{m\,s}^{-1}$ although the temperature may be as high as 20°C. Mortality under adverse weather conditions is about three times as high in small lambs weighing less than 3 kg than it is in lambs of 3–5 kg, and mortality is related to the demand on the animal to produce metabolic heat (Starr, 1980).

Both wind speed and rainfall in the first 6 h after birth are related to lamb mortality. Mortality in one series of observations was over 70% during the first 3 days after birth when the wind speed exceeded 5 m s^{-1} in the initial period and rainfall was greater than $1 \cdot 5$ mm in 6 h, but with wind up to 2 m s^{-1} under dry conditions mortality was reduced to 5–10% (Obst and Ellis, 1977). The importance of shelter provided by hedges and fences in reducing lamb mortality has been demonstrated (Egan *et al.*, 1972; Lynch and Alexander, 1977); shelter reduces heat losses both from animals and from houses. Estimates made on red deer have shown that heat loss from the animals when they are exposed on a hillside is about twice the heat loss when they are in woodland in which wind speed is reduced to about 5% of that found in the exposed situations (Grace and Easterbee, 1979).

Pigs

Pigs are now nearly entirely housed in animal production practice, but some observations have been made on the effects of weather variations on the animal. In one study of this sort, pigs that were free to move about in a grass paddock had heat-flow discs attached to the trunk, with the signal transmitted by telemetry. There was a six-fold range in the amplitude of the sensible heat loss, from 60 to 350 W m^{-2}, depending on conditions, the two most important environmental factors being the mean radiant temperature and the wind speed (Ingram *et al.*, 1975).

Behavioural responses on the part of the pig allow it to find conditions of thermal neutrality in a suitable micro-environment even under unpromising conditions, and the methods of multiple choice and operant conditioning have in general indicated that animals seek the thermal environment that demands minimum heat production (Baldwin, 1974; Mount, 1968; 1979). Pigs kept on straw and in simple shelters which provide a diversity of environment can achieve satisfactory micro-environments through behavioural adaptation. On the other hand, animals in houses with closely controlled non-diverse environments have less chance to vary their immediate environments and so to minimise adverse fluctuations, such as draughts of air, so that the responsibility for providing a suitable environment falls on the house designers and operators.

Increasing wind speed from $0 \cdot 15$ to $0 \cdot 45 \text{ m s}^{-1}$ has no effect on heat loss from groups of pigs at an environmental temperature of 20°C, but at 15°C the same increase in wind speed is equivalent to a $1 \cdot 4$°C fall in temperature (Verstegen and van der Hel, 1976). Other work has shown that although variation in temperature from 8 to 20°C has no significant effect on weight gain, increasing wind speed from 0·1 to 0·8 m s⁻¹ at 12°C results in reduced weight gain (Mount *et al.*, 1980). When allowed to, the pig seeks conditions which approach those of thermal neutrality, both by moving between different areas and by operating on its environment, for example, by digging into straw. This principle probably applies generally, that appropriate environments are selected to the degree that the animal has freedom of choice.

Poultry

Amongst chickens, poorly feathered birds are at a disadvantage in the cold because the feathers are the fowl's principal thermal insulation; poorly feathered birds eat more than well-feathered birds at the same temperature (Richards, 1977; Sykes, 1977). In general, the optimal temperature for maximum growth in the chicken is 32–34°C at 1 day old, falling by about 0·5°C per day to 19°C at 32 days old (Charles and Spencer, 1976).

Animal behaviour

The behavioural responses that an animal makes under different weather conditions are sometimes not those that would be expected from observations made in the laboratory. When young pigs were allowed free movement in an area of woodland and pasture with a hut provided for shelter they did not begin to take shelter in dry weather until the environmental temperature was below 5°C, although laboratory measurements had shown the *CT* for such pigs to be about 25°C. The interaction of drives affecting the pig in a diverse environment out of doors was indicated when the animals stayed in the region of lowest air movement unless food was available *ad libitum* in troughs in a windy area, when they spend more time there (Ingram and Legge, 1970).

The patterns of feeding and activity, and therefore of energy exchange, vary throughout the 24 h, and depend on the environmental temperature. For example, although the pig is normally a diurnal mammal, under hot conditions the animal is active by night and quiet by day. Similarly, when cattle are exposed to hot sun they tend to seek shelter during the day and graze at night. There is sometimes a tendency to ignore the considerable behavioural adaptations of which animals are capable. Such adaptations are commonly observed under both laboratory and field conditions; for example, when the environmental temperature is lowered an animal's heat production does not rise to the expected level, and it is found that the animal has changed its posture, or orientation to wind or sun, sought shelter or huddled with its fellows (Mount, 1960). Birds also make behavioural and metabolic responses to environmental variations (Rising, 1979; Siegel, 1979); poorly feathered chickens are particularly susceptible to the effects of cold (Richards, 1977).

The orientation and behaviour of sheep and cattle is important in reducing heat loss in the cold. Wind impinging on the hindquarters of ewes has 25% less cooling effect than it has on the flank (Blaxter, 1964); ewes have been found to orientate themselves in relation to wind when wind speed exceeds $1\cdot7\,\text{m s}^{-1}$ with rain, and to move into groups when the wind speed exceeds about $3\,\text{m s}^{-1}$ (Obst and Ellis, 1977). In one study, sheltering behaviour in a flock of Blackface ewes was largely dependent on wind speed over about $10\,\text{m s}^{-1}$, and increased at temperatures below 0°C; temperatures over 0°C, and rain, had little effect on shelter seeking (Munro, 1962).

The variations in solar radiation intercepted by the sheep during the course of the day also depend on orientation, and even in the west of Scotland the total solar heat load on a sheep can exceed $300\,\text{W m}^{-2}$, which is about four times the animal's minimal heat production (Clapperton et al., 1965). Hill sheep seek out the protection from wind that is offered by rocks and vegetation. Surface roughness can measurably reduce surface wind speed and removal of such roughness can lead to a harsher micro-climate near the ground (Gloyne, 1976).

Man

The responses that man makes to his thermal environment show some differences from those that have so far been discussed in respect of farm animals. The differences are determined by three principal factors. The first of these lies in man's bare skin and his consequent lack of thermal insulation, a deficiency that would confine him to tropical or subtropical regions of the world if he did not wear clothes. The second factor is the very high level of sweating of which man is capable which makes him well suited to survive in hotter regions. Of the animals discussed earlier, only cattle approach man in their ability to sweat, and their maximum rate of sweating is only about 10% that of man. The third factor is that man does not adapt to different thermal environments primarily by physiological means but instead by building shelter of different types and by engineering methods that allow him to exist in environments that are hostile to mammalian life.

However, although there are these peculiarities, man's responses to his thermal environment are characteristically homeothermic and mammalian in type. The thermoneutral metabolic rate is about 45 W m^{-2}, which for the surface area of about 1·8 m^2 in a 70 kg man gives a resting metabolism of close to 80 W for the individual, of which usually about 25% is lost as evaporative heat. The deep body temperature during exercise is related to the metabolic rate and not to the environmental temperature; it can rise from the usual level of 37°C to 38·5°C with heavy work.

The critical temperature is 27–29°C for the naked subject, a high level that is in accordance with the lack of thermal insulation and consequent susceptibility to cold, with a cold limit as high as 14°C, very much higher than the cold limits of the mature sheep or even mature pig (see Table 1). In the newborn human infant and the elderly person, cold susceptibility is even more marked (Mount, 1979).

Some recent observations on adult volunteers, each of whom lived in a calorimeter for periods of 28–30 h, have indicated that the metabolic responses of man to variation in the level of food intake and to depression of the environmental temperature correspond to those found in other mammals. The mean 24-h rates of heat production were close to 9, 8 and 7 MJ when energy intakes were about 14, 8 and 4 MJ, respectively, and the resting metabolic rate was affected by the previous day's energy intake (Dauncey, 1980). When subjects clothed in a thin cotton garment were exposed to environmental temperatures of 22 or 28°C, the heat production over 24 h was significantly higher by 7% at 22°C, and there was some indication of substitution of diet-induced for cold-induced thermogenesis (Dauncey, 1981).

Although acclimatisation to cold is limited, acclimatisation to heat is much more in evidence. It takes the form of increased sweating, with a diminution in the increased skin temperature and heart rate that accompany the initial exposure to high temperatures. The maximum sweating rates that have been measured are about 2 kg h^{-1} for the 70 kg subject. The effects of hot environments and heat stress have been comprehensively discussed by Kerslake (1972).

THE ASSESSMENT OF THE THERMAL ENVIRONMENT

The collective designation of the thermal characteristics of the environment in terms of the air temperature taken as the environmental temperature (as in Figs 1, 2 and 3) is appropriate only in the case of a standardised environment in which

1. The air and mean radiant temperatures are equal to each other
2. There is a regimen of natural convection with no forced air currents
3. The floor where animals may lie is insulated
4. There is no solar radiation or precipitation.

Such conditions are often established for experimental work, but normally these strict requirements are not met in houses for either people or livestock, or out of doors, where the closest approach occurs under dry calm overcast conditions.

In any other than a standardised environment, variations in the quantities in Table 2 result in variations in heat transfer through the several channels. Air temperature by itself then becomes an incomplete thermal indicator, and must be replaced by a more comprehensive value. There have been many approaches to the formulation of equations and the construction of meters that would give equivalent temperatures (Newburgh, 1949; Burton and Edholm, 1955; Monteith, 1973; 1974; Webster, 1974; Mount, 1979).

One assessment of the effects of the thermal environment based on the calculation of the external insulation of sheep out of doors, from measurements on sheep in the laboratory, was used by Joyce et al. (1966). The values of insulation that they calculated for the sheep under conditions of both high and low levels of radiation showed good agreement with experimental measurements, and could be used to predict the needs of sheep for food energy under different weather conditions. Other approaches to the problem have included the use of simulated animals, usually in the form of cylinders in which the energy required to maintain a given temperature can be measured.

In his discussion on human bioclimate, Landsberg (1972) has reviewed the various indices for assessing the effects of heat and cold on man. He concludes that under warm conditions effective temperature (combining the effects of temperature, humidity and wind), and under cold conditions wind chill (temperature and wind speed) or cooling power (also including radiation), have proved adequate for many biometeorological purposes.

Micro-environment

An animal out of doors is not necessarily exposed to the general weather environment that is described by meteorological measurements. The animal's relations to environment take place in the micro-environment immediately around the animal, a zone that may have characteristics that are quite different from those of the general environment, for example if the animal is behind a wind-break, or in shade or under shelter, or more particularly in a house (Bond, 1967). The effects of weather are then modified by the factors that produce the micro-environment, so that it is necessary to consider highly localised sites. An additional factor is that the micro-climates of mammals and birds are affected to a large degree by their own metabolic heat production.

REFERENCES

Alexander, G. (1974). Heat loss from sheep. In: *Heat Loss from Animals and Man: Assessment and Control* (Eds J. L. Monteith and L. E. Mount). Butterworths, London, p. 173.

Arnold, G. W. and Birrell, H. A. (1977). Food intake and grazing behaviour of sheep varying in body condition. *Anim. Prod.* **24,** 343.

Baldwin, B. A. (1974). Behavioural thermoregulation. In: *Heat Loss from Animals and Man: Assessment and Control* (Eds J. L. Monteith and L. E. Mount). Butterworths, London, p. 97.

Baldwin, B. A. and Ingram, D. L. (1968). The effects of food intake and acclimatization to temperature on behavioural thermoregulation in pigs and mice. *Physiol. Behav.* **3,** 395.

Benedict, F. G. (1938). *Vital Energetics.* Carnegie Inst. Publ. 503, Washington.

Bennett, J. W. (1972). The maximum metabolic response of sheep to cold: effects of rectal temperature, shearing, feed consumption, body posture and body weight. *Aust. J. agric. Res.* **23,** 1045.

Bennett, J. W. and Hutchinson, J. C. D. (1964). Thermal insulation of short lengths of Merino fleece. *Aust. J. agric. Res.* **15,** 427.

Bianca, W. (1968). Thermoregulation. In: *Adaptation of Domestic Animals* (Ed. E. S. E. Hafez). Lea and Febiger, Philadelphia, p. 97.

Blaxter, K. L. (1958). Nutrition and climatic stress in farm animals. *Proc. Nutr. Soc.* **17,** 191.

Blaxter, K. L. (1962). The reactions of cattle and sheep to the stress of cold environments. *MAFF Symposium on Shelter Research*, Aberystwyth, p. 31.

Blaxter, K. L. (1964). The effect of outdoor climate in Scotland on sheep and cattle. *Vet. Rec.* **76,** 1445.

Blaxter, K. L. (1967). *The Energy Metabolism of Ruminants,* 2nd edn. Charles C. Thomas, Springfield, Illinois.

Blaxter, K. L. and Wainman, F. W. (1966). The fasting metabolism of cattle. *Br. J. Nutr.* **20,** 103.

Blaxter, K. L., Graham, N. McC. and Wainman, F. W. (1957). Energy retention of sheep in relation to environmental temperature. *Proc. Nutr. Soc.* **16,** iii.

Blaxter, K. L., Graham, N. McC., Wainman, F. W. and Armstrong, D. G. (1959). Environmental temperature, energy metabolism and heat regulation in sheep. II. The partition of heat losses in closely clipped sheep. *J. agric. Sci., Camb.* **52,** 25.

Blaxter, K. L., Joyce, J. P. and Webster, A. J. F. (1964). Investigations of environmental stress in sheep and cattle. *Proc. 2nd Symposium Shelter Research,* MAFF, Edinburgh.

Bond, T. E. (1967). Microclimate and livestock performance in hot climates. In: *Ground Level Climatology* (Ed. R. H. Shaw). Publ. No. 86, Am. Ass. Adv. Sci., Washington DC, p. 207.

Brody, S. (1945). *Bioenergetics and Growth.* Reinhold, New York.

Brown, G. D. and Hutchinson, J. C. D. (1973). Climate and animal production. In: *The Pastoral Industries of Australia* (Eds G. Alexander and O. B. Williams). Sydney University Press, Australia, p. 336.

Burton, A. C. and Edholm, O. G. (1955). *Man in a Cold Environment.* Edward Arnold, London (reprinted 1969, Hafner Publishing Company, New York and London).

Cena, K. and Monteith, J. L. (1976). Heat transfer through animal coats. In: *Progress in Animal Biometeorology,* Vol. 1, Part 1, (Ed. H. D. Johnson). Swets and Zeitlinger, Amsterdam, p. 343.

Charles, D. R. and Spencer, P. G. (1976). *The Climatic Environment of Poultry Houses.* MAFF Bulletin 212. HMSO, London.

Christopherson, R. J. (1976). Effects of prolonged cold and the outdoor winter environment on apparent digestibility in sheep and cattle. *Can. J. Anim. Sci.* **56,** 201.

Clapperton, J. L., Joyce, J. P. and Blaxter, K. L. (1965). Estimates of the contribution of solar radiation to the thermal exchanges of sheep at a latitude of 55° north. *J. agric. Sci., Camb.* **64,** 37.

Close, W. H. and Mount, L. E. (1975). The rate of heat loss during fasting in the growing pig. *Br. J. Nutr.* **34,** 279.

Close, W. H. and Mount, L. E. (1978). The effects of plane of nutrition and environmental temperature on the energy metabolism of the growing pig. 1. Heat loss and critical temperature. *Br. J. Nutr.* **40,** 413.

Dauncey, M. J. (1980). Metabolic effects of altering the 24 h energy intake in man, using direct and indirect calorimetry. *Br. J. Nutr.* **43,** 257.

Dauncey, M. J. (1981). Influence of mild cold on 24 h energy expenditure, resting metabolism and diet-induced thermogenesis, *Br. J. Nutr.* **45,** 257.

Donnelly, J. B., Lynch, J. J. and Webster, M. E. D. (1974). Climatic adaptation in recently shorn Merino sheep. *Int. J. Biometeor.* **18,** 233.

Duckham, A. N. (1963). *Agricultural Synthesis: The Farming Year*. Chatto and Windus, London.

Egan, J. K., McLaughlin, J. W., Thompson, R. L. and McIntyre, J. S. (1972). The importance of shelter in reducing neonatal lamb deaths. *Aust. J. exp. Agric. Anim. Husb.* **12**, 470.

Folk, G. E. (1974). *Textbook of Environmental Physiology*. Lea and Febiger, Philadelphia.

Fox, R. H., Woodward, P. M., Exton-Smith, A. N., Green, M. F., Donnison, D. V. and Wicks, M. H. (1973). Body temperatures in the elderly; a national study of physiological, social, and environmental conditions. *Br. med. J.* **1**, 200.

Gagge, A. P. (1970). Effective radiant flux, an independent variable that describes thermal radiation on man. In: *Physiological and Behavioral Temperature Regulation* (Eds J. D. Hardy, A. P. Gagge and J. A. J. Stolwijk). Charles C. Thomas, Springfield, Illinois, p. 34.

Gatenby, R. M. (1977). Conduction of heat from sheep to ground. *Agricultural Meteorology* **18**, 387.

Gloyne, R. W. (1976). Shelter in agriculture, forestry and horticulture—a review of some recent work and trends. *ADAS A. Rev.* **21**, 197.

Grace, J. and Easterbee, N. (1979). The natural shelter for red deer (*Cervus elaphus*) in a Scottish glen. *J. Appl. Ecol.* **16**, 37.

Graham, N. McC., Wainman, F. W., Blaxter, K. L. and Armstrong, D. G. (1959). Environmental temperature, energy metabolism and heat regulation in sheep. I. Energy metabolism in closely clipped sheep. *J. agric. Sci., Camb.* **52**, 13.

Hales, J. R. S. (1976). Interaction between respiratory and thermoregulatory systems of domestic animals in hot environments. In: *Progress in Animal Biometeorology*, Vol. 1, Part 1 (Ed. H. D. Johnson). Swets and Zeitlinger, Amsterdam, p. 123.

Heldmaier, G. (1971). Zitterfreie, Wärmebildung und Körpergrösse bei Saugetierern. *Z. vergl. Physiologie*, **73**, 222.

Hey, E. N. (1974). Physiological control over body temperature. In *Heat Loss from Animals and Man: Assessment and Control* (Eds J. L. Monteith and L. E. Mount). Butterworths, London, p. 77.

Holmes, C. W. and McLean, N. R. (1975). Effects of air temperature and air movement on the heat produced by young Friesian and Jersey calves, with some measurements of the effects of artificial rain. *N. Z. J. Agric. Res.* **18**, 277.

Hull, D. (1973). Thermoregulation in young mammals. In: *Comparative Physiology of Thermoregulation, Vol. III. Special Aspects of Thermoregulation* (Ed. G. Causey Whittow). Academic Press, New York, p. 167.

Huxley, J. S. (1932). *Problems of Relative Growth*. The Dial Press, New York.

Ingram, D. L. and Legge, K. F. (1970). The thermoregulatory behaviour of young pigs in a natural environment. *Physiol. Behav.* **5**, 981.

Ingram, D. L. and Mount, L. E. (1975). *Man and Animals in Hot Environments*. Springer-Verlag, New York.

Ingram, D. L., Heal, J. W. and Legge, K. F. (1975). Heat loss from young unrestrained pigs in an outdoor environment. *Comp. Biochem. Physiol.* **50A,** 71.

Jakob, M. (1957). *Heat Transfer,* Vol. II. Wiley, New York.

Jansky, L. (1973). Non-shivering thermogenesis and its thermoregulatory significance. *Biol. Rev.* **48,** 85.

Jessen, C. (1977). Interaction of air temperature and core temperature in thermoregulation of the goat. *J. Physiol., Lond.* **264,** 585.

Joyce, J. P. and Blaxter, K. L. (1964). The effect of air movement, air temperature and infra-red radiation on the energy requirements of sheep. *Br. J. Nutr.* **18,** 5.

Joyce, J. P., Blaxter, K. L. and Park, C. (1966). The effect of natural outdoor environments on the energy requirements of sheep. *Res. vet. Sci.* **7,** 342.

Kerslake, D. McK. (1972). *The Stress of Hot Environments.* Cambridge University Press, London.

Kleiber, M. (1932). Body size and metabolism. *Hilgardia* **6,** 315.

Kleiber, M. (1975). *The Fire of Life,* 2nd edn. John Wiley, New York.

Landsberg, H. E. (1972). *The Assessment of Human Bioclimate.* Technical Note No. 123. World Meteorological Organization, Geneva.

Lynch, J. J. and Alexander, G. (1977). Sheltering behaviour of lambing Merino sheep in relation to grass hedges and artificial windbreaks. *Aust. J. Agric. Res.* **28,** 691.

McDowell, R. E. (1972). *Improvement of Livestock Production in Warm Climates.* W. H. Freeman & Co., San Francisco.

Milligan, J. D. and Christison, G. I. (1974). Effects of severe winter conditions on performance of feedlot steers. *Can. J. Anim. Sci.* **54,** 605.

Monteith, J. L. (1973). *Principles of Environmental Physics.* Edward Arnold, London.

Monteith, J. L. (1974). Specification of the environment for thermal physiology. In: *Heat Loss from Animals and Man: Assessment and Control* (Eds J. L. Monteith and L. E. Mount). Butterworths, London, p. 1.

Mount, L. E. (1960). The influence of huddling and body size on the metabolic rate of the young pig. *J. agric. Sci., Camb.* **55,** 101.

Mount, L. E. (1964). Radiant and convective heat loss from the new-born pig. *J. Physiol., Lond.* **173,** 96.

Mount, L. E. (1968). *The Climatic Physiology of the Pig.* Edward Arnold, London.

Mount, L. E. (1974). Thermal neutrality. In: *Heat Loss from Animals and Man: Assessment and Control* (Eds J. L. Monteith and L. E. Mount). Butterworths, London, p. 425.

Mount, L. E. (1976). Energy expenditure during the growing period. In: *Early Nutrition and Later Development* (Ed. A. W. Wilkinson). Pitman, London, p. 156.

Mount, L. E. (1977). The use of heat transfer coefficients in estimating sensible heat loss from the pig. *Anim. Prod.* **25,** 271.

Mount, L. E. (1979). *Adaptation to Thermal Environment: Man and His Productive Animals.* Edward Arnold, London.

Mount, L. E. (1980). Growth and the thermal environment. In: *Growth in Animals* (Ed. T. L. J. Lawrence). Butterworths, London, p. 47.

Mount, L. E., Start, I. B. and Brown, D. (1980). A note on the effects of forced air movement and environmental temperature on weight gain in the pig after weaning. *Anim. Prod.* **30,** 295.

Munro, J. (1962). The use of natural shelter by hill sheep. *Anim. Prod.* **4,** 343.

Newburgh, L. H. (Ed.) (1949). *Physiology of Heat Regulation and Science of Clothing.* Saunders, Philadelphia.

Obst, J. M. and Ellis, J. V. (1977). Weather, ewe behaviour and lamb mortality. *Agricultural Record* **4,** 44.

Pringle, W. L. and Tsukamoto, J. Y. (1974). Wintering beef cows in the far north. *Can. J. Anim. Sci.* **54,** 709.

Richards, S. A. (1970). The biology and comparative physiology of thermal panting. *Biol. Rev.* **45,** 223.

Richards, S. A. (1977). The influence of loss of plumage on temperature regulation in laying hens. *J. agric. Sci., Camb.* **89,** 393.

Rising, J. D. (1979). Recent observations on the thermoregulatory mechanisms of birds. In: *Biometeorological Survey, Vol.* 1, 1973–1978; *Part B, Animal Biometeorology* (Ed. S. W. Tromp). Heyden, London, p. 34.

Sarrus and Rameaux (1839). Mémoire addressé à l'Académie Royale. *Bulletin de l'académie royale de médecine* **3,** 1094.

Siegel, H. S. (1979). Influence of temperature on the metabolism of birds. In: *Biometeorological Survey, Vol.* 1, 1973–1978; *Part B, Animal Biometeorology* (Ed. S. W. Tromp). Heyden, London, p. 44.

Slee, J. (1974). The retention of cold acclimatization in sheep. *Anim. Prod.* **19,** 201.

Slee, J. (1978). The effects of breed, birthcoat and body weight on the cold resistance of newborn lambs. *Anim. Prod.* **27,** 43.

Slee, J. (1979). Mortality and resistance to hypothermia in young lambs. In: *Biometeorological Survey, Vol.* 1, 1973–1978; *Part B, Animal Biometeorology* (Ed. S. W. Tromp). Heyden, London, p. 60.

Starr, J. R. (1980). Lamb mortality in a commercial lowland sheep flock. Submitted to *Vet. Rec.*

Sykes, A. H. (1977). Nutrition–environment interactions in poultry. In: *Nutrition and the Climatic Environment* (Eds W. Haresign, H. Swan and D. Lewis) Butterworths, London, p. 17.

Sykes, A. R., Griffiths, R. G. and Slee, J. (1976). Influence of breed, birth weight and weather on the body temperature of newborn lambs. *Anim. Prod.* **22,** 395.

Taylor, C. R. (1974). Exercise and thermoregulation. In: *Environmental Physiology* (Ed. D. Robertshaw). Butterworths, London, p. 163.

Templeton, J. R. (1970). Reptiles. In: *Comparative Physiology of Thermoregulation* (Ed. G. C. Whittow). Academic Press, New York, p. 167.

Thompson, G. E. (1979). Recent observations on thermoregulation in cattle in relation to weather and climate. In: *Biometeorological Survey, Vol.* 1, 1973–1978; *Part B, Animal Biometeorology* (Ed. S. W. Tromp). Heyden, London, p. 66.

Underwood, C. R. and Ward, E. J. (1966). The solar radiation area of man. *Ergonomics* **9,** 155.

Verstegen, M. W. A. and van der Hel, W. (1974). The effects of temperature and type of floor on metabolic rate and effective critical temperature in groups of growing pigs. *Anim. Prod.* **18,** 1.

Verstegen, M. W. A. and van der Hel, W. (1976). Energy balances in groups of pigs in relation to air velocity and ambient temperature. In: *Energy Metabolism of Farm Animals* (Ed. M. Vermorel). EAAP Publ. No. 19, p. 347.

Voit, E. (1901). Über die Grösse des Energiebedarfs der Tiere in Hungerzustande. *Ztschr. Biol.* **41,** 113.

Webster, A. J. F. (1974). Heat loss from cattle with particular emphasis on the effects of cold. In: *Heat Loss from Animals and Man: Assessment and Control* (Eds J. L. Monteith and L. E. Mount). Butterworths, London, p. 205.

Webster, A. J. F. (1978). Prediction of the energy requirements for growth in beef cattle. *World Rev. Nutr. Diet.* **30,** 189.

Webster, A. J. F., Gordon, J. G. and Smith, J. S. (1976). Energy exchanges of veal calves in relation to body weight, food intake and air temperature. *Anim. Prod.* **23,** 35.

Webster, A. J. F., Gordon, J. G. and McGregor, R. (1978). The cold tolerance of beef and dairy type calves in the first weeks of life. *Anim. Prod.* **26,** 85.

Wiener, G., Deeble, F. K., Broadbent, J. S. and Talbot, M. (1973). Breed variations in lambing performance and lamb mortality in commercial sheep flocks. *Anim. Prod.* **17,** 229.

Discussion

Referring to the experiments on man kept at two temperatures and given different amounts of food, *Dr Elia* asked whether the change in insulation could be related to an effect of food, to which *Professor Mount* replied that the overall efficiency of food utilisation was probably not changed by temperature.

Professor Kaufman asked whether extra heat produced by physical exercise may be used to maintain body temperature when environmental temperature falls and *Professor Mount* cited work with mice which showed that there was a substitution; however the calorimeter measures total heat and does not distinguish between external work done by the subject and heat released within the tissues. On this point, *Sir Kenneth Blaxter* stated that experiments with animals walking on tread-mills had shown that even that component of the total heat emission which was generated within the tissues and not evident in external work could not be used to keep the body warm under cold. When an animal walks, the convective environment changes markedly and increases heat loss, while the action of the larger muscles in locomotion does change tissue insulation to an extent. As far as sheep confronted with cold are concerned, it is far more sensible to stand still and shiver than to walk about to keep warm, to which idea *Professor Mount* added the remark that this is equally so of survival in water. Swimming, and thereby increasing convective loss, reduces survival time.

Professor Monteith pointed out that while man has been classified by Professor Mount as a tropical animal due to his ability to sweat profusely, sweat secretion is limited by the vapour pressure gradient. As the Symposium was considering the possibility of increased agricultural production in tropical and subtropical countries characterised by humid environments, he wondered how far the rate of work might become a limiting factor determined by the difficulty of evaporating moisture at high temperatures and high humidities. *Professor Mount* stated that it was very important not to neglect considerations of humidity. Even under cool conditions, relative humidity was of importance in animals with respect to the drying out of fleeces after rain and he too thought that humidity could be a real limiting factor in terms of man working in tropical conditions.

Dr Fox asked Professor Mount to enlarge on the high and sustained expenditure of the human subjects in the calorimeter during the night and asked how far people could adjust metabolism to burn off energy. Equally, how much inter-subject variation had been found in the night metabolism of the high energy uptake group, for it was common experience that some people were able to eat a lot and others comparatively little and yet remain in body weight equilibrium. *Professor Mount* said that it may well be that there were data from the individual subjects in the experiment which would enable partial answers to be made to these questions. He doubted, however, whether there were very real differences between man and animals in terms of the way in which they utilised food. He continued that while it was very useful to work with people in experimental situations insofar that they were highly cooperative and would undertake tasks, such as exercise, for particular periods, interpretation of behavioural observations was sometimes difficult because the subjects were, by virtue of their cooperation, not free to behave and react to the environment in subtle ways. Experience with animals kept under close observation but not disturbed, for example, showed that as nutritional plane was increased so the animals spread out and adopted extended postures characteristic of exposure to temperature above the critical temperature. In man, under the conditions of the calorimeter, activity was to a very large extent controlled in that people exercised when they were told. *Professor Jarvis* said that he was very impressed by the importance attributed to wind in determining environmental thermal demand. It was worth emphasising that extra windiness was one of the main characteristics of the British climate, especially in upland areas. Very recently one of his colleagues, Dr Mutch at Edinburgh, had been looking at the economic effects on animal production of providing shelter through integration of agriculture with forestry. On a number of estates in upland situations, an average of 15% of the agricultural land had been converted to forestry. In all instances, agricultural production had increased on the reduced area as a result of increased rate of stocking and higher productivity, with the consequence that there was a higher economic return because of the provision of shelter.

Food Animals and Climate

SIR KENNETH BLAXTER

Director, Rowett Research Institute, Aberdeen, UK

Many experimental and observational studies of the reactions of mammals and birds to the environments in which they live have shown the wide variety of adaptive mechanisms they employ. These range from that of the camel, which has an ability to tolerate high osmotic pressure in its body fluids so to survive dehydration in its desert environment, to that of musk oxen, which have developed behavioural patterns which suggest that they employ the cloud of water vapour they emit to increase incoming infra-red radiation in Arctic cold. However interesting and informative comparative studies of a wide range of species in widely ranging environments might be, I will largely confine my remarks to grazing livestock and to our cold temperate climates. Excellent comprehensive reviews of the physiological responses of domesticated species have been published in volumes by Monteith and Mount (1974), Robertshaw (1974), Haresign *et al.* (1977) and by Mount (1979).

SEASONAL EFFECTS ON REPRODUCTION

The most obvious attribute of climate is that it embraces the seasons. Some equatorial climates are characterised by wet or dry seasons, but as one moves north or south the more conventional seasons of spring, summer, autumn and winter emerge, and the further north or south so, broadly speaking, does the growing season for plants diminish and thus the availability of food for animals during the remainder of the year reduces. Mammals and birds living in the high latitudes have adapted to the seasonal availability of food by adjustment of their breeding season. Commonly, young are produced at or about the time at which

247

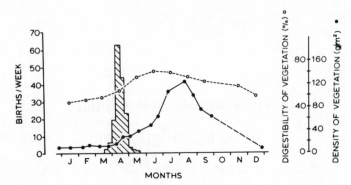

F IG. 1. The lambing of Soay sheep on the Island of St. Kilda in relation to the quality and amount of herbage available (after Jewell and Grubb, 1974).

food becomes available. Figure 1 shows, as example, the reproductive behaviour of the primitive Soay sheep of St. Kilda. These have been left to their own devices since the last islanders left in the 1930s and the Soay sheep breed to drop their lambs at a time when herbage supply is beginning to increase (Jewell and Grubb, 1974). In birds, the studies by Baker (1939) show that as one moves north in the temperate latitudes so the advent of the egg-laying season advances by 20 to 30 days per 10° of latitude.

The strength of the link between the seasonal availability of food and the time at which the young are born is particularly strong in the Soay sheep and also in the red deer. The red deer herds of Scotland calve in the first two weeks of June (Mitchell *et al.* 1977) with very few 'stragglers' and the latter calves have poorer chances of survival (Blaxter and Hamilton, 1980). Other breeds of sheep exhibit a wider range of lambing time than the Soay and with domesticated cattle calving can occur at any time of the year. The primitive wild White Cattle of the Chillingham herd, however, calve in about April (Wallace, 1907), and even in our common cattle breeds it is usual for cows, although they may have commenced reproductive life as autumn calving heifers, to assume a spring calving pattern as they age.

Several studies, the most recent being that by Roy *et al.* (1980), have shown that puberty in cattle is related to the season of birth. The age at first oestrus, determined by progesterone assay, occurs two months earlier in animals born in autumn than in those born in spring. The onset of first oestrus in sheep is also affected by the time of birth (Dýrmundsson, 1973; Quirke, 1978).

Similar reproductive patterns to those in large ruminants are seen in small rodents (Amoroso and Marshall, 1960); young are produced in the spring and in winter none are born. Again, as with the cow, domestication extends or even obliterates seasonal breeding. The domestic rabbit will breed throughout the year but the wild rabbit shows peaks of reproduction in the spring and summer. Conversely, in equatorial regions most mammals do not exhibit the same periodicity of reproduction. Tropical and subtropical breeds of sheep, for example, reproduce throughout the year and so do pigs.

Clearly, reproduction to ensure that the young have a sufficient food supply has survival value in an evolutionary sense; ensured conditions for the young are thus what Baker (1938) called an ultimate cause of reproductive timing. The proximal cause is the factor which causes the parents to breed so to produce young at the favoured time.

When sheep or deer are transferred from the UK to Australia or New Zealand they eventually adopt a breeding season which accords with the climatic seasons in their new environment. Studies by the Duke of Bedford and Marshall (1942) showed this very well and part of their data (from Sadleir, 1972) is shown in Fig. 2. Red deer transferred from Britain to New Zealand and back again adopted the reproductive pattern shown by deer in the countries concerned. Transfer of equatorial species of deer, such as the Indian Axis deer which breeds at any time of year, to Woburn in the UK does not impart a seasonal breeding pattern; nor does the pig, being of tropical origin, respond to the seasons of high latitudes by becoming a seasonal breeder.

The proximal cause of these adaptations of reproduction is the

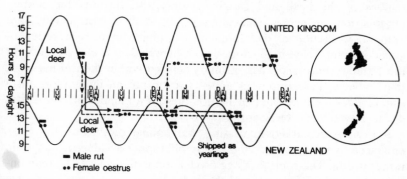

FIG. 2. Reproduction in red deer transferred from Britain to New Zealand and back again (after Sadleir, 1972).

photoperiod. This was first shown experimentally by Rowan in 1925 in birds, first with the junco and later with canaries and crows. Rowan, by exposing juncos kept outside in the cold Canadian winter to electric light, showed that testis size increased in a comparable way to that seen normally when day length increases in the spring. This finding, together with the Duke of Bedford and Marshall's observations on transfer of animals to the Antipodes, led to confirmation of the effect of seasonal light patterns on reproduction in farm mammals, notably by Yeates (1949) in the sheep. Whether species are long-day breeders such as rodents and carnivores, beginning to breed as the days lengthen, or short-day breeders such as sheep and deer which breed as the day length shortens, the photoperiod is the proximal cause of the close adaptation of the animal to the seasonal availability of food.

The photoperiod-dependence of reproduction infers that light induces hormonal changes and it is known that the secretion by the pituitary of follicle-stimulating hormone (FSH), luteinizing hormone (LH) and prolactin are all influenced by changes in day length (Pelletier, 1973). In the ram, testosterone levels also rise and testicular size increases. Figure 3, derived from Lincoln's (1979) experiments, shows the sequence of events when rams were exposed to either 16-h light or 8-h light in successive periods of 16 weeks. The overall mechanism involved is complex. The receptor organ is the eye; severing the optic nerve abolishes seasonal control. The neural pathways involve the suprachiasmatic nucleus in the rostral part of the hypothalamus (Domanski *et al.*, 1980) which modulates the 24-h rhythmic activity of the pineal. The pineal may be inactivated by superior cervical ganglionectomy since this removes the sympathetic innervation of all regions of the head and ganglionectomy also disrupts the normal photoperiod response (Lincoln, 1979). Subsequent events are humoral—secretion of melatonin by the pineal induces secretion of gonadotrophin-releasing factors by the hypothalamus and secretion of the pituitary hormones. The primary sensing within the diurnal cycle that initiates these responses appears to be not an integration but a simple assessment of whether light is present a number of hours after dawn (Ravault and Ortavant, 1977).

It may be remarked in passing that animal production has been enhanced by taking into account these photoperiod-induced changes in reproduction. The control of egg production in the chicken by manipulation of artificial lighting, and the induction of twice-yearly breeding in sheep by light control (Robinson and Ørskov, 1975) are examples. It

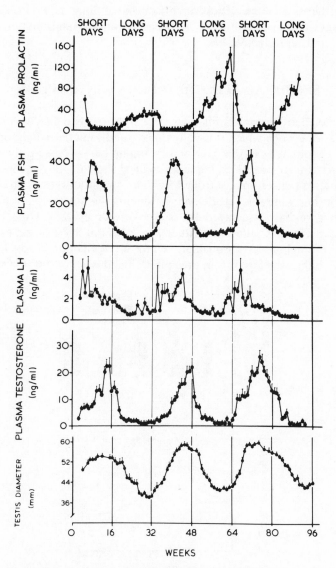

FIG. 3. Endocrine changes in rams subjected to alternating long days (16-h light) and short days (8-h light) (after Lincoln, 1979).

may also be remarked that there is no similar sexual periodicity in man
in northern climates. Zuckerman concluded long ago (1932) that
'monkeys and apes like man experience a smooth and uninterrupted
sexual and reproductive life'.

SEASONAL EFFECTS ON COAT INSULATION

Most northern mammals characteristically grow two hair coats each
year, a winter one which is usually thicker and sometimes light or even
white in colour, as in red deer and mountain hares respectively, and a
shorter summer coat. This implies a cyclical shedding of the coats, and
all these responses are controlled by light. In cattle, rate of growth of
hair during winter is unaffected by environmental temperature but
shedding of hair is delayed by cold (Webster *et al.*, 1970). This is
shown in Fig. 4. Cattle were either kept warm at 20°C or kept out of
doors throughout the Canadian winter at temperatures as low as
−29°C, either sheltered from precipitation and wind or not. Growth of

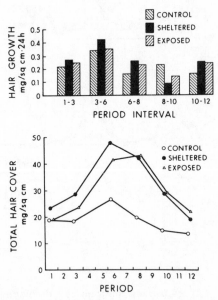

Fig. 4. The growth rate of cattle coats in the Canadian winter and the weight
of coat per unit area. The control animals were kept at 20°C and the others at
temperatures as low as −29°C (after Webster *et al.*, 1970).

hair was unaffected by cold but weight of hair per unit area increased in the exposed groups, thereby increasing the animals' resistance to cold.

Sheep exhibit a seasonal growth of fleece and of follicular activity which is independent of temperature and controlled by the light environment (Ryder, 1973; Nagorcka, 1978). Figure 5, from Ryder's (1969) study, illustrates the seasonal changes in wool follicle activity in sheep, showing the complete quiescence of primary and secondary follicles in the depth of winter. Under these circumstances, dietary

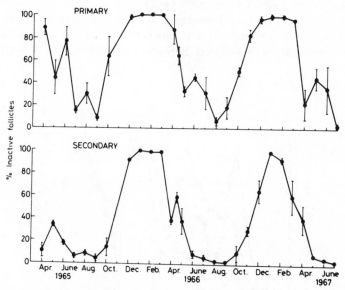

FIG. 5. Wool follicle activity in sheep in relation to the seasons in Scotland (after Ryder, 1969).

protein and energy-yielding nutrients are not diverted to wool production. The seasonal amplitude of the growth rate of the fleece varies with breed and in the Merino, which has origins in the South Mediterranean, seasonal amplitude is small relative to that in Cheviots (Doney, 1966). The primitive Soay has a moult, characteristically losing its fleece in the late spring, and there is evidence that this characteristic survives in a vestigial from in other breeds. Teleologically this could be regarded as a device to reduce body insulation in the warm summer.

SEASONAL EFFECTS ON APPETITE

It was noted by Gordon (1964) and by Tarttelin (1968) that the
voluntary intake of the same feed by sheep in winter was less than in
summer. A similar phenomenon was noted in red deer stags, hinds and
castrates (Blaxter *et al.*, 1974; Simpson, 1976) and there is evidence
(Kilkenny, 1974; Hudson, 1980) that a small difference in voluntary
intake with smaller intakes in winter occurs in cattle. Again, the
determinant is the photoperiod. The effect can be induced by an
artificial six-month photoperiod in deer and sheep (Kay, 1979) and the
magnitude of the effect varies with breed. Kay's studies show that the
amplitude in the primitive Soay sheep is such that the winter depression of intake is to amounts less than 30% of those consumed in
summer whereas in cross-bred Suffolk × Finn × Dorset it is only to

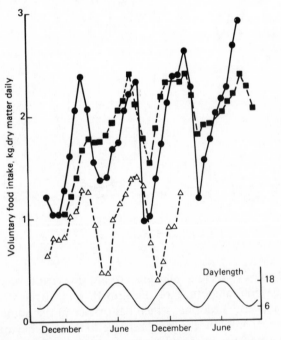

FIG. 6. The voluntary intake of pelleted concentrate by red deer (●), and
Finn × Dorset × Suffolk sheep (■) and of pelleted roughage–concentrate by
Soay sheep (△) subjected to an artificial six-month photoperiod (unpublished
work by Kay and associates).

about 85% (Blaxter and Gill, 1979). In growing lambs, a series of studies by Forbes and his associates (Forbes *et al.*, 1979; Forbes *et al.*, 1981) show that growth in body weight is stimulated by an 18-h day compared with an 8-h day. A large part of this increase, however, was due to an increase in the contents of the digestive tract. In non-ruminants, exposure to cold results in an increase in voluntary intake of feed. In ruminants, however, exposure to cold in any season of the year does not invariably increase intake. The latter is largely determined by the 'space-filling' attributes of feed rather than by the demands of metabolism.

Figure 6 summarises the observations made by Kay and his colleagues at the Rowett Institute (Kay, Simpson, Suttie and Goodall, 1974–78 unpublished) on red deer, Soay sheep and Finn × Dorset × Suffolk sheep subjected to six-month light cycles. The considerable amplitude of the responses of red deer and Soay sheep are evident.

THE PHOTOPERIOD AND WINTER COLD

The weather in the winters of high latitudes varies considerably; in some years there is reasonable feed available in much of the winter and early spring, but in others the reverse is true. Animals in high latitudes have not used the weather-dependent signals of cold and absence of feed to cue many of their responses but rather the climate-dependent cycle of day length. The use of this signal obviously has advantage in evolutionary terms since the seasons are constant but their weathers are not. Considering these seasonal cycles in relation to winter coldness and summer warmth in evolutionary terms, there is obvious advantage in young being born at the most propitious time; one can visualise an advantage accruing in natural selection for the summer breeder in high latitudes. There is an advantage too in a preparation for winter by growth in autumn of a winter coat. Survival value may also be inferred from the absence of coat growth in winter, for the demand for amino acids and energy for the synthesis of keratins of the hair coat and fleece during the winter when feed is likely to be scarce is thereby reduced.

What is difficult to understand in terms of its survival value is the reduction in feed intake during winter. This reduction inevitably reduces heat production and thus the ability of the animal with constant insulation and deep body temperature to survive cold. The paradox is

even more curious in that the digestibility of feed by both sheep
(Graham *et al.*, 1959) and cattle (Blaxter and Wainman, 1961) was
found to be reduced by cold and hence the smaller amount consumed
resulted in less heat produced per unit. Reduction of digestibility by
cold has been confirmed and shown to be related to the rate of
contraction of the forestomachs and to an enhanced passage of feed
through the digestive tract (Christopherson, 1976; Kennedy *et al.*
1976; Westra and Christopherson, 1976). The effect is large; the
depression of percentage digestibility is 0·3% units per °C in sheep and
only slightly less in cattle, implying that at winter environmental
temperatures of −5°C the energy obtained from the same amount of
feed is at least 10% less than that noted at summer temperatures of
20°C. There is nothing to suggest that this phenomenon of reduced
digestibility is linked to light cycles. It is simply induced by cold.

Perhaps resolution of the paradox of light-dependent appetite regulation is best obtained by stating it in the reverse way. There may well
be survival value in the ability of grazing livestock to consume more
than that sufficient for survival when feed is plentiful and to be able to
store it as depot fats which can be drawn on when feed is scarce. The
low winter feed consumption can then be regarded as simply that
amount sufficient for survival under some average winter weather.
Perhaps the paradox illustrates certain of the unsatisfactory aspects of
the Darwinian hypothesis; not only is it incapable of falsification but
the transposition of testable hypotheses apparently results in proof
acceptable to some people and hence its continued existence.

CONCOMITANT ENVIRONMENTAL EFFECTS
ON ANIMALS

The environment, besides having direct effects on animals or on their
feed supply, indirectly affects them through influences on organisms
which cause disease. The effects of environment on the resistance of
animals to infection and on the virulence of organisms and their
survival has recently been reviewed by Webster (1981). These interesting aspects are not commented on further; rather factors related to the
dissemination of infections are considered. The most spectacular example of this is the spread of foot-and-mouth disease. Following upon the
major outbreak of 1967–1968 in the UK, epidemiological studies
showed a clear association of the spread of the disease, to give

outbreaks more than 60 km from the main epidemic area, with wind velocity and direction and with precipitation (Smith and Hugh-Jones, 1969; Hugh-Jones and Wright, 1970). Spread of disease is certainly in part determined by the occurrence of a particular weather pattern at the time the virus is being excreted by infected animals. Short-term forecasting of the weather is clearly of value in terms of precautionary measures.

Much work has been undertaken to relate the variation in the occurrence of diseases of grazing stock to the variation in aggregated attributes of weather from year to year. An example is the series of studies of *Nematodirus battus* infestation in lambs (Smith and Thomas, 1972; Ollerenshaw, 1980). This disease occurs in spring and early summer. Infested lambs excrete worm eggs and by autumn these eggs contain third-stage larvae. These do not hatch until after the following winter to infect the next year's lamb crop. Adult sheep play no part in maintaining the life cycle, and timing of the larval hatch is critical. Cold winters and late springs mean a delay in hatching and hence the larvae are more likely to be consumed by grazing lambs, born early in the year. Figure 7 shows the association over a 25-year period of incidence of *Nematodirus* with the preceding winter weather.

Wide variations from year to year equally occur with respect to the incidence and severity of infestation of sheep with parasitic nematodes of the genera, *Ostertagia*, *Trichostrongylus* and *Cooperia*. Here the effect of weather, though discernible, is more complex than that for *Nematodirus*. The major factor is surface wetness of pasture in summer

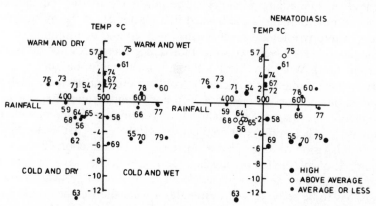

Fɪɢ. 7. The pattern of winter weather in England and Wales and the pattern of severity of *Nematodirus* infestation in lambs (after Ollerenshaw, 1980).

and the duration of such wetness into autumn, but additionally cold dry weather in winter appears to prolong survival of overwintering larvae (Ollerenshaw *et al.*, 1978; Thomas and Starr, 1978).

In both nematodiasis and parasitic gastroenteritis, and also in fascioliasis or liver fluke disease, forecasts based on long-term weather patterns are necessary if outbreaks of disease in grazing stock are to be combated by preventative medication. Animal disease forecasts, based on meteorological data, have in fact been issued by MAFF from the Central Veterinary Laboratory at Weybridge for some years. As Ollerenshaw (1980) has pointed out, however, the space allotted to them in farming publications is minute compared with that sold to manufacturers for display of information on anthelmintics and uptake of the forecasts has been poor.

CLIMATE, WEATHER AND PLANNING IN ANIMAL PRODUCTION

Animals are affected by the climate as evidenced by their responses to the photoperiod. They also react to antecedent weather as evidenced by the incidence of parasitism or by the effects of the previous summer's weather on the amount and quality of feed available in winter. All responses are long-term ones. The responses of the animal to what may be termed the 'coldness' of the environment, however, are immediate and rapid. A change in the convective or radiative environment elicits immediate physiological response and thermal equilibrium in a new environment is established in a matter of, at the most, a few hours. The physiological mechanisms involved and quantitation of the basic parameters have been well studied (see references quoted in the Introduction). What is critical is how to use the information.

If an environment is sufficiently 'cold' to elicit an increase in heat production and thereby maintain deep body temperature, then a loss in production occurs; weight gain in a growing or fattening animal diminishes. These effects of cold can be combated in two ways, firstly by the provision of more feed to increase heat production or secondly by provision of shelter or housing. Both approaches involve forward planning. In the one instance stocks of feed have to be available and there has to be some forward estimate of what the weather is likely to be. Storm feeding of sheep, for example, entails provision of hay stocks and an appreciation of whether a snow fall is likely to be but a shower or sufficient to prevent grazing for a long period. In the second instance, capital has to be invested in shelter and the criterion to be used to ascertain how much can be invested relates to the savings that accrue by sheltering the stock. This entails estimating the likely effect of the weather over the lifetime of the building on the productivity of stock. Both approaches involve forecasting of the weather, one on the short-term basis of a single winter or winter week or month, the other on the basis of many years of winters. Apart from selection of the best time at which to commence additional feeding during the winter, both approaches really entail estimating the effects of what can be called the average winter, for decisions on what feed to conserve or purchase have to be made on a long-term basis to fit farm policy rather than be specifically geared to each particular winter.

There is no difficulty in predicting heat loss using information on wind speed, solar radiation incidence and cloud cover (the latter providing a method of estimating incoming long-wave radiation) (Joyce *et al.*, 1966). Some initial attempts to apply these to meteorological records have been made (Joyce and Blaxter, 1964), but at present we lack complete data on the joint probabilities of occurrence of environmental components so to transform them into estimates of what might be called the 'climatic demand' of an average winter. Since such estimates of the environment are available, the problem then becomes one of translating them to the wide conditions in which animals are kept, for meteorological observations are made at a limited number of locations and under highly standardised conditions.

An alternative approach to estimating the climatic demand from conventional meteorological observations is to use a probe which can be located at a particular site. Construction of a thermostated model of the animal and measurement of the power required to maintain it at constant internal temperature enables this to be done. The principle is based on the contention that the insulation between the deep body and skin in a completely vasoconstricted animal can be regarded as constant; insulation defined as a temperature gradient divided by a heat flux is then only determined by attributes of the coat, which may be fixed, and by the environmental variables of radiation, convection and precipitation. There is now a family of such probes. The first was ASS—the artificial sensing sheep (Blaxter and Joyce, 1963); the next the Canadian MOOCOW—the model ox for observing cold obnoxious weather (Webster, 1971); and later MABEL—the model analogue bovine energy logger (Burnett and Bruce, 1978). Professor Monteith has not given a name to his latest sheep probe (McArthur and Monteith, 1980); surely it should have one!

Dr Bruce has run MABEL for two successive winters and we have fitted to the results a polynomial in time. This describes the sensible heat loss of MABEL during the winter. We have combined these estimates with those which estimate the effect of diet on appetite, heat production and body gain (Blaxter and Boyne, 1978). We can thus predict what effects on animal production accrue in an Aberdeen winter, admittedly from the slender base of two observed winters. The results are given in Figs 8 and 9. They show that well fed animals

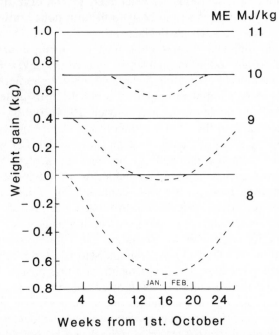

Fig. 8. Predicted daily gain of cattle weighing initially 250 kg when given feed of different quality throughout the Aberdeen winter. ——, No climatic stress; – – –, outdoor conditions.

consuming all they wish of high quality diets suffer no production loss, but those offered low quality diets show diminished growth. The analysis permits estimates to be made of the amounts of additional feed required to maintain growth rate. For an animal gaining in equitable surroundings $0.5–0.55$ kg day^{-1} the winter causes a loss of

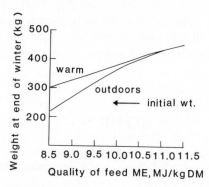

FIG. 9. Final body weights of cattle derived from Fig. 8.

29 kg of weight, worth about £25 at current prices. The additional feed required to combat cold is equivalent to 41 kg barley, which costs currently £3·9. Even with current interest rates one can buy sufficient capital to erect a simple shelter at £25 per beast. The alternative, however, in this instance is to give more feed, and this may well be the more sensible course. However, protection from the weather is only one reason why stock is housed; housing eases winter feeding and prevents attrition on pastures due to 'poaching', the action of feet on wet land.

The model, though it gives results in accord with farming experience, has limitations. The artificial animal does not delay shedding of its coat when it is cold, nor does it exhibit a protective vasodilatation at very low temperatures so to prevent freezing damage to its extremities. The latter response in the live animal reduces its tissue insulation at sub-zero temperatures (Webster and Blaxter, 1966). The model animal does not seek shelter nor orient itself to the sun or reduce the profile it presents to the wind. Additionally, the models do not have a heat capacity analogous to the heat storage term in the identity relating heat production to heat loss. Clearly, we need living probes and many of them to measure the effects of the average winter weather more precisely and ascertain the saving that accrues for different types of shelter.

In conclusion, it is quite certain that long-term climate and short-term weather have considerable effects on animal production under northern temperate conditions. Many of the effects are not direct ones related to temperature regulation, indeed the influence of the environment on the feed available for livestock in winter is probably the most important climatic effect of all in terms of animal production. A fuller understanding of all these effects and their economic implications are obviously of considerable importance in using our resources more efficiently.

REFERENCES

Amoroso, E. C. and Marshall, F. H. A. (1960). External factors in sexual periodicity. In: *Marshall's Physiology of Reproduction*, Vol. 1, Part 2 (Ed. A. S. Parkes). Longmans, London, pp. 707–831.

Baker, J. R. (1938). The evolution of breeding seasons. In: *Evolution: Essays on Aspects of Evolutionary Biology* (Ed. G. R. de Beer). Univ. Press, Oxford.

Baker, J. R. (1939). The relation between latitude and breeding season in birds. *Proc. Zool. Soc. Lond. A* **108,** 557.

Bedford, Duke of and Marshall, F. H. A. (1942). On the incidence of the breeding season of mammals after transference to a new latitude. *Proc. Roy. Soc. London B,* **132,** 306.

Blaxter, K. L. and Boyne, A. W. (1978). The estimation of the nutritive value of feeds as energy sources for ruminants and the derivation of feeding systems. *J. agric. Sci., Camb.* **90,** 47.

Blaxter, K. L. and Gill, J. C. (1979). Voluntary intake of feed and equilibrium body weight in sheep. *Proc. Nutr. Soc.* **38,** 150A.

Blaxter, K. L. and Hamilton, W. J. (1980). Reproduction in farmed red deer. 2. Calf growth and mortality. *J. agric. Sci., Camb.* **95,** 275.

Blaxter, K. L. and Joyce, J. P. (1963). Artificial sheep. *Anim. Prod.* **5,** 216.

Blaxter, K. L., Kay, R. N. B., Sharman, G. A. M., Cunningham, J. M. M. and Hamilton, W. J. (1974). *Farming the Red Deer.* HMSO, Edinburgh.

Blaxter, K. L. and Wainman, F. W. (1961). Environmental temperature and the energy metabolism and heat emission of steers. *J. agric. Sci., Camb.* **56,** 81.

Burnett, G. A. and Bruce, J. M. (1978). Thermal simulation of a suckler cow. *Farm Buildings Progr.* **54,** 11.

Christopherson, R. J. (1976). Effects of prolonged cold and the outdoor environment on apparent digestibility in sheep and cattle. *Can. J. Anim. Sci.* **56,** 201.

Domanski, E., Przekop, F. and Polkowska, J. (1980). Hypothalamic centres involved in the control of gonadotrophin secretion. *J. reprod. Fert.* **58,** 493.

Doney, J. M. (1966). Breed differences in response of wool growth to annual nutritional and climatic cycles. *J. agric. Sci., Camb.* **67,** 25.

Dýrmundsson, O. R. (1973). Puberty and early reproductive performance in sheep. 1. Ewe lambs. *Anim. Breeding Abstr.* **41,** 273.

Forbes, J. M., Brown, W. B., Al Banna, A. G. M. and Jones, R. (1981). The effect of day length on the growth of lambs. 3. Level of feeding, age of lamb and speed of gut fill response. *Anim. Prod.* **32,** 23.

Forbes, J. M., El Shahat, A. A., Jones, R., Duncan, J. G. S. and Boaz, G. (1979). The effect of day length on the growth of lambs. 1. Comparisons of sex, level of feeding, shearing and breed of sire. *Anim. Prod.* **29,** 33.

Gordon, J. G. (1964). Effect of time of year on the roughage intake of housed sheep. *Nature, Lond.* **204,** 798.

Graham, N. McC., Wainman, F. W., Blaxter, K. L. and Armstrong, D. G. (1959). Energy metabolism and heat regulation in closely clipped sheep. *J. agric. Sci., Camb.* **52,** 13.

Haresign, W., Swan, H. and Lewis, D. (1977). *Nutrition and the Climatic Environment.* Butterworths, London.

Hudson, H. G. (1980). Private communication relating to his commercial beef enterprise.

Hugh-Jones, M. E. and Wright, P. B. (1970). Studies on the 1967–68 foot-and-mouth disease epidemic. *J. Hyg., Camb.* **68,** 253.

Jewell, P. A. and Grubb, P. (1974). In *Island Survivors* (Eds P. A. Jewell, C. Milner and J. Morton-Boyd). Oxford Univ. Press. London.

Joyce, J. P. and Blaxter, K. L. (1964). The effects of air movement, air temperature and infra-red radiation on the energy requirements of sheep. *Br. J. Nutr.* **18,** 5.

Joyce, J. P., Blaxter, K. L. and Park, C. (1966). The effect of natural outdoor environments on the energy requirements of sheep. *Res. vet. Sci.* **7,** 342.

Kay, R. N. B. (1979). Seasonal changes of appetite in deer and sheep. *ARC Res. Rev.* **5,** 13.

Kennedy, P. M., Christopherson, R. J. and Milligan, L. P. (1976). Effects of cold exposure of sheep on digestion, rumen turnover time and efficiency of microbial synthesis. *Br. J. Nutr.* **36,** 231.

Kilkenny, J. B. (1974). Housing and equipment. In: *Beef Production, Meat and Livestock Commission Handbook No. 2.* p. 49.

Lincoln, G. A. (1979). Photoperiodic control of seasonal breeding in the ram: participation of the cranial sympathetic nervous system. *J. endocrinol.* **82,** 135.

McArthur, A. J. and Monteith, J. L. (1980). Air movement and heat loss from sheep. 1. Boundary layer insulation of a model sheep with and without fleece. *Proc. Roy. Soc. Lond. B.* **209,** 187.

Mitchell, B., Staines, B. W. and Welch, D. (1977). *Ecology of the Red Deer.* Inst. Terrestrial Ecol., Natural Environment Research Council.

Monteith, J. L. and Mount, L. E. (1974). *Heat Losses from Animals and Man.* Butterworths, London.

Mount, L. E. (1979). *Adaptation to the Thermal Environment: Man and his Productive Animals.* Edward Arnold, London.

Nagorcka, B. N. (1978). The effect of photoperiod on wool growth. In: *Physiological and Environmental Limitations to Wool Growth* (Eds J. L. Black and P. J. Reis). Univ. New Eng. Pub. Unit, Armidale, N.S.W., p. 127.

Ollerenshaw, C. B. (1980). Animal disease forecasts—reflections on the winter of 1978–79. *ADAS Quart. Rev.* **37,** 87.

Ollerenshaw, C. B., Graham, E. G. and Smith, L. P. (1978). Forecasting the incidence of parasitic gastroenteritis in lambs in England and Wales. *Vet. Rec.* **103,** 461.

Pelletier, J. (1973). Evidence for the photoperiodic control of prolactin release in rams. *J. reprod. Fert.* **35,** 143.

Quirke, J. F. (1978). Onset of puberty and oestrus activity in Galway, Finnish Landrace and Finn-cross ewe lambs during their first breeding season. *Irish J. Agric. Res.* **17,** 15.

Ravault, J.-P. and Ortavant, R. (1977). Light control of prolactin secretion in sheep. Evidence for a photo-inducible phase during a diurnal rhythm. *Ann. Biol. Bioch. Biophys.* **17,** 459.

Robertshaw, D. (1974). *Environmental Physiology: MTP International Review of Science, Vol. 7.* Butterworths, London.

Robinson, J. J. and Ørskov, E. R. (1975). An integrated approach to improving the biological efficiency of sheep meat production. *World Rev. Anim. Prod.* **11,** 63.

Rowan, W. (1925). Relation of light to bird migration and developmental changes. *Nature, Lond.* **115,** 494.

Roy, J. H. B., Gillies, C. M., Perfitt, M. W. and Stobo, I. J. F. (1980). Effect of season of the year and phase of the moon on puberty and on the occurrence of oestrus and conception in dairy heifers reared on high planes of nutrition. *Anim. Prod.* **31,** 13.

Ryder, M. L. (1969). The development and structure of and seasonal change in the coat of some Wiltshire sheep. *Anim. Prod.* **11,** 467.

Ryder, M. L. (1973). *Hair.* Inst. Biol. Studies in Biology. No. 41. Edward Arnold, London.

Sadleir, R. M. F. S. (1972). Environmental effects. In: *Reproduction in Mammals. 4. Reproductive Patterns.* (Eds C. R. Austin and R. V. Short). Univ. Press, Cambridge.

Simpson, A. M. (1976). Energy metabolism and seasonal cycles of captive red deer. Ph.D. Thesis, Univ. Aberdeen.

Smith, L. P. and Hugh-Jones, M. E. (1969). The weather factor in foot-and-mouth disease epidemics. *Nature, Lond.* **223,** 713.

Smith, L. P. and Thomas, R. J. (1972). Forecasting the spring hatch of *Nematodirus battus* by the use of soil temperature data. *Vet. Rec.* **90,** 188.

Tarttelin, M. F. (1968). Cyclical variations in food and water intakes in ewes. *J. Physiol., Lond.* **195,** 29P.

Thomas, R. J. and Starr, J. R. (1978). Forecasting the peak of gastrointestinal nematode infection in lambs. *Vet. Rec.* **103,** 465.

Wallace, R. (1907). *Farm Livestock of Great Britain,* 4th edn. Oliver and Boyd, Edinburgh.

Webster, A. J. F. (1971). Prediction of heat losses from cattle exposed to cold outdoor environments. *J. appl. Physiol.* **30,** 684.

Webster, A. J. F. (1981). Weather and infectious disease in cattle. *Vet. Rec.* **108,** 183.

Webster, A. J. F. and Blaxter, K. L. (1966). The thermal regulation of two breeds of sheep exposed to air temperatures below freezing point. *Res. vet. Sci.* **7,** 466.

Webster, A. J. F., Chlumecky, J. and Young, B. A. (1970). Effects of cold environments on the energy exchanges of young beef cattle. *Can. J. Anim. Sci.* **50,** 89.

Westra, R. and Christopherson, R. J. (1976). Effects of cold on digestibility retention time of digesta, reticulum mobility and thyroid hormones in sheep. *Can. J. Anim. Sci.* **56,** 699.

Yeates, N. T. M. (1949). The breeding season of the sheep with particular reference to its modification by artificial means using light. *J. agric. Sci., Camb.* **39,** 1.

Zuckerman, S. (1932). *The Social Life of Monkeys and Apes.* Keegan, Paul and Co., London.

Discussion

Mr Smith stated that he did not think that there was much to be gained by trying to increase the precision of the correlation-type models by including more variables if the simplest approach was satisfactory. In the instance of the prediction of *Nematodirus* infestation in lambs, his opinion was that the original idea of taking simply the March soil temperature was adequate for general guidance. *Dr Booth* asked whether there was any indication of effects of environmental temperature on cellular turnover in the gut. Information on small animals suggests that turnover of cells increased on reduction of environmental temperature. To this *Sir Kenneth* replied that as far as he was aware no experiments of a similar nature had been done in large farm livestock. *Professor Waterlow* asked whether there was any indication that rates of protein synthesis increased in ruminants during sleep and whether, in the long summer days, food acquisition was limited by the necessity to sleep. *Sir Kenneth* stated that while there was clear evidence that the state of central nervous system vigilance changed in ruminants and while similar or analogous changes could be seen in them, like paradoxical sleep or REM sleep, there was no indication that the ability of an animal to harvest food was in any way inhibited by CNS vigilance or sleep. Conventional sleep in ruminants is very short in duration.

Professor Monteith stated that he thought that the value of models such as MABEL was not so much as probes but as means whereby one could obtain the fundamental parameters relating to the energy exchanges from very complex surfaces. It could be argued that it would be more sensible, rather than to clone artificial animals, to build simple recording automatic weather stations to provide standardised variables which could then be used in computer models to evaluate heat loss for a much wider range of parameters. Even more elements of behaviour could be included in a computer model. *Sir Kenneth* stated that he thought that such automated stations would have very considerable advantages provided they could be installed in relative profusion. They had advantages insofar that the data could be used for a variety of different purposes. Once the basic physics of the energy exchanges had been worked out in any situation, then it should be possible to relate these to a variety of situations. An automatic weather station, for example, could be used to accumulate information relevant to the design and insulation to be placed on animal buildings, or indeed buildings of any sort, and obviously the data could be used to predict the heat exchanges of not one single type of animal but a variety of them.

Professor Bunting asked about the response of animals to day length, and what particularly were they able to measure. *Sir Kenneth* replied that much work was taking place in this field and that French workers had shown fairly unequivocally that the sensing was of the nature of an on–off signal. The animal sensed at a particular time after dawn whether or not light was present. There did not seem to be anything in the nature of an integration of the day-to-day responses or a measurement of rate of change of day length. The signal which was analysed was simply the on–off signal.

Professor Webster returned to the question of the limitations of models and pointed out that another limitation was that they failed to acclimate to seasonal changes and to cold *per se*. On the prairies in Canada it was found that exposure of animals to very low temperatures during the winter changed both lower and upper critical temperatures by somewhere near 20°C and it was possible to induce panting in cold-adapted animals at temperatures as low as 3°C. *Sir Kenneth* thought that the experiments to which Professor Webster referred could largely be explained by the change in coat shedding pattern and an increase in external insulation, to which *Professor Webster* replied that his impression was that at most 50% of the change in critical temperature could be accounted for in this fashion.

Mr. Jackson asked about the effects of shearing ewes in the autumn of the year and the extent of breed differences in these respects. *Sir Kenneth* replied that in Australia it was commonplace to muster sheep, hold them without food for a while before shearing, remove very efficiently the whole of their fleece, and hold them again without food before returning them to their grazings. Under these conditions, if there was slight rain and wind, very many deaths occurred. These were entirely due to the animals' heat production not being able to cope with the massively increased thermal demand. The device of using a snow-comb on the shears had left an extra few millimetres of residual fleece and this had had the result of reducing death rate.

Dr. Elia suggested that there could well be hypotheses to explain the winter depression of appetite of the ruminants under cold circumstances. *Sir Kenneth* replied that he agreed there were a number of possible explanations that could be put forward and this was really at the bottom of the unsatisfactory nature of the teleological argument. It had to be admitted that explaining matters in terms of survival value while no doubt satisfactory did not really advance understanding very greatly.

Nutrient Needs for Man in Different Environments

J. C. WATERLOW

London School of Hygiene and Tropical Medicine, UK

The title of this symposium is 'Food, Nutrition and Climate' and I have to discuss the effect of environment on man's nutrient needs. This is a large task: environment includes climate, but also a great deal more. In the health field we include in the environment factors such as the water supply, the prevalence of vector-borne diseases, etc. A very common phrase nowadays is the socio-economic environment. Then there is what people are now calling the 'micro-environment'—the relations within the family and the level of stimulation in the home. The pioneer work of Cravioto (1977) in Mexico and of Richardson (1976) and Grantham-McGregor *et al.* (1980) in Jamaica has shown how important this is in determining whether or not a child becomes malnourished.

To begin with, we might consider the findings from Nepal shown in Fig. 1. The seasonal variations in the growth rate of children depend on the availability of food, the prevalence of infection, water-borne or respiratory, the amount of time the mother has to spend working in the fields or collecting fuel and water rather than looking after the children, and so on. These in turn depend on seasonal and climatic factors such as the monsoon and the planting season. All these factors are inter-related—it is impossible to separate them. Therefore, as is obvious, the environmental effects on nutrition are very complicated. Equally, the concept of requirements is not a simple one. Classically, the requirement is supposed to be the amount of a nutrient needed for health, which we can only define by criteria which are partial and inadequate. It may be more practical to think of a range of intakes which are acceptable under different conditions, rather than of a single target level.

I am dividing this paper into two parts. The first provides some

271

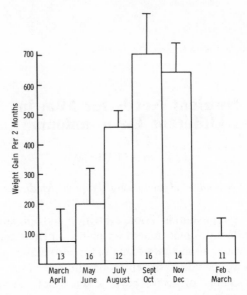

Fig. 1. Mean and standard error of weight gain of individual children aged 5–32 months in Chuliban village, Dhankuta, Nepal over successive two-month periods. A difference of 300 g is significant.

examples of fairly direct and obvious effects of climate and environment on requirements, and of situations in which people may be unable to meet their requirements. In the second, and more diffuse part I want to consider some environmental situations in which our estimates of requirements do not seem to work very well. In general, in the present state of knowledge it would usually be better to talk of 'estimates of requirements' rather than 'requirements', but the phrase is rather cumbersome.

EXAMPLES OF DIRECT EFFECTS OF ENVIRONMENT ON NUTRIENT NEEDS

Salt

The most obvious example of these direct effects is the increased need for sodium chloride in hot climates, to replace that lost in sweat. This essential need has had important economic and political consequences, such as the development of trade routes for salt across the

Sahara, and the use in India of a salt monopoly and a salt tax as a major means of raising revenue. In fact, the word 'salary' comes from the Latin for salt. I do not know whether anyone has written a history of salt from this point of view, comparable to Salaman's history of the potato (Salaman, 1949).

The losses of salt in a hot climate can be very large. When I was working on heat stroke and heat exhaustion in Iraq during the War the late Dr W. S. Ladell and I found that an active man in that climate (140°F in the shade) might lose 9 litres of sweat in a day, containing about 0·3% NaCl, giving a salt loss of nearly 30 g day^{-1}. These observations were made on men who were at least partially acclimatised. It is well known that with acclimatisation the salt content of sweat falls, but I do not think that it can go much below 0·2%, so that losses under these severe conditions will always be considerable. Another interesting point, which to my knowledge has not been much investigated, is that individuals seem to differ in their ability to conserve salt. Although it was contrary to Army regulations, I myself never took extra salt, other than that in food, and felt no ill effects, while others found it necessary to take substantial amounts. Is there possibly some link here with the apparent constitutional differences between individuals in the way their blood pressure reacts to salt intake?

Iodine and endemic goitre

I do not know whether it is correct to include geography as a component of the environment, but if it is, then mention should be made of the prevalence of endemic goitre in mountainous regions. That this is due mainly to iodine deficiency in soil and water, and hence in food, is clearly established by measurements of iodine status and by the prophylactic effect of the iodination of salt. If we include in our terms of reference the social environment and the extent to which it allows the application of scientific knowledge, then it is interesting to recall that in a previous Symposium of this series Elton (1978) pointed out that in southern Germany endemic goitre still has a prevalence of 32%, although it has virtually been eliminated from Switzerland and New Zealand.

It is also becoming clear that in less privileged countries iodine deficiency is not the only factor. There appears to be a clear relationship to a toxic factor in some foods, such as cassava (Ermans *et al.*,

1980); moreover, protein–energy malnutrition predisposes to, or makes worse, the defects of thyroid function which are characteristic of iodine deficiency goitre (Ingenbleek *et al.*, 1980).

Iron

Needs for iron are influenced by environmental factors in two ways, though perhaps it is stretching it a bit to describe the effects as direct. First, in tropical countries iron requirements are increased by parasites, e.g. the direct blood loss produced by hookworm and the haemolytic anaemia of malaria. These parasites, or their vectors, cannot easily survive in more temperate climates. I say easily, because malaria was at one time indigenous in East Anglia in the UK, Holland, Russia— countries which can hardly be described as tropical.

The second cause of increased iron needs in the tropics is that the iron in the prevailing vegetable diets is very poorly absorbed. Most of this iron is in the inorganic form, whereas in animal foods it is mostly present as haem. It was shown some years ago that external labelling, by simply adding radioactive iron to foods, gives exactly the same result as giving foods containing biosynthetically labelled iron. This has made measurement of iron absorption very easy, and it is now clear that with most vegetable sources only about 5% of the iron is absorbed. Perhaps it is not fair to say that this is an effect of the environment, except in so far as the environment conditions the diet.

Vitamin D and rickets

Colleagues who are slightly older than me, who practised paediatrics in cities such as Glasgow in the years before the War, tell me that rickets was then one of the commonest of children's diseases, in spite of the fact that, from the work of Mellanby and of Chick, the cause and prevention of rickets seemed to be quite well understood. Since then the prevalence has greatly decreased, but it is hard to disentangle the reasons because several things have happened. The diets of children have improved; the welfare services provide vitamin D; and the clean air acts have reduced atmospheric pollution. The prevailing opinion among the experts in this field is that sunlight is a far more important source of vitamin D than intake in the food (Poskitt *et al.*, 1979). It is now well established that rickets in the UK is found almost exclusively in the children of immigrants from the Asian subcontinent, and osteomalacia is most common in Asian women (Department of Health and Social Security, 1980). In a recent study which we carried out on pregnant women in South London, the serum vitamin D level in Asian mothers was only half that of West Indians or Europeans (D. I. Thurnham, unpublished). It is difficult to understand why this should be, on the sunlight theory, since we are all under the same sky. It has been suggested that for cultural reasons Asian women and children are more covered up, but for infants at any rate this seems rather a thin explanation. There are, of course, differences in diet, but again these differences are less for infants than for adults.

One question which has arisen is whether the immigrants brought the rickets with them. When the Asian people were expelled from Uganda and lodged for a time in camps in this country, we had the opportunity, in collaboration with Professor T. P. Whitehead and Dr Trevor Stamp, to examine four biochemical variables: calcium, phosphorus, alkaline phosphatase and 25-Hydroxycholecalciferol (25-HCC), in a fairly large sample. Absolutely no abnormalities were found (Stamp, 1980). These people came from a region—Uganda—of reasonably high altitude, with plenty of sunlight. This seems to rule out any genetic factor.

It is now becoming clear, although the epidemiology is so far poor, that rickets, although rare in the true tropics, is common throughout the subtropical zone, extending from northern India through the Middle East and Turkey to North Africa, and even Greece. WHO now regards rickets as an important public health problem. All this seems very odd, since many of these countries are ones to which people from the North go to for holidays in the sun. The explanation must lie in an interaction between climate and cultural factors. I shall end this section with two examples of this.

Some years ago, Groen et al. (1965) described osteomalacia among Bedouin women of the Negev desert. At that time custom demanded that the women lived inside tents or that when they went outside they were fully covered with black clothes. A change in social behaviour seems to have occurred: the women nowadays work unveiled, with head, arms and feet exposed to the sun. Perhaps as a consequence, in a small sample studied by Shany et al. (1976) serum concentrations of 25-HCC were found to be well above the range typical of osteomalacia.

Another example comes from the other side of the world. In 20 years in Jamaica I never saw a clear case of vitamin D deficiency rickets. In recent years the condition has been observed in children living in high-rise flats, with little opportunity to go outside, particularly if the lifts break down (Miller and Chutkan, 1976).

PROTEIN AND ENERGY REQUIREMENTS IN DIFFERENT ENVIRONMENTS

I come now to a more difficult and less easily definable problem. Estimates of protein and energy requirements, such as those of FAO/WHO (1973) have in general been based on observations made in developed countries. When we come to apply these estimates in less favourable environments, a number of problems arise, of which I shall try to give examples. Undoubtedly, over a certain range, human beings can adapt to different dietary conditions. However, adaptation is a relative term. Often when we use it we seem to be implying that, 'I am normal, but you are adapted', and there is a further implication that the adaptation must involve some sacrifice or limitation of function. This is often unjustified. The Swiss physiologist Alexander von Muralt once said that if a textbook of physiology had been produced by an inhabitant of the high Andes, he might have written: 'With us when a child is born, it emerges from the low oxygen tension of the uterine environment to a similarly low tension in the outside world. How marvellous it is that a child born at sea level can adapt so rapidly to the high oxygen tension which it finds down there'.

The point I want to make is that adaptation is a two-way process. If requirements appear to be different in different environments, there is no justification for supposing that one is the norm and the other a deviation from it. We have got into the habit of thinking in this way, and therefore of producing recommendations which may be inappropriate for situations other than our own.

PROTEIN REQUIREMENTS

Young children

Current estimates (FAO/WHO, 1973) of the protein requirements of young infants are based on observed intakes of breast milk, which has a protein:energy ratio of 7–8%. The figure, appropriate to the child who is growing very rapidly, provides at least one fixed point on which we can rely. The only condition in which the protein requirement, in relation to energy, is greater than this is lactation.

After six months of age the protein requirement has been calculated by adding together the maintenance requirement (assessed from the basal metabolic rate at $2\,mg\,N\,kcal^{-1}$) and the amount of N required for the formation of new tissue. As the rate of growth falls off, so this growth complement rapidly becomes quite small, and the estimated protein requirement in the second year of life falls to about 5% of total energy (Waterlow and Payne, 1975). Are these figures realistic? In the 1960s, because of the interest all over the world in kwashiorkor, there was great emphasis on the *protein* gap and how to fill it. Then, when it was realised that the diets of most children everywhere contain sufficient protein to meet these requirements, provided that enough food is eaten to satisfy energy needs, the protein gap turned into the protein fiasco (McLaren, 1975). The emphasis changed to the fulfilment of energy needs.

I now begin to wonder whether the pendulum has not swung too far, for the following reason. In almost every Third World country there are very large numbers of pre-school children whose growth in height is retarded, by our standards (Waterlow, 1978). There is possibly some inherited element in this, since in developed as well as developing countries the height of children is related to that of the mother. Nevertheless, there is strong evidence of an environmental influence also, for example the secular increase in height of children which has occurred in many countries. We do not know whether this stunting, as I have called it, matters in any biological sense, nor do we know its cause. When we estimate protein requirements in the way that I have mentioned, we take account of gains in weight, but no-one knows the protein requirements for growth in height. Everyone here will remember the comparison which Orr and Gilks (1931) drew in Kenya between the tall, well-grown Masai, who live on meat and blood and milk, and the short Kikuyu, whose staple is maize. Rutishauser and Whitehead (1969) found a similar difference between the Karamoja and Buganda tribes in Uganda, the former living on meat and milk, the latter having plantain as their staple. Could the stunting which is so common result from a deficiency of protein, or of calcium, or of some factor associated with animal protein, such as zinc? Golden and Golden (1981) have shown that in children recovering from malnutrition on a diet containing soya protein rather than milk, the rate of weight gain was limited by shortage of zinc. I am here talking about growth in height rather than weight, but his finding illustrates the point that diets for young children which do not contain milk may be deficient in this trace element.

Alternatively, stunting could be regarded as a reasonably successful adaptation to a hostile environment, because a small child needs less food. There are certainly risks and handicaps associated with stunting, for example, these children have a lower developmental quotient (Richardson, 1976), but presumably this is another effect of the environment, and not a consequence of growth retardation *per se*. To summarise this point: our criteria for the protein requirements of children may be inadequate, because they do not allow for growth in height. However, we do not know whether this inadequacy is of any real importance.

Another criticism of the current estimates of the protein requirements of children is that they take no account of the infections which are so prevalent in children in developing countries. One way of quantifying the effect of infection is by plotting the weight gains of children against the proportion of time that they are suffering from an infection. Rowland *et al.* (1977) did this for children in the Gambia, and showed that on average children were infected for 14% of the time during the rainy season, and that there was a deficit in weight gain of $3 \text{ g kg}^{-1} \text{ day}^{-1}$ infected.

This deficit has to be restored during the 86% of the time that the child is not infected, i.e. the diet should support an additional weight gain, on top of normal growth, of $(3 \times 14)/86$—about $0 \cdot 5 \text{ g kg}^{-1} \text{ day}^{-1}$. The extra requirements for this are about $2 \cdot 5$ kcal and $0 \cdot 13$ g protein $\text{kg}^{-1} \text{ day}^{-1}$. These are not large amounts, and if the figures are correct the conclusion seems to be that the main problem for these children is not so much the infection, but their generally low intake. Martorell *et al.* (1980) in Guatemala obtained very similar results. The conclusion is rather surprising. All one can say is that if children are on marginal intakes, the extra stress, although not very great, tips them over the edge.

PROTEIN REQUIREMENTS OF ADULTS

The last FAO/WHO Expert Committee on Protein Requirements (FAO/WHO, 1973), basing its estimates on all the available data from balance studies, concluded that the safe level of protein intake, which would meet the needs of 97·5% of the population, was approximately $0 \cdot 6 \text{ g kg}^{-1} \text{ day}^{-1}$, in terms of top quality protein (egg). After that,

Scrimshaw and his colleagues, in a series of studies at MIT on healthy young American adults, found that in general his subjects did not come into N balance on this level of intake, and over long periods there were some signs of harmful effects (raised serum transaminases) (Young *et al.*, 1973; Garza *et al.*, 1977). On the other hand, Nicol and Phillips (1976) carried out a very similar study on farmers in northern Nigeria and found that they did come into balance on the safe level of egg protein. The very important question then is whether the Nigerians were depleted, as Scrimshaw has maintained, or adapted. At the biochemical level, the adaptation to low protein intakes must depend on a reduction in activity of the enzymes which irreversibly oxidise amino acids. We know that in experimental animals these adaptive changes take place, even in the enzymes in muscle which oxidise branched chain amino acids, but we do not know the extent or the speed with which they occur in man. This is a question which could now be investigated with modern techniques (see Waterlow and Stephen, 1981). In the meantime, in order to resolve the discrepancies, the UNU has organised balance studies in a number of Third World countries, with subjects receiving the safe level of protein derived from their habitual diets. We shall await the results of these studies with interest.

PROBLEMS RELATED TO ENERGY REQUIREMENTS

Energy requirements have been estimated in two ways: from observed intakes and from measurements of energy expenditure for basal metabolism, physical activity, etc. All the original measurements were World War One. Orr and Leitch (1938), in a review which I think is often overlooked, showed that physiological estimates of energy requirements for various occupations agree very well with what on average we actually eat. Other workers since then have amply confirmed this. It is important, of course, to recognise the enormous variability that there is in intakes (Widdowson, 1962), and presumably also in requirements.

Energy requirements of young children

One of the problems of determining the energy requirements of young children is that it is difficult to measure the amount of energy expended on physical activity. The usual recommendation is that a child of one to two years needs on average about 90 kcal kg^{-1} day^{-1}. Some people think that this is too high, because many children can grow satisfactorily on lower intakes. They think that we are using inappropriate Western standards for weight gain, which include many children who are overweight or even obese. I fully agree that weight gain is not everything. Ferro-Luzzi et al. (1979), in a comparison of young children from the rural south of Italy with children from Rome showed that the former, in spite of significantly lower energy intakes, had a slightly greater lean body mass and performed better in a physical fitness test, i.e. they were thinner but fitter. However, it does seem that when energy intake is limiting, physical activity is the first thing to be sacrificed. Torun (1980) and co-workers in Guatemala showed that when the net energy intake of preschool children was reduced from 90 to 80 kcal kg^{-1} day^{-1}, growth and N balance were not impaired, but there was a decrease in energy expenditure. Rutishauser and Whitehead (1972) compared the energy expenditure of Ugandan and European children of one to three years old. The Ugandan children spent most of their time sitting or standing around, with very little walking or running about. On average, they expended 20 kcal kg^{-1} day^{-1} less than the European children; their intake at 70 kcal kg^{-1} day^{-1}, was just enough to cover maintenance and growth. The reduction in activity could be regarded as an adaptation to restricted energy intake, which is necessary for the preservation of life. However, this adaptation is certainly not harmless, because it means decreased exploratory activity and, as a result, retardation in mental and social development. In this situation quite small deficits, of the order of 10–20% of the requirement, can have very serious consequences.

Lactating women

This is the group in which there is the biggest gap between what people actually eat and physiological estimates of what they need. In the UK the fit is quite good. Thomson et al. (1970) compared the intakes of mothers with young infants, some of whom were breast feeding and others bottle feeding. The intake of the bottle-feeding mothers was on average 2200 kcal day^{-1}, while the breast-feeding mothers consumed 600 kcal day^{-1} more. Although the output of breast milk was not measured, this difference corresponds very well with the expected energy content of the breast milk.

In developing countries the picture is quite different. Results summarised by Prentice (1980) show intakes of lactating women in the Gambia which range from 1200 kcal day^{-1} in the wet season to 1750 kcal day^{-1} in the dry season. Equally low intakes have been recorded in India (Prentice, 1980) and in New Guinea (Norgan et al., 1974). These intakes are incredibly low, and one's first instinct is to doubt their accuracy. However, they have been determined by very experienced investigators, and in my view we have to accept them as correct. Nor can we say that lactation performance is entirely unsatisfactory, although it may not be optimal. It therefore remains a mystery how these women can not only produce milk but also work in the fields on such low intakes. We cannot say simply that our methods are wrong, if they work in the UK but not in the Gambia. If some kind of adaptation has occurred, we need to know its mechanism and its cost. This is one of the most important challenges for nutrition at the present time.

REFERENCES

Cravioto, J. (1977). Not by bread alone: effect of early malnutrition and stimuli deprivation on mental development. In: *Perspectives in Pediatrics* (Ed. O. P. Ghai). Interprint, New Delhi, India, pp. 87–104.

Department of Health and Social Security (1980). *Rickets and Osteomalacia.* Report of The Working Party on Fortification of Food with Vitamin D. Committee on Medical Aspects of Food Policy. HMSO, London.

Elton, G. A. H. (1978). European diets in relation to standards of need. In: *Diet of Man: Needs and Wants* (Ed. J. Yudkin). Applied Science Publishers, London, pp. 25–40.

Ermans, A. M., Mbulamoko, N. M., Delange, F. and Ahluwalia, R. (1980). *Role of Cassava in the Etiology of Endemic Goitre and Cretinism.* International Development Research Centre, Ottawa, Canada.

FAO/WHO (1973). *Energy and Protein Requirements.* Report of a Joint FAO/WHO Ad Hoc Expert Committee. FAO Nutrition Meetings Rep. Ser. 52. FAO, Rome, Italy.

Ferro-Luzzi, A., d'Amicis, A., Ferrini, A. M. and Maiale, G. (1979). Nutrition, environment and physical performance of preschool children in Italy. *Biblthca Nutr Dieta* **27,** 85–106.

Garza, C., Scrimshaw, N. S. and Young, V. R. (1977). Human protein requirements: a long term metabolic nitrogen balance study in young men to evaluate the 1973 FAO/WHO safe level of egg protein intake. *J. Nutr.* **107,** 335–52.

Golden, M. H. N. and Golden, B. E. (1981). Trace elements: potential importance in human nutrition, with particular reference to zinc and vanadium. *Br. Med. Bull.* **37,** 31–6.

Grantham-McGregor, S. M., Stewart, M. E. and Desai, P. (1980). The relationship between hospitalization, social background, severe protein energy malnutrition and mental development in young Jamaican children. *Ecology of Food and Nutrition* 151–6.

Groen, J. J., Eshchar, J., Ben-Ishay, D., Alkan, W. J. and Ben Assa, B. I. (1965). Osteomalacia among the Bedouin of the Negev desert. *Archs Intern. Med.* **116,** 195–204.

Ingenbleek, Y., Luypaert, B. and De Nayer, Ph. (1980). Nutritional status and endemic goitre. *Lancet* i, 388–92.

Martorell, R., Yarbrough, C., Yarbrough, S. and Klein, R. E. (1980). The impact of ordinary illness on the dietary intakes of malnourished children. *Am. J. Clin. Nutr.* **33,** 345–54.

McLaren, D. S. (1975). The protein fiasco. *Lancet* ii, 93–6.

Miller, C. G. and Chutkan, W. (1976). Vitamin D deficiency rickets in Jamaican children. *Archs Dis. Chldh.* **51,** 214–18.

Nicol, B. M. and Phillips, P. G. (1976). Endogenous nitrogen excretion and utilization of dietary protein. *Br. J. Nutr.* **35,** 181–93.

Norgan, N. G., Ferro-Luzzi, A. and Durnin, J. V. G. A. (1974). The energy and nutrient intake and the energy expenditure of 204 New Guinean adults. *Phil. Trans. R. Soc. Lond. B* **268,** 309–48.

Orr, J. B. and Gilks, J. L. (1931). *Studies of Nutrition. The Physique and Health of Two African Tribes.* Spec. Rep. Ser. Med. Res. Counc. No. 155. HMSO, London.

Orr, J. B. and Leitch, I. (1938). The determination of the calorie requirements of man. *Nutr. Abstr. Rev.* **7,** 509–29.

Poskitt, E. M. E., Cole, T. J. and Lawson, D. E. M. (1979). Diet, sunlight and 25-hydroxyvitamin D in health of children and adults. *Br. Med. J.* i, 221–3.

Prentice, A. M. (1980). Variation in maternal dietary intake, birthweight and breast milk output in the Gambia. In: *Maternal Nutrition During Pregnancy and Lactation* (Eds H. Aebi and R. G. Whitehead). Hans Huber, Bern, pp. 167–83.

Richardson, S. A. (1976). The relation of severe malnutrition in infancy to the intelligence of school children with differing life histories. *Pediat. Res.* **10,** 57–61.

Rowland, M. G. M., Cole, T. J. and Whitehead, R. G. (1977). A quantitative study into the role of infection in determining nutrition status in Gambian village children. *Br. J. Nutr.* **37,** 441–50.

Rutishauser, I. H. E. and Whitehead, R. G. (1969). Field evaluation of two biochemical tests which may reflect nutritional status in three areas of Uganda. *Br. J. Nutr.* **23,** 1–13.

Rutishauser, I. H. E. and Whitehead, R. G. (1972). Energy intake and expenditure in 1–3 year old Ugandan children living in a rural environment. *Br. J. Nutr.* **28,** 145–52.

Salaman, R. N. (1949). *The History and Social Influence of the Potato.* Cambridge University Press, London.

Shany, S., Hirsh, J. and Berlyne, G. M. (1976). 25-Hydroxycholecalciferol levels in Bedouins in the Negev. *Am. J. Clin. Nutr.* **29,** 1104–7.

Stamp, T. C. B. (1980). Sources of vitamin D nutrition. *Lancet* i, 316.

Thomson, A. M., Hytten, F. E. and Billewicz, W. Z. (1970). The energy cost of human lactation. *Br. J. Nutr.* **24,** 565–72.

Torun, B. (1980). Unpublished observations in: Report on the informal gathering of investigators to review the collaborative research programme on protein requirements and energy intake. ESN/Misc/80/3. FAO, Rome.

Waterlow, J. C. (1978). Observations on the assessment of protein–energy malnutrition with special reference to stunting. *Courrier* **28,** 455–60.

Waterlow, J. C. and Payne, P. R. (1975). The protein gap. *Nature,* **258,** 113–17.

Waterlow, J. C. and Stephen, J. M. L. (Eds) (1981). *Nitrogen Metabolism in Man.* Applied Science Publishers, London.

Widdowson, E. M. (1962). Nutritional individuality. *Proc. Nutr. Soc.* **21,** 121–69.

Young, V. R., Taylor, Y. S. M., Rand, W. M. and Scrimshaw, N. S. (1973). Protein requirements of man: efficiency of egg protein utilization at maintenance and submaintenance levels in young men. *J. Nutr.* **103,** 1164–74.

Discussion

Dr Collins raised a number of problems related to salt and water requirements under hot environmental conditions. Many statements were made, particularly in text books, which could not be substantiated. There is, for example, no evidence that man can reduce his water requirement in hot environments and in tropical situations water turnover does increase markedly. Similarly, the suggestion that there should be abundant salt intake at all times, and this approaches $30 \, g \, day^{-1}$, is clearly not correct. A requirement of this order is only apparent for a day or so before acclimation takes place. Furthermore, he was of the opinion that much of the work done on water and salt metabolism under conditions of heavy work could be criticised because of faulty methodology. Studies that have recently been made on man in which 72-h balances were performed relating to potassium, nitrogen and iron showed that cutaneous losses from the body were quite small, even in heat acclimatised states with high sweat rates. With respect to the salt problem, *Professor Waterlow* stated that it may well be that there has been an over-estimation of salt need, but the fact remains that considerable importance is attached to salt in tropical countries. It is an essential article of trade and he was of the opinion that this long accumulated knowledge could not be ignored. *Dr Booth* wondered whether the differences in salt economy in tropical areas related to the incidence of high blood pressure in developing countries. *Professor Waterlow* replied that there is a large variation and the cause of the higher blood pressure was completely unknown.

Dr Ulbricht said that the fundamental assumption of most nutritionists, which needed to be questioned, was that the desirable rate of growth of children is the fastest rate of growth. Should not work be done to define the optimal rate of growth which may not necessarily be the maximal? *Professor Waterlow* agreed that this assumption was implicit but pointed out that one needed a very long time in order to test whether there was a deviation of the optimal from the maximal.

The continuing studies in the UK should provide some information of this sort, but only after many years.

Sir Kenneth Blaxter stated that Scrimshaw's studies on balance in man really confirmed Dr Calloway's studies in California, namely that the nitrogen balance was dependent on concomitant energy supply and that to obtain balance more energy had to be used by the young men concerned and this gave rise to an increase in body weight and presumptively body fatness. The subjects, however, were kept under confinement and it could be argued that under natural conditions of exercise this apparent discrepancy would not occur. *Professor Waterlow* stated that the Scrimshaw experiments were open to this criticism, but Dr Scrimshaw was now conducting collaborative studies in several countries using natural diets rather than the rather unpalatable whole egg diets. He thought that these balance studies with natural diets together with studies on the fate of labelled amino acids might enable us to get closer to estimates of need.

Professor Taylor commented on the incidence of rickets in tropical countries with high solar radiation. Firstly, the incidence of rickets appeared to be more common in female than in male children and the experience in northern countries was that the matter was more serious in northern cities than in southern ones. The observations in Saudi Arabia had shown that rickets was quite common despite the high intensity of solar radiation and much of this was related to the shrouding of women and the keeping of children and infants indoors away from direct sunlight. *Professor Waterlow* stated that he still had difficulty in accounting for the incidence of rickets in Mediterranean-type countries and other countries with high solar radiation. Admittedly, the absorption of calcium from unleavened bread might be involved through the phytate–phosphorus mechanism, but he could hardly conceive that the solar radiation story and the way in which children were kept in tropical and subtropical countries was the factor responsible.

Professor MacKey asked whether there were differences in racial groups with respect to digestive efficiency and whether any reliable parameter is available, such as length of digestive tract. *Professor Waterlow* replied saying that all the evidence suggested that the obligatory losses of nitrogen showed no differences as between racial groups when corrected to similar body size, and as far as one could see, there were no clear differences in physiological needs. The difficulty which he had outlined in his paper thus remained.

Shelter, Clothing and Climate

R. H. FOX

26 St. Peters Way, Chorleywood, Herts, UK

INTRODUCTION

Man is unique amongst the homeotherms in the success he has achieved in maintaining his deep body temperature constant in hostile thermal environments. This is due to the application of his intellect and inventiveness to use and modify the environment in which he lives, rather than the evolution of superior physiological mechanisms.

Nevertheless, physiological mechanisms remain essential for the fine control of body temperature, and the clothing/shelter combinations man has evolved are simply designed to protect them from overloading.

Over millennia primitive men evolved simple, but effective, techniques to live and work in particular hostile climates, thus enabling them to colonise ever greater areas of the earth's surface. In more recent times these specialised life styles have been increasingly supplanted by a reliance on energy intensive building and air conditioning. In the western world this has led to increasing demands on unreplenishable energy sources and poses serious problems for future generations. The rapidity of these changes has also thrown great strain on the normally slow process of social evolution and adaptation, which may well be placing some of the more vulnerable members of our community at risk. One example is the plight of many elderly folk in England in the winter months.

HOMEOTHERMY AS AN EVOLUTIONARY ADVANCE

Homeothermy is an advantage in permitting the chemical processes of the body to operate at one temperature level over a range of environmental conditions. Some creatures can only control their body temperature very crudely—by adopting specialised behavioural patterns (e.g. the poikilotherms)—and can become torpid in the cold and risk overheating in hot conditions. This imposes penalties of restricted territorial limits and vulnerability in the fight for survival.

To maintain the whole body at a constant optimum temperature would be very costly in energy; the evolutionary compromise was to control the temperature of the deep body or 'core', using the more superficial tissues or body 'shell' as a variable insulator or heat sink. The vital organs are included in the 'core', thus both protecting them from temperature fluctuations and from injury. Since the vital organs are responsible for the greater part of the metabolic heat production in resting man, it facilitates a control system based on regulating heat loss.

BODY TEMPERATURE

Just why man controls his deep body temperature at around 37°C (98·6°F) we do not know, the answer may be a biochemical requirement, or perhaps man evolved in a tropical climate. It is nevertheless

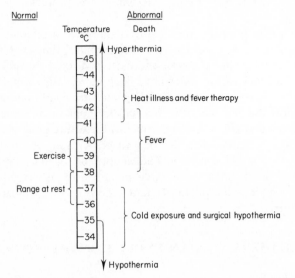

FIG. 1. Body temperature variations (after du Bois (1936)).

clear that the temperature of the core must be above the temperature of the environment for a controlled heat loss system to function.

With exercise there is an increase in body temperature (see Fig. 1), and the increase is proportional to the increase in metabolism. There is a small diurnal variation in the core temperature, with the temperature falling during sleep at night and rising again the following day.

An excessive fall in deep body temperature is termed 'hypothermia' and is defined as being present when the core temperature falls below 35°C (95°F) (BMA, 1964; Royal College of Physicians, 1966). Patients suffering from hypothermia with temperatures between 30°C and 34·9°C have been reported to have a mortality of 32%, and below 30°C the mortality rose to 70%.

An excessively high body temperature, or 'hyperthermia', is less easily defined. Heat stroke has been diagnosed with a body temperature as low as 40·6°C (105°F) (Kew et al., 1967), but most individuals can survive a rise in body temperature several degrees higher without apparent harm. The diagnosis of heat stroke depends on the clinical findings, with the classical trio of cardinal signs being: (a) hyperpyrexia; (b) severe central nervous disturbance, and (c) cessation of sweating (MRC, 1958). However, heat stroke frequently occurs without cessation of sweating (Shibolet et al., 1967). In both severe hypo- and hyperthermia, there are profound metabolic disturbances which, if prolonged, lead to irreversible pathological changes in the vital organs such as heart, brain, liver, kidneys and pancreas.

THE CONTROLLING SYSTEM

A simple model to illustrate the more important features of human thermoregulation is given in Fig. 2 (Fox, 1974). The model emphasises the control of heat loss from the core of the body to the periphery by varying the blood flow through the skin and especially the extremities. The control centre is in the hypothalamus of the brain, and is itself sensitive to local changes in the blood temperature. It also receives inputs from deep temperature receptors, as well as hot and cold temperature receptors in the skin. The outputs from the controller influence the amount of blood flowing through the cutaneous blood vessels, increasing or decreasing the transport of heat in the bloodstream from the core to the periphery, as required to maintain homeostasis. There are additional outputs to activate sweating, which

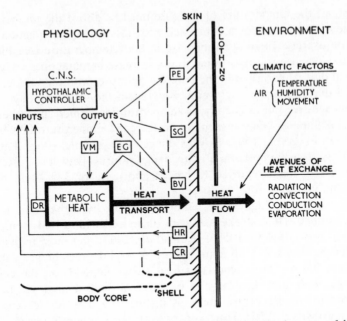

Fig. 2. A simple model to illustrate the more important features of human thermoregulation. PE = piloerection, SG = sweat gland, BV = blood vessel, HR = hot receptor, CR = cold receptor, VM = voluntary muscle, EG = endocrine glands, DR = deep receptor.

is the body's principal mechanism against overheating, and to stimulate heat production by shivering and increasing metabolism, which is the main defence mechanism against cooling.

Piloerection, or 'goose pimples', represents the vestigial mechanism for trapping air close to the body which in other animals, with feathers or fur covering, plays a vital role in retarding heat loss.

As a result of the changes in blood flow from the core to the periphery, there is a constantly changing relationship between the core and the shell. In warm conditions, and during exercise, the shell shrinks, while the core expands; conversely, to conserve heat the body core shrinks and is protected by a thicker shell (see Fig. 2). From Fig. 2 we can also see how the heat flow from the body is modified by the environment surrounding the body. Firstly, man has become adept at surrounding his body with portable insulation in the form of clothing. This is a much more versatile technique for adapting to changing circumstances than the thick hair, or fur, of most mammals, or the feathers of birds. The heat loss from the body into the environment depends on the rate of heat flow through the avenues of thermal exchange. This is set out in the conventional heat balance equation based on the first law of thermodynamics which can be written:

$$M + R + Cv + Cd + E = S = 0$$

where M is the metabolic heat production; S is the heat storage; R, Cv, Cd, and E are the rates of heat transfer by radiation, convection, conduction, and evaporation respectively. The rates of heat flow through each avenue are determined by the environmental variables of temperature, humidity and air movement surrounding the body. This technique of quantifying thermal exchange pioneered by Winslow et al. (1936) has become one of the cornerstones of thermal physiology, but is dealt with in detail elsewhere in this volume (see the paper by Mount), and will therefore not be expanded on here. Suffice to say that the clothing barrier, and the shelter, or built environments, are designed to favour a heat flow equal to the metabolic heat production from the body surface, with the minimum of physiological effort or disturbance.

ACCLIMATISATION TO HEAT AND COLD

Heat acclimatisation is a familiar experience for travellers to hot climates, and was well described by Adolph (1943): 'Acclimatisation to the desert is as rapid as it is dramatic. For 2 or 3 days in the summer desert a man is uncomfortable and lazy. Upon about the fourth day he suddenly finds life enjoyable again. He wants to be vigorous. In some individuals changes can still be detected after 10 days'. The changes observed were readier and more copious sweating and the maintenance of a lower body temperature. These changes are illustrated in Fig. 3 from experiments in which men were exposed to a carefully controlled hot climate for a number of hours daily, during which they performed a known amount of physical work.

Such experiments have shown that the sweating mechanism responds to repeated stimulation by a progressively quicker onset of sweating and a more copious production of sweat for a given heat exposure. There is a decrease in the electrolytes, especially sodium chloride, in the sweat, thus conserving essential body nutrients. The blood flow through the extremities, for a given rise in deep body temperature, also

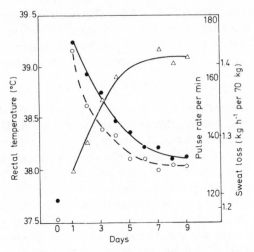

FIG. 3. Typical average rectal temperatures (●), pulse rates (○) and sweat losses (△) of a group of men during the development of acclimatisation to heat. On day 0, the men worked for 100 min at an energy expenditure of 350 W in a cool climate; the exposure was repeated on days 1 to 9 but in a hot climate with dry-bulb and wet-bulb temperatures of 48·9°C and 26·7°C (120°F and 80°F) (after Leithead and Lind (1964)).

increases, thereby facilitating the loss of heat by convection and radiation, as well as sweating. The overall effect of these changes is a lessened sensation of stress which is caused by rises in body temperature in a hot climate, and a greater capacity to dissipate the heat released by metabolism during work. In general, the indigenous members of hot countries do not exhibit a highly trained sweating response. Although the reasons for this are not entirely clear, it is undoubtedly largely behavioural adaptation which enables them to avoid excessive heat exposure.

Acclimatisation to cold through physiological changes has proved less easy to define. A lessened awareness of discomfort on repeated exposure to cold is well established (Scholander et al., 1958). The evidence for increased basal metabolic rate or insulative changes in the shell are not conclusive (Goldsmith, 1974). Some of the clearest evidence for adaptation to cold has come from the studies on bushmen, who sleep naked in the desert cold with only a small fire to warm their feet (Hammel, 1964). These primitive people are able to sleep without shivering and allow their body temperature to decrease during the night, rewarming early the following day. It is not altogether surprising that physiological mechanisms to adapt against cold are less developed than those for heat, because it is much easier to protect the body from cooling by adding insulation or seeking shelter, than to protect the body from overheating.

SHELTER AND CLOTHING IN PRIMITIVE CULTURES

Man differs from the monkeys and apes in his intellectual ability, in being able to walk erect with legs fully extended and loss of body hair. The increasing loss of hair was an advantage in promoting heat loss in hot conditions, or when fight or flight required reliance on the sweating mechanism to dissipate heat. Man compensated for the disadvantages of a relatively hairless skin by using his superior brain power to adopt behavioural patterns to protect the surface of the body from physical injury and cold exposure. Wearing the skins from animals slaughtered for food or in self-defence, provided crude protection from cold exposure and physical injury.

The genitalia were particularly sensitive parts of the body, and so some form of loin cloth was an early acquisition. Superstition played an important role, with the belief that evil spirits could be warded off by wearing charms or amulets, as bracelets or strung round the neck or waist. Sexual modesty is a much more recent influence on clothing, although the genitalia were probably considered prime targets for evil spirits in some communities.

The changing climate, associated with the advancing and receding ice ages, may well have played an important role in the evolution of primitive clothing and shelter combinations. This would have favoured the survival of the more inventive and resourceful early races. What we know of these early days in man's prehistory has been culled at great labour by anthropologists from cave dwellings, burial sites and through chance preservation by sudden embalming in natural catastrophes, such as earthquakes, floods or lava flows. It is a fragmentary picture, but we can see how man began to use and modify the materials he found in his environment to provide both clothing and shelter. The forms this took were dictated partly by the climate and partly by the readily available materials.

Primitive cultures living off the land, untouched by the technology of western culture, have virtually disappeared. There may still be some tribes in New Guinea, in isolated valleys, who have had no contact with European culture, but otherwise, all the so-called 'primitive races' still in existence today are in transition, having adopted varying degrees of western culture and technology. Even so, we can still learn a great deal by studying how they live, and how they have adapted western technology into their cultures.

Hot climates

Even though man is generally considered to have emerged in warm or tropical climates, he still had to evolve specialised clothing and shelter in the fight for survival and the search for comfort. This is particularly true of desert people, where it becomes quite cold at night, as well as very hot in the daytime. Desert people also need to be mobile, so that as the meagre resources of one area are used or dry up, they can move on to another area. Shelter in the desert frequently takes the form of a simple tent formed by slender poles set in the ground to form a circle and bound together at the top. The outside of this simple framework is then covered by skins. This gives a measure of protection from heat at the hottest time of the day and from cold at night. For desert living, clothing is helpful by absorbing radiation and releasing it to the environment, as well as providing insulative comfort at night. To perform its day time function of reducing the radiant heat load and allowing sweat to evaporate usefully from the skin surface, it has to be loosely applied to the body. At first sight, white clothing with its superior reflective properties would seem preferable to dark, but the latter is better for intercepting radiation and converting it into heat, which is then lost from the clothing by convection into the environment instead of from the skin.

Since water is scarce, the nomadic Arab avoids activity in the heat of the day which would cause sweating. For transport he depends on the camel, itself almost a unique animal in its ability to store water in the body and permit body temperature to rise by day and fall at night.

The bushmen of the Kalahari Desert and the Bindibu of the Australian Central–Western Desert are traditionally naked, apart from possible adornment with a necklace and loin cloth. They are both hunters and food gatherers and essentially nomadic. For shelter in the heat of the day they build primitive erections of twigs or grasses, which provide shade. For warmth at night they light a fire and sleep huddled together with their feet towards the fire.

Cold climates

The Eskimo and the Lapp are two examples of a highly specialised adaptation to life in cold climates. In both cases the traditional shelter and clothing are determined by what is available in the environment, and modified to enable them to hunt or use the animals which make life possible.

Lappish people

The Lapp reindeer herdsman is Europe's last surviving aboriginal. The forbears of the present day Lapp were entirely nomadic, following their herds from the winter retreat to summer pasture. They hunted and trapped other creatures, but the reindeer provided them with almost all their material needs. Reindeer skins covered the conical tents they erected for shelter and warmth. The reindeer provides milk, and his carcass all the food that is required. The reindeer skins originally provided the clothing, together with furs from other animals, and the reindeers' antlers and bones were fashioned into tools.

Lapp clothing consists of a smock and breeches, with a belt. Hands are protected with gloves, and feet with boots, made of reindeer skin. Heat loss is reduced by a cap with flaps which covers the whole head except the face. Additional insulation in gloves, and especially boots, is achieved using dry, soft grass, which is carefully inserted to form an even layer. Like the Eskimo in very cold conditions, the Lapp some-times wears a second smock and breeches as an outer garment, with the fur outside, instead of turned inwards, to give maximum insulation.

Brightly coloured and embroidered woollen garments have been added to supplement the skin and furs. The bright red colouring adds a note of cheerfulness in the otherwise bleak greyness of the arctic tundra, and enables the herdsmen to see each other from a great distance, as well as making it easier to find a child who has strayed too far.

Few Lapps are now truly nomadic, many live in permanent settle-ments and exist more on the earnings from tourists than by herding and hunting. Some have permanent wooden cabins in the reindeers' winter feeding grounds, but still migrate with their flocks to fresh pastures in the mountains or down to the lowlands in the summer, using traditional tents. The Lappish way of life is ultimately dependent on the reindeer, and its uncanny ability to locate good patches of lichen by the scent, through a thick layer of snow, and then paw a way down to eat it.

Eskimos

The origin of the Eskimo way of life is still debated, although it seems most likely to have evolved during the last ice age, when much of the northern hemisphere was frozen. The survivors were those who had learned to live in an arctic environment and hunt the musk ox and caribou driven south by the ice, and then followed them back as the glaciers retreated.

The Eskimo's traditional dress is an outer two-piece garment of seal skin or reindeer, with the hair outside. The hooded jacket can be loosened at the neck to increase or decrease heat loss. It very effectively increases heat loss during activity by the 'bellows' action of the air drawn in and out by movement; loosening a belt at the waist increases this further. The trousers are of similar material and long enough to overlap the boots with soles of reindeer skin. Like the Lapp, the Eskimo may use moss or dried grass to increase the insulation of the untrimmed hair of the sole. The protection of the foot is particularly important because pressure squeezes the insulating air out, and heat is rapidly lost through conduction to the snow.

The inner layer of clothing consists of a fur upper garment, with trousers and leggings, or socks, with the hair on the inside. The hands are protected in a similar way to the feet and in very cold conditions both hands and feet may be covered with three or more layers. During work one or more of these layers may be removed to avoid overheating and sweating.

The popular image of the Eskimo home is an igloo, fashioned from blocks of compressed snow to form a dome shaped dwelling. The entrance is an elongated tunnel dipping below the floor level of the dwelling and only high enough to crawl along. The snow igloo is used for travelling and can be erected remarkably quickly. It provides effective shelter from the wind and is thermally efficient. The heating is entirely dependent on the metabolic heat production of the occupants, with only a small blubber or oil lamp for illumination. The inner surface of the igloo turns to ice and helps to absorb the moisture from the breath and bodies of the occupants. With the entrance below the living area the warm air is trapped and the occupants remain warm even after removing most of their clothing.

Although the snow igloo is commonly thought of as the typical Eskimo home, it was not used in Alaska and only used as a permanent dwelling by the Canadian Eskimo. Most Eskimos lived in dwellings constructed of stone which were often partially sunk into the ground

(Page, 1938). Outside the stone, or slate, roof and walls of the house, sods of earth were used to provide insulation and held in place by a further layer of stones. A tunnel or short passage, at a low level, formed the entrance. A small vent in the roof allowed air and fumes to escape; and the floor was stone. Ledges at the sides, well insulated with skins or moss, provided sleeping platforms. In the summer, and when hunting, skin tents were commonly used. With the advent of driftwood, rather crude wooden cabins became commonplace, and now, of course, the modern Eskimo is more likely to be found living in a comfortable prefabricated and well insulated dwelling. The absurdity of selling refrigerators to the Eskimo is no longer the joke it once was!

In a short paper it is not possible to review all the ways in which primitive cultures have contrived to protect themselves from hostile climates, but a pattern of skilful use of available materials is common to all. So also is a minimal use of irreplaceable energy resources.

MODERN AFFLUENT SOCIETIES

Before taking the big step from the so-called primitive societies to modern affluent societies, we must at least acknowledge a continuum between the two. It is possible to trace the developing technology of clothing, and the increasing complexity of the built environment, from primitive beginnings in the ancient civilisations.

The change, from nomadic hunters and gatherers to settled agrarian communities, made permanent buildings and cities possible. It would seem that Jericho was a city covering 10 acres of land well before 7000 BC. A Mesopotamian town house built 4000 years ago shows many of the features of Middle Eastern houses today. It was built with a central courtyard shielded by high walls from the sun and radiation. It had few windows on the perimeter walls, and the walls themselves were thick. With the increasing size of buildings the effects of diurnal variations in temperature were reduced, both in temperate as well as in hot climates. Thus, before there were effective means of artificially heating and cooling buildings, increasing their size and mass contributed to thermal comfort. Building into cliffs or rocks served the same purpose of achieving thermal stability. For example, this must have done much to make Herod's palace, hewn into its barren Judean rock fortress at Massada, a bearable place to live.

Long before man could express heat flow in terms of the thermal exchange avenues, he had learnt their principles through trial and error. In hot climates he learnt how to avoid excessive heat gain by siting buildings correctly, to shield them from radiation; how to scoop the cool night breezes into buildings in order to convect away the previous day's stored heat. The cooling and shading effects of planting vegetation close to buildings, and cooling, by humidifying, the air entering buildings were known and used from early times. Ventilated roof spaces and architectural designs to create thermal air flows through buildings are all to be found in early civilisations in the Middle East and elsewhere.

In cooler climates, and especially in the temperate zone, we can see the principles of insulation and draught exclusion employed throughout recorded history. In general, there was less need to design buildings for thermal comfort, because artificial warming of at least part of the building, with a wood or peat fire, was available from the outset. Furthermore, the resident in cool or temperate climates had the option of achieving thermal comfort through clothing; which was an option not open to man living in hot climates. Although coal has been used as fuel from very early days, and in the UK probably even in the Bronze age, it was not until the Industrial Revolution that it was widely used in homes. Coal fuelled the Industrial Revolution, and by harnessing it to produce steam, mining itself became easier and coal could be transported cheaply.

Ever since the advent of coal as a cheap energy source for heating, man's reliance on clothing for thermal comfort has declined, while the demand for heat in his shelter has increased. This is of course true, not only in the UK and America, but in all the modern western cultures in the northern hemisphere. Even more recently, advances in technology, and the same cheap energy from coal supplemented by oil, gas and hydroelectric power, have made it possible for man to air-condition his sheltered environment in hot and cold climates, and have enabled him to choose a climate in which to live and work, anywhere in the world. The rapidity with which these changes have occurred emphasises the importance man places on his thermal comfort, The close agreement in the chosen temperature for comfort throughout the world underlines the essential physiological similarity of men of all races, irrespective of the colour of their skin, or the climate in which their ancestors evolved. Many people are now becoming increasingly concerned that energy resources will not be capable of maintaining this trend into the foreseeable future. It is already leading to some anomalies in our own society, and both these problems will be examined in the closing sections of this paper.

The old and the cold

In recent years there has been increasing concern over the incidence of hypothermia in elderly people during the winter months in the UK. Estimates of the incidence of deaths due to hypothermia vary from a few hundred returns on the Registrar General's death certificates, to over 20 000 annually (Taylor, 1964). The trouble is that hypothermia leaves no visiting card and, once rewarmed, there are no specific signs of the previous serious condition. If the patient dies from bronchopneumonia this becomes the cause of death reported on the death certificate. Many patients who are admitted to hospital with hypothermia have coexisting serious pathology, and it is difficult to decide the real cause of death.

Perhaps even more disturbing, have been the persistent reports showing the prevalence of low room temperatures in the homes of elderly people in the winter months (Williams, 1968; Allen, 1969; Eddy *et al.*, 1970; Corkhill *et al.*, 1972).

To help throw more light on these problems a multidisciplinary study was mounted in the UK by the Medical Research Council, The Centre for Environmental Studies and the Departments of Geriatric Medicine at University College and the Royal Free Hospitals in 1972 (Fox *et al.*, 1973). In all some 2000 individuals aged 65 and over were visited by a nurse–interviewer, who recorded temperatures and filled in a questionnaire. The temperatures measured were the deep body (using a special urine temperature recording technique), mouth, hand, room and outdoors. The main areas of enquiry in the questionnaire were the basic demographic situation, household composition, heating technique, contact with medical and social services, degree of isolation and financial circumstances. The individuals' thermal comfort was elicited by asking them to identify, on a seven point scale, how cold or warm they felt generally. Hand comfort was identified on a similar scale. Each individual was also asked whether they would prefer to be warmer or cooler, on a five point scale.

The results of the study showed that body temperature declines with age, but it revealed no case of severe hypothermia, and only some nine individuals with morning temperatures at, or below, the critical level of 35·0°C for diagnosing hypothermia. This may well indicate that 35·0°C is the critical level below which an individual is recognised as ill and admitted to hospital, or other appropriate action is taken. More disturbing was the finding that 10% of the whole sample had deep body temperatures below 35·5°C. When this 'low' body temperature group was compared with the individuals having 'normal' body temperatures ($\geq 36\cdot0$°C) they were also found to have a reduced temperature difference between the hand and the core, indicating that they were failing to try to conserve body heat. Such individuals are at risk of developing hypothermia, since they are not only already close to the critical deep body temperature level, but also show some evidence of thermoregulatory failure. The receipt of supplementary benefits was significantly associated with a low body temperature, partly reflecting the identification of those with a low income, but also infirmity and age. These findings are illustrated in Fig. 4.

The living room temperatures at the time of the nurses' morning visits were clearly much too cold for comfort, with 75% at, or below,

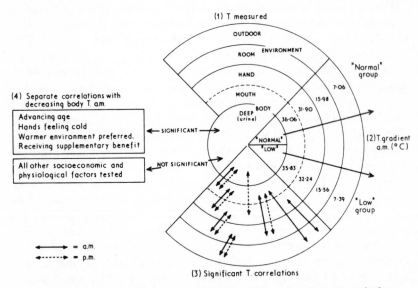

FIG. 4. Body and environmental temperature (T) and socio-economic factors (national survey). (1) Summary of many important relationships between temperatures forming a gradient from body core to external environment. (2) Comparison of the mean (a.m.) temperatures (°C) for the 'low' and 'normal' groups. (3) Significant correlations (a.m., p.m.) between temperatures. (4) Important significant correlations with certain physiological and socio-economic factors.

18·3°C (the minimum level recommended by the Parker Morris Report on Council Housing (Ministry of Housing and Local Government, 1961)). Very few achieved the target of 21·1°C recommended (although subsequently dropped) for the elderly by the Department of Health and Social Security (DHSS, 1972). Over half the rooms were below the minimum specified by the Offices, Shops and Railway Premises Act (1963) and in 10% the room temperatures were at, or below, 12·0°C.

Against this background of unacceptably cold room temperatures, it was quite surprising to find that the majority of the elderly subjects expressed themselves as comfortable or warm. Nevertheless, between a fifth and a quarter expressed themselves as feeling cool, too cool, or much too cool. Similarly, when asked their preference for living room temperatures the majority voted for 'no change' and only just over a quarter expressed a desire for warmer conditions.

This apparent lack of appreciation that they were living in cold conditions has a number of possible explanations, including

1. A degree of adaptation to the cold
2. A lessened awareness of discomfort with ageing
3. A desire to save on heating to spend elsewhere
4. Greater reliance on insulation from clothing

Probably all of these factors play a role, although the contribution from each is impossible to define.

We are left with the important conclusion that large numbers of the elderly are living in much colder conditions than the younger and generally more affluent members of our society consider acceptable.

SHELTER AND CLOTHING, TODAY AND IN THE FUTURE

The immense complexity and bulk of the built environment in the advanced western societies today is available for all to see and assess. It is the product of a technological explosion which has been gathering strength and speed of change for over a century. The explosion itself shows no sign of being spent; indeed, it is probably still gathering momentum. Although our ability to evolve quicker and more effective methods of changing the face of the earth seems to have no limits, other constraints may well begin to operate. More and more we are beginning to question the effects of the pressures we are placing on the ecology of the world; we question the possible effects of CO_2 on climate; we question the effects of pollution of the environment, but above all we are beginning to question whether energy resources are adequate to sustain the new civilisation we are developing.

It would be tedious to try and catalogue all the factors involved, but a few simple comparisons between the modern and primitive ways of life show quite clearly why energy resources are critical. In primitive cultures the shelter or dwelling was small; it usually housed whole families and sometimes more than one. Warmth in cold climates was achieved by controlling heat loss from the body with clothing, supplemented by small fires burning fuel that was being continually regenerated. Each individual in a modern society occupies much more space and relies on energy to warm or cool the environment in which he lives. This now includes not only his home, but where he works, the vehicle he uses to travel and many of his leisure activities. The reliance on clothing for insulation has been greatly reduced and that worn is dictated by fashion and social circumstances. Similarly, in hot climates, there is a rapidly rising demand for energy from the fossilised fuels to air condition man's living and working environments. The reserves of these fuels are not limitless and many organisations have become very active in trying to assess and evaluate the possible solutions to the energy problem. The figures and estimates which follow are largely drawn from documents prepared by the Building Research Establishment. Overall, it is estimated that between 40–50% of the national primary energy output is associated with building services.

If individual living standards in our own and other modern societies continue to increase, so that everyone enjoys the same high standards of living, we can expect a further huge rise in total demand (Fig. 5).

If those living in the less highly developed parts of the world were to demand similar standards of living, a further huge increase in energy consumption would occur.

The importance of the built environment in energy consumption, based on data available in 1972, is illustrated graphically in Fig. 6 and although industry is shown as the largest single user, a substantial proportion of this is really committed to providing a comfortable working environment.

The estimated gross energy input and net energy output of the UK economy in 1972 is illustrated in Fig. 7 and shows the very small contributions to input from nuclear and hydroelectric power, as well as

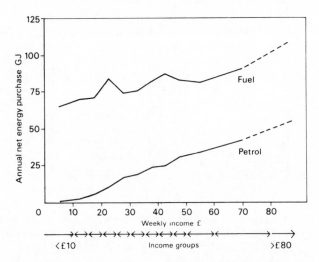

FIG. 5. Estimated annual net energy purchases per household based on 1972 family expenditure survey. (Crown copyright. Reproduced from *Building Research Establishment Digest* **191** (1976) by permission of the controller of HMSO.)

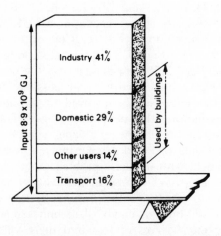

FIG. 6. Gross energy used by final users. (Crown copyright. Reproduced from *Building Research Establishment Digest* **191** (1976) by permission of the controller of HMSO.)

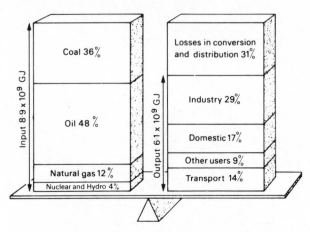

Fig. 7. Gross energy input and net energy output of UK economy. (Crown copyright. Reproduced from *Building Research Establishment Digest* **191** (1976) by permission of the controller of HMSO.)

the huge losses of energy in conversion and distribution. Electricity is the main culprit for waste through conversion and distribution, with a ratio between gross energy used and net energy delivered of 3·82, compared with 1·03 for coal and 1·09 for oil.

An attempt to forecast energy needs in the UK up to 1990 was made in evidence given to the Select Committee on Science and Technology in 1975 (see Fig. 8). This depended on assuming possible growth rates of 2·7 and 3·3% per annum over the next 15 years. The wide shaded envelopes associated with the possible usage of different fuels, illustrate the uncertainties involved in any such projections. However, it does indicate that dependence on certain fuels, such as natural gas, is expected to decline, and dependence on nuclear energy will increase. The time taken to develop nuclear energy is relatively long and still fraught with immense problems of acceptability, which may retard its progress. We know that the assumptions of the growth in demand were too high for the last five years, because of the world-wide recession, but this may well be only temporary.

Just how long the reserves of fossilised fuels will last is again a matter of guesswork but even the most optimistic forecast only gives us the shortest breathing space in the evolutionary time scale. Even now the increasing costs of extracting the dwindling supplies have made energy increasingly expensive, and eventually reliance on alternative sources will be forced upon us. Much research and thought has been

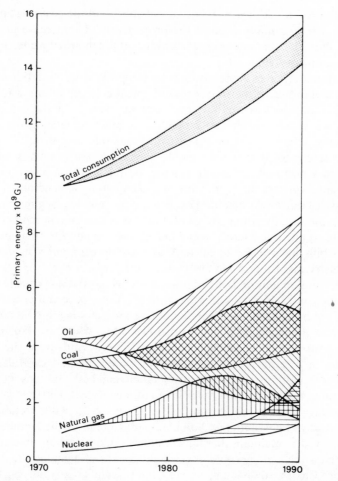

FIG. 8. Envelopes of Department of Energy consumption forecasts (1974).
The figure shows the range of primary energy inputs under a number of
different assumptions for an economic growth rate of between 2·7% and 3·3%
per annum. (Crown copyright. Reproduced from *Building Research Establishment Digest* **191** (1976) by permission of the controller of HMSO.)

applied to considering how we could economise and yet maintain our
environmental standards. It has been estimated that it should be
possible to save 15% of the total UK consumption of primary energy
by action taken in buildings alone, using technically feasible options.
Using only the well established technologies applied to the existing
housing stock, and the direct use of fossil fuels for heating instead of

electricity, would bring savings of only 6%, and the cost is estimated at over £3000 million. Against the projected annual increase in demand for the UK, this once for all saving, although worthwhile, does not solve our problem.

Ultimately, new methods of harnessing the solar radiation reaching our planet may come to our rescue, but this is still a long way off and most authorities expect nuclear power will have to fill the gap. If this is so, we should surely be expending a much greater effort now to develop it and to ensure that it will be as safe as possible.

It seems likely that the steadily increasing cost of energy will bring about substantial changes in our way of living, with a return to greater reliance on clothing for achieving comfort in a generally less well heated built environment. This change has already begun in the UK, with the rapidly rising cost of all fuels. It is unfortunately affecting the more vulnerable elderly members of the community first, but rising fuel bills have made us all look at possible economies in the house, industry and other buildings with a more critical eye.

To end on a more hopeful note, it seems more than possible that the science and technology that has produced the space suit can transform our everyday clothing. Heated clothing for everyday use may not be as silly as it sounds. It is not even a new idea, when we remember the Kashmir custom of carrying a Kangri. The warmth from the glowing coals in a metal pan, enclosed in a wicker basket, carefully placed beneath clothing, is an effective, albeit cumbersome way of supplementing body warmth. Quite tiny amounts of heat delivered within the clothing barrier will ensure adequate warmth, while retaining the comfort of light clothing. Automatic adjustment of the amount of heat delivered to maintain thermal comfort should be relatively simple, and perhaps technology could develop the means of beaming the necessary energy to the individual, or very lightweight energy stores, to avoid trailing wires. Throughout his history man has always managed to come up with new solutions to overcome new problems, and we may be sure he will do so again.

REFERENCES

Adolph, E. F. (1943). Physiological fitness for the desert. *Proc. Fedn Am. Socs exp. Biol.* **2,** 158.

Allen, W. H. (1969). Accidental hypothermia in Hertfordshire during the winters of 1966/7 and 1967/8. *Publ. Hlth, Lond.* **83,** 229.

BMA (1964). Accidental hypothermia in the elderly. *Br. med. J.* **2,** 1255.

Building Research Establishment (1976). Energy consumption and conservation in buildings. *Building Research Establishment Digest.* **191,** 1.

Corkhill, R. T., Holland, W. W., Fox, R. H. and Mee, M. S. R. (1972). A study of exposure to environmental temperatures in a population sample, using the temperature SAMI. *Br. J. Prev. Soc. Med.* **26,** 40.

DHSS (1972). *Keeping Warm in Winter.* HMSO, London.

du Bois, E. F. (1936). *Basal Metabolism in Health and Disease,* 3rd edn. Bailliers, Tindall and Co., London.

Eddy, T. P. *et al.* (1970). Body temperatures in the elderly. *Lancet* **2,** 1088.

Fox, R. H. (1974). *Temperature Regulation with Special Reference to Man. Recent Advances Series, Physiology,* Vol. 9 (Ed. R. J. Linden). Churchill Livingstone, London.

Fox, R. H., Woodward, P. M., Exton-Smith, A. N., Green, M. F., Donnison, D. V. and Wicks, M. H. (1973). Body temperatures in the elderly: a national study of physiology, social and environmental conditions. *Br. med. J.* **1,** 200.

Goldsmith, R. (1974). Acclimatisation to cold in man. In *Heat Loss from Animals and Man* (Eds J. L. Monteith and L. E. Mount). Butterworths, London, Ch. 15.

Hammel, H. T. (1964). Terrestrial animals in cold: recent studies of primitive man. In *Adaptation to the Environment* (Eds D. B. Dill, E. F. Adolph and C. G. Wilber), (*Handbook of Physiology,* section 4). Am. Physiol. Soc., Washington DC, p. 413.

Kew, M. C., Abrahams, C., Levin, N. W., Seftel, H. C., Rubenstein, A. H. and Hersohn, I. (1967). The effects of heatstroke on the function and structure of the kidney. *Quart. J. Med.* **36,** 277.

Leithead, C. S. and Lind, A. R. (1964). *Heat Stress and Heat Disorders.* Cassell, London.

Ministry of Housing and Local Government (1961). *Homes for Today and Tomorrow.* HMSO, London.

MRC (1958). A classification of heat illness. *Br. med. J.* **1,** 1533.

Offices, Shops and Railway Premises Act (1963). HMSO, London.

Page, J. W. (1938). *Primitive Races of Today.* George Harrap and Co., London, p. 153.

Royal College of Physicians (1966). *Report of Committee on Accidental Hypothermia.* Royal College of Physicians, London.

Scholander, P. F., Hammel, H. T., Andersen, K. L. and Lönying, Y. (1958). Metabolic acclimation to cold in man. *J. appl. Physiol.* **12,** 1.

Shibolet, S., Coll, R., Gilat, T. and Sohar, E. (1967). Heatstroke, its clinical picture and mechanism in 36 cases. *Quart. J. Med.* **36,** 525.

Society of Medical Officers of Health (1968). A pilot survey into the occurrence of hypothermia in elderly people living at home. *Publ. Hlth. Lond.* **82,** 223.

Taylor, G. (1964). The problem of hypothermia in the elderly. *Practitioner* **193,** 761.

Williams, B. T. (1968). Oral temperatures of elderly applicants for welfare services. *Gerontologia Clinica* **10,** 281.

Winslow, C. E. A., Herrington, L. P. and Gagge, A. P. (1936) A new method of partitional calorimetry. *Am. J. Physiol.* **116,** 641.

Discussion

Professor Cena asked whether old people who were potential sufferers from hypothermia had the same ability as younger people to sense the change in temperature. In young, normal people, it was possible for them to sense a difference per 1°C, but in older people this difference rose to 2–3°C. *Dr Fox* said that there was certainly a decline in the ability of older people to distinguish the differences in temperature between two plates. The decline in this acuity arose in the over-sixties. *Professor Cena* then continued by asking whether the preferred temperatures of the environment for young and old were the same, to which *Dr Fox* replied that when people were exposed to different temperatures it would appear that they reacted in the same way. He admitted, however, that there was really a very serious paucity of data on the behaviour of the elderly and while some work had been done, the subject was not as well studied as it should be.

Professor Monteith drew attention to the situation of the bushmen sleeping out of doors with their feet to the fire under a blanket. He pointed out that the mean radiant temperature of a clear sky at night would be about 20°C below air temperature and the thermal demand that this imposed was about 100 W m^{-2}. He put forward the idea that, through evolution, the minimal metabolism of man and other homeotherms during the night had increased to meet this thermal demand. This was probably why we were not animals which burrow into the ground at night! *Dr Fox* stated that the adaptation of the Aboriginal in Australia was not a refutation of any laws of physics. The reaction was to drop skin temperature just as in normal man, but there was a physiological adaptation insofar that the Aboriginal would allow his deep body temperature to fall and not make the response seen in temperate peoples of increasing muscular activity in shivering. *Professor Heide* stated that when he was in the UK in 1962 he was told that despite the coldest winter for 70 years people in the UK did not regard

309

the insulation of their houses as a problem and he was surprised that Dr Fox had suggested that there could only be some 15% of saving through better house construction and design of heating systems. *Dr Fox* stated that he would agree absolutely with Professor Heide that the British are extremely prodigal in terms of the use of energy for keeping themselves warm and went on to state that it was extremely difficult when the attitude was to build houses with presumptive lives of a hundred years to cater for eventualities. It is extremely difficult, for example, to insulate curtain wall buildings and he thought it was the height of folly to build buildings at the present time without considering the present energy problems and take them fully into account. Continuing this aspect of the discussion, *Professor Cena* stated that 30% of all the energy use in Poland was employed in heating buildings and it had been calculated that if buildings could be heated so that their mean temperature was 1°C lower they could save the energy output from three of their coal mines. This suggestion of reduction of the heat in buildings was, however, highly unpopular. *Sir Kenneth Blaxter*, taking up the point that Dr Fox had made about the alternative of increasing the amount of clothing worn, asked why it was that there was such a resistance to increasing the insulation value of clothing. *Dr Fox* stated that there were several reasons. First, thicker clothing was obviously more cumbersome; second, with more insulation it was more difficult to change insulation according to differences in activity and heat production, and third, it would appear that there is a great liking for light clothing and heated rooms. Whether we could afford this or not was another matter. It was of some interest that at the end of the Second World War the definitions of comfort zones in the United States were very different to those which Bedford had calculated as suitable in the UK, but now the two have moved together. One might almost say that it is a status symbol to walk about in shirt sleeves in a house in the middle of winter and, quite frankly, it would be necessary for such attitudes to change. *Mr Smith* stated that on the basis of experience in the Middle East it would seem that man responded also to changes in temperature as well as to mean temperatures and pointed out that the best insulated house was one which was surrounded by other houses. *Dr Lake* raised the question about the clothing–food substitution. One could reduce food intake somewhat and use energy supplies to increase insulation. *Dr Fox* pointed out that it was difficult to do this substitution in hot climates and while in cold climates one could design clothing which had an internal heating component, it would be very difficult to design clothing with an internal refrigerator. He suggested that perhaps the solution to some of these problems would be to devote the subtropics and tropics to food production and move the population into the more northern and cooler climates.

Man's Impact on Climate

A. J. CRANE

*Central Electricity Research Laboratories,
Leatherhead, Surrey, UK*

INTRODUCTION

As our understanding of the mechanisms which control climate increases, it is becoming apparent that man may be capable of modifying
climate not only locally but also on regional and global scales. It is
possible that some man-induced climatic changes could already be
occurring, but with present magnitudes not large enough to be detected above the natural climatic variability. Nevertheless, with continuing increases in population and energy consumption, it is likely that
such effects on climate would grow. It would clearly not be prudent to
wait until they became manifest before researching their likely influence.

Our understanding of the causes of natural climatic variability on
time scales of less than 1000 years is not good enough to allow
precise prediction of natural variations over the next few centuries. On
the other hand, we do have some idea of the likely amplitudes and
rates of change of future natural variations, based on our knowledge of
past climatic variation. What we must, therefore, be concerned about
are those activities of man which, either singly or together, could lead
to climatic changes occurring more rapidly or having greater magnitude than likely natural variations.

The major tools at our disposal in the investigation of man's influence on climate are the mathematical models which simulate well
the major features of the present climate. While such models are still
far from perfect, they are probably good enough to indicate how the
gross aspects of the global-scale climate might respond to specified
changes in the boundary conditions, such as a change in the chemical
composition of the atmosphere.

Much of our later discussion will be based on the results of these models. It will therefore be useful to examine briefly the main features of the climate system and how the various components interact, and then describe the principles of climate modelling and the way in which the models are generally used. This should provide a suitable framework for our discussion of the possible influence of man on climate and the changes we could experience as a result over the next 50–100 years.

THE CLIMATE SYSTEM

The climate system comprises the atmosphere, oceans, cryosphere (ice and snow), land surface and biosphere. The source of heat for the system is solar radiation, which, in the global average and over a sufficiently long period of time (years), is balanced by the outgoing infra-red emission of the planetary system. The latter is temperature dependent and so this balance determines the mean temperature of the Earth–atmosphere system. The vertical distribution of temperature in the atmosphere and the temperature at the surface, again in the global average, are controlled by the way in which the components of the climate system redistribute the incoming solar radiation and the outgoing infra-red radiation. The mechanisms involved are illustrated schematically in Fig. 1.

The presence in the atmosphere of trace gases which are largely transparent to solar radiation but which absorb strongly in the infra-red leads to a mean surface temperature some 30 K warmer than the mean temperature of the planetary system. This feature is known as the 'greenhouse' effect, an analogy being drawn with the once supposed role of glass in a greenhouse. As we shall discuss later, it is man's inadvertent alteration of the concentrations of these gases which poses the largest threat to the maintenance of the present climate.

Over shorter periods of time and on space scales smaller than that of the globe, a balance between solar and infra-red radiation does not occur. For example, the polar regions have a net radiative deficit while the tropical regions have a net radiative surplus. The resulting differential heating leads to pressure gradients and hence motions in the atmosphere and ocean which are modified in a major way by the rotation of the planet. The circulations which develop transport heat, both sensible and latent, from those regions where there is net radiative heating to those where there is net radiative cooling, and in so

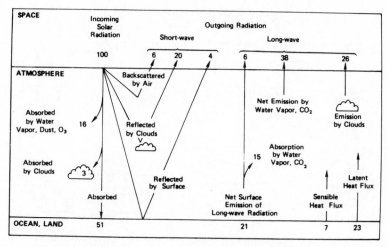

FIG. 1. The mean annual radiation balance of the atmosphere, relative to 100 units of incoming radiation, based on satellite measurements and conventional observations. (Reproduced from NAS (1975) with the permission of the National Academy of Sciences, Washington, DC.)

doing regulate the distribution of temperature, precipitation and cloudiness.

The various physical processes operating in the climate system are highly coupled as illustrated in Fig. 2. This coupling leads to numerous feedback mechanisms which make extremely complex the task of predicting the effects of a specified perturbation to the system. One example of the more easily traced linkages is the positive ice albedo–temperature feedback, whereby an increase in ice cover leads to an increase in reflected solar radiation and thus a decrease in surface temperature followed by a further increase in ice cover. Many others may be traced in Fig. 2. In view of the complicated nature of these interactions and the very wide range of time scales over which they operate, it is not surprising that the climate exhibits an inherent variability characterised by fluctuations of a similarly wide range of frequencies. The very long period cycles, of the order 10^4–10^5 years, evident in the climatic records are almost certainly due to periodicities in the characteristics of the Earth's orbit. Shorter period variations are much more difficult to explain, and many must result from interactions of the internal climatic process. The panel on climatic variations of the Global Atmospheric Research Programme (GARP) have examined paleoclimatic records spanning the last 700 000 years. They have

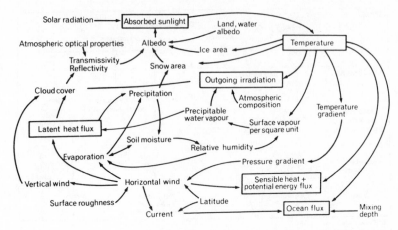

FIG. 2. Schematic illustration of many of the potential climatic feedback interactions which give rise to inherent climatic variability and which need to be taken into account in mathematical modelling of climate. (Reproduced from Kellogg and Schneider (1974) and published with the permission of *Science*. Copyright 1974 by the American Association for the Advancement of Science.)

analysed the surface temperature in terms of a supposition of five periodic functions (as illustrated in Fig. 3), quasi-periodic cycles of the chosen periods being evident in the climatic record. The reconstructed temperature curve displays the major variations in surface temperature over the last 10 000 years. The present trend in global mean temperature of -0.15 K per decade indicated by the reconstruction agrees well with the observed cooling trend since the 1940s, and is seen to be dominated by the shorter-period fluctuations. It is known that some historical changes in climate have been abrupt rather than cyclical especially those occurring on a regional scale. However, even if rates of change an order of magnitude larger were assumed, it seems unlikely that the large-amplitude longer-period variations could contribute much to the temperature changes over the next century. The trend of -0.15 K per decade gives a yardstick against which to measure likely anthropogenic temperature changes.

Long-term trends are not the only climatic characteristics of importance. Of equal or greater concern in some circumstances is a knowledge of possible changes in climatic variability, whether this be from season to season, year to year or over any other periodic interval of interest. There is an often quoted belief that the level of variability is

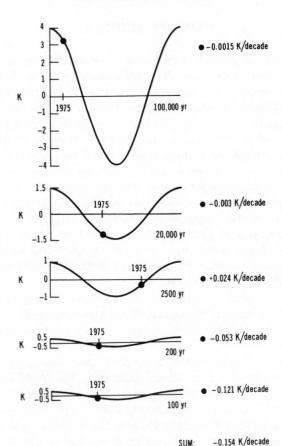

FIG. 3. Potential contribution of sinusoidal fluctuations of various time periods (indicated beneath time axis) to the rate of change of present-day global mean temperature. The five periodic functions were derived by the GARP panel on climatic variations (NAS, 1975) from a wide variety of paleoclimatic records.

related to the mean state. For example, many suggest that the apparently greater frequency of extreme climatic events in the last decade or two is related to the general cooling in the northern hemisphere that occurred between the 1940s and the 1970s. However, such relationships are not always borne out by the instrumental records. As I shall show, the prospects for estimating the influence of man's activities on the *variability* of climate are far less good than those for estimating their effect on the *mean* state.

CLIMATE MODELS

Climate models of interest in the present context may be divided into two classes. First there are the 'mechanistic' models that aim to investigate particular mechanisms operating in the climate system. Important examples are the *radiative–convective* models used to study the fundamental role of radiative processes in determining the one-dimensional global mean vertical temperature structure of the atmosphere. Such models can include very detailed representations of the radiative processes and are useful in assessing the sensitivity of the global mean surface temperature to changes in atmospheric composition. Assumptions must be made about the temperature lapse rate and the humidity of the troposphere which are largely controlled by dynamical processes and so cannot be modelled by radiative processes alone. Other features of these models, such as the treatment of cloud-top variations, pose problems and different assumptions, may lead to significantly different results.

The second class of models comprise the 'simulation' models, which try to include as many of the interacting climatic processes as possible. We shall be concerned with the most elaborate of these, the *general circulation models* (GCMs). In these the meteorological variables which define the state of the atmosphere are usually held at the intersection points of a three-dimensional grid. The set of mathematical equations based on the physical laws which govern the behaviour of the atmosphere are integrated forward in time-steps of perhaps 10 min of model atmosphere time to yield the atmospheric state at future times. In principle all the interactions illustrated in Fig. 2 could be included explicitly in the model in terms of mathematical equations. However, since these processes cover a range of time and space scales of at least 10 orders of magnitude this is not possible in practice. The horizontal grid spacing is chosen so that the smallest meteorological processes of interest may be resolved. This choice determines the maximum value of the time-step needed for computational stability of the integration. A higher spatial resolution generally requires a shorter time-step.

For global climate models in which integrations of several years are necessary the horizontal grid is chosen to resolve the synoptic scale motions (anticyclones and depressions) and usually has a grid spacing of a few hundred kilometres. This means that all processes of smaller scales which are known to interact in important ways with the resolvable processes, such as cumulus convection, cloud formation and dissipation processes, precipitation, turbulence, etc., must be 'parametrised'—i.e. the average effect of the 'subgrid scale' processes within an elemental volume of the grid must be expressed in terms of the variables held at the grid scale. The development of satisfactory parametrisation schemes is often the most difficult aspect in the development of climatic models. The problem of representing clouds realistically in climate models, for example, is very far from being solved. This is a particularly serious deficiency since clouds play a crucial role in the Earth's radiation balance.

At the other end of the scale those components of the climate system which vary only very slowly relative to the atmosphere may be regarded as fixed boundary conditions.

Any model intended to simulate climate must contain a representation of the oceans. Oceans are the major source of moisture for the atmosphere, they act as a thermal regulator on account of their large heat capacity, and they transport about as much heat polewards by their currents as does the atmosphere. The development of oceanic general circulation models is considerably less advanced than those of the atmosphere. A particular difficulty with oceanic modelling is that while the characteristic time scales of the ocean circulation are much longer than those of the atmosphere the size of the eddy motions which contain the bulk of the ocean's kinetic energy are an order of magnitude smaller than their atmospheric equivalents.

The simplest way of including the oceanic moisture source in a climate model is to assume that the atmosphere is underlain by a wet surface. Such a model is known as a 'swamp' model. If it is intended to model seasonal variations it is essential to include the thermal capacity of that part of the ocean—the surface mixed layer—which responds to the seasonal cycle. Later we shall look at the results of a coupled atmosphere–mixed layer model which has been used to study the seasonal effects of increased carbon dioxide but even in this it was not possible to include ocean currents, a deficiency which leads to inaccuracies in regional climate simulation.

Most general circulation model studies of climate have been in the form of sensitivity experiments. The model is run using present day climatic boundary conditions from a prescribed initial state, which may often be a stationary isothermal atmosphere, until an equilibrium climate is achieved. This may require from about 4–15 model years, depending on the complexity of the model. The experiment is repeated with a specified change in the boundary conditions, such as a doubling of carbon dioxide. The differences between the two final equilibrium states are regarded as representing the changes which would occur if the prescribed change in boundary conditions occurred in the real climate system.

The reason why these experiments are preferred to more realistic time-dependent simulations of the evolution of the climate in response to a varying boundary condition is principally one of computational expense. In the case of carbon dioxide increases, for example, it would be necessary to run a simulation for 50–100 model years to obtain useful results, an impossible task with present day computer facilities. Furthermore, in time-dependent simulations it would be necessary to include the thermal interaction between the mixed layer and the deeper layers of the ocean which have an increasingly important bearing on the climate system beyond a period of a decade or so. Suitable models are being developed for such experiments but it will be some time before their full potential can be realised. The coupling of an atmospheric and an oceanic model in itself is difficult on account of their different characteristic time scales. While various time-saving, asynchronous coupling schemes have been used successfully in sensitivity experiments, such schemes are unlikely to give a correct simulation of the time-dependent evolution of climate (Ramanathan, 1981). Nothing short of a fully coupled atmosphere–ocean model, involving vast computational expense, would appear to be adequate in this case.

The prohibitive computational expense of long simulations has also largely prevented the detailed comparison of the *variability* of simulated present day climate with that of the real climate. Moreover, on account of the regional nature of the climatic variability, it will be necessary to improve the simulation of regional climate itself before models can be relied upon to simulate variability. Eventually it should be possible to carry out sufficiently long integrations to determine whether the variability of climate obtained with perturbed climatic boundary conditions is statistically significantly different from that of the control run. Considerable advances in computer power will undoubtedly be necessary for such a task.

ANTHROPOGENIC INFLUENCES ON CLIMATE

Addition to the atmosphere of infra-red-absorbing trace gases with long residence times has the potential for producing sustained, global perturbations in climate. At present this appears to be the means

TABLE 1

POSSIBLE ANTHROPOGENIC INFLUENCES ON CLIMATE (ADAPTED FROM KELLOGG
(1979))

Anthropogenic factor	Climatic element primarily affected	Probable direct effect	Scale[a]	Potential importance
CO_2	Temperature	Warming	G	Major
Trace gases in troposphere	Temperature	Warming	G	Significant
Tropospheric aerosols	Albedo	Warming	R	Significant
Tropospheric aerosols	Cloud processes	Alter rainfall	L/R	Uncertain
Trace gases in stratosphere	Ozone concentration	Increased UV at surface	G	Uncertain
Thermal release	Temperature	Warming	L/R	Major/ significant
Land-use change	Albedo, evapotranspiration	Various	R/G	Significant/ speculative
Kr-85	Conductivity	Alter rainfall	G	Highly speculative

[a] G = global, R = regional, L = local.

whereby man is likely to make his greatest impact on climate. On regional and local scales, however, other factors may be more important now and for some time to come. Table 1, based on the summary given by Kellogg (1979), gives an indication of the scale and likely importance of possible anthropogenic impacts on climate. The increase in atmospheric carbon dioxide concentration is widely thought to represent the largest single threat to the maintenance of the present climate and will be discussed in detail in the following section. Here we look at some of the other ways in which man may modify climate.

Thermal pollution

The most obvious local perturbation to climate has resulted from the building of towns and cities. Direct warming of the air as a result of energy generation and consumption leads to higher temperatures within cities compared with surrounding countryside. This is particularly so in winter, when the anthropogenic heat emissions may be comparable with solar energy input, and at night when buildings retain much of the heat accumulated during the day on account of their large thermal capacity.

Averaged over the globe, anthropogenic heat emissions are some four orders of magnitude smaller than the heating from the sun, and it would require an increase in emissions by at least a factor of 50 to yield a global increase in temperature of 1 K. Most estimates of future energy use suggest increases by a factor of only 3 to 5 by the middle of the next century. Nevertheless, it is possible that the concentration of power generation plants into 'power parks' could in the future influence regional climate by displacing atmospheric flow patterns, but most model simulations indicate that the effects are unlikely to be very significant. It is worth noting that if fossil fuels remain a major source of power, the release of carbon dioxide associated with increased energy consumption could be of much greater significance than the effects of thermal pollution.

Industrial aerosols

Industrialisation, together with 'slash and burn' agricultural practices, have led to increased injection of aerosols into the atmosphere. Aerosols reflect and absorb solar radiation so their presence reduces the intensity at the surface of incoming solar radiation. Some have argued that, if distributed uniformly across the globe, aerosols should give rise to general cooling. Kellogg et al. (1975) and others have questioned the relevance of this suggestion on the grounds that most industrial aerosols and aerosols generated by land clearance tend to remain airborne on average for only about 5 days and are thus likely to be concentrated over the land regions. If the ratio of the solar radiation absorbed to that reflected is sufficiently high, the aerosols may effectively lower the albedo of the underlying surfaces, leading to a net warming of the system. Radiative transfer models have been used to calculate the critical aerosol absorption to backscatter ratios for various underlying surfaces. Combining these results with observations of aerosol optical properties and surface albedo indicates that the majority of low-level tropospheric aerosols over land should provide net warming of the surface–lower troposphere system (Kellogg, 1980), although where these aerosols do spread over the oceans their effect is likely to be one of cooling. Estimates of the possible warming effect are difficult to quantify. Kellogg (1980) suggests that at present, on a regional scale, aerosol warming is probably larger than the warming due to increased carbon dioxide concentration, although this situation could reverse in the future.

More important may be the alteration of the atmospheric stability consequent upon the heating of the aerosol layer by day and its cooling by night. Increased daytime stability and reduced nighttime stability could lead to a reduction in convective rainfall where this occurs by day and an enhancement in those areas subject to rainfall at night.

Whether over land or ocean, the presence of aerosols within clouds usually reduces their reflectivity and provides a further source of tropospheric warming. The ability of some aerosols to act as freezing and condensation nuclei in the formation of cloud ice crystals and water droplets may influence the formation of precipitation. Whether an increase or decrease in local rainfall results from this effect depends on the concentrations of nuclei present together with other meteorological factors. Considerable uncertainty remains in this field of research.

If aerosols are carried upwards into the stratosphere they tend to become uniformly distributed around the globe and remain there for several years. Their effect is generally to cool the troposphere as is evident following major volcanic eruptions. Most stratospheric aerosols consist of sulphate particles and sulphuric acid droplets and for this reason are thought to be of terrestrial origin (Cadle, 1973). Since anthropogenic sources contribute significantly to the atmospheric sulphur loading (Georgii, 1979) the possibility exists that increased sulphur dioxide emissions could lead to higher stratospheric aerosol concentrations. However, the transport mechanisms are not well understood, and there is little doubt that the major perturbations to the stratospheric aerosol loading result from volcanic eruptions (Castleman et al., 1974).

Land-use changes

As mentioned earlier, the thermal characteristics of the surface may be altered by urbanisation. However, built-up areas cover only about 1×10^6 km^2, i.e. 0·2% of the Earth's surface area. Much more important changes in the land surface are brought about through conversion of forests to agricultural land, overgrazing of marginal lands and irrigation schemes, all of which alter the surface albedo and the exchanges of moisture between the surface and the atmosphere. The rate at which deforestation is taking place in the tropics is notoriously difficult to estimate, and is, as we shall see, a problem closely tied in with the carbon dioxide issue. Hampicke (1979) quotes a reduction in the area of closed tropical forest from $17 \times 10^6 \, \text{km}^2$ in 1950 to $10 \times 10^6 \, \text{km}^2$ in 1977. In other parts of the globe, reforestation and re-growth have probably led to small increases in the forested area, and even in the tropics other forms of vegetation will have taken the place of the cleared forest. However, the overall reduction in stored carbon has probably been large and the new vegetative cover has a significantly higher albedo than the virgin forest it replaced.

The complex atmospheric feedback mechanisms which might follow surface albedo changes have been examined using general circulation models. One classic study by Charney *et al.* (1975), of relevance to agricultural practices, suggested how a decrease in vegetative cover could be reinforced by a consequent reduction in rainfall. The biogeophysical feedback envisaged comprised the following sequence of events. A decrease in plant cover increases the albedo which leads to a decrease in the net incoming radiation and a cooling of the atmospheric column. To compensate for the cooling the air sinks and warms adiabatically. Convection is thereby suppressed and convective rainfall is reduced, which in turn enhances the original decrease in plant cover. Charney examined this hypothesis using a general circulation model to simulate the rainy season over the Sahara. Starting with the observed atmospheric state of 18 June 1973 two runs were carried out, one in which the albedo of the Sahara was set at 14%, corresponding to plant cover, and one in which an albedo of 35% was used, appropriate for bare, light soil. Figure 4 illustrates the area-averaged weekly rainfall rates during the 7-week simulations. A southward shift in the rainfall distribution in the high albedo case is evident in Fig. 5. The greatest reduction in rainfall occurred in the region 18–22°N which corresponds with the Sahel. The experiment, although by no means conclusive, suggests that overgrazing may play a significant role in causing droughts and extending desert regions. The persistence of droughts of natural origin in desert regions could also be explained by this mechanism.

The possibility of land-use changes affecting the global scale climate has also been studied by Potter *et al.* (1980). Their modelling experiments show how albedo changes due to large scale desertification and deforestation in the tropics could have sufficient influences on the Hadley circulation and the low-latitude heat and moisture budgets to reduce the poleward heat transport in the northern hemisphere, thereby causing a cooling in higher latitudes. On the basis of these results it may be concluded that if land-use changes were carried to

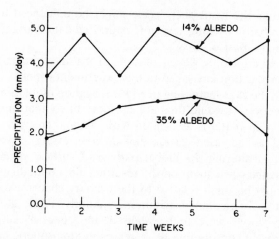

FIG. 4. Simulated weekly mean rainfall rates in the Sahara for two values of surface albedo during the 7-week biogeophysical feedback experiment. (Reproduced from Charney *et al.* (1975) and published with the permission of *Science.* Copyright 1975 by the American Association for the Advancement of Science.)

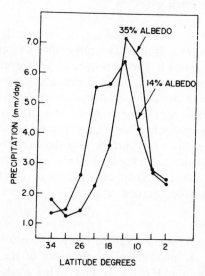

FIG. 5. Latitudinal distribution of mean rainfall during July in North Africa in the biogeophysical feedback experiment. (Reproduced from Charney *et al.* (1975) and published with the permission of *Science.* Copyright 1975 by the American Association for the Advancement of Science.)

extreme limits the hemisphere-scale might be influenced to an extent just observable above the level of natural climatic variability experienced over the past century.

It could be argued, however, that the probability of man causing the major desertification envisaged in this experiment cannot be very high, considering the ever increasing need for irrigation of marginal areas for food production. It would then appear more likely that future changes in precipitation patterns associated with climatic changes of different origin, such as increased carbon dioxide concentrations, would play a larger part in altering the global pattern of surface vegetation. Any climatic change consequent on the resulting albedo modification would then probably be small relative to the primary change which initiated the alteration in rainfall distribution. Similarly, if the global climate model predictions were to be realised, the effect of major tropical deforestation in contributing to increases in atmospheric carbon dioxide concentrations would indirectly lead to a bigger change in climate than that associated with the changes in surface albedo (Baumgartner and Kirchner, 1980).

Radiatively active trace gases

The injection into the atmosphere of man-made trace gases has caused concern on two fronts. The possibility has arisen that certain long-lived species, inert in the troposphere, may eventually be carried into the stratosphere where their dissociation by solar ultra-violet radiation into chemically active constituents could seriously perturb the stratospheric ozone layer. While resident in the troposphere, these and some other anthropogenic trace gases absorb strongly the outgoing infra-red radiation from the surface and the underlying layers of the atmosphere. This leads to an increase in the temperature of the Earth's surface and the lower atmosphere, and thus enhances the natural greenhouse effect noted earlier.

Stratospheric ozone

The chief concern over a decrease in the ozone concentration is that it would lead to an increase in the intensity of the solar ultra-violet radiation reaching the Earth's surface. This could upset biological processes and increase the incidence of skin cancer in humans, although such effects are by no means proven. The effect of a reduction in ozone on climate is less certain. An increase in short-wave radiation at the surface would lead to an increase in temperature. However, the cooling in the stratosphere arising from a reduction in ozone concentration would reduce the infra-red flux from the stratosphere to the troposphere and, according to Ehalt (1980), provide a roughly compensatory cooling. Nevertheless, changes in the stratospheric circulation associated with ozone depletion could influence the tropospheric circulation and climate.

The prime candidates for ozone destruction are the oxides of nitrogen, hydrogen and chlorine. The possibility that large concentrations of the oxides of nitrogen would be injected into the stratosphere by high-flying aircraft is no longer considered a problem since detailed research programmes have concluded that the emissions in the foreseeable future are likely to be too small to have a noticeable effect. Another potential source of nitrous oxide for the stratosphere stems from the increasing use of fertilisers. Nitrous oxide is released naturally from the soil and the oceans and has a sink in the stratosphere. Its residence time in the atmosphere is at least several decades from which Bolin (1980) deduces that the maintenance of a concentration twice that existing today would require an annual injection of about 10^8 tonnes. This figure is comparable with the present production rate of nitrogen fertilisers, which is still rapidly increasing. It is conceivable, therefore, that anthropogenic nitrous oxide formation could exceed natural sources. However, the natural nitrogen cycle is still not well understood and it is plausible (Ellsaesser, 1977) that better agricultural land management has, despite the use of fertilisers, reduced the release of nitrous oxide from the soil.

Most attention in the last 7 years has focused on the release in the troposphere of chlorofluorocarbons (CFCs) from aerosol spray cans. Some of these compounds are completely inert in the troposphere and therefore eventually diffuse into the stratosphere where they are broken down to release chlorine species which enter into a series of reactions leading to the destruction of ozone. The process is not at all simple and photochemical schemes involving well over 100 reactions between naturally occurring and anthropogenic species of oxygen, nitrogen, hydrogen and chlorine have been used in modelling the effects of CFCs in one-dimensional radiative–photochemical column models. Estimates of the eventual ozone depletion obtained from these models, assuming CFC release rates remaining close to present levels, are in the region of 10–20% (see, for example, Ehalt (1980)) with a corresponding 20–40% increase in ultra-violet intensity at the surfaces.

One-dimensional models are, however, unable to take proper account of the dynamical processes which are important in controlling the distributions of ozone and other species in the lower stratosphere, and which are themselves influenced by the interaction of photochemical, radiative and dynamical processes. We shall therefore look briefly at the results obtained using a time-dependent two-dimensional (height–latitude) model of the atmosphere (Haigh and Pyle, 1979; Pyle, 1980; Haigh and Pyle, 1981) in which dynamics are included, but which, for reasons of computational expense, employs a somewhat simple photochemical scheme (51 reactions) compared with those used in some one-dimensional models. Figure 6 shows a latitude–time

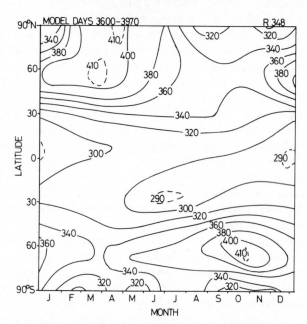

FIG. 6. Latitude–time section for one year of the total atmospheric ozone amount in Dobson units (m atm cm) from the control run of a two-dimensional, time-dependent circulation model. (Reproduced from Pyle (1980) with the permission of Birkhauser Verlag.)

section of the total ozone in the atmosphere, as simulated in the model for unperturbed conditions, which is in good agreement with the observed pattern of time and space variations, although the amplitude of the seasonal variation is a little small. A similar section (see Fig. 7)

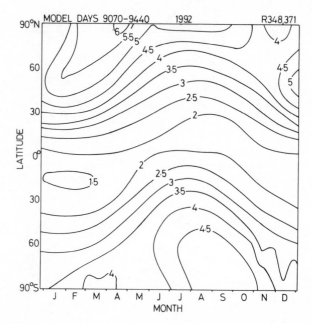

FIG. 7. Latitude–time section of the percentage reduction in total ozone due to CFCs, corresponding with the year 1992 for the particular release history adopted. (Reproduced from Pyle (1980) with the permission of Birkhauser Verlag.)

gives the percentage reduction in total ozone for the year 1992 using a specified CFC release history. The important feature to note is that regions of greatest and smallest reduction coincide with regions of high and low ozone respectively, as seen in Fig. 6. This result becomes more significant in the light of a similar calculation examining the percentage increase in ozone following a doubling of atmospheric carbon dioxide. (Ozone concentration is inversely correlated with temperature, so increased carbon dioxide, which leads to stratospheric cooling, leads to increased ozone concentrations.) Figure 8 indicates an almost identical pattern of ozone increase with that of ozone decrease due to CFCs, the largest increases occurring where ozone concentrations are naturally largest. There is thus an apparent tendency for the effects on ozone of CFCs and carbon dioxide to oppose one another on a seasonal and latitudinal basis. A further experiment, however, in which both pertur-bations were modelled individually and together showed that the effects are not linearly additive. In this experiment, which was run to

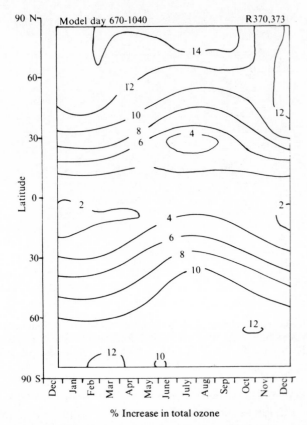

FIG. 8. Latitude–time section of the percentage increase in total ozone follow-
ing a doubling of carbon dioxide concentration from 320 to 640 ppmv.
(Reproduced from Haigh and Pyle (1979) with permission from *Nature*.
Copyright 1979 Macmillan Journals Ltd.)

the year 2045, a doubling of carbon dioxide gave an 8·8% increase in
global total ozone, while a specified accumulation rate for CFCs
resulted in a 12·8% decrease. When both were modelled simultaneously the decrease was 8·1% rather than the 4·0% which would be
obtained by adding the changes resulting from the two separate
perturbations. The reason was that the presence of chlorine species
reduced the temperature dependence of ozone and hence the influence
of the carbon dioxide perturbation. These experiments demonstrate
well the importance of photochemical and dynamical interactions in

producing seasonal and latitudinal variations in the ozone perturbation, and also the complex interdependence of the photochemical processes involved. They should not, however, be regarded as predictive since the model contains of necessity many simplifications and is a mechanistic rather than a simulation model.

A further potential threat to ozone is an increase in stratospheric water vapour. This could arise from increased production of methane, but more likely of greater importance would be an increase in the natural transport of water vapour from the troposphere to the stratosphere initiated by changes in tropospheric temperature and circulation associated with a natural or man-induced climatic change.

Tropospheric greenhouse gases

Table 2, adapted from Wang *et al.* (1976), summarises the estimated globally averaged greenhouse warming at the surface which would

TABLE 2

THE GREENHOUSE EFFECT DUE TO VARIATIONS IN THE CONCENTRATION OF VARIOUS MINOR CONSTITUENTS OF THE ATMOSPHERE (AFTER WANG *et al.* (1976))

Constituent	Multiple of present concentration	Greenhouse effect (K) FCT^a	FCA^b
N_2O	2	0·68	0·44
CH_4	2	0·28	0·20
NH_3	2	0·12	0·09
HNO_3	2	0·08	0·06
C_2H_4	2	0·01	0·01
SO_2	2	0·03	0·02
$CCl_2F_2 + CCl_3F$	20	0·54	0·36
$CH_3Cl + CCl_4$	2	0·02	0·01
CO_2	1·25	0·79	0·53

[a] FCT = fixed cloud-top temperature.
[b] FCA = fixed cloud-top altitude.

result from the specified increases in the concentrations of a number of important infra-red-absorbing trace gases to which man is contributing. The calculations were made with a one-dimensional radiative–convective model and results are given for both the assumptions of fixed cloud-top temperature (FCT) and fixed cloud-top altitude (FCA). It is immediately apparent that while carbon dioxide has by far the largest impact, nitrous oxide, methane, ammonia and perhaps CFCs could also make significant contributions to tropospheric warming in addition to their impact on stratospheric photochemistry.

Recently Ramanathan (1980) has drawn attention to the fact that methane, carbon monoxide and nitric oxide, released from fossil fuel combustion, may lead to significant increases in the production of tropospheric ozone which is itself an important infra-red absorber and thus able to contribute to the greenhouse effect. From available estimates of future increases in these gases together with nitrous oxide and CFCs, Ramanathan indicates that they may contribute as much as 40% to the combined warming due to carbon dioxide and these other trace gases. In other words the warming due to carbon dioxide may only be 60% of the total warming due to anthropogenic gas releases. The results could be subject to considerable error, however, since only 25% of the warming effect of the trace gases other than carbon dioxide was directly due to anthropogenic emission of radiatively active gases. The remaining 75% was a result of anthropogenic emission of photochemically active species which, via complex chemical reactions, led to increases in radiatively active trace gases. Understanding of tropospheric chemistry is extremely limited at present. Considering also the lack of knowledge concerning natural sources and sinks of methane, carbon monoxide and nitric oxide, and the general limitations of one-dimensional models discussed earlier, the results must be taken only as an indication of the potential climatic importance of a wide range of trace gases in the troposphere, and not as a quantitative prediction of future warming.

Krypton-85

An anthropogenic perturbation to climate of a rather different kind has been suggested by Boeck (1976). Release of radioactive Krypton-85 from extensive use and reprocessing of nuclear fuels could lead to atmospheric ionisation rates which are significant relative to the rate of natural production of ions by cosmic rays. This could increase the electrical conductivity of the atmosphere and modify thunderstorm electrification processes. Krypton-85 has a half-life of 10·7 years. Thus any effects would be global, although the effects would be of greatest importance in those areas where thunderstorms provide most of the rainfall. This effect is at present highly speculative since current knowledge of the interaction between the Earth's electric field and thunderstorms is very limited.

CARBON DIOXIDE

Anthropogenic carbon dioxide release

The increase in atmospheric carbon dioxide from burning fossil fuels is the one single anthropogenic influence which could produce global climatic changes observable above the natural climatic noise within the next 50 years. Between 1860 and the early 1970s emissions of carbon dioxide increased at a rate of just over 4% per year, except during the world wars and the depression in the 1930s (Fig. 9). The pre-industrial

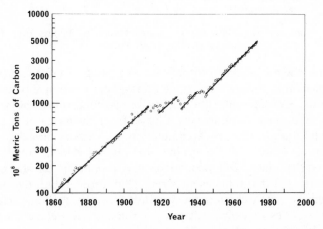

FIG. 9. Annual production of carbon dioxide from fossil fuels and cement (after Rotty, 1979).

atmospheric concentration of carbon dioxide is uncertain, but it is thought to have been in the range of 265–295 ppmv. Continuous observations did not begin until 1957 (Keeling *et al.*, 1976). Since then the atmospheric concentration has risen from about 315 to 337 ppmv. This rate of increase is equivalent to just over half the rate of input of fossil fuel carbon dioxide to the atmosphere. Figure 10 shows the first 19 years of the record from Mauna Loa, the original monitoring station. On the secular trend is superimposed the annual cycle of atmosphere–biosphere exchange of carbon dioxide. The fossil fuel carbon dioxide that does not remain in the atmosphere is thought to be absorbed by the oceans, which is potentially a large sink, and by the

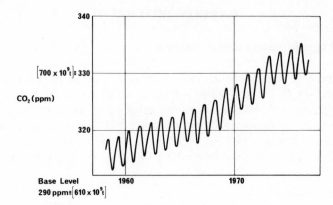

FIG. 10. Atmospheric carbon dioxide concentration at Mauna Loa, Hawaii (after Keeling *et al.*, 1976).

biosphere which is assumed to increase as a result of enhanced photosynthesis in the presence of larger atmospheric carbon dioxide concentrations. Considerable uncertainty exists concerning the relative importance of these natural sinks. Clearly for a given rate of fossil fuel usage, the future rate of accumulation of carbon dioxide in the atmosphere, which will determine the rate at which any climatic damage takes place, will depend on the proportion of the carbon dioxide released that remains airborne. This consideration has prompted extensive research into the operation of the carbon cycle, the relevant features of which will now be summarised before discussing the possible climatic effects of increased carbon dioxide.

Man's impact on the carbon cycle

Prior to the industrial revolution man's impact on the cycling of carbon between the natural reservoirs was negligible. Figure 11 gives estimates of the carbon contents of each of the major reservoirs and of the annual fluxes of carbon between them. The oceans are seen to have an enormous potential capacity to absorb excess atmospheric carbon dioxide, not only by reaction with dissolved carbonate ions to form bicarbonate ions but also by dissolution of sedimentary carbonate minerals. However, in the short-term their full potential cannot be realised because mixing between the surface and deep waters is very slow, the residence time of water in the deep ocean being of the order of 1000 years. Moreover, although the surface waters, which mix rather

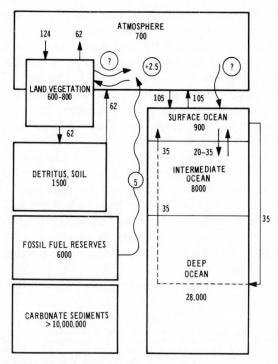

FIG. 11. The global carbon cycle. Estimates of the carbon contents (Gtonnes of carbon) of each reservoir and of the annual transfers (Gtonnes year^{-1}) are indicated. Circles denote transfers resulting from man's intervention (after Bjorkstrom, 1979).

rapidly, have a carbon content comparable with that of the atmosphere, the chemical characteristics of the seawater carbonate system prevents them from serving as a major sink for carbon dioxide. Indeed their limited capacity will be further reduced as carbon dioxide concentrations increase. The overall capacity of the oceans for taking up excess carbon dioxide at any given time would seem to depend on the rate at which carbon can be transported from the surface to the deep ocean relative to the rate of input of fossil fuel carbon dioxide to the atmosphere. Most models of oceanic uptake suggest that the ocean has been capable of absorbing most, but certainly not all, of the fossil fuel carbon dioxide that has not remained airborne, implying that the biosphere has taken up the remainder. This implication has led to considerable controversy, however, since many now believe that the biosphere cannot have acted as a sink for carbon dioxide. The hypothesis that increased carbon dioxide concentrations lead to greater rates of photosynthesis may not be valid in regions where nutrients or water supplies are growth-limiting factors. More important still is the probability that large scale deforestation has led to a significant additional source of atmospheric carbon dioxide. During deforestation, not only is carbon dioxide released to the atmosphere as a result of both burning and accelerated decomposition of soil organic matter, but the forest ecosystem, which is an effective abstractor of carbon dioxide, is replaced by urban or agricultural developments which store very little carbon. It is difficult to estimate by how much the biosphere has changed and is changing now. Some argue for a biospheric source of carbon dioxide equivalent to that from fossil fuels. Most authorities opt for a lower figure but there are few who believe that the biosphere has been a sufficiently large net sink to meet the requirements of the ocean models. Figure 12 summarises the present state of uncertainty in the

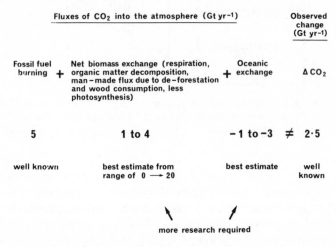

FIG. 12. Uncertainty in the global carbon cycle.

global carbon budget. One possible explanation for the apparent imbalance in the carbon cycle is that many processes, which on their own are not significant in comparison with the major sinks discussed, may together provide an important sink. Dissolution of sediments in coastal waters and enhanced biological fixation in association with increased supplies to the oceans of phosphorus and nitrogen of agricultural origin are possible examples.

Future carbon dioxide concentrations

While the uncertainties in the partitioning of the carbon dioxide additions are important factors in the assessment of the long-term future, increases in atmospheric carbon dioxide concentrations, uncertainties in future rates of fossil fuel usage and man-induced biospheric carbon dioxide emission provide the largest sources of error in estimating the accumulation of carbon dioxide over the next 50–100 years. The time scales of the carbon reservoirs are such that changes from the currently observed airborne fraction of near 50% of emissions are likely to be rather slow, whereas predictions of energy consumption beyond a decade or so and future rates of deforestation vary very considerably. Admitting the impossibility of making reliable predictions, several energy analysis groups have developed scenarios for use in assessing the possible impact of carbon dioxide. One scenario from the Institute of Energy Analysis at Oak Ridge (Rotty and Marland, 1980) suggests that world primary energy consumption will be 27 terawatt-year per year ($TWy\, y^{-1}$) in the year 2025. Similar scenarios from the Energy Group at IIASA (1980) indicate energy consumption in 2025 in the range 18–36 $TWy\, y^{-1}$. Present world consumption is about $8\cdot2\, TWy\, y^{-1}$. On the basis of these scenarios the Joint WMO/ICSU/UNEP Meeting of Experts in November 1980 (WMO, 1981) concluded that the average rate of increase in carbon dioxide emissions over the next 50 years will be 2% per year, giving a cumulative emission between now and 2025 of 400 ± 60 Gtonnes of carbon from fossil fuel combustion. Assuming an additional release of 50–150 Gtonnes from the biosphere between 1980 and 2025 and a value for the airborne fraction of 40–55% yields an atmospheric concentration of carbon dioxide in 2025 of between 410 and 490 ppmv with a most likely value of 450 ppmv. The increase due solely to fossil fuel usage would yield a concentration of 425 ± 25 ppmv. However, if emissions were to grow at the past long-term average rate of just over 4% per year the concentration would be double its pre-industrial level by about the year 2030. For the next decade at least the World Bank predicts an increase in world energy production at a rate of $3\cdot9\%$ per year, so the 2% per year value adopted by WMO may be optimistic and represent a lower limit for carbon dioxide increases.

Climatic change due to increased carbon dioxide concentrations

In our discussion of climate models, attention was drawn to their present inadequacies. We recall that using the most realistic models, the general circulation models, only climate sensitivity experiments are today feasible, giving no indication of the transient response of the climatic system to carbon dioxide increases. In particular it was noted that neither the role of the oceans nor the interactions between clouds and radiation have yet been treated adequately. Nevertheless, the GCMs are capable of simulating the gross features of the present seasonal cycle of the global climate, a fact which lends some credence to their predictions of the major impacts of man on climate.

Owing to the expense of running climate models the number of experiments assessing the sensitivity of climate to increased carbon dioxide has been small. They may be divided into those using one-dimensional radiative–convective equilibrium models and those using GCMs. The joint WMO/ICSU/UNEP Meeting of Experts (WMO, 1981) quoted results from five models of the first category which gave global average total increases in surface air temperature in the range 1·5–2·3 K for a doubling of the carbon dioxide concentration. All the models include the water vapour–temperature feedback, in which the initial surface warming due to increased carbon dioxide leads to an increase in the water vapour content of the lower atmosphere which substantially amplifies the greenhouse warming. The equivalent temperature increases given by GCMs are somewhat higher since these models include various latitude-dependent feedback processes, the net effect of which enhance the warming. The range of increase given by those GCMs which permit atmosphere–ocean interaction is from 2·0 to 3·5 K. The value of 2·0 K was implied by Manabe and Stouffer (1979, 1980) who obtained a 4·0 K increase for a quadrupling of carbon dioxide using a global model with realistic geography, seasonal variations and a mixed-layer ocean. The 3·5 K global warming was simulated by Hansen (see NAS, 1979) also using a seasonal model with realistic geography and a mixed-layer ocean but with model-determined cloud cover. Manabe and Wetherald (1975, 1980) predicted global mean increases of 3·0 and 2·9 K using a northern hemisphere model with idealised geography, annual mean conditions and a swamp ocean. The earlier model used fixed cloud cover while the latter included model-determined cloudiness. The apparently minor effect of cloud changes arose from the tendency for the changes to produce compensatory effects in the solar and infra-red radiation budgets. That such compensation occurs in the real climate may be suggested by the ability of the Manabe and Stouffer model to reproduce the observed seasonal cycle using fixed annual mean cloud cover.

It could then be argued that more sophisticated modelling of cloud feedback interactions will not change the general aspects of the simulated carbon dioxide-induced climatic change (WMO, 1981). On the other hand specified cloud changes in radiative–convective models illustrate the extreme sensitivity of climate to cloud amounts. Hunt (1981) found that a 10% increase in low cloud cover could completely compensate for the warming caused by a doubling of carbon dioxide. This is not to suggest that such a change in cloud cover would occur, but serves to indicate that very high accuracy is required for model-generated cloud cover in GCMs. Other cloud characteristics, such as liquid water content, albedo and emissivity have not yet been considered as variables in GCM cloud prediction schemes. Paltridge (1980), for example, suggests that increases in liquid water content could be as influential as increased low cloud cover. Clearly the role of cloud–climate interactions could be vital and warrants a great deal more research.

According to the report of the *ad hoc* study group of the National Academy of Sciences (NAS, 1979) the differences between the Manabe and Stouffer and the Manabe and Wetherald models can be explained by the inclusion in the former of seasonal effects and realistic geography with a southern hemisphere. Differences in ice- and snow-cover, with the associated ice albedo–temperature feedback, and in the interactive cloud schemes used probably explains the differences between the Manabe and the Hansen models. A value for the global mean warming of near 3 K with an error of ±1·5 K is concluded by the *ad hoc* study group.

The measure of agreement amongst the GCMs, and between the GCMs and the one-dimensional models when account is taken of the feedback processes that cannot be simulated in the latter, suggests that the GCMs are probably reliable qualitatively in their prediction of at least the gross features of the seasonal and spatial variations of the carbon dioxide-induced climatic changes. Hunt (1981) points out that while a variety of potentially important feedback mechanisms, including those associated with cloud properties and air–ocean exchange, are not yet adequately included in GCMs, nothing is to be gained by disparaging the performance of existing models because they lack these mechanisms. Many of the latter are as likely to enhance as to diminish the currently predicted climatic change.

The annual mean latitudinal variation of the temperature increase in the northern hemisphere for doubled carbon dioxide deduced by

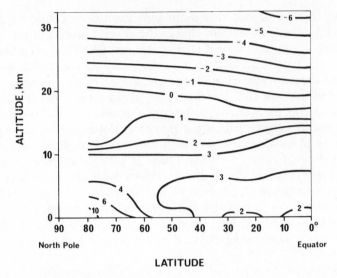

FIG. 13. Latitude–height distribution of the increase in zonal mean temperature (K) resulting from a doubling of carbon dioxide concentration (after
Manabe and Wetherald, 1975).

Manabe and Wetherald (1975) is shown in Fig. 13. The considerably
larger warming in high latitudes is a feature of all the GCMs simulations. This is due to the enhancement of the radiatively induced
warming by retreat of highly reflective snow- and ice-cover (the ice
albedo–temperature feedback), the confinement of heating to the
lowest layers due to the vertical stability of the polar atmosphere, and
increased transport toward the poles of latent heat due to the overall
warming and moistening of the atmosphere. The latter process is
illustrated in Fig. 14 which shows changes in the latitudinal distributions of precipitation and evaporation as calculated by Manabe and
Wetherald (1980). The enhanced moisture flux toward the poles is
shown to produce significant increases in precipitation north of 50°N
which exceeded the increase in evaporation rate which also occurred.
Conversely a surface moisture deficit is indicated for the band 40–
50°N. The models are not yet sophisticated enough to simulate regional climate with any reliability. Nevertheless, some indications of the
spatial scale of the possible changes are available. Figure 15 shows the
horizontal distribution of the change in precipitation rate minus evaporation rate $(P - E)$ in response to a doubling of carbon dioxide in the

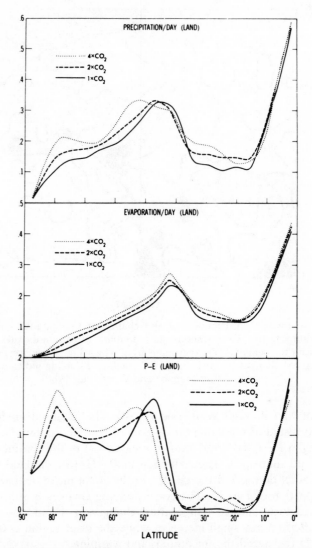

FIG. 14. Latitudinal distributions of zonal mean values of precipitation rate, evaporation rate and precipitation rate minus evaporation rate $(P-E)$, over the continent of a GCM with idealised northern hemisphere geography, for present day, doubled and quadrupled carbon dioxide concentrations. Units are cm day^{-1}. (Reproduced with permission from Manabe and Wetherald, 1980.)

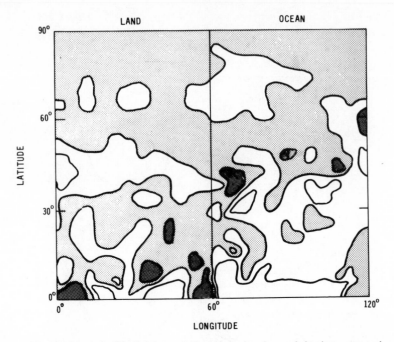

FIG. 15. Horizontal distribution of the change of precipitation rate minus evaporation rate $(P-E)$ in response to a doubling of carbon dioxide concentration, from the same GCM experiment from which Fig. 14 derives. Contours are drawn for changes of $-0\cdot1$, 0 and $0\cdot1$ cm day^{-1}; shading indicates positive changes (after Manabe and Wetherald, 1980).

model of Manabe and Wetherald (1980). The idealised model geography consisted of repeating 60° sectors of land and ocean. Noticeable increases in $P-E$ occurred along the east coast of the continent in the tropics and subtropics. The reduction in $P-E$ over the land between 40 and 50°N dominated the change in the zonal mean depicted in the lowest portion of Fig. 14. The corresponding changes in soil moisture influenced local surface temperature changes in the model, the east coast suffering only small increases while the drier region between 40 and 50°N registered the maximum land warming.

The lower global mean in temperature found in the global seasonal model of Manabe and Stouffer (1979, 1980), as compared with the non-seasonal, idealised northern hemisphere models of Manabe and Wetherald (1975, 1980), was due in part to the relative absence of ice albedo–temperature feedback in the Antarctic. This resulted in a

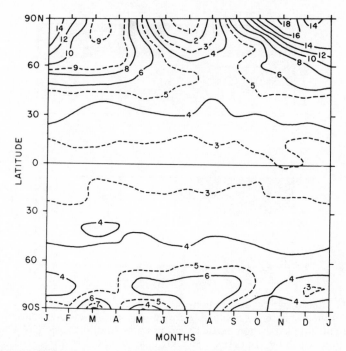

Fig. 16. Latitude–time distribution of the difference in zonal mean surface air temperature between present day and quadrupled carbon dioxide concentrations as deduced from a seasonal GCM with realistic, global geography and a mixed-layer ocean. (Reproduced from Manabe and Stouffer (1979) with permission from *Nature*. Copyright 1979 Macmillan Journals Ltd.)

considerably smaller warming in southern high latitudes than in northern high latitudes. The seasonal variation in temperature change (Fig. 16) illustrates the importance of sea ice and continental snow cover in the northern hemisphere. The results shown are for quadrupled carbon dioxide concentration, but the same pattern, showing zonally averaged winter and spring warming considerably larger than summer warming, would be expected for smaller increases in carbon dioxide. This seasonal pattern is explained by the utilisation in summer of the additional heating to reduce sea ice thickness and to warm ice-free surface waters rather than to warm the air. During autumn the lack of, or reduced thickness of, the ice allows heat to be transferred from the warmed ocean to the atmosphere, arresting the usual seasonal cooling of the atmosphere. Figure 17 shows the difference in the seasonal

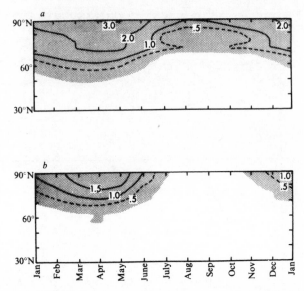

FIG. 17. Latitude–time distributions of zonal mean thickness of sea ice for the northern hemisphere oceans for (a) present-day carbon dioxide concentration and (b) quadrupled carbon dioxide concentration, from the same GCM experiment from which Fig. 16 derives. Shading indicates areas where sea ice is more than 0·1 m thick. (Reproduced from Manabe and Stouffer (1979) with permission from *Nature*. Copyright 1979 Macmillan Journals Ltd.)

variation in sea ice thickness between the control and quadrupled carbon dioxide runs. While a considerably less exaggerated effect would result from a doubling of carbon dioxide, a mechanism capable of having a major influence on the seasonal variation of a climatic warming has been identified in this experiment.

The relatively large warming in spring in northern high latitudes arises from earlier removal of snow cover than in the control run and subsequent operation of the snow albedo–temperature feedback. It will be recalled that the modelling of snow- and ice-cover was deemed by the *ad hoc* study group to be a major cause of the differences in global mean temperature changes predicted by the Manabe and the Hansen models. Clearly, accurate ice and snow modelling is equally important for simulating the seasonal and regional changes in climate.

It is pertinent at this stage to summarise the main climatic effects which, on the basis of the climate sensitivity experiments discussed, could occur as a consequence of a doubling of carbon dioxide. These include:

1. A significant warming of global climate during the next century. An increase of 2–3 K due to carbon dioxide could be augmented by an increase of up to about 1 K due to the accumulation of other infra-red absorbing trace gases emitted by man

2. A warming greater in high latitudes than in the tropics, and greater in the Arctic than in the Antarctic

3. In northern temperate and high latitudes a warming likely to be larger in winter and spring than in summer

4. An intensification of the hydrological cycle due to the general warming

5. Changes in the general circulation of the atmosphere due to (2) which would ensure regional changes in temperature and precipitation larger than the changes in the zonal mean

Since climate models cannot yet predict the character of regional climatic change, several authors have examined past, warmer climates or past anomalously warm years or seasons, in an attempt to obtain some idea of the likely scale of regional change. Kellogg (1977) collected evidence from the hypsithermal period between 4000 and 8000 years ago, and Fig. 18 shows differences between the summertime climate that prevailed then and that of today. The patterns of

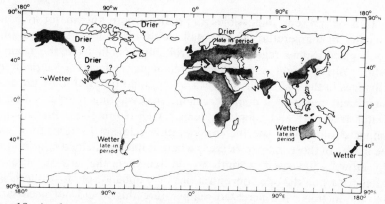

FIG. 18. A schematic map of the distribution of rainfall, relative to the present climate, predominantly during the summer season in the Altithermal period 4000–8000 years ago when the world was generally warmer than now by several degrees. Shaded areas, wetter. Blank areas are not necessarily regions of no rainfall change; information is still far from complete. (Reproduced from Kellogg (1978) with permission of Cambridge University Press.)

change shown cannot be regarded as a prediction of future climatic change for many reasons. It is probable, for example, that the various regional differences occurred at different times and that the climatic boundary conditions were somewhat different then than now. The cause of the warmer climate in the hypsithermal period was probably not higher carbon dioxide concentrations. Nevertheless, indications are beginning to emerge from the climate models (Manabe and Wetherald, 1980) that the climatic responses to different types of climatic forcing may bear strong similarities since the effects of internal feedback mechanisms dominate the effects of the initial perturbation to the climate system. This suggests that study of past, warm climates may be of greater relevance to the future than once thought. Other analogue studies using instrumental data have concentrated on temperature and rainfall anomalies in the northern hemisphere which have been associated with extreme warmth in high northern latitudes. From studying a variety of assumed analogues it may eventually be possible to identify certain features of regional climatic change that tend to recur, and which, therefore, may be expected in a carbon dioxide-induced warm climate.

Impact of carbon dioxide-induced climatic change on agriculture and fisheries

It is at present impossible to predict where the major regional changes in temperature and rainfall would occur if a global warming took place. Some regions would probably benefit from the changes while others might suffer severe, damaging effects on agriculture. Changes in the availability of fresh water could turn out to be the most significant result of a climatic change necessitating reorganisation of water transport and supply systems. Aside from these fundamental impacts some more specific consideration relevant to agriculture may be made. In those temperate areas where rainfall remained non-limiting to growth, increased warmth would lengthen the growing season. Higher carbon dioxide concentrations may enhance photosynthesis but in conjunction with increased temperature this would not necessarily lead to higher crop yields. In the case of some crops grown widely in the tropics and subtropics (such as sorghum, maize, cotton and sunflower) yields could be reduced (WMO, 1981). Skills in developing strains able to withstand, and moreover capitalise upon, the stresses imposed by prevailing local climate will doubtless be increasingly valuable in the future.

Possibly a more serious problem would be the tendency for higher temperatures to increase the spread of diseases and the speed of multiplication of agricultural pests. The influence of higher temperatures on bacterial decomposition of dead vegetation is to reduce the formation of humus, resulting in slow deterioration of soils. It may be significant that almost all the world's poorer countries lie in areas with an annual mean temperature above 20°C, the temperature above which decay of vegetation proceeds more rapidly than humus production (Tonge, 1981).

Fisheries might be at risk from both the chemical and dynamical changes which could occur in the oceans. The slow increase in the acidity of seawater might upset links in the marine food chain, while ocean circulation changes, particularly in coastal waters, could influence the patterns of upwelling of nutrient-rich deeper waters upon which many fisheries depend.

Detecting carbon dioxide-induced climatic change

It should be remembered that the present climate sensitivity experiments give no indication of the timing of the climatic changes which they predict. A doubling of the atmospheric carbon dioxide concentration, if it occurs, may not be realised until late in the next century. Nevertheless, if the models are broadly correct and if fossil fuels continue to be a major source of energy, some noticeable effects on climate should be apparent well before then. Indeed, on the basis of the GCM results the warming should already be detectable above the natural climatic noise, according to Madden and Ramanathan (1980). However, in a careful study of monthly mean data at 60°N for the period 1906–1977 they failed to detect a warming signal. They suggested that this may be due to compensating cooling associated with other, unidentified climatic factors, or a delay of more than a decade in the appearance of the warming arising from the thermal inertia of the oceans. Considering the uncertainties in the models and in the oceanic response, Madden and Ramanathan suggested that an extension of the period for detection to the year 2000 was reasonable. Even then it may be difficult to show unambiguously that any warming is due to carbon dioxide or that a lack of warming is not indicative of a compensating cooling. Consequently, validation or otherwise of the climatic model predictions may not be possible for several decades.

CONCLUDING REMARKS

As yet no changes in the global climate which can be attributed to man's activities have been observed. Climate models, however, indicate that significant changes might occur in the next century if fossil fuel consumption and large scale tropical deforestation continue to expand. Considerable uncertainty remains in their predictions and several potentially important feedback processes have yet to be included in the models. Nevertheless, the possible consequences of the climatic changes which they currently predict are sufficiently serious to have attracted world-wide attention. Until observational evidence of a climatic warming is available it will be difficult to make any firm conclusions about the validity of the model predictions. Strategies aimed at the earliest possible detection of a carbon dioxide-induced climatic change therefore need to be developed. During the intervening period it is desirable that research be continued to improve our understanding of the physical processes involved in climatic change so that uncertainty in model predictions may be reduced and a better indication of possible regional climatic change may be obtained. Research, too, must be carried out into the possible implications for both industrialised and developing nations of the climatic changes predicted. If, as a result of an unacceptable carbon dioxide-induced climatic change, it should be deemed necessary to reduce consumption of fossil fuels, the nations of the world would be better able to respond if their quest for alternative energy sources have been given a high priority.

ACKNOWLEDGEMENT

This paper was written at the Central Electricity Research Laboratories and is published by permission of the Central Electricity Generating Board.

REFERENCES

Baumgartner, A. and Kirchner, M. (1980). Impacts due to deforestation. In: *Interactions of Energy and Climate* (Eds W. Bach, J. Pankrath and J. Williams). D. Reidel Publishing Company, Dordrecht, p. 305.

Bjorkstrom, A. (1979). Man's global redistribution of carbon. *Ambio* **8**, 254.

Boeck, W. L. (1976). Meteorological consequences of atmospheric Krypton-85. *Science* **193**, 195.

Bolin, B. (1980). *Man's Impact on Climate*. Presented at the International Conference on Climate and Offshore Energy Resources, Royal Society, London, 21–23 October.

Cadle, R. D. (1973). Composition of the stratospheric 'sulphate layer'. In: *Climatic Impact Assessment Program, Proceedings of the Survey Conf.*, Cambridge, Mass., 15–16 February 1972 (Ed. A. E. Barrington). NTIS, Springfield, p. 130.

Castleman, A. W., Munkelwitz, H. R. and Manowitz, B. (1974). Isotopic studies of the S compound of the stratospheric aerosol layer. *Tellus* **26**, 222.

Charney, J. G., Stone, P. H. and Quirk, W. J. (1975). Drought in the Sahara: A biogeophysical feedback mechanism. *Science* **187**, 434.

Ehalt, D. H. (1980). The effects of chlorofluoromethanes on climate. In: *Interactions of Energy and Climate* (Eds W. Bach, J. Pankrath and J. Williams). D. Reidel Publishing Company, Dordrecht, p. 243.

Ellsaesser, H. W. (1977). Has man increased stratospheric ozone? *Nature* **270**, 592.

Georgii, H.-W. (1979). Large-scale distribution of gaseous and particulate sulphur compounds and its impact on climate. In: *Man's Impact on Climate* (Eds W. Bach, J. Pankrath and W. W. Kellogg) Elsevier, Amsterdam, p. 181.

Haigh, J. D. and Pyle, J. A. (1979). A two-dimensional calculation including atmospheric carbon dioxide and stratospheric ozone. *Nature* **279**, 222.

Haigh, J. D. and Pyle, J. A. (1981). Ozone perturbation experiments in a two-dimensional circulation model. Submitted to *Quart. J. R. Met. Soc.*

Hampicke, U. (1979). Man's impact on the Earth's vegetation cover and its effect on carbon cycle and climate. In: *Man's Impact on Climate* (Eds W. Bach, J. Pankrath and W. W. Kellogg). Elsevier, Amsterdam, p. 139.

Hunt, B. G. (1981). An examination of some feedback mechanisms in the carbon dioxide problem. *Tellus* **33**, 78.

IIASA (1980). *Energy in a Finite World*. International Institute for Applied Systems Analysis, Ballinger Publishing Company.

Keeling, C. D., Bacastow, R. B., Bainbridge, A. E., Ekdahl, C. A., Guenther, P. R., Waterman, L. S. and Chin, J. F. S. (1976). Atmospheric carbon dioxide variations at Mauna Loa Observatory, Hawaii. *Tellus* **28**, 538.

Kellogg, W. W. (1977). Effects of human activities on global climate. *WMO Tech. Note No. 156*. WMO No. 486, Geneva.

Kellogg, W. W. (1978). Global influences of mankind on the climate. In: *Climatic Change* (Ed. J. Gribbin). Cambridge University Press, London, p. 205.

Kellogg, W. W. (1979). Influences of mankind on climate. *Ann. Rev. Earth Planet Sci.* **7**, 63.

Kellogg, W. W. (1980). Aerosols and climate (and report of Workshop discussion on impact of aerosols). In: *Interactions of Energy and Climate*, (Eds W. Bach, J. Pankrath and J. Williams). D. Reidel Publishing Company, Dordrecht, pp. 281 and 301.

Kellogg, W. W., Coakley, J. A. and Grams, G. W. (1975). Effect of anthropogenic aerosols on the global climate. *Proc. WMO/IAMAP Symposium on Long-Term Climatic Fluctuations*, Norwich, UK WMO No. 421, Geneva, p. 323.

Kellogg, W. W. and Schneider, S. H. (1974). Climate stabilization: for better or for worse? *Science* **186**, 1163.

Madden, R. and Ramanathan, V. (1980). Detecting climate change due to increasing carbon dioxide. *Science* **209**, 763.

Manabe, S. and Stouffer, R. J. (1979). A CO_2-climate sensitivity study with a mathematical model of the global climate. *Nature* **282**, 491.

Manabe, S. and Stouffer, R. J. (1980). Sensitivity of a global climate model to an increase of CO_2 concentration in the atmosphere. *J. Geophys. Res.* **85**, 5529.

Manabe, S. and Wetherald, R. T. (1975). The effects of doubling the CO_2 concentration on the climate of a general circulation model. *J. Atmos. Sci.* **32**, 3.

Manabe, S. and Wetherald, R. T. (1980). On the distribution of climate change resulting from an increase in CO_2 content of the atmosphere. *J. Atmos. Sci.* **37**, 99.

NAS (1975). *Understanding Climatic Change: A Program For Action.* US Committee for GARP, National Academy of Sciences, Washington DC.

NAS (1979). *Carbon Dioxide and Climate: A Scientific Assessment.* Report of an *ad hoc* study group on carbon dioxide and climate to the Climate Research Board of the National Research Council. National Academy of Sciences, Washington DC.

Paltridge, G. W. (1980). Cloud-radiation feedback to climate. *Quart. J. R. Met. Soc.* **106**, 895.

Potter, G. L., Ellsaesser, H. W., MacCracken, M. C., Ellis, J. S. and Luther, F. M. (1980). Climate change due to anthropogenic surface albedo modification. In: *Interactions of Energy and Climate* (Eds W. Bach, J. Pankrath and J. Williams). D. Reidel Publishing Company, Dordrecht, p. 317.

Pyle, J. A. (1980). A calculation of the possible depletion of ozone by chlorofluorocarbons using a two-dimensional model. *Pure and Applied Geophysics* **118**, 355.

Ramanathan, V. (1980). Climatic effects of anthropogenic trace gases. In: *Interactions of Energy and Climate* (Eds W. Bach, J. Pankrath and J. Williams). D. Reidel Publishing Company, Dordrecht, p. 269.

Ramanathan, V. (1981). The role of ocean–atmosphere interactions in the CO_2-climate problem. *J. Atmos. Sci.* **38**, 918.

Rotty, R. M. (1979). Present and future production of CO_2 from fossil fuels—a global appraisal. In: *Workshop on the Global Effects of Carbon Dioxide from Fossil Fuels.* US Dept. of Energy Carbon Dioxide Effects Research and Assessment Program No. 001, Washington DC.

Rotty, R. M. and Marland, G. (1980). *Constraints on Carbon Dioxide Production from Fossil Fuel Use.* Research Memorandum ORAU/IEA 80–89, Oak Ridge Associated Universities.

Tonge, D. (1981). Dangers from the 'greenhouse effect'. Energy review: carbon dioxide from fossil fuels. *Financial Times* 13 February.

Wang, W. C., Young, J. L., Lacis, A. A., Mo, T. and Hansen, J. E. (1976). Greenhouse effects due to manmade perturbation of trace gases. *Science* **194**, 685.

WMO (1981). *On the Assessment of the Role of CO_2 on Climate Variations and their Impact.* Report of the Joint WMO/ICSU/UNEP Meeting of Experts, Villach, Austria, 17–21 November, World Climate Programme, WMO, Geneva.

Discussion

Professor Van Eimern pointed out that there was a slight anomaly in calling the effect of carbon dioxide 'a greenhouse effect'. In a greenhouse the major effect is through the warming of the trapped air. He then raised the question of whether assumptions about albedo in relation to land use were altogether relevant. In Germany the increase in maize production had entailed that the crop cover was not complete in the early part of the year and the soil was exposed in April, May and June. Lastly, he pointed out the anomaly that although there had been an increase in the CO_2 content of the atmosphere in the last few years there had in fact been a decrease in global temperature. *Dr Crane* replied stating that he quite agreed that the ordinary greenhouse was effective through air trapping and while the albedo was locally variable, most of the models dealt with much larger aspects. He pointed out that he had emphasised throughout the extent of the natural variation in climate and that the absence of a measurable effect of CO_2 concentration over the last years was operating in a situation in which there was considerable climatic noise. *Dr Thompson* raised the problems associated with models, notably those associated with cloud cover and the neglect of the ocean circulation. He pointed out that quite small errors in initial assumptions could give rise to large errors later on. *Dr Crane* stated that the assumption of fixed cloud cover had, in some models, not prevented a realistic simulation of the seasonal climatic cycle, although he agreed that the problem was one of great importance. He also agreed that models did not include circulation of the ocean waters and emphasised that the various models were estimates and were subject to a number of errors. *Dr Flood* again advised caution, pointing out that any changes will necessarily be very slow giving people a chance to react and that they could still be swamped by the year-to-year variability in the climate which Dr Crane had referred to as climatic noise. *Dr Crane* agreed with this and once again stated that one could not predict climatic change with any precision and all estimates had to be treated with caution. *Professor Jarvis* raised questions about the two-fold effect of burning fossil fuels. Not only did fossil fuel burning increase the CO_2 content of the atmosphere, it also increased the number of dust and solid particles which could quite well reflect solar radiation and thus cancel out in part the carbon dioxide effect. *Dr Crane* stated that the current feeling was that aerosols in the troposphere appeared to be of short residence time and would probably cause only regional disturbances. Some of these particles, however, did enter the stratosphere where residence times could be long and these could conceivably result in some of the effects which Professor Jarvis was predicating.

The Economic Cost of Climatic Variation

P. A. ORAM

International Food Policy Research Institute,
Washington DC, USA

CLIMATIC VARIABILITY AND ECONOMIC STABILITY

Climate and its variability has, until recently, not received the attention it merits in economic studies, particularly in those which attempt to determine the future potential of large areas of the world to provide food and food security to an expanding population. Although a good many geographically localised micro-level studies have been published (for example, those summarised by McQuigg (1975*b*) under the title *Economic Impacts of Weather Variability*) most predictive efforts—even long-range ones such as those of the FAO (1970, 1980)—treat climate as a constant on an assumption of normality. Only a few attempts have been made to treat climate as a stochastic variable or to take account of climatic change in a scenario approach. One of the most recent (*The Global 2000 Report*, 1980) states that 'none of the global long-term models used . . . are capable of accepting climatological inputs. The energy, food, water, and forestry projections all assume implicitly a continuation of the nearly ideal climate of the 1950s and 1960s.' Nevertheless, although no provision was made for long-term climatic change, some weather assumptions, i.e. unchanged, more and less favorable than the last 25 years, were built into the three alternative yield assumptions for grains in this study.

Some analysts (Collis, 1975; National Research Council, 1976) attribute the apparent neglect of the effects of climate in economic analyses to the fact that a combination of exceptionally favorable

355

weather with advancing technology in the world's major grain-producing regions for the 25 years from the end of the Second World War until the beginning of the 1970s, produced a situation where weather-induced deviations from the rapidly rising trend of production were relatively insignificant in global terms. The impact of climate was therefore either ignored or discounted as unimportant. While this is probably true, I also suspect that the unsatisfactory data base and the contradictory nature of expert climatic forecasts may have engendered a feeling of uncertainty among economists as to the usefulness or technical feasibility of trying to build such data into economic models.

Whatever the underlying causes of this weakness, I am not going to try and redress the balance here. Nor am I going to attempt to review and assess all the possible economic costs of climatic variation. These are so large and pervasive as to be incalculable.

Instead I will look mainly at the implications of climatic variation for the future of world food supply, particularly in the poorer countries, and what measures might be taken to assist those countries in dealing with climatic instability. Many Third World countries are located in a relatively harsh environment, with high climatic variability compounded by economic poverty and lack of infrastructure, and it is the poor, who spend most of their meagre income on food, who suffer most from the resultant uncertainties of food supply.

The measure of the task ahead is illustrated by Fig. 1 and Tables 1 and 2. These show first that although production performance in the developing regions, with the exception of Sub-Saharan Africa, has not been inferior to that in the industrialised countries in recent years, higher rates of population growth in most Third World countries have made it difficult to improve their generally inadequate levels of nutrition in *per capita* terms. Looking ahead to 1990, Table 2 defines the magnitudes of the deficits between supply and economic demand for food that could build up if the growth rate of production cannot be accelerated. These are vast, particularly in Asia, and would be even larger, as Fig. 1 demonstrates, if the maldistribution of food between rich and poor were to be corrected, and malnutrition significantly reduced. I must stress that these are based on projections of past trends of production into the future, compared to various assumptions of demand based on population and income growth. They are not predictions of what will happen, and of course we hope that the gaps will close and not widen. But they *are* predicted on a continuation of normal, i.e. past trends of weather, and not on a worsening of climate;

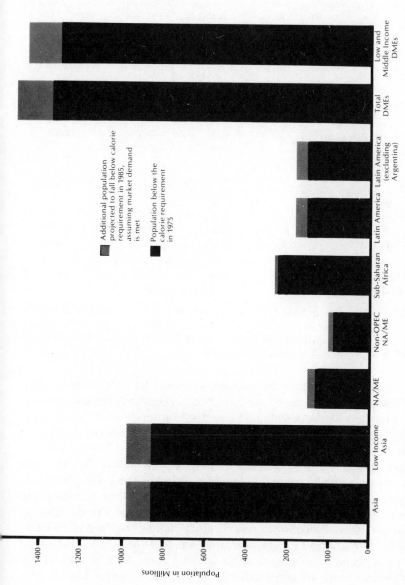

Fig. 1. Undernourished population in DME regions in 1975 and projected 1985. NA/ME = North Africa/Middle East. DMEs = Developing market economies.

TABLE 1
ESTIMATED AVERAGE ANNUAL GROWTH RATES OF POPULATION AND OF CEREAL
PRODUCTION AND DOMESTIC USE, BY REGION AND ECONOMIC GROUP, 1970–
1977[a]

Region/economic group	Population	Cereal production (%)	Cereal domestic use (%)
World total[b]	1·8	2·4	1·9
Region			
North America	0·9	3·3	−1·1
Europe	0·6	2·0	2·1
USSR	1·0	1·0	2·2
North Africa/Middle East	2·8	3·5	4·0
Sub-Saharan Africa	2·7	0·6	1·5
Latin America	2·7	3·9	4·1
Asia and Oceania	2·0	2·5	2·5
ASPAC Group	(2·2)	(1·7)	(2·4)
Others	(1·9)	(2·6)	(2·5)
Economic group[c]			
Developed	0·9	2·2	1·2
Developing	2·2	2·7	2·8

[a] The growth rates of cereal production and domestic use include all cereals
and were calculated based on the averages for 1969–1971 and 1975–1977.
[b] For 130 countries with available data on cereal production and domestic use.
[c] Following the FAO country classification.

and if that were to happen the situation could be even more serious.

Whatever complacency may have been engendered among economists or others about climate and its effects on food supply prior to the 1970s, during the 1970s that complacency was shattered when four major weather-related food crises occurred—the 1970 corn blight attack in the USA (estimated to have cost a billion dollars); bad harvests in a number of major countries including the USSR, India and China in 1972; bad harvests again in 1974, this time including the USA; and finally in 1980, when world production dropped by 50 million tonnes. Twice world reserve stocks fell below the danger level; and in 1974 a World Food Conference was convened in an atmosphere of panic when grain prices, aggravated by rising fuel, transport, and input costs, rose to unprecedented levels, as shown in Fig. 2. This demonstrated dramatically the destabilising influence which climate can have on the world economy.

TABLE 2

GROSS DEFICITS OF MAJOR STAPLES (MILLION TONNES) IN DEVELOPING MARKET ECONOMIES, BY IFPRI CATEGORY AND REGION, 1977 AND 1990[a]

IFPRI category	1977	1990		
		At 1977 per capita level	Low income growth	High income growth
Food Deficit	54·0	75·1	121·0	142·1
Low income	15·2	32·4	54·5	66·1
Middle income	21·1	18·1	31·3	36·6
High income	17·7	24·6	35·2	39·4
Grain Exporters	0·2	–	–	–
Total DMEs[b]	54·2	75·1	121·0	142·1
Region				
Asia	16·8	22·3	40·1	49·8
North Africa/ Middle East	17·4	23·8	33·0	37·0
Sub-Saharan Africa	3·6	14·9	24·6	28·7
Latin America	16·4	14·1	23·3	26·6
Total DMEs[b]	54·2	75·1	121·0	142·1

[a] Gross deficit represents the sum of the production deficits of major staples in food-short countries of the indicated groups of DMEs.
[b] Developing market economies.

A further striking example of the economic impact of climatic variation is the effect of frost in Brazil on world coffee prices. As a result of a southward shift in the focus of coffee production in Brazil in the late 1950s frost damage to coffee there has increased, and severe frosts cut output by around 50% in 1964–1965, 1970–1971, 1973–1974, and by two-thirds in 1976–1977. Because of the biennial cycle a low crop is often followed by a large one (unless, as in 1975, the frost has been exceptionally severe); and as Brazil produces almost 30% of world coffee, the effect is to make prices highly volatile (see Fig. 3).

In addition to these global effects, climatic variability led to serious, if more localised crises; including famines in the Sahelian Zone of Africa and Ethiopia in the early 1970s, in a much wider area of semi-arid Sub-Saharan Africa in the late 1970s and 1980, and in Bangladesh in 1974–1975. These demonstrated that in addition to

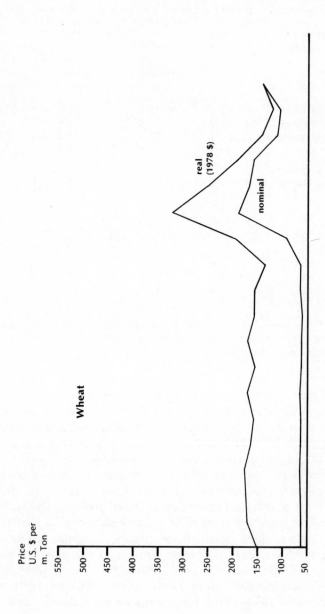

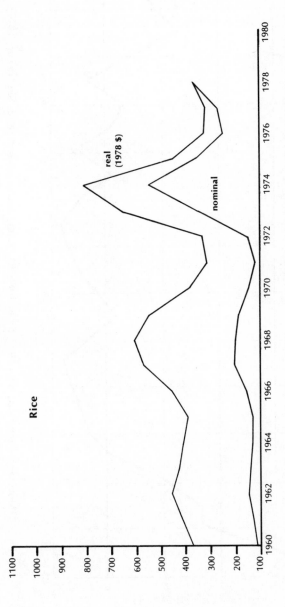

Fig. 2. World price of wheat and rice. Wheat, single average of fob prices (from Morrow, 1979). Rice, 5% broken fob Bangkok (from IBRD, 1979). For both wheat and rice, the deflator used to produce real prices was the index of US dollar unit value of manufactured exports from developed to developing countries (cif index) from IBRD (1979).

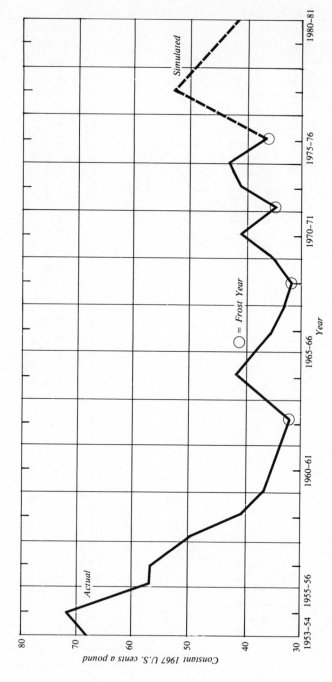

FIG. 3. Movements in coffee prices 1953–54 to 1980–81 (actual and simulated) (after Singh et al., 1977).

quantifiable economic losses, climatic events can have sweeping social and political repercussions, ranging from increasing marginality and loss of livelihood among small farmers and migratory herdsmen, to the overthrow of governments. Between 1960 and 1980 at least 15 countries of Africa suffered revolutions, coups, liberation struggles or external aggression, and 13 of those countries had almost zero or negative growth of grain yields (Table 3).

TABLE 3

GROWTH RATES OF AREA, YIELD AND PRODUCTION FOODCROP FOR 1961–1977 BY GEOGRAPHICAL REGION OF AFRICA. CHANGE IN CEREAL YIELDS FOR 1977– 1979 AS A PERCENTAGE OF 1961–1971

Country	Area	Yield	Production	Change in cereal yield
Sahel				
Chad[a]	−1·20	−0·67	−1·86	77
Gambia	2·08	−0·24	1·33	81
Mali	−1·12	1·73	0·59	81
Mauritania[a]	−4·33	−0·71	−5·02	104
Niger	2·45	−2·62	−0·24	100
Senegal	0·45	−0·37	0·08	112
Upper Volta	0·89	0·60	1·50	111
West Africa				
Benin	−1·39	2·27	0·85	136
Cameron	2·70	−0·24	2·45	99
Ghana[a]	3·15	−1·91	1·18	97
Guinea[a]	2·40	−1·00	1·37	98
Guinea Bissau[a]	−2·72	−1·01	−3·70	124
Ivory Coast	3·33	0·77	4·12	84
Liberia[a]	2·57	0·89	3·48	108
Nigeria[a]	1·26	−0·72	0·53	107
Sierra Leone	1·51	1·57	3·10	71
Togo	−2·93	2·58	−0·42	105
Central Africa				
Angola[a]	1·05	−0·13	0·92	69
Central Afr. Rep.[a]	3·01	−0·58	2·41	69
Congo	−0·07	1·38	1·31	105
Zaire[a]	2·94	−0·22	2·71	97
Eastern Africa				
Burundi	1·46	0·54	2·01	101
Ethiopia[a]	−0·17	1·40	1·22	107
Kenya	2·37	2·54	4·97	95

TABLE 3 (*continued*)

Country	Area	Yield	Production	Change in cereal yield
Rwanda	3·36	3·58	7·06	103
Somalia[a]	1·16	−0·42	0·74	76
Tanzania	2·73	−0·53	2·19	101
Uganda[a]	2·39	0·39	2·79	99
Southern Africa				
Botswana	3·79	1·64	5·49	148
Lesotho	−1·79	0·71	−1·10	194
Madagascar	1·80	0·17	1·97	101
Malawi	0·57	1·95	2·53	119
Mozambique[a]	1·55	−0·42	1·13	69
Namibia[a]	−1·50	0·92	−0·59	107
Swaziland	−1·98	9·41	7·25	151
Zambia	1·46	0·80	2·27	99
Zimbabwe[a]	0·51	2·54	3·06	111

[a] Countries which have experienced political disturbances between 1961 and 1979.

A recent study shows that although technology was found to have an insignificant influence on yield compared to meteorological variability in crop yield models developed for the drought-prone countries of Sub-Saharan Africa, 'random noise' generated by events of the type described above was a very important factor (USAID 1979). In a number of cases political instability can be attributed directly to food shortages and/or high food prices as a result of climatic instability. However, even where these were not the trigger, progress in raising food production is usually impeded, hunger aggravated, and relief efforts hampered by short-run political uncertainties, even though their longer-run effects may prove to be beneficial.

Both economic and socio-political factors, therefore, have to be taken into account in determining how best to offset the potentially damaging effects of climatic variability; conversely, since climate has a dominant influence on land use, farming systems, and production techniques, any policies designed to improve food security by increasing or stabilising production also have to be designed with climate as a major factor in the equation.

TYPES OF CLIMATIC VARIABILITY

Climatic variability is not uniform in time or space, and any measures to cope with it also have to bear these differences in mind. I shall be dealing later with geoclimatic differences, for example between the temperate zone where frost is a major cause of economic loss, and the inter-tropical zone where, except at high altitudes, low temperature is not a problem. I have distinguished four main time-scales of climatic variability and will discuss their geoclimatic significance briefly in order of their duration. They are:

1. Long-term climatic change
2. Cyclical patterns of change covering several years within a basically unchanged regional climate
3. Year-to-year and within-year variability
4. Sudden disasters

Major shifts in climate during the late Quaternary period are well documented, and Grove (1977) has shown that during the last 20 000 years and up until 5000 years ago large parts of Africa were both drier and significantly wetter than they are today. The effect of these major changes is retrospective; it lies in their influence on soils and land forms, and what these imply for fertility and agricultural management in the different climatic and socio-economic regime of the twentieth century.

The issue of major climatic change within recorded history is more controversial. Despite evidence of famine and pestilence from warm, humid weather and consequent consumption of blighted grain (aflatoxins) in the Middle Ages, the rigours of the Little Ice Age between 1550 and 1700, and the warming and cooling trends of the present century, indications of a lasting climatic impact on the agricultural environment comparable to that in the Pleistocene seem to be lacking. Despite plagues, famines, fat and lean years as reported in the Bible, the basic Mediterranean scenario depicted there is much the same as today; changes are mainly the result of human interference. Indeed, the intervention of man on a scale unprecedented in the past, has superimposed a new element of uncertainty on to the natural warming and cooling processes which have mainly determined the nature and variability of global climate until the present century. Monitoring and predictive analysis of the possible direction of human influence on climate is a field in which economists should play a role in collaboration with other scientists.

Historical evidence seems to bear out the hypothesis that the human race can adapt without too much pain to a *gradual* climatic transition (Anon, 1976). Unfortunately the corollary argument that contingency plans can therefore be worked out to cope with such a transition in an orderly manner rather than on the basis of expediency, is *not* supported by recent experience, which suggests that our ability to identify long-term changes far enough ahead to do anything effective about them remains very weak. Each new short-term crisis gives rise to predictions of fundamental climatic change, but agreement as to their direction is lacking (NOAA/NDF, 1978). Perhaps this is why economists prefer to assume 'normal' weather, even though climatologists warn them that it doesn't exist (McQuigg, 1975a).

This does not mean that nothing should be done. Continuing attempts must be made to strengthen our understanding of the factors which influence climate in the long- and short-term, and to improve predictive capability and global information systems. The incorporation of probabilistic climatic scenarios into indicative planning studies at the global and regional level would give planners a better sense of likely contingencies. An assumption that the best year of the 1980s will be no better than the average of the 1970s and that absolute year-to-year fluctuations in production may be greater, might not be an unrealistic basis for calculating food security needs. A start might be made on contingency biological research to improve the tolerance of crops to the types of climatic stress foreseen as most likely by predictive climatic studies. This task might be undertaken as part of the more speculative research planned in the long-term programmes of the International Agricultural Research Centres.

Of an intermediate order in the time-scale are the cyclical patterns, which tend to be shorter and more narrowly confined geographically— for example, the recurring runs of wet and dry years in the Sahelian Zone of Africa. While these events are linked to global weather patterns such as the movement of the inter-tropical convergence zone, they do not necessarily have the same economic impact around the world; poor weather in the Sahel may mean more favorable conditions for crops in the wetter areas of West Africa.

Because the adverse effects tend to be cumulative in the affected countries, they may persist long after the climatic anomaly which caused them has ended. Their long-term economic impact may be mainly through degradation of the physical environment (overgrazing, erosion, desertification, depletion of the water table), but it may also be reflected in sweeping social change. Large-scale migration to the cities followed the decimation of animal populations and human famine in the Sahel; in Ireland over a million people died of hunger and disease, and a similar number emigrated in the years of the potato famine, which halved the population. Nevertheless, to the extent that an approximate pattern and duration of the cycles can be established from meteorological records, it may be possible to plan precautionary measures on a more rational basis than for long-term climatic change.

However, the main problem most farmers have to cope with in their daily lives is between- and within-season variability around a normal trend. The dominant crops and livestock, and how these fit into farming systems, are determined by the climatic norms; crop yields in any given season, farmers' decisions as to how much land to plant, how much fertiliser to apply, what equipment to invest in, are determined more by their assessment of risk due to departures from the norms. The degree of variability differs widely among geoclimatic regions, but it is of key economic importance both nationally and internationally; affecting domestic self-sufficiency, export availabilities, trade, price, and reserve stock policy. According to Konandreas et al. (1978), over half of the 65 developing countries which they surveyed have more than a 30% chance of expecting a production shortfall greater than 5% in any given year. A main objective of agricultural policy is therefore to smooth out the more extreme shortfalls or surpluses arising from deviations from the trend.

The last and most short-lived type of climatic anomaly (but not necessarily the least damaging) is a violent natural disaster, e.g. catastrophic floods, tidal waves, typhoons, hurricanes, tornadoes, hailstorms, etc. Even though these tend to be more frequent in some geographical areas and at certain seasons of the year than others, they vary greatly in frequency and intensity in any one year, their occurrence is random, and their sheer violence often makes them difficult to counter. It is often unclear what (if any) level of expenditure would be effective in coping with such haphazard occurrences; or whether it is better to rely on good luck, improved weather predictions, and perhaps attempts at weather modification, insurance policies, and evasive action (such as evacuation of threatened areas), rather than trying to meet unknown levels of natural challenge head-on by expensive (and perhaps ultimately ineffective) physical action. The internal rates of return on massive flood control structures, for example, are pretty low.

Evidence suggests that the largest, most costly (both economically and socially), and the most tragic effects of climatic variation are the cyclical and season-to-season departures from expected patterns. These are also the ones which are most susceptible to statistical analysis, to actuarial–type insurance precautions, and to contingency planning; and even though cyclical and seasonal deviations occur on a different time-scale, the measures that can be taken to counter them are often broadly similar. I will therefore focus in the rest of my paper mainly on the sources of vulnerability of world food supplies to such climatic anomalies and on the types of counter-measures which are needed to mitigate them.

SOURCES OF VULNERABILITY OF WORLD FOOD SUPPLY

The narrow geographical concentration of grain exporters

In 1938 all geographical regions other than western Europe were net grain exporters; by 1977 all but North America, Australia, and marginally Latin America were net *importers*. Table 4 shows that in that year North America, with under 6% of the world population, produced 23% of world cereal output and 76% of the total exportable surplus of about 150 million tonnes. Since grain is the basis for intensive livestock production this dominance extends to meat, milk, and egg production. Political considerations aside, the effects of any major weather-induced shortfall in North America would be felt more severely in Moscow, USSR than Moscow, Idaho.

If this situation is uncomfortable for the more affluent countries, it is even more so for the poor ones, whose bargaining power is weak in a crisis. This is particularly true for the rice-dependent economies, since the world rice trade (with a carry-over of only a few million tonnes) is much more narrowly based than that for wheat or feedgrains. This is one reason that many tropical countries which cannot grow wheat are becoming increasingly dependent on it (Table 5).

Although it is unlikely that all major grain producers would have a simultaneous failure, and although the United States has a wide,

TABLE 4

ESTIMATES OF ANNUAL CEREAL SURPLUS AND DEFICIT BY REGION AND ECONOMIC GROUP 1969–1971 AND 1975–1977 AVERAGES (IN MILLION TONNES)[a]

Region/economic group	1969–1971 Average			1975–1977 Average		
	Gross surplus	Gross deficit	Net surplus/deficit[b]	Gross surplus	Gross deficit	Net surplus/deficit[b]
World total[c]	77·3	81·8	−4·5	153·1	123·3	29·8
Region						
North America	52·0	–	52·0	116·5	–	116·5
Europe	1·1	28·3	−27·2	5·3	38·1	−32·8
USSR	–	4·4	−4·4	–	18·1	−18·1
North Africa/Middle East	–	9·3	−9·3	–	13·3	−13·3
Sub-Saharan Africa	3·1	2·0	1·1	2·3	3·3	−1·0
Latin America	8·3	7·3	1·0	12·5	12·2	0·3
Asia and Oceania	12·8	30·5	−17·7	16·5	38·3	−21·8
ASPAC group	(11·9)	(21·7)	(−9·8)	(15·2)	(29·9)	(−14·7)
Others	(0·9)	(8·8)	(−7·9)	(1·3)	(8·4)	(−7·1)
Economic group[d]						
Developed	64·8	49·1	15·7	135·5	77·3	58·2
Developing	12·5	32·7	−20·2	17·6	46·0	−28·4

[a] Including all cereals; aggregated from country-level estimates of production and domestic use.
[b] Gross surplus minus gross deficit.
[c] For 130 countries with available data on cereal production and domestic use.
[d] Following the FAO classification.

TABLE 5

PERCENTAGE SHARE OF DIFFERENT FOOD ITEMS IN CALORIE INTAKE OF DEVELOPING COUNTRIES BY REGIONAL GROUP, 1965, 1976 (SOURCE: FAO)

Regional group/year	Wheat	Rice	Maize	Millet and sorghum	Total cereals	Roots and tubers	Pulses	Groundnuts	Sugar	Fruit and vegetables	Meat and milk	Fish
I. China[a]												
1965[b]	13·1	34·1	10·2	7·1	67·6	11·0	3·2	0·3	1·7	1·9	6·8	0·7
1976[b]	14·9	34·5	7·6	5·3	65·5	8·8	4·4	0·5	1·7	2·1	7·9	0·5
Relative change	+13·7	1·2	−25·5	−25·4	−3·1	−20·0	+37·5	+66·7	0·0	+10·5	+16·2	−28·6
II. South/South-east Asia												
1965	7·9	51·0	9·2	2·0	73·0	4·8	2·1	0·4	4·4	3·0	4·1	1·3
1976	7·0	52·6	5·5	0·8	73·1	3·7	1·3	0·4	4·4	3·1	3·4	1·8
Relative change	−11·4	3·1	−40·2	−60·0	10·1	−22·9	−38·1	0·0	0·0	+3·3	−17·1	+38·5
III. India[a]												
1965	13·9	31·5	3·7	14·2	64·4	1·5	8·5	0·3	10·3	3·2	4·3	0·2
1976	16·9	31·3	3·7	12·0	65·3	2·2	7·5	0·2	9·4	3·2	3·3	0·3
Relative change	+21·6	−0·6	0·0	−15·5	+1·4	+46·7	−11·8	−33·3	−8·7	0·0	−23·2	+50·0
IV. Temperate North Africa/ Middle East												
1965	42·3	8·5	2·7	0·9	62·1	2·2	2·6	0·2	8·9	6·0	7·7	0·3
1976	46·2	4·9	3·4	0·6	57·8	1·4	2·5	0·4	9·9	5·5	9·6	0·3
Relative change	+9·2	−42·4	+25·9	−33·3	−6·9	−36·4	−3·8	+100·0	+11·2	−8·3	+24·7	0·0
V. Africa/Middle East/ semi-arid tropics												
1965	6·2	10·0	7·5	37·6	64·0	5·9	3·8	2·1	5·8	2·2	9·0	0·7
1976	7·8	10·3	7·1	31·5	59·9	4·7	4·1	2·3	5·1	3·7	9·5	1·0
Relative change	+25·8	+3·0	−5·3	−16·2	−6·4	−20·3	+7·9	+9·5	−12·1	+68·2	+5·6	+42·9

VI. Equatorial Africa												
1965	2·6	15·1	11·5	7·0	37·0	39·8	5·0	2·7	2·4	2·0	3·5	1·2
1976	3·4	13·9	10·2	5·6	33·3	30·5	4·3	3·4	2·5	9·3	3·4	1·2
Relative change	+30·8	−7·9	−11·3	−20·0	−10·0	−23·4	−14·0	+25·9	+4·2	+65·0	−2·9	0·0
VII. East and southern Africa												
1965	5·8	1·5	42·2	8·3	57·9	15·3	4·6	1·4	6·9	1·6	7·6	0·8
1976	6·9	1·6	39·6	6·0	54·5	14·3	3·9	1·5	7·9	3·3	6·4	0·6
Relative change	+19·0	+6·7	−6·2	−27·7	−5·9	−6·5	−15·2	+7·1	+14·5	+106·3	−15·8	−25·0
VIII. Central America/Caribbean[c]												
1965	6·3	3·3	33·8	4·8	54·6	5·3	7·0	0·2	13·9	3·4	7·1	0·2
1976	7·6	4·1	34·7	4·3	51·5	1·7	5·5	0·1	15·5	5·9	8·1	0·2
Relative change	+20·6	+24·2	+2·7	−10·4	−5·7	−67·9	−21·4	−50·0	11·5	+73·5	+14·1	0·0
IX. Central America/Caribbean[d]												
1965	26·8	35·9	10·7	e	73·5	14·7	7·0	0·4	27·4	6·6	18·4	2·1
1976	13·8	22·8	3·8	—	41·0	3·7	3·2	0·2	18·4	7·2	11·6	0·8
Relative change	−48·5	−36·5	−64·5	—	−44·2	−74·8	−54·3	−50·0	−32·8	+9·1	−37·0	−61·9
X. Tropical South America												
1965	12·0	8·2	14·4	f	36·0	17·3	4·4	0·7	14·4	4·2	14·0	0·7
1976	11·9	9·6	12·5	—	35·0	10·7	3·9	0·6	16·4	8·4	12·9	0·6
Relative change	−0·8	17·1	−13·2	—	−2·8	−38·2	−11·4	−14·3	+13·9	+100·0	−7·9	−14·3
XI. Temperate South America												
1965	35·7	2·4	0·2	—	38·5	5·3	1·2	d	13·1	3·6	27·2	0·5
1976	32·3	2·3	2·0	—	37·2	3·9	1·0	d	12·6	3·8	25·1	0·3
Relative change	−9·5	−4·2	+900·0	—	−3·4	−26·4	−16·7	d	−3·8	+5·8	−7·7	−40·0
XII. All regions												
1965	14·7	16·2	13·0	9·5	56·7	13·2	4·0	1·2	8·0	3·4	8·4	0·8
1976	15·7	15·8	11·1	7·1	52·1	9·3	3·3	1·3	8·3	5·5	8·2	0·8
Relative change	+6·8	−2·5	−14·6	−25·3	−8·1	−29·5	−17·5	+8·3	+3·8	+61·8	−2·4	0·0

[a] China and India, because of their size, population and range of crops are regarded as separate regions.
[b] 1965 and 1976 reflect averages for 1964–1966 and 1975–1977, respectively.
[c] Maize diets. [d] Mixed cereal diets.
[e] —, Negligible or not applicable. [f] Indicates less than 0·05%.

TABLE 6
DEVELOPED COUNTRY GRAIN EXPORTERS: GROWTH RATES OF PRODUCTION, AREA AND YIELD OF CEREALS 1961–1978, AND PREDICTED 1990 VALUES

Country	Production				Area harvested				Yield			
	Growth rate 1961–1978	Growth rate 1970–1978	Predicted values[a] 1978	1990	Growth rate 1961–1978	Growth rate 1970–1978	Predicted values[a] 1978	1990	Growth rate 1961–1978	Growth rate 1970–1978	Predicted values[a] 1978	1990
Wheat												
Australia	0.027	0.083	14 327 091	37 138 397	0.021	0.053	10 304 911	19 163 212	0.005	0.027	1.39	1.92
Canada	0.018	0.094	22 921 433	67 425 918	−0.011	0.073	11 743 562	27 392 266	0.029	0.019	1.95	2.45
US	0.036	0.046	57 717 782	99 039 313	0.019	0.053	28 438 000	53 009 751	0.016	−0.007	2.03	1.87
Rice												
Australia	0.092	0.100	524 630	1 646 332	0.101	0.132	97 961	434 769	−0.008	−0.029	5.35	3.78
Canada	–	–	–	–	–	–	–	–	–	–	–	–
US	0.039	0.058	5 841 755	11 433 144	0.028	0.062	1 167 180	2 402 423	0.012	−0.004	5.01	4.76
Barley												
Australia	0.089	0.045	3 165 095	5 384 376	0.083	0.039	2 663 831	4 213 688	0.006	0.005	1.19	1.27
Canada	0.083	0.002	10 488 751	10 692 589	0.054	−0.010	4 464 377	3 916 094	0.028	0.012	2.35	2.72
US	−0.0003	−0.006	8 515 692	7 926 098	−0.016	−0.014	3 526 291	2 971 664	0.016	0.008	2.41	2.67
Maize												
Australia	−0.017	−0.060	118 009	55 839	−0.037	−0.077	42 505	16 102	0.020	0.018	2.78	3.46
Canada	0.102	0.069	4 169 338	9 287 127	0.092	0.056	761 069	1 456 686	0.009	0.013	5.48	6.39
US	0.038	0.047	172 540 518	301 034 616	0.014	0.027	29 250 053	40 343 694	0.023	0.019	5.90	7.46
Sorghum												
Australia	0.128	−0.002	943 879	915 743	0.111	−0.008	497 972	448 950	0.016	−0.006	1.90	2.05
Canada	–	–	–	–	–	–	–	–	–	–	–	–
US	0.024	−0.005	18 971 694	17 787 714	0.013	−0.003	5 759 007	5 522 944	0.011	−0.002	3.29	3.22

[a] Based on a semi-log trend.

diverse and mainly favorable grain-producing environment, there is no cause for complacency. A recent Kettering Foundation (1976) study shows that, assuming constant 1975 area and technology, a recurrence of weather similar to that in 1933–1936 could reduce North American grain and soya production by 71 million tonnes. Some evidence has been put forward that relative variability of yield there is increasing. In any case, as production increases overall its absolute variation (the standard deviation) tends to rise, making stock and price management policy more tricky. Finally, as Table 6 shows, the growth of production in the 1970s has been maintained more by bringing additional land under the plough than by improvements in yield-increasing technology. By and large this also seems to be true of Australia, Canada, and the USSR, raising doubts as to how long such a land-extensive pattern of growth can be maintained. Expanding the number and geographical spread of grain surplus countries therefore seems highly desirable.

The heavy dependence on agriculture as a base for economic growth in the Third World

Although dependence of the economy on agriculture is decreasing in the Third World, especially in the Near East and South America, the agricultural sector is still the main source of income and employment, as well as of food and foreign exchange earnings in many countries. While there is strong empirical evidence (Mellor, 1976; Mundlak, 1979; etc.) that a buoyant agriculture is essential to underpin broad-based economic growth, the greater vulnerability of agriculture to weather variability compared to industry or minerals, makes economic management more difficult in most developing countries than in industrialised economies. This is particularly true where foreign exchange earnings also depend heavily on agricultural commodities, because of the nature of the growth process as it affects demand for food.

In a largely subsistence society climate is the predominant influence determining the nature of the diet (Fig. 4), and one reason for slow growth of food production in some tropical countries is that their diet is still based largely on crops for which little research has been undertaken. As urbanisation increases, a market economy develops, and incomes rise, the nature of demand for food changes: food grains, which form 60–70% of the diet of low-income people become less predominant, and fruit, vegetables and livestock products increase.

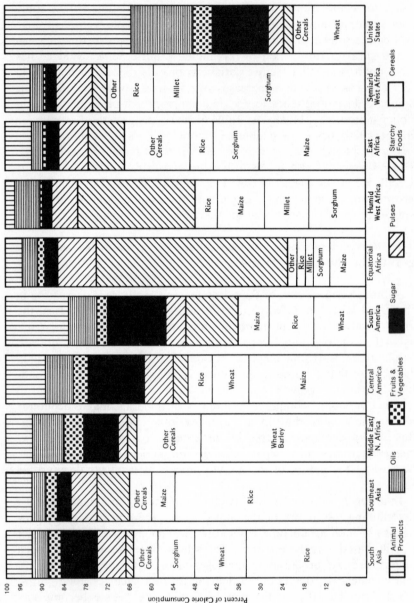

FIG. 4. Major commodities as a percentage of total calorie consumption.

While diversification of the diet may reduce vulnerability to climatic variation in terms of traditional locally produced foods, it often increases dependence on foreign sources of supply; and, to the extent that foreign exchange earnings depend on agricultural exports, it merely shifts the vulnerability to climate to those commodities.

In fact, the combination of high population growth in low-income Third World countries, and high population and fast economic growth in

TABLE 7

RATIO OF FOOD IMPORTS TO TOTAL EXPORT REVENUE (1965–1976) (AFTER VALDES AND KONANDREAS, 1981)

	Mean (%)	Maximum (%)
Asia		
Bangladesh[a]	88·4	119·4
India[b]	22·4	44·5
Indonesia	9·5	19·9
Korea, Rep. of	13·5	21·4
Philippines	4·9	9·1
Sri Lanka	27·2	49·2
North Africa/Middle East		
Algeria[c]	6·0	9·3
Egypt[d]	14·0	27·0
Jordan[d]	10·6	15·4
Libya[d]	1·4	2·3
Morocco	7·0	13·4
Syria[d]	5·7	18·4
Sub-Saharan Africa		
Ghana[d]	3·7	5·4
Nigeria[d]	1·9	2·5
Senegal[b]	12·2	17·8
Tanzania[d]	5·5	22·2
Upper Volta[e]	7·4	13·0
Zaire[b]	3·1	6·9
Latin America		
Brazil	3·9	8·5
Chile	5·3	13·9
Colombia	2·8	4·9
Guatemala	2·4	3·3
Mexico	0·4	9·3
Peru	6·6	10·5

Time period of analysis [a] 1973–1976; [b] 1965–1975; [c] 1966–1976; [d] 1967–1976; [e] 1968–1976.

many middle to high-income developing countries, with relatively low production growth, is widening the food gap and forcing them to spend a significant proportion of their foreign currency earnings on food imports (Table 7). Work at IFPRI (Bachman and Paulino, 1979) shows that even sustained high levels of growth of food production do not necessarily increase domestic self-sufficiency in food because of these income–growth effects. Climate affects the economic position here in two ways, first, unpredictable shortfalls in food production, due to climatic variability, hamper an orderly fiscal policy and may siphon off foreign exchange needed for development objectives, including agricultural inputs and investments such as irrigation designed to reduce climatic instability and increase yields.

Second, climate dictates what export crops can be grown and their quality (some have much more favorable trade prospects than others); and thus the nature and magnitude of foreign exchange earnings from agriculture. Certain countries (usually in the humid tropics such as Malaysia), are favorably placed for export crop production, but not so well placed for food self-sufficiency. Those with a broader ecological spectrum (e.g. Brazil) may be able to develop a substantial base of export production without competing significantly with their ability to produce food. Others, particularly in the more marginal areas, have limited scope for either; thus land used to produce jute in Bangladesh or cotton and groundnuts for export from Sahelian Africa is likely to be at the expense of its use for food. Since countries with marginal climates also tend to have the greatest relative variability of production, their dilemma is severe, and unless they have other sources of export revenue such as minerals, oil, or tourism, they are among the poorest and most vulnerable of all.

High climatic risk and variability in the tropics and subtropics

Climatic variability shows marked differences both within and between countries, in general being three to four times as high in semi-arid areas of the subtropics and tropics as in temperate Europe or the United States.

Variability is strikingly high (20–40%) in many countries of North Africa and the Near East, most of which lie in the Mediterranean climatic zone; high in the drier countries of the semi-arid tropics of Africa (usually over 15%); fairly high in the countries of Central

TABLE 8

VARIABILITY IN STAPLE FOOD PRODUCTION, 1961–1976

	Staple food production instability		Probability of actual production falling below 95% of trend (%)	Correlation coefficient between total staple food production and consumption	Correlation coefficient between cereal production and total staple food production
	Standard deviations[a] (thousand tonnes)	Coefficient of variation[b] (%)			
Asia					
Bangladesh	765	6·4	22	0·90	0·99
India	6 653	6·4	22	0·89	0·99
Indonesia	1 040	5·4	18	0·92	0·94
Korea, Rep. of	445	7·1	24	0·20	0·96
Philippines	346	5·7	19	0·03	0·99
Sri Lanka	107	9·3	29	0·56	0·91
North Africa/Middle East					
Algeria	531	28·9	43	0·78	1·00
Egypt	282	4·5	13	0·29	0·96
Jordan	119	65·6	47	0·63	1·00
Libya	56	28·0	43	0·62	1·00
Morocco	1 156	27·2	43	0·98	0·96
Syria	702	38·8	45	0·92	1·00
Sub-Saharan Africa					
Ghana	121	5·8	20	0·98	0·93
Nigeria	958	5·7	19	0·99	0·92
Senegal	325	18·6	39	0·99	0·81
Tanzania	430	12·7	35	0·98	0·09
Upper Volta	128	9·8	30	0·95	0·99
Zaire	190	4·9	15	0·96	−0·21
Latin America					
Brazil	1 631	5·2	17	0·92	0·60
Chile	215	11·1	33	0·54	0·99
Colombia	126	4·4	13	0·51	0·85
Guatemala	56	6·5	22	0·51	0·99
Mexico	1 060	7·7	26	0·53	1·00
Peru	197	9·8	30	0·37	0·97

[a] Defined as the standard deviation of the variable $Q_t - \hat{Q}_t$.

[b] Defined as the standard deviation of the variable $\dfrac{Q_t - \hat{Q}_t}{\hat{Q}_t} \times 100$.

America and the Caribbean (10–30%); and relatively low in Southeast Asia, the humid tropics of Africa, and South America (Table 8). Inter-regional comparisons are revealing. Although the winter rainfall regime of the semi-arid countries with a Mediterranean climate is often held to be more efficient for crop growth than the summer rainfall pattern of the semi-arid tropics, the relative variability of the Mediterranean is actually considerably higher. It is also noteworthy that the colder climate of the steppe regions of West Asia in Turkey, Iran, and Afghanistan appears to be more favorable, or at least less unreliable, for crop production than that of the milder countries around the Mediterranean littoral in the same geographical region. Variability of yield in the countries with a large area of steppe is markedly and consistently lower, and their climate appears more comparable with the plains of the Pacific north-west of the United States than with the Mediterranean. In this respect there has been an important increase in winter wheat yields in plateau areas of Turkey consequent on adaptation of North American technology to conditions there, and the introduction of winter-hardy wheat varieties from the USSR.

Crops grown in more humid regions of the tropics (rice, cassava, and yams) tend to have low coefficients of variability compared to the food staples of the drier tropics and subtropics (millet, sorghum, and pulses). Maize, which is grown over an enormous ecological range, fluctuates greatly, but generally its variability is lower in more humid countries or where it is largely grown under irrigation.

The widely held tenet that irrigation helps to stabilise yields has recently been challenged by Barker et al. (1981), who argue that absolute variance must increase as yields increase due to the combination of irrigation with modern seed/fertilizer technology; and that relative variability may also be increased by greater crop losses due to pests and diseases under more intensive agriculture, or because irrigation by itself does not automatically ensure good water control. The latter may be the key, since Tsujii (1976) states that where irrigation is combined with drainage and flood regulation it is effective in reducing the yield variability of paddy rice in monsoon Asia. Another analysis, based on Indian data, concludes 'new technology has the effect of increasing the absolute variance, and in many cases even the relative variance, in yield. However, assured irrigation can neutralise, or even more than neutralise, the variance increasing effect of new technology (S. Mehra, private communication).

The data cited for irrigation by Barker et al. are mainly derived from

South-east Asia, where paddy is the dominant food crop and coefficients of variability are generally low; probably due partly to irrigation and partly to the generally humid conditions under which paddy rice is grown there. The latter would tend to reduce variability compared to that found in drier climatic regions even without irrigation, and thus to mask the irrigation effect.

In drier climatic regions, which generally tend to have a highly erratic rainfall pattern both in quantity and distribution, the stabilising effect of irrigation on yield could be expected to be more clearcut, and this in fact seems to be the case. Countries with a high proportion of their cultivated area in arid or semi-arid regions, but with a significant portion of that land under irrigation (Afghanistan, Egypt, India, Iran, Mexico and Pakistan), tend to have relatively low coefficients of variability (even though the absolute variability of some of them may be large because of the sheer size of their production). In a number of these countries relative variability seems to have decreased in recent years compared to the 1960s, at least for rice and to some extent for wheat, both of which are frequently irrigated (Table 9).

The issue of whether the wider use of seed/fertiliser technology (with or without irrigation) improves or reduces yield stability is very crucial, since at the moment modern technology has an insignificant influence in many developing countries (especially in Africa); and considerable hopes have been built on the expectation that its wider use would help to combat climatic variability. This is partly based on the United States' experience, but also on claims that high-yielding cereal varieties generally perform better than traditional ones, even under conditions of low fertility and rainfall. The fact that the absolute magnitudes of deviations from the trend increase as production expands with the adoption of yield-increasing technology is to be expected. This may not be too worrying, although it implies more tricky stock and price management, provided the relative variability does not also increase; especially if (as Barker *et al.* suggest), technology shifts the skewness of yield distribution from being positive to negative, perhaps creating a more favorable risk environment. Clearly there is room for more research on this issue.

The economic importance of reducing the variability of production goes beyond its measurable impact on yield, or on the improvement of self-sufficiency. Greater stability of production implies reduced risk; and risk and uncertainty are widely recognised to be major disincentives to agricultural innovation, particularly by small farmers.

Although higher population pressure is a key driving force in Asia,

TABLE 9

COEFFICIENTS OF VARIABILITY: MAJOR STAPLE FOOD CROPS OF ASIA AND NORTH AFRICA, 1961–1969 AND 1970–1977 (IFPRI/FAO DATA)

	Percentage arable irrigated	Wheat		Rice		Maize	
		1961–1969	1970–1977	1961–1969	1970–1977	1961–1969	1970–1977
S.E. Asia							
Pakistan	80	9·75	3·21	10·02	3·80	8·34	3·40
China	60	7·28	5·56	1·93	1·22	4·32	7·16
Korea	37	8·95	7·73	7·93	5·18	12·18	14·38
India	20	10·78	5·64	8·64	6·81	4·78	12·09
Bangladesh	16	7·85	18·44	4·31	4·19	5·74	9·76
Burma	10	13·43	14·85	4·44	2·89	18·46	28·23
West Asia							
Afghanistan	28	9·77	12·90	5·95	2·02	4·62	2·91
Iran	37	7·62	6·72	10·17	4·64	8·49	30·54
Turkey	8	8·15	11·63	10·38	3·71	5·59	3·60
Near East/North Africa							
Sudan	20	11·61	16·89	29·63	7·83	20·92	14·40
Yemen AR	15	4·78	14·76	—	—	1·96	25·65
Syria	10	16·04	38·50	9·58	N.A.	8·78	11·34
Algeria	5	24·33	17·10	12·11	10·57	18·68	20·17
Jordan	5	33·60	38·18	—	—	14·50	33·01
Morocco	6	28·65	15·44	11·54	22·26	32·32	30·76
Tunisia	4	18·16	20·11	—	—	—	—

TABLE 10
POPULATION DENSITY, AGRICULTURAL INPUTS, AND GROWTH RATES IN AREAS IN SELECTED ASIAN, AFRICAN AND LATIN AMERICAN COUNTRIES[a]

Region[b]	1975 Economically active agricultural population per square kilometre of arable land	1976 Arable and pasture (hectares per animal unit)	1975 Irrigated area as percentage of arable land	1975 Fertiliser kilograms per hectare arable land (units NPK)	1975 Tractors per 1 000 hectares arable land	1975 Cropping intensity (%)
Asia	104	0·9	24·8	22·5	2·6	96
North Africa/Middle East	47	3·1	17·7	28·7	6·3	61
West Africa	37	6·5	0·4	1·4	0·2	54
East Africa	97	3·6	2·0	3·6	0·6	66
South America	24	2·6	8·2	32·9	7·3	68
50 Country average	69	2·2	15·8	22·3	3·5	77

a Source IFPRI Research Report No. 10, 1979.
b FAO and other reports; regional average for 10 countries of each region.

the fact that so high a proportion of its cropped area—30%—is now irrigated and that irrigation reduces risk, is undoubtedly a major reason for the much higher crop intensities, fertiliser use, and area under high-yielding varieties in Asia compared to Sub-Saharan Africa (Table 10).

In addition to increasing risk, high climatic variability blunts the impact of price incentives and subsidies. The higher yields of rice in East Asia compared to South-east Asia in the mid-1960s, are often attributed to more favorable rice/fertiliser price ratios in Japan, the Republic of Korea, and Taiwan. This is an over-simplification. Their favorable price ratios were certainly an incentive to the adoption of modern technology but they are also subtropical or temperate countries where irrigated rice yields tend to be higher and more stable than in the tropics (probably due to lower pest/disease incidence and lower cloudiness). Also, they grow mainly *Japonica* rice varieties which are highly fertiliser-responsive, but can only be grown with good water control. Until the last few years these conditions did not apply in South-east Asia, where the irrigated area was much lower. On large areas deeply flooded each year, short-strawed *Indica* varieties could not be grown (indeed did not exist), fertiliser responses were poor, and the potential for area expansion was limited. Under these circumstances, and until these fundamental constraints on increasing productivity were alleviated by flood control, irrigation and plant breeding, price was an ineffective instrument of change.

Weak infrastructural linkages

Many developing countries lack adequate infrastructure: this increases their vulnerability to climatic variation by hampering distribution and marketing of food (whether locally produced or imported), increasing waste and losses, raising input costs, and frustrating national price support and incentive policies. CIMMYT studies (see reference list) have shown how difficult topography and poor communications frustrate the adoption of improved technology; and Glantz (1977) has pointed out that even if there had been perfect warning of the Sahelian drought six months in advance, large losses of livestock could not have been prevented because of the inadequacies of the transportation and marketing system in West Africa. Table 11 illustrates this very clearly.

The ruminant livestock sector appears particularly vulnerable, since in North Africa, the Near East, and the Sahel (all high climatic risk

TABLE 11
ROAD AND RAIL NETWORKS IN SUB-SAHARAN AFRICA 1977 (SOURCE: USAID)

	Number of countries	Total road network (km)	Paved roads (km)	Percentage of total network paved	Railroad network (km)	Number of countries with		Total road per capita (km)	Hectares cropped per km road	Hectares cropped per km paved road
						no railway	no port			
Sahelian Africa	8	87 416	8 497	9·7	3 498	4	4	0·003	180	1 956
Humid West Africa	10	249 936	44 096	17·9	8 697	1	0	0·002	182	1 006
Central Africa	1 (Zaire)	168 979	2 654	1·6	4 859	–	–	0·006	37	2 345
Eastern Africa	8	143 464	16 265	11·3	13 295	3	3	0·001	263	2 348
Southern Africa	9	231 675	29 102	12·5	13 806	1	6	0·006	79	632

areas) many of the animals are kept by migratory herdsmen who do not own land, there is little stratification between range and settled farming systems, and no organised marketing. Squeezed between the desert and the sown areas, with little reserve or alternative occupation, it is not surprising that the United Nations desertification conference rated these people as at the highest climatic risk.

MEASURES TO REDUCE THE ECONOMIC COSTS OF CLIMATIC VARIATION

In the light of these problems, five approaches might form the base of a strategy for reducing the hazards imposed on agriculture by climate. These are:

1. Undertaking a systematic classification of areas of maximum vulnerability both on a national and regional basis, as a means of identifying action needed to forestall major crises
2. Accelerating agricultural production and improving its stability
3. Building an international food security system
4. The improvement of climatic analysis, weather forecasting, early warning procedures, and research in related fields
5. Developing more effective national food distribution systems

In conclusion, I would like to deal briefly with each.

Establishing areas of maximum vulnerability

This would require the establishment of a set of criteria or variables which might be incorporated into a linear programme or other model; or which might possibly form the basis of a simpler means of classification. Climatic variability (relative and absolute); self-sufficiency levels; foreign exchange availability and its origin; population and income growth; population density; dietary patterns; infrastructure; irrigation; and the availability of potential arable land, ought to be among the criteria. A trial run using such criteria based on a scoring system, shows that some regions with a highly variable climate, e.g. the Mediterranean climatic zone, are not necessarily at the highest social risk because of a strong economic base; and that there are also important differences in the aggregate degree of vulnerability (taking account both of climatic and socio-economic criteria), between countries within relatively homogeneous climatic zones. Sheer size of population is very important: India and China have lower coefficients of variability than many countries, but very large absolute deviations of production from trend. Without going into more detail, I would rate South Asia, the semi-arid tropics of West and East Africa, China, and the smaller, non-industrial Central American and non-oil Near Eastern countries as highly vulnerable.

Accelerating food production and increasing its stability

This is crucial if the widening foodgap shown in Table 1, which would result in an unmanageable crisis for the low-income countries, is to be averted.

Despite the controversy over the effects of irrigation to which I referred earlier, I still believe that the provision of good water control is probably the single most important means of achieving faster and more diversified agricultural growth, while at the same time reducing risk and the relative instability of yield. In addition, a number of recent studies have shown that irrigation increases employment opportunities, both within farming systems and in related off-farm activities, thus providing purchasing power for additional food. There are, however, great differences in the energy and other economics of ground and surface water use, as well as in the efficiency of systems, which merit careful watching. Energy for irrigation, and competition for water between agriculture and other uses, which are already serious problems in the USA, will become more critical constraints in developing countries as their economies evolve.

A further problem is that both the existing location of irrigated land and the irrigation potential are very maldistributed. As Table 12 shows, 65% of the present 198 million ha of world irrigated area lies in China, West, South and South-east Asia; only 4% in Africa; and 6% in Latin America.

While irrigation is clearly crucial in Asia, where the man–land ratio is extremely tight, it cannot be expected to provide a major input either to increasing food production or stabilising yield in most countries of Africa in the foreseeable future. Very few Sub-Saharan African countries have more than 1% of their arable area irrigated today, and given the long gestation of surface irrigation, its high cost and the lack of experience both of administrators and farmers in the planning,

TABLE 12

REGIONAL DISTRIBUTION AND IMPORTANCE OF IRRIGATION (MILLION HECTARES) FOR 1977 (SOURCE: FAO PRODUCTION YEARBOOK 1978)

Asia	Area	Africa	Area	America	Area	Europe	Area	Oceania	Area	World
South-east and East	14·6	West	0·4ᵃ	South	6·5ᵃ	South	7·6ᵃ	Australia	1·5ᵃ	—
Japan	3·3	East/Central	2·5ᵃ	Central	6·3ᵃ	West	1·7	Others	0·2	—
P.R. China	48·7	South	1·0ᵃ	North	17·7ᵃ	East	3·7		1·7	—
India and Pakistan	49·0ᵃ	North	3·8ᵃ	—		USSR	16·0ᵃ			—
West Asia	13·1ᵃ	—		—		—				
Total	128·7		7·7		30·5		29·0		3·4	199·3
Percentage of world total	65		4		15		15		1	100
Percentage in developing countries	97		87		42		0		0	73
Percentage of arable area irrigated	28		3		8		8		4	13

ᵃ Largely in dry areas. Estimated total approximately 115 million ha (6·5 million ha in Asia, 9·5 million ha in Africa, 14 million ha in Latin America, 7 million ha in North America, 6 million ha in South Europe, 10 million ha in USSR, 1·5 million ha in Australia).

management, and use of irrigation water, the solution to Africa's difficult food problems must be found in rainfed agriculture.

This is likely to be a tough proposition, since about 50% of the potential arable area is semi-arid, and population pressure on the recuperative fallow is already leading to declining yields in several countries.

No single solution is likely to be adequate technically; and in addition the social and demographic pattern varies widely. In parts of Africa, and in South America (which also depends heavily for the future on the development of improved systems of rainfed farming) there are actually labour constraints. Extending the cultivated area using mechanisation or ox ploughs, and more stress-tolerant and disease-resistant varieties may be possible, although (as Barker *et al.* (1981) have pointed out) pushing out the margins of cultivation often increases climatic variability and risk. Risk may increase at either end of the rainfall spectrum; but while most attention seems to have been focused in recent years on desertification in low rainfall areas, the progressive destruction of the tropical rain forests (whether for cultivation or timber extraction) perhaps has an even more serious potential for long-term environmental deterioration through its effects on rainfall and the CO_2 balance, and thus on global climatic change.

In order to combat erosion, increase stability of production, and provide risk insurance, various means of diversifying farm enterprises, both new and traditional, are being examined. These include agro-forestry, mixed and multiple cropping, and the introduction of livestock into crop-based farming systems. However, these often require new or improved systems of land management to conserve soil moisture, maintain fertility, control weeds, minimise tillage, and facilitate timely operations, if they are to succeed or even be feasible; stable systems of managing some difficult marginal environments have yet to be evolved. Problems include widespread soil acidity and chemical infertility in the humid tropics; diseases which preclude ruminant livestock, especially *Trypanosomiasis*, in Africa; and lack of cheap cultivation tools for moisture conservation and improved tillage suited to use by small farmers.

Clearly, whatever can be done to improve yield stability is important, and in high risk situations it should probably be given priority over raising yields. However, the need to achieve higher rates of agricultural growth in most developing countries is so desperate that a risk-avoiding strategy alone will not suffice. Difficult decisions of research priorities and wider policy issues are involved. If higher productivity can only be achieved at some cost of additional vulnerability to climatic variability, this trade-off may have to be accepted and other means sought to increase food security.

International food security schemes

Attempting to maintain large domestic grain reserves to cover yearly fluctuations is not only difficult for food-deficit countries, but has been shown to be an expensive solution where trade is an alternative. Efforts are therefore being made to devise internationally supported measures which would ensure poor countries fair access to world export availabilities in times of weather-induced crisis.

Schemes being studied include regional reserve stocks at strategic points, minimum emergency stock policies at the national level, a 'food facility' insurance-type scheme (possibly under the aegis of the IMF), which would provide foreign exchange to protect countries from excessive price fluctuations in years of above-trend food imports, and to enable them to buy food when their own production is adversely affected by weather; or some combination of these measures with conventional food aid. The latter alone is not considered adequate, partly because the total quantity made available by donors is so insufficient and demands so much administration, and partly because it is often least available when needed most. Donor pledges are at best niggardly compared to their commercial exports, and food aid is less attractive to them when world supplies are tight and prices high, as in 1973–1974 when aid actually declined.

None of the schemes proposed is without snags, but according to Siamwalla and Valdes (1980), compensatory financing is a much more effective approach to providing security than an international grain reserve scheme; especially as prices now represent a very much higher component of the fluctuations of food import bills. A combination of a financial insurance type scheme with a small strategic reserve of 20 million tonnes to be drawn on only in years of exceptionally high prices might be a good solution and less dependent on political bias than aid or international grain reserves as a sole solution. According to Konandreas et al. (1978) such a scheme would cost approximately $5 billion for a five-year period. To be effective any insurance-type scheme would need to be supported by early and reasonably accurate information on production shortfalls.

Improved weather warning systems

Better information on weather would be useful, both to farmers and to economists. Early warning of conditions which increased risk of frost, drought, pest, or disease attack (or conversely, which made precautionary treatment unnecessary), could be of immediate economic value to growers, and would help in forecasting harvest probabilities, prices, and export availabilities.

In addition to these more obvious practical applications of improved climatological information, there is an urgent need to develop a better understanding of the underlying atmospheric and terrestrial forces affecting climate, and the means by which man, consciously or accidentally, influences them. Analysis and diagnosis of climate/productivity relationships (including yield, energy, vegetation dynamics, and the identification of areas of high climatic vulnerability) would also be valuable and would help in short- and long-term monitoring, modelling, and designing research to improve agricultural management. Much of this work, particularly if it involved global monitoring, or research on weather modification, might have to be undertaken and funded by advanced countries with sophisticated equipment; but the results should be made available to all countries, and people from the Third World should be trained in its interpretation and operational application. International Agencies such as WMO and FAO could play a valuable role in respect of the latter, as well as in helping to establish instrumentation to co-ordinate the recording of basic information from meteorological stations around the world.

The cost of a more comprehensive world weather monitoring and climate research system has not, to my knowledge, been assessed. However, the United States climate programme, including research, was budgeted at $100 million for 1980, and the initial budget of the Joint WMO/ICSU Climate Research Fund for the same year was only just over $1 million. Set against the enormous annual losses from weather-related events, the billions of dollars being invested in irrigation and other measures to reduce weather variability, and the incalculable and poorly understood costs of ongoing human and other forces on longer-term trends in climate, these, or even much larger, sums appear trifling. According to Sah (1979), the cost of creating a major centre for weather prediction is $10–$15 million. However, he suggests that the benefits of improved predictive capability for a country like India could be as high as $200 million a year in food production alone. Other estimates show very high benefit–cost ratios to climatological analysis.

Developing coherent national food policies

It is clear that a passive political attitude to accepting climatic variability as an inevitable fact of life is no longer good enough. A conscious effort to reduce economic and social vulnerability to climate is essential in an increasingly crowded world. This is required both at the international level, because of the imbalances between exporting countries and potential food importers, and *within* countries because of the skewed nature of income distribution and access to food. Although in the last analysis the solutions must begin at the national level, donor countries could do a great deal to help alleviate climatic insecurity in the poorer regions of the world by more liberal trade policies for agricultural exports; by easing the foreign exchange burden of food imports; and by technical and financial aid to improve food delivery systems.

At the same time developing countries must recognise that increasing food production, even to the level of self-sufficiency, may not in itself be a sufficient guarantee of food security, although it *can* play an important part in raising purchasing power. There must be an infrastructure, sound marketing institutions, storage at the right place, and a distributive system which makes food available in times of crisis to those who need it most. Speed is crucial to effective food security. There are many causes of hunger other than climate. Poverty is the most widespread of all. Even the most favorable climate will not ensure social justice, full employment, and fair access to assets, and Garcia (1979) has argued that the real cause of distress in climatic adversity is not so much climate as social disequilibria and faulty socio-economic policies.

It is therefore essential to develop a sound framework within which strategies for food security can be planned, but although many countries have *agricultural* policies, most have no real *food* policy in the sense that the production, trade/aid, price, transportation, and food distribution systems are integrated within a national plan which also provides access to food by socially disadvantaged groups. The lack of such a coherent policy is why projects are often established *ad hoc*, why input supplies are not available when needed, why transport and storage systems break down (both when there is too much food available in a favorable year and in years of shortage and adversity), why price policies often lag behind events, and why starvation occurs even amid abundance.

Recently there has been a move, supported by the World Food Council with the collaboration of both developed and developing countries, to prepare national food strategies for all Third World countries wishing to develop them. To the extent that these are realistic and well-prepared, they should help to cut the economic and human cost of climatic variation, and to increase the effectiveness of counter-measures.

REFERENCES

Anon (1976). *Climate Change, Food Production, and Interstate Conflict, A Bellagio Conference 1975.* The Rockefeller Foundation.

Bachman, K. and Paulino, L. (1979). Rapid Food Production Growth in Selected Development Countries. A Comparative Analysis of Underlying Trends, 1961–76. IFPRI Research Report No. 11, October.

Barker, R., Gabler, E. C., and Winkelmann, D. (1981). Long-term consequences of technical change on crop yield stability. In: *Food Security for Developing Countries* (Ed. A. Valdes). Westview Press, Boulder, Colorado, pp. 53–78.

CIMMYT (Centro Internacional de Mejoramiento de Maiz y Trigo, El Batan, Mexico) studies:

Colmenares, J. H. (1975). *Adoption of Hybrid Seeds and Fertilizer among Colombian Corn Growers.*

Cutie, J. (1975). *Diffusion of Hybrid Corn Technology: The Case of El Salvador.*

Gerhart, J. (1975). *The Diffusion of Hybrid Maize in Western Kenya.*

Gafsi, S. (1976). *Green Revolution: The Tunisian Experience.*

Collis, R. T. H. (1975). Weather and world food. *Bulletin of American Meteorological Society* **56**(10).

FAO (1970). *Provisional Indicative World Plan for Agricultural Development.* Food and Agriculture Organization of the United Nations, Rome.

FAO (1980). *Agriculture Towards 2000.* Food and Agriculture Organization of the United Nations, Rome.

Garcia, R. V. (1979). Nature pleads not guilty. Abstracted in: *Food and Climate Review.* Aspen Institute for Humanistic Studies, Boulder, Colorado.

Glantz, M. H. (1977). The value of long-range weather forecast for the western Sahel. *Bulletin of American Meteorological Society* **58**, (2), 150–8. (See also *The Politics of Natural Disaster: The Case of the Sahel Drought.* Praeger Publishers, New York, 1976.)

The Global 2000 Report. Entering the Twenty-First Century. (1980). Prepared by the US Council on Environmental Quality and the Department of State.

Grove, A. T. (1977) The geography of semiarid lands. *Phil. Trans. R. Soc., London,* B **278**.

IBRD (1979). *Commodity Trade and Price Trends,* August, 42.

IFIAS (1974). *The Impact of Man on Climatic Change.* Workshop, University of Bonn. (Ed. C. Ramaswamy). International Federation of Institutes for Advanced Study, Stockholm.

Kettering Foundation (1976). *Impact of Climatic Fluctuations of Major North American Crops.* The Institute of Ecology, Charles F. Kettering Foundation, Dayton, Ohio.

Konandreas, P., Huddleston, B. and Ramangkura, V. (1978) *Food Security, an Insurance Approach.* International Food Policy Research Institute Research Report No. 4.

McQuigg, J. D. (1975a) *Effective Use of Weather Information in Projections of Global Grain Production.* Symposium on Food and Population, FAO, Rome.

McQuigg, J. D. (Ed.) (1975b). *Economic Impacts of Weather Variability.* University of Missouri.

Mellor, J. W. (1976). *The New Economics of Growth.* Cornell University Press.

Morrow, D. (1979). *The Economics of the International Stockholding of Wheat.* IFPRI, Washington, DC.

Mundlak, Y. (1979). Intersectoral Factor Mobility and Agricultural Growth. Research Report No. 6, International Food Policy Research Institute, Washington, DC, 1977.

National Research Council (1976). *Climate and Food.* National Academy of Sciences, Washington, DC.

NOAA/NDF (1978). *Climate Change to the Year 2000. A Survey of Expert Opinion.* National Oceanic and Atmospheric Administration/National Defense University, Washington, DC.

Sah, R. (1979). Priorities of developing countries in weather and climate. *World Development,* Vol. 7. Pergamon Press, London. pp. 337–47.

Siamwalla, A. and Valdes, A. (1980). Food insecurity in developing countries. *Food Policy* **5**(4).

Singh, S., de Vries, J., Hulley, J. C. L. and Yeung, P. (1977) *Coffee, Tea and Cocoa,* World Bank Staff Occasional Papers No. 22. John Hopkins Univ. Press, Baltimore, pp. 106–7.

Tsujii, H. (1976). Effect of climatic fluctuation on rice production in continental Thailand. In: *Climatic Change and Food Production* (Ed. K. Takahashi), pp. 167–79.

USAID (1979). Weather–Crop–Field Relationships in Drought-Prone Countries of Sub-Saharan Africa. US Agency for International Development, Office of Foreign Disaster Assistance, Washington, DC. (Prepared by NOAA and the University of Missouri.)

Valdes, A. and Konandreas, P. (1981). Assessing food insecurity based on national aggregates in developing countries. In: *Food Security for Developing Countries* (Ed. A. Valdes). Westview Press, Boulder, Colorado.

Where Should the World's Food be Grown?

IAN CARRUTHERS

Agrarian Development Unit, Wye College, University of London, UK

FOOD POLITICS

In the 1970s food became a political commodity. Despite much rhetoric which abhorred food being used as a political lever it was significant that the main USA response to the Afghanistan crisis was to withhold substantial grain shipments. Conversely, in early 1981 we find the EEC food surplus being justified on the grounds that they are being used to service western interests in Poland.

It was a series of weather events in the early 1970s that helped to reveal the potency of the food weapon. Whilst there is an established statistical correlation between poor weather in the Soviet Union grain areas and an unsatisfactory South Asian monsoon, between 1972 and 1974 poor Soviet weather coincided for the first time in 50 years with poor North American weather. With Japan and USSR unwilling to cut either cereal or feed grain consumption it was inevitable that there would be a massive rise in prices.

There are some important trends which make the food weapon a growing source of power for food exporting countries:

1. Volume of world cereal trade is increasing
2. The percentage of world crop entering trade is rising ($> 14\%$)
3. The number of countries becoming net importers is rising

These trends arise largely because of failure of domestic agricultural policies to increase food production sufficiently to match population growth.

The political and financial shocks of the 1970s may have some beneficial long-term effects for agriculture. It may be the final lesson to show developing nations that the vision of an industry led, or export cash crop led, development policy is illusory. Perhaps urban elites, who generally control development policy in developing countries, will recognise that it is now vitally important for national independence and integrity to commit scarce resources to agricultural investment on an unprecedented, massive scale.

In the 1980s less developed countries (LDCs) would be advised to continue to rely upon food imports or to move to import dependency only if:

1. They are certain not to be denied supplies in a crisis
2. They can be insulated from wide swings in prices
3. They are confident food will never be withheld as a political weapon
4. They are sure that the long-term potential export earnings will generate sufficient revenue over other needs (e.g. energy) to pay for food imports

It is suggested that few developing countries can afford to be confident on these counts and therefore their strategic interests will require a shift in emphasis toward agriculture. About 5 billion people or 79% of the 6·35 billion people expected to be alive in the year 2000 will live in LDCs. Nearly 92% of population growth up to then will be in LDCs (*The Global 2000 Report*, 1980). Investment in LDC agriculture will be necessary to satisfy food, employment and income goals unless a vast global welfare scheme is envisaged or Malthusian predictions are to become a reality.

The central thesis of this paper is that only by strengthening domestic agriculture will the impact of the food weapon be blunted. Furthermore, it is not only good politics to seek food security but also good economics. However, such a strategy will require many governments to change their development philosophy, their investment and research priorities and new levels and forms of aid to agriculture will need to be agreed.

There are greater risks associated with this strategy of increased emphasis upon domestic production. A shift from reliance upon global trade to domestic agriculture will in most instances make domestic food supplies more and not less vulnerable to weather events. If a country relies upon many regions of the world for food it is less likely to experience an overall inter-year variation in supply. Therefore national governments who pursue food self-sufficiency should adopt policies to help alleviate national weather sensitivity. In this paper stress will be placed upon an improved research base for rainfed agriculture and investment in existing irrigation works. In addition countries must have financial reserves, be prepared to import if and when necessary, and maintain adequate national strategic food reserves.

Within developing countries there are two important forms of adaptations to population growth which increase the risk of domestic agriculture not being able to cope with adverse weather events.

First, many farmers have been and will be forced to move to the extensive margin of cultivation. The extensive margin typically has either less favourable climate and edaphic conditions or it is a hillside with high rainfall and erosion-prone soils. Where the margin is a low rainfall area there is often a higher variance associated with it and consequently large inter-seasonal production variation.

Second, rural people have migrated to cities (over 200 million in 20 years) adding to the growing urban population and squalor. The large and increasing urban population is a major contributing factor to the world trade in cereals. Within developing countries the capacity to produce food, and perhaps more important to market it efficiently, has not kept pace with urban demands. The political dominance of urban folk, the civil servants, industrial workers and the armed forces, have made food imports the soft option with first call on foreign exchange. But this option is going to become increasingly expensive. The projection of *The Global 2000 Report* (1980) is for the real price of food to double over the period 1970–2000. This forecast rests on the fairly modest projections of energy price increases and an increase in LDC food production of 148%. If energy prices increase more rapidly or if agriculture fails to supply the needs there will be greater price rises.

Whilst the real price of food will increase, the degree of self-sufficiency is expected to fall substantially. FAO projections (UNFAO, 1979) expect a fall from 92% self-sufficiency at present to only 80%—and this level will only be maintained if domestic production expands at 2·7% annually.

Economic arguments are not the only reasons for putting an emphasis on food production where people already live. Food production is always close to the heart of any human culture. Furthermore, more practical arguments hold for producing food in the LDCs where more people and needs exist. Table 1 shows an estimate of land and water resources in various agroclimatic zones. It shows the predominance of

TABLE 1
LAND AND WATER RESOURCES IN MILLIONS OF HECTARES (AFTER NORSE, 1979)

Agroclimatic zone	Present arable area		Additional potential arable area	Additional irrigable area in columns 1 and 3	Total potentially cultivable area
	Non-irrigated	Irrigated			
Developed countries					
Wet tropics	1	0	2	0	3
Dry tropics	10	1	7	5	18
Warm humid	43	3	20	4	69
Warm dry	69	17	20	23	103
Cool humid	367	13	240	8	630
Cool dry	106	20	46	58	170
Cold temperate and polar	20	0	30	0	50
Total	616	54	365	98	1 043
Developing countries					
Wet tropics	76	9	414	–	499
Dry tropics	373	40	733	–	1 146
Warm humid	28	26	58	6	112
Warm dry	94	44	90	9	228
Cool humid	26	32	12	20	70
Cool dry	20	11	10	4	41
Total	617	162	1 317	39	2 096
Grand total	1 233	216	1 682	137	3 139

irrigation in developing countries as well as most of the potential arable and irrigable area. It is hard not to conclude that all possible encouragement should be given to production in developing countries where most people live, where food needs are greatest and where the technical potential is high.

FOOD SECURITY

In view of the foregoing analysis it is hardly surprising that at the end of the 1970s the apt phrase at international political as well as agricultural conferences was 'food security'. This largely replaced talk of ecology, environment, habitat and other worthy but less essential matters. Food security was a focus of attention despite a series of good harvests, and high cereal stocks in the second half of the 1970s. Indeed world food production in the last 20 years has experienced unprecedented growth. On a *per capita* basis the developing world produces 5% more food today than in 1960. But as *Global 2000* and UNFAO (1979) studies have shown, considerable progress is needed to maintain present levels of *per capita* food supplies.

Aggregate statistics can hide grave local problems. There are disturbing statistics from Asia where food production (mainly rice) is barely keeping pace with population growth, and from sub-Saharan Africa where average consumption of food per head has probably fallen in the last two decades. In many countries the growing number of landless people and farmers with very small holdings create apparently intractable problems. Political upheavals in countries as distant as Poland, Afghanistan, Kampuchea, Uganda and El Salvador, and unwise policies toward agriculture in Tanzania, Nigeria and elsewhere, have exacerbated food supply problems. And in many instances politically inspired problems have overshadowed problems arising from unfavourable weather.

OPTIMISM FROM INDIA

There is one recent notable and significant exception to the general increased vulnerability of low-income countries to weather events. This is the Indian case. India is now self-sufficient in cereals. Grain production is 20% higher than in the period 1972–1974. Most significantly, yield increases now contribute more to growth in cereal production than do crop area increases. Furthermore, there is a large and growing proportion of crops under irrigation (a quarter overall but up to three quarters in key grain producing states such as the Punjab) and much of the irrigation is from reliable groundwater sources. In consequence the poor 1979–1980 monsoon, which would have been disastrous in the 1960s, did not result in food shortages.

Indeed, the undoubted success in negating the impact of a poor monsoon has created new problems. Farmers have long appreciated a fact that tends to elude governments, namely that it is often in years of poor crops that they make most money. Over the last year (1980–1981) there has been very effective farmer agitation in many states in India, sparked off by the failure of price rises to compensate for the poor yield of crops after the unsatisfactory 1979–1980 monsoon. Prices did not rise because government and private stocks were high. Furthermore, aggregate production was not in fact so depressed as rainfall statistics would suggest because of the impact of irrigation. In future it is possible that India will only be able to regulate the profitability of food production if export outlets are developed. Agricultural policies in developed countries inhibit this. India was one of the first developing countries to take its agriculture seriously and give it a reasonable share of public investment. It was forced into adopting this strategy by circumstances which included failure of industry to match expectations and humiliating levels of food aid.

India had certain advantages: it had a large number of high calibre agricultural scientists and institutions to apply global scientific advance locally and in a wise way. It had a form of irrigated agriculture ready to benefit from modern scientific innovations. But, India was exceptional and it still has serious agricultural, social and political problems.

Food supply is seldom the real problem, even where severe malnutrition exists. It is a lack of purchasing power–effective demand that creates the hardship. As Norse (1979) pointed out there are historical precedents. For example, wheat was being exported from Ireland during the 1840s when the last European famine raged because the impoverished could not pay for the grain. In recent years India has exported grain, although malnutrition exists in many areas. Even Argentina, a regular grain exporter, has pockets of malnutrition.

Obtaining a greater purchasing power among low income groups is an unresolved problem. 'Food for work' programmes and subsidised 'fair price shops', as in Egypt, India and Sri Lanka, are fairly successful.

However, without food aid they can develop into a massive budgetary commitment, particularly during weather-induced global grain shortages. (For a comprehensive review of policy measures required to increase food supplies see Scrimshaw and Taylor, 1980.) A shift in opinion is detectable among many development specialists, away from excessive concern with 'second generation problems' of agricultural modernisation, over-ambitious integrated rural development programmes and what looks increasingly like Utopian basic needs for all. More modest goals of agricultural development, a rehabilitation of trickle-down concepts and a realisation that much needed improvements in rural and indeed urban welfare must stem from a technically and economically sound agriculture base are needed. The inequalities within existing institutions can seldom be tackled effectively without seriously impairing food supplies.

Modernisation of agriculture should reduce weather impact. To the extent that irrigation alleviates drought or crop protection reduces the incidence or effects of weather-related pests and diseases, modernisation should reduce weather-induced production variation. As Oram discusses (this volume) it is hard to verify this proposition empirically even in regard to irrigation. This is partly because the operation of much irrigation is sub-standard (Carruthers, 1981). Modern inputs are so sparsely and irregularly applied, and the weight of vulnerable farmers at the subsistence margin is so great that no relationships between modern input use and weather-induced variation can be detected.

Although considerable progress has been made in measuring and analysing the effect of weather on agricultures in developed countries (see Shaw and Durost (1962) for an early example) there is a dearth of such work in developing countries. In western Europe and North America, where climatic variations seldom have serious economic social consequences, there is considerable work on constructing and using weather indices, but in vulnerable zones such as South Asia there is relatively little serious study.

Successful adoption of modern agricultural technology in LDCs certainly requires more application of established climate science. Sah (1979) in a state-of-the art review puts a convincing case on economic grounds for additional investment in applied climatology for agriculture and a reallocation of resources away from the aviation matters which have dominated meteorology in LDCs for the last 30 years. Notable progress is being made (Omar, 1980; Robertson, 1980) but

the needs far exceed the likely level of achievement with present
resources and orientation.

NEGLECT OF CLIMATE AND WEATHER

Kamark (1976) reviewed the literature on development and economics
and noted the absence of serious climatic analysis. The standard text
The Economics of Agricultural Development does not include an index
entry for weather, climate or the tropics. There are exceptions but few
give climatic influences the thorough treatment the topic evidently
merits.

Part of the problem is that climate is an essentially ungovernable
variable. In the optimistic development phase which can be stated to
be from 1950 to 1973 it was argued that what Malthus missed in his
pessimistic prognosis was the role of technology in alleviating poverty
and in offsetting the negative effects of population growth. Whilst the
'white hot scientific revolution' was driving men from industrial countries to the moon, in developing countries the hope remained that
technology (notably industrial technology) would drive them along a
similar path to sustained economic take-off. For its part, the agricultural sector would benefit from adopting new technology and the
planners in their search for means were in no mood to be baulked by
uncontrollable impediments such as climate.

But it is now abundantly clear that climatic problems were not just a
colonial rationalisation, linking assumptions of racial inferiority, ethnic
and cultural constraints and justifying minimal investment. It is evident
that tropical climates are often a harsh environment for agriculture,
requiring more capital for infrastructure such as irrigation and all-
weather roads, creating more problems related to the eradication and
prevention of diseases, lowering the work efficiency of animals and
humans and adding to management problems. Our knowledge of the
climatic constraints contains gaps and biases. In particular there are
deficiencies associated with the tropical wet season. This is the period
when maximum work is demanded of farm families but also the period
of food scarcity, when food prices are highest. The wet season is the
period of most avoidable human suffering in the form of increased
malnutrition, morbidity and mortality. Part of the reason for the
neglect of this aspect are the practical difficulties of conducting and the
unpleasant working conditions for field investigations. Dry season
research biases need to be countered (Chambers *et al.*, 1979). Streeten
and Myrdal say that to neglect such realities is 'opportunistic'.

Neglecting for a moment political matters there should be no false hopes that efficient temperate agriculture can supply, on food aid terms, the needs of poor countries. Institutional devices for transferring food aid on the scale needed are inconceivable. Arguments often put forward by temperate agriculturists that in a hungry world they have a moral duty to expand production are at best simplistic and too often hypocritical cant. Indeed in many ways by depressing the market for agricultural products the temperate country agricultural lobby can be seen to be part of the problem. Temperate producers can create market problems with a false appearance of efficiency.

Prices offered to grain producers in the EEC are normally at least twice those received by North American farmers and Japanese farmers receive nine times world grain prices. In contrast, in India since 1973 grain prices to farmers have generally been below world prices. In many LDCs agricultural returns are depressed by various policies designed to tax the agricultural production base to raise revenue for use elsewhere.

On the input side fertiliser prices in developing countries are (usually) much higher than in developed market economies although shortages of credit, unreliable fertiliser supplies and lack of appropriate advice are at least equally important disincentives to application. Fertiliser use is growing but it is still inadequate on irrigated land despite very high marginal returns in physical terms to its application. Admittedly, in the last decade US agriculture has gone from being heavily subsidised to a leading sector employing 14 million people, virtually propping-up the US economy during the world recession. However, energy prices to agriculture in North America were until this year notoriously low. It is too early to forecast the impact of deregulating energy prices on US agriculture. If the low-income Asian farmer had North American energy prices and Japanese or even European product prices there would probably be grain mountains in Asia irrespective of monsoon conditions.

The main reason to invest and tackle effectively the problems of LDC agriculture is that real opportunities exist. But the incentive to increase developing countries' agriculture would be enhanced if subsidised 'greenhouse' agriculture in more developed countries, including cereals, sugar and other competing products, were to be somewhat curbed.

This conclusion has implications relating to the type, scale and form of scientific research activity in developed and developing countries alike. In the industrialised world it is arguable that we have 'scientific overkill' in relation to agriculture. There is a trend toward over-production. Yet output-generating research on specific problems on a customer–client basis is continuing with less emphasis upon basic research. It seems likely that fewer of the products of current research are transferable to developing countries.

RESEARCH NEEDS OF RAINFED AGRICULTURE

Agricultural research in many tropical countries has low status and, with notable exceptions, relatively low calibre staff and poor facilities are provided. Whereas in the UK biological science competes pretty well for talent and facilities, in LDCs I suspect it does not.

Problems of rainfed agriculture are complex and the recommendation domain is small. Site-specific recommendations, often for only a few square kilometres are needed. Local problems are not easily or adequately dealt with by a few international centres with outstations. Food crop research lags far behind cash crop research. This is particularly the case for food crops grown in climatically drier and more risky environments.

Regional agricultural stations often cater for single crops, cash crops rather than food crops, they seek to achieve maximum yield per unit of land and they are concerned with academic and not applied research. They often neglect indigenous technical knowledge and are generally short on recurrent budget support.

This situation needs to be remedied particularly in Africa. Whilst fairly applied or practical and location-specific work is needed, more theoretical needs also exist. We need to integrate scientific knowledge for tropical agriculture, to find and verify what general principles apply. Climate and weather will have a much more central place in this theoretical development than hitherto. We need to know what general principles of temperate agricultural science can be transferred and what modifications of them need to be made.

MORE IRRIGATION OR BETTER MANAGEMENT

Irrigation development is the most obvious way of eliminating or reducing climatic problems in Asia. The potential of irrigation is not being realised. Most of the 200 million ha presently irrigated operate well below the levels of productivity predicted by the planners. There is an agreement emerging but not yet convincingly proven with well documented case histories, that the greatest potential for increased agricultural production lies in reorganising, rehabilitating, modernising and improving the management of the existing irrigation networks. New irrigation investment is still continuing (at a rate of about 4 million ha year^{-1}) and considerable scope still exists, particularly in the rice growing areas of Asia where two-thirds of the world's malnourished live. Nevertheless, it is the presently irrigated land to which attention is increasingly directed.

Despite not coming up to expectations in performance new irrigation development still commands powerful interest group support (Carruthers and Clark, 1981). Recently the Brandt Commission (1980) concluded that additional and improved irrigation in large river basins should receive special international attention and a Trilateral Commission report recommended that to help eliminate hunger there should be concentration upon physical investments in canal distribution and on-farm water control structure (Colombo et al., 1978). Another report sponsored by IDRC recommended that additional irrigation investment opportunities would occur if various scientific and technical problems were tackled (Pereira et al., 1979) and played down the institutional problems of managing the water supply system. They recommended 30 topics for research to help promote irrigation development, but as Chambers and Wade (1980) note they omitted reference to main system management problems.

Social scientists have recently given much greater stress to management and institutional problems. Bromley et al. (1980), Taylor and Wickham (1979) and Chambers (1981) all provide extensive bibliographies on these topics. But from the civil engineering profession, who still have major responsibility for devising and implementing irrigation systems there is scarcely a word. The degree to which engineers can play down sub-optimal scheme working, being either blind to or ignorant of the systems faults is illustrated in Ali's (1981) remarkably frank and revealing paper describing his attempts at irrigation reform in Andhra Pradesh. In my own work I have laid stress upon adequate recurrent finance and the opportunities for aid agencies in finding novel means of resource transfer (Carruthers, 1981).

CONCLUSION

Climatic disadvantages and adverse weather events can be conquered by modern scientific approaches to agriculture. It is concluded that the world's food should be grown where consumers live. The greatest population and food need is in the LDCs. There are three ways which may be suggested which would assist a larger (but not necessarily more stable) global food production system:

1. Marked reduction of developed (so-called market) economy subsidy and support for agricultural production, especially where it impinges upon LDC agriculture markets
2. More basic research on tropical rainfed agricultural systems and more local research efforts
3. Rehabilitation of existing irrigation systems, improved management and reconsideration of aid support for recurrent budgeting for irrigation

REFERENCES

Ali, H. (1981). Practical experience in irrigation reform, Andhra Pradesh, India. *Water Supply and Management* **5**(1), 19–30.

Brandt Commission (1980). *North–South. A Programme for Survival. Report of the Independent Commission on International Development Issues.* Pan Books, London.

Bromley, D. W., Taylor, D. C. and Parker, D. E. (1980). Water reform and economic development: institutional aspects of water management in the developing countries. *Economic Development and Cultural Change* **28**(2), 365–87.

Carruthers, I. (1981). Neglect of O & M in irrigation. The need for new sources and forms of support. *Water Supply and Management* **5**(1), 53–65.

Carruthers, I. and Clark, C. (1981). *The Economics of Irrigation.* Liverpool University Press, Liverpool.

Chambers, R. (1981). In search of a water revolution: questions for managing canal irrigation in the 1980s. *Water Supply and Management* **5**(1), 5–18.

Chambers, R. and Wade, R. (1980). Managing the main system: canal irrigation's blind spot (mimeo report). Institute of Development Studies, University of Sussex.

Chambers, R. C., Longhurst, R., Bradley, D. and Feachem, R. (1979). Seasonal dimensions to rural poverty: analysis and practical implications. Discussion Paper 142. Institute of Development Studies, University of Sussex.

Colombo, U., Johnson, D. Gale and Shishido, T. (1978). *Reducing Malnutrition in the Developing Countries: Increasing Rice Production in South and South East Asia.* The Trilateral Commission, New York.

The Global 2000 Report. Entering the Twenty-First Century (1980). A report prepared by the Council on Environmental Quality and the Department of State, Washington DC.

Kamark, A. (1976). *The Tropics and Economic Development.* Johns Hopkins Univ. Press, Baltimore.

Norse, D. (1979). In: *Food, Climate and Man* (Eds. M. R. Biswas and A. K. Biswas). Wiley, Chichester.

Omar, M. H. (1980). *The Economic Value of Agrometeorological Information and Advice.* (WMO 256), Geneva.

Pereira, C., Aboukhaled, A., Felleke, A., Billal, D. and Moursi, A. (1979). Opportunities for increase of world food production from the irrigated lands of developing countries. Report to Technical Advisory Committee of the Consultative Group on International Agricultural Research. IDRC Ottawa (mimeo).

Robertson, G. W. (1980). *The Role of Agrometeorology in Agricultural Development.* (WMO 536), Geneva.

Sah, R. (1979). Priorities of developing countries in weather and climate. *World Development* **7,** 337–47.

Scrimshaw, N. S. and Taylor, L. (1980). Food. *Scientific American* **243**(3), 74–84.

Shaw, L. H. and Durost, D. D. (1962). Measuring the effects of weather on agricultural output. USDA ERS-72 Washington DC.

Taylor, D. C. and Wickham, T. H. (Eds) (1979). *Irrigation Policy and the Management of Irrigation Systems in South East Asia.* The Agricultural Development Council, Bangkok.

UNFAO (1979). *Agriculture Towards 2000.* UNFAO, Rome.

Discussion

Dr Darling agreed broadly with Dr Carruthers' conclusions. He stated that the Consultative Group of the International Agricultural Research Organisation were now probably moving in this direction. It was quite true that national research organisations cannot at present be relied upon to undertake the research that was needed because of shortage of resources and this is why international effort is of such importance. Criticisms will naturally be levied against this change and criticisms suggesting that the objective is to do research and not to undertake development work and application study have already emerged. The compromise solution which is being reached is that the international agencies should strengthen national research. *Dr Darling* also commented on the problems of rainfed agriculture indicating that this was a major problem. In his own Institute the approach was to study the local system and to improve it rather than to attempt injection of new technologies. In this respect, he agreed completely with Dr Pereira's analysis referred to by Dr Carruthers about the need for reclamation work in existing irrigation areas. *Dr Ulbricht* also agreed with the analysis which Dr Carruthers had given but pointed out that a number of other factors had to be considered. The leaders of the developing countries are mostly urban people trained mostly in the West and tended to be unsympathetic to the need to start from an agricultural base. He was not optimistic about changes of heart in many of the LDCs. *Professor MacKey* pointed out the problems which might occur in attempts to transfer technology, optimalising the production of food by changing field size to accommodate machinery would have a serious social impact. *Dr Carruthers*, in reply, pointed out that large-scale mechanised agriculture was certainly not on in many of the developing countries. The smaller the farms usually the greater the yield in most countries in the developing world. There has indeed recently been a fall in interest in land reform generally, a matter for which the Green Revolution is stated to have been responsible. *Professor MacKey*,

407

however, stated that small farms as a whole have lower yield, particularly if they were catering only for their own needs. It may well be that co-operation is the answer so that a small farm social structure can be achieved and yet the advantages of scale could be retained. *Dr Carruthers*, however, thought that most modern technology is scale neutral. This is particularly so of crop protection and fertiliser application. He questioned whether farmers indeed worked to a particular target income. *Dr Wilkinson*, while he applauded the analysis given by Dr Carruthers, doubted very much whether it was clearly a feasible solution to reduce agricultural production in the developed countries. Firstly, one had to consider that this would simply transfer political insecurity to the developed countries, secondly it had to be remembered that the agricultural industry, in the UK at any rate, had a strategic role, and in any event there were not at present the financial structures which would enable the developed countries to help. *Dr Carruthers*, in reply, pointed out that our own agricultural development services in the UK had had a massive effect on the agricultural industry. This arose from the original decision to have a basic strategy and this decision was taken more than 30 years ago. It had led to the considerable increases in productivity that had taken place. Something analogous was required in the developing countries. The critical matter would appear to be that the developing countries have now reached the point that they begin to require export markets largely because our farming has been pushed to the point of satisfaction of the internal demand and increasingly would be pushed to low real returns for the farming community. *Dr Oram* agreed with the point relating to the productivity of small farms and stated that the environmental problem is really the over-riding one. On the transferability of technology from the developed countries to the least developed ones, *Mr Anthony* thought the most cost effective way would be to support basic work and the long term furtherance of work in the LDCs and in this respect pointed out that the Overseas Development Administration had regarded this as a central feature of their work. Finally, *Dr Carruthers* pointed out that there is probably now a considerable coincidence of interest on the part of the developed and developing world and that it was in our power to underpin this by sensible policy decisions.

Participants

Aggett, P. J. A., MSc., MRCP., *University of Aberdeen, Physiology Department, Marischal College, Aberdeen AB9 1AS, UK.*

Anthony, K. R. M., BSc., AICTA., FIBiol., *Overseas Development Administration, Eland House, Stag Place, London SW1E 5DH, UK.*

Austin, R. B., BSc., DSc., *Plant Breeding Institute, Maris Lane, Trumpington, Cambridge CB2 2LQ, UK.*

Blaxter, Sir Kenneth, FRS., *Rowett Research Institute, Greenburn Road, Bucksburn, Aberdeen AB2 9SB, UK.*

Booth, C. C., MD., FRCP., *Clinical Research Centre, Northwick Park Hospital, Watford Row, Harrow, Middlesex HA1 3UJ, UK.*

Britton, D. K., BSc., MA., Hon.D. Agric., CBE., Hon. FRASE., *Agricultural Economics Unit., Wye College, Nr. Ashford, Kent, TN25 5AH, UK.*

Bunting, A. H., CMG., MSc., D.Phil., L.LD., FIBiol., *Plant Science Laboratories, University of Reading, Whiteknights, Reading RG6 2AS, UK.*

Buringh, P., *Agricultural University Wageningen, Duivendaal 10, PO Box 37, 6700 AA, Wageningen, The Netherlands.*

Bushuk., W., BSc., MSc., Ph.D., FCIC., *Research Administration, Department of Plant Science, University of Manitoba, Winnipeg R3T 2NZ, Canada.*

Carruthers, I. D., BSc., D.Phil., *Agrarian Development Unit, Wye College, Nr. Ashford, Kent TN25 5AH, UK.*

Cena, K., Ph.D., DSc., *Department of Environmental Physics, Institute of Building Science, 1–2 Technical University of Wroclaw, Wyb, Wysplanskiego 27, 50–370 Wroclaw, Poland.*

Collins, K. J., MB., D.Phil., BS., MRCS., LRCP., *Department of Geriatric Medicine, University College London, St. Pancras Hospital, London NW1 0PE, UK.*

Cooke, G. W., CBE., Ph.D., FRSC., FRS., *33 Topstreet Way, Harpenden, Herts AL5 5TU, UK.*

Cooper, J. P., FRS., *Welsh Plant Breeding Station, University College of Wales, Plas Gogerddan, Nr. Aberystwyth, Dyfed SY23 3EB, UK.*

Cowey, C. B., BSc., MA., *Institute of Marine Biochemistry, St. Fittick's Road, Aberdeen AB1 3RA, UK.*

Crane, A. J., BSc., D.Phil., *CEGB Research Laboratories, Kelvin Avenue, Leatherhead, Surrey KT22 7SE, UK.*

Cunningham, J. M. M., CBE., BSc., Ph.D., FIBiol., FRSE., *West of Scotland Agricultural College, Auchincruive, Ayr KA6 5HW, UK.*

Curtis, R. F., BSc., Ph.D., DSc., FRSC., FIFST., *Agricultural Research Council, Food Research Institute, Colney Lane, Norwich NR4 7UA, UK.*

Darling, H. S., Ph.D., M.Agr., AICTA., FIBiol., CBE., *Icarda, PO Box 114/5055, Beirut, Lebanon.*

Dennett, M. D., Ph.D., *Department of Agricultural Botany, University of Reading, Whiteknights, Reading RG6 2AS, UK.*

Eadie, J., BSc. (Agr.), *Hill Farming Research Organisation, Bush Estate, Penicuik, Midlothian EH26 0PY, UK.*

Edelman, J., Ph.D., DSc., ARCS., *Rank Hovis McDougall Ltd, High Wycombe, Bucks. HP12 3QR, UK.*

Elia, M., MD., *MRC Dunn Nutrition Unit, Dunn Clinical Nutrition Centre, Addenbrooke's Hospital, Trumpington Street, Cambridge CB2 1QE, UK.*

Elston, J., BSc., Ph.D., FIBiol, *Department of Plant Sciences, University of Leeds, Leeds LS2 9JT, UK.*

Flood, C., MA., *Meteorological Office, London Road, Bracknell RG12 2SZ, UK.*

Fowden, L., Ph.D., FRS., *Rothamsted Experimental Station, Harpenden, Herts. AL5 2JQ, UK.*

Fox, R. H., Ph.D., DSc., MRCP., MB., BS., MRCS., *26 St. Peters Way, Chorleywood, Herts. WD3 5QE, UK.*

Gasser, J. K. R., MSc., Ph.D., FRSC., *Agricultural Research Council, 160 Great Portland Street, London W1N 6DT, UK.*

Gormley, T. R., BSc., Ph.D., *Department of Food Science and Technology, AFT, The Agricultural Research Institute, Kinsealy Research Centre, Malahide Road, Dublin 5, Ireland.*

Gregory, S., MA., Ph.D., *Department of Geography, University of Sheffield, Sheffield S10 2TN, UK.*

Hatch, M. D., BSc., Ph.D., AM., FAA., FRS., *Division of Plant Industry, CSIRO, PO Box 1600, Canberra City, ACT 2601, Canberra, Australia.*

Hawthorn, J., FRSE., *Department of Food Science and Nutrition, University of Strathclyde, 131 Albion Street, Glasgow G1 1SD UK.*

Heide, O. M., D.Agric., MSc., *The Agricultural University of Norway, Oslo, Norway.*

Henderson, Sir William, FRS., *Yarnton Cottage, High Street, Streatley, Berks RG8 9HY, UK.*

Hirst, J. M., FRS., *Long Ashton Research Station, Long Ashton, Bristol BS18 9AF, UK.*

Jackson, G. H., BSc., MIBiol., FBIM., *Royal Agricultural Society of England, Stoneleigh, Kenilworth, Warwickshire CV8 2LZ, UK.*

Jarvis, P. G., MA., Ph.D., Fil.Doc., FRSE., *Department of Forestry and Natural Resources, University of Edinburgh, Darwin Building, The King's Buildings, Mayfield Road, Edinburgh EH9 3JU, UK.*

Jones, R., BSc., *Department of Agriculture and Fisheries for Scotland, Marine Laboratory, Victoria Road, Aberdeen AB9 8DB, UK.*

Kaufman, N. A., MD., *Department of Nutrition, The Hebrew University, Haddassah Medical School, Jerusalem, Israel.*

Kortschak, H. P., BSc., Ph.D., *Lyon Arboritorium, University of Hawaii, 2428 Ferdinand Avenue, Honolulu 96822, USA.*

Lake, J. V., Ph.D., FIBiol, *Agricultural Research Council, Letcombe Laboratory, Wantage, Oxon OX12 9JT, UK.*

Landsberg, J. J., BSc., MSc., Ph.D., *Long Ashton Research Station, Long Ashton, Bristol BS18 9AF, UK.*

Lester, E., BSc., *Plant Pathology, Rothamsted Experimental Station, Harpenden, Herts AL5 2JQ, UK.*

MacKey, J., MSc. (Agr.)., D.Ph. (Agr.), DSc. (Agr.), *Department of Genetics and Plant Breeding, Royal Agricultural College of Sweden, Box 7003, 750 07 Uppsala, Sweden.*

McLoughlin, J. V., BSc., MSc., Ph.D., FICD., MRIA., *Department of Physiology, University of Dublin, Trinity College, Dublin 2, Ireland.*

Monteith, J. L., FRS., *Department of Physiology and Environmental Studies, University of Nottingham, School of Agriculture, Sutton Bonington, Loughborough LE12 5RD, UK.*

Moorby, J., BSc., Ph.D., *Agricultural Research Council, 160 Great Portland Street, London W1N 6DT, UK.*

Morton, I. D., MSc., Ph.D., C.Chem., FRIC., FIFST., FNZIC., *Department of Food Science, Queen Elizabeth College, University of London, Campden Hill Road, London W8 7AH, UK.*

Mount, L. E., MB., BS., MD., CM., *Agricultural Research Council, Institute of Animal Physiology, Babraham, Cambridge, CB2 4AT, UK.*

Oram, P., MA., Dip.Agric.Sci.(Cantab.), *International Food Policy Research Institute, 1776 Massachusetts Avenue N.W., Washington DC 20036, USA.*

Pons, L. J., *Department of Soil Science and Geology, Wageningen Agricultural University, Duivendaal 10, PO Box 37, 6700 AA Wageningen, The Netherlands.*

Raymond, W. F., MA., FRIC., C.Chem., CBE., *Ministry of Agriculture Fisheries and Food, Great Westminster House, Horseferry Road, London SW1P 2AE, UK.*

Scott, R. K., Ph.D., FIBiol., *Broom's Barn Experimental Station, Higham, Bury St. Edmunds, Suffolk IP28 6NP, UK.*

Slack, C. R., BSc., Ph.D., *Department of Scientific and Industrial Research, Plant Physiology Division, Private Bag, Palmerston North, New Zealand.*

Smith, L. P., BA., *2 Greenway, Berkhamsted, Herts HP4 3JD, UK.*

Speed, C. B., *Department of Agricultural Botany, University of Reading, Whiteknights, Reading RG6 2AS, UK.*

Swinburne, T. R., DSc., Ph.D., ARCS., DIC., *Crop Protection Division, East Malling Research Station, Nr. Maidstone, Kent ME19 6BJ, UK.*

Taylor, T. G., MA., Ph.D., FIBiol, *Department of Nutrition, School of Biochemical and Physiological Sciences, University of Southampton, Southampton SO9 5NH, UK.*

Thompson, N., Ph.D., *Meteorological Office, London Road, Bracknell RG12 2SZ, UK.*

Truszczynski, M., *Veterinary Research Institute, Partyzantwo 57, 24-100 Pulway, Poland.*

Ulbricht, T., Ph.D., DSc., FRSC., *Agricultural Research Council, 160 Great Portland Street, London W1N 6DT, UK.*

Van Eimern, J., *Lehrstuhl fuer Bioklimatologie, Der Universitaet, Buesgenweg 5, D-3400 Goettingen-Weende, W. Germany.*

Waterlow, J., CMG., MD., Sc.D., FRCP., *Department of Human Nutrition, London School of Hygiene and Tropical Medicine, Keppel Street (Gower Street), London WC1E 7HT, UK.*

Wareing, P. F., DSc., FRS., *Department of Botany and Microbiology, University College of Wales, Aberystwyth SY23 3DA, UK.*

Webster, A. J. F., MRCVS., *Department of Animal Husbandry, University of Bristol, Langford House, Langford, Bristol BS18 7DU, UK.*

Wilkinson, B., BSc., MSc., Dip.Agr. Chem., *Agricultural Development and Advisory Service, Block 2 Government Buildings, Lawnswood, Leeds LS16 5PY, UK.*

Williams, W., MSc., DSc., FIBiol., *Department of Agricultural Botany, University of Reading, Whiteknights, Reading RG6 2AS, UK.*

Woodhead, T., Ph.D., BSc., F.Inst.P., FRAS., *Physics Department, Rothamsted Experimental Station, Harpenden, Herts AL5 2JQ, UK.*

Index